Minds, Memes, and Manipulation

In an era where battles are fought not only with code but also with culture, this book explores the evolving landscape of cyber conflict through the lens of psychology, cognition, and information warfare. It delves into the hidden war waged across digital platforms: a war for attention, belief, and behavioural control.

Drawing on research from psychology, the book examines how online spaces have become fertile ground for memetic warfare, disinformation campaigns, and cognitive manipulation. It investigates the psychological mechanisms that make individuals susceptible to digital influence, including cognitive dissonance, confirmation bias, and personality traits that shape vulnerability. From the motivations of hackers and propagandists to the architecture of viral misinformation, the strategic use of digital tools to exploit human cognition is unpacked. It also explores the role of personality psychology in understanding who is most at risk – and why – in the age of digital persuasion.

Whether you're a researcher, policymaker, professional, or simply a curious reader, this book offers a compelling and timely analysis of the new terrain of cyber conflict, where minds are the battlefield and memes are the weapons.

Lee Hadlington is Associate Professor of Cyberpsychology at Nottingham Trent University, UK, and a member of the Cyberpsychology Research Group. His research focuses on aspects of risk and resilience in cyberspace, with a particular emphasis on susceptibility to cybercrime, fake news and misinformation, cybersecurity, and information security. He has published extensively on the topic of human factors and cybersecurity, as well as other work focusing on the role of individuals in the proliferation of misinformation and attitudes towards AI in defence settings.

Minds, Memes, and Manipulation

Psychological, Cognitive and Information Warfare in the Digital Space

Lee Hadlington

Routledge
Taylor & Francis Group
LONDON AND NEW YORK

Designed cover image: Getty Images / Peter Dazeley

First published 2026
by Routledge
4 Park Square, Milton Park, Abingdon, Oxon OX14 4RN

and by Routledge
605 Third Avenue, New York, NY 10158

Routledge is an imprint of the Taylor & Francis Group, an informa business

British Library Cataloguing-in-Publication Data
A catalogue record for this book is available from the British Library

ISBN: 978-1-041-27037-9 (hbk)
ISBN: 978-1-041-27036-2 (pbk)
ISBN: 978-1-003-75240-0 (ebk)

DOI: 10.4324/9781003752400

Typeset in Times New Roman
by Apex CoVantage, LLC

Contents

Preface

Imagine waking up one morning to discover that you have been fighting an invisible war. However, there are no trenches to speak of, no physical battlelines, no tanks and missiles, just screens, clicks, and whispers of information. This is the reality of digital warfare: a conflict without borders, fought in the shadows of algorithms and the vulnerabilities of human psychology.

You have no doubt already survived countless skirmishes on the digital front line, perhaps without even realising it. You have binned emails that looked almost legitimate but never quite sat right with your gut. You have been pinged by a long-lost acquaintance who suddenly wants to discuss a "can't-miss" cryptocurrency opportunity. You have liked and shared a meme lampooning policy, and you have scrolled past unverified footage that blurred crucial details while stoking outrage. In each of these moments, you navigated a battlefield that is globally accessible, endlessly inventive, and perpetually primed for attack.

This book is not about firewalls, technology, and malware payloads. It is about *people*, about how minds are targeted, nudged, and sometimes overwhelmed. I distinguish *digital warfare* from *cyberwarfare* deliberately: the latter primarily assaults systems and infrastructures; the former takes aim at the human mind, manipulating perception, emotion, and cognition at scale. Digital operations are low cost, highly scalable, and often invisible, making them irresistible to both state and non-state actors. The most consequential battles today are fought over *attention*, *memory*, and *belief*, not servers and switches.

The lineage of psychological manipulation runs deep. Consider the story of Gideon taken from the Old Testament: 300 men, each with a torch and trumpet, multiplied into the *appearance* of 30,000. Panic ensued; victory followed, and no pitched battle was required. The tactic was simple: engineer confusion, magnify fear, and compel a misreading of reality. The digital age repeats this pattern: botnets masquerade as masses, troll farms fabricate consensus, and "viral" content ambushes the night watch. Modern illusions are brighter, faster, and more pervasive, but they exploit the same frailties that were documented in the Old Testament over 2,000 years ago.

These frailties are meticulously mapped by behavioural science. Repetition breeds belief (the illusory truth effect); framing steers judgement; novelty and emotional salience etch memories deeper than dull facts; primacy and recency position ideas on cognitive pedestals. Flood enough feeds, and attention fractures. Wait long enough, and you can allow memories to decay, allowing old information to be supplanted by new, crafted information. The seeding of artful contradictions and influencing the likelihood of cognitive dissonance pushes people to defend old beliefs with new biases. In the hands of a skilled adversary, these mechanisms become weapons; they are precise, patient, and devastating.

Our adversaries are not machines. They are communities, tribes, hierarchies, and loose federations of talent, where *reputation* and *skill* determine rank. "Elites" craft exploits; "technocrafters" adapt what they inherit; and "script kiddies" amplify noise. Motivations range from curiosity and status to ideology and profit. In parallel sits the *insider threat*: trusted, credentialed, and context-rich actors who can destabilise systems from within, either intentionally or inadvertently, serving to blur the boundary between external attack and internal compromise. Understanding the psychology of these people and the culture of their networks is as vital as patching vulnerabilities.

Misinformation, whether it is created accidentally or engineered, can spread like a pathogen. During crises, when fear is ambient and facts are fluid, deceptive content accelerates through community ties and emotional cues, piggybacking on our social instincts. Viral artefacts need little more than a nudge: a like, a retweet, or a forwarding gesture that promises care or belonging. Memes mutate as they travel, bending to each context while preserving a recognisable core; repetition simulates truth; and engagement simulates consensus. Architecture matters: platforms curate what you see, rank what you feel, and subtly shape what you believe.

To navigate this terrain, we must look squarely at the architecture of human cognition. We are *active* information processors with very *limited* cognitive resources. As cognitive misers, we satisfice; we grasp at heuristics; and we seek "good-enough" answers when the world presents us with too much, too quickly. Attention toggles between goal-driven focus and stimulus-driven capture. Memory reconstructs; it does not replay. Decision-making rushes through intuitive, affect-laden pathways when time is scarce and stakes feel high. Fatigue in various forms can serve to silence our scepticism and tempt us into compliance. Adversaries know this; they design for it.

And then there is the *wetware* of susceptibility, the dispositional lattice of personality, age, gender, and culture. Traits such as neuroticism, conscientiousness, extraversion, and openness bias what we attend to, how we appraise risk, and when we succumb to urgency. Dark triad traits sharpen adversarial intent; the same overconfidence that fuels attackers can make targets underestimate threats. Risk attitudes are malleable under stress; locus of control colours agency and resignation. Cultural frames, such as those of collectivism or individualism, high power distance or low, can bend trust and authority into different shapes. More than demographics, these are levers that influence *how* people engage and *why* they comply.

Bias does not travel alone. It travels in *packs*. In-group favouritism, out-group homogeneity, bandwagon effects, false consensus, and pluralistic ignorance are primed by social signalling and algorithmic amplification. Emotional contagion turns fear and outrage into accelerants; social contagion converts private judgement into public imitation. In "hot" emotional states, we mispredict a calmer, cooler future; under the aura of authority, we outsource our scepticism. These dynamics are not theoretical footnotes; they are the operating system of modern manipulation, powering the mobilisation of crowds and the hardening of belief.

You will meet these mechanics repeatedly in the pages ahead, first as concepts, then as tactics, and finally as case studies that show their collateral in the real world. You will see how agenda setting shifts what we think *about*, while framing shifts *how* we think. You will learn why deepfakes succeed even when their artefacts are detectable, how "choice architecture" nudges behaviour without removing options, and why echo chambers feel safe until they are weaponised. You will see how fatigue is not merely an outcome of overload but also a *designed* condition of modern information environments.

If this sounds disquieting, it is. But disquiet is the beginning of resilience. Resilience begins with naming the tactics, recognising your cognitive defaults, and building routine defences: *slowing down* under urgency cues, *seeking provenance* under authority signals, *switching channels* when content feels engineered for outrage, and *checking your state* when a decision invites sprinting rather than thinking. It continues in organisations that understand insider risk as psychological as much as technical, in platforms that treat virality not as a virtue but as a vector, and in classrooms that teach scepticism as a skill rather than as cynicism.

The pages you are about to read offer a structured guide to this battlespace. We begin by defining the theatre, mapping psychological, informational, and cognitive warfare as overlapping campaigns against perception, meaning, and memory. We profile adversaries not as caricatures but as human agents embedded in cultures of skill and status. We chart the contagion of falsehoods and the architecture that helps them travel. We dissect the cognitive vulnerabilities that make those travels efficient. We examine dispositional levers that adversaries pull, and we show how social and emotional biases can be orchestrated into movements that feel organic but are engineered. The book's aim is not to sermonise about truth but to illuminate *mechanism*: once you can see the machinery, you can resist its rhythm.

If you have ever felt the "too muchness" of our information age, the fatigue of constant sorting, or the vertigo of competing claims, you are not alone. That sensation is not merely a symptom; it is frequently a strategy deployed against you. The antidote is not withdrawal but *aware engagement*: cultivating habits that slow impulses, enrich context, and keep your judgements portable across frames and states. We cannot remove emotion from decision-making, nor should we, but we can keep our emotional moments from deciding *for* us. We cannot dismantle algorithms overnight, but we can diversify our inputs, interrogate our feeds, and rebuild our own sense-making networks.

This book is your field guide to understanding that battlefield: its weapons, its tactics, and the psychology that makes it so effective. Turn the page and let us explore the war you never signed up for but have been fighting all along.

1 The Digital Battlefield

Introduction

Cyberspace is not a stable, static environment; it is constantly changing and evolving. Some of the changes that take place extend its uses for the good, engaging the core aspects of creativity, connectivity, and freedom that underlie the utility of digital technologies. The internet and associated technologies offer us a great number of ways in which we can interact with individuals and information, sharing ideas, forming like-minded groups, and growing communities. However, there is another side to digital technology that we are sometimes reticent to acknowledge, even though it sits there in plain sight. There is a set of darker, more sinister uses that cyberspace can mask, usually associated with more nefarious actions by multiple unseen forces. Such actions can be categorised under the overarching theme of digital warfare, and although we may not perceive offensive activities occurring in cyberspace as being strategically planned to destabilise our societies, they are, in reality, occurring daily. In this first chapter, we set out to identify the key components of psychological warfare and plot the use of such tactics and strategies in traditional warfare settings, leading to the current explosion in the use of such mechanics in the digital domain.

Digital Warfare Versus Cyberwarfare

There is an unavoidable issue at the heart of discussions about cyberspace: the terminology used to describe offensive operations is often inconsistent, contested, or poorly defined. In this chapter, we aim to clarify this conceptual landscape by outlining the key terms and establishing the focus of this book. Cyberwarfare, in the terms of the most predominant use of the term, refers to the use of digital technologies and network-based attacks to disrupt, damage, or gain unauthorised access to systems, infrastructure, or data (Groš, 2024; Robinson et al., 2015). These actions are typically carried out for strategic, military, or political purposes and encompass a range of techniques, including hacking, denial-of-service

DOI: 10.4324/9781003752400-1

(DDoS) attacks, malware deployment, and the sabotage of digital infrastructure. In traditional cyberwarfare, the primary targets are technological, such as digital systems and the infrastructures that support them. In this context, psychological tactics play only a limited role, often restricted to social engineering methods used to bypass security barriers that are otherwise resistant to technical intrusion.

In contrast to traditional cyberwarfare, *digital warfare*, as it is defined in this book, refers to a set of tactics aimed not at systems or infrastructure but at the minds of individuals who engage with digital technologies. These tactics target the psychological and cognitive vulnerabilities of users behind screens, whether on computers or smartphones. Digital warfare encompasses a range of strategies, including the dissemination of misinformation and propaganda, the execution of digital psychological operations (*DiPsyOPs*), the use of memetics as a tool for manipulation, and the biased framing of narratives. In this context, the primary targets are the hearts and minds of individuals inhabiting cyberspace, as well as the broader social systems and belief structures that underpin social cohesion.

To frame *digital warfare* within the parameters of this text, it is defined as the strategic deployment of psychological, cognitive, and informational operations within digital environments. Its primary aim is to influence, disrupt, or control the thoughts, emotions, and behaviours of individuals, either collectively or as targeted entities. Unlike *cyberwarfare*, which focuses on compromising systems and infrastructure, digital warfare targets the human mind. Digital warfare operates through digital platforms to manipulate perception, exploit cognitive biases, and influence emotional responses. These operations are typically covert, scalable, and low cost, often occurring without the target's direct awareness. As such, digital warfare represents a powerful mechanism for destabilisation, persuasion, and social control that can be executed without physical confrontation yet is capable of producing profound psychological and societal effects.

There are a variety of methods that are aligned with the concept of digital warfare that we will explore in more detail throughout this book, but here we will delve into an overview of each of the key pillars for psychological warfare alongside an exploration of the key tactics that are employed in each.

The Art of Psychological Warfare

Psychological warfare, which is often referred to as either "psywar" or "psychological operations" (PsyOPs), has been seen as a central tool in the context of conflict and diplomacy. Very broadly speaking, PsyOPs have been broadly seen as the use of communication(s) to influence both human behaviour and attitudes, which can in turn shape behaviour, emotions, and attitudes, which in turn fulfil a strategic objective for the originator (Narula, 2004). Communication can come in a variety of forms and be something as simple as word of mouth and escalate to the use of mass media, cyberspace, and its associated technologies. Importantly, psychological warfare does not happen as a function of conventional conflict or occur as a concurrent offensive strategy alongside traditional aspects of war (e.g., ground-based attacks and missile launches). Psychological warfare is distinct from conventional warfare, as it can be conducted as a prelude to war, during, and after a war has taken place (Linebarger, 1946). There are also no defined laws or rules that accompany the use of psychological warfare tactics, and the actual battlefields upon which such techniques can be deployed are ill-defined and limitless. The temporal mechanics of psychological warfare also make it stand apart from more traditional kinetic methods of attack. Typically, such strategies can take months or even years to reach their full potential, and even then, there is no guarantee of success (Linebarger, 1946). However, as Linebarger (1946) was keen to note, to under-estimate the potential for psychological warfare to achieve its overarching goals is a "mortal" mistake.

One of the earliest uses of psychological tactics in warfare was documented in Judges 7:15–24, the seventh book of the Old Testament. The story is recounted of Gideon, who commanded a meagre force of 300 men against a vastly superior Midianite army. Knowing that he was outnumbered and understanding that traditional combat would result in certain defeat, he turned to the use of psychological tactics. The tactic utilised a well-known technological aspect of warfare at the time, namely that there should be one light carrier and one torchbearer for every 100 men. By giving the 300 men a torch and a trumpet, he could create the illusion that 30,000 men were present on the battlefield. The torches were hidden until the soldiers were in position on the battlefield, and at a specified time, when they were near the enemy camp, they broke the jars (thus suddenly revealing hundreds of lights) and blew their trumpets. The Midianites were thrown into a blind panic, startled by the sudden appearance of the lights and accompanying sounds, believing they were under attack by a massive enemy force. As a result, many of the Midianite soldiers fled the battlefield, and Gideon secured victory without any actual battle taking place. The key tactics of confusion, fear, and panic, elicited through a process of perception and an awareness of current real-world information, made light work of a superior fighting force (Linebarger, 1946). Gideon's tactics mirror modern digital psychological warfare, where disinformation is used to amplify the feelings of fear; perception is manipulated to create feelings of confusion and chaos; and there is the capacity to spread discontent within groups. All this comes with minimal direct engagement with the individuals who were targeted, but the results leveraged maximum psychological impact.

There are many concurrent examples of how such tactics have been used in recent years. For example, the proposed interference by Russian disinformation operatives during the 2016 U.S. election has been well-documented using a mixture of bots and troll farms to generate the illusion of widespread support for one side while portraying dissent in other camps. The use of botnets to simulate the opinion of the masses is akin to Gideon's use of lamps to mimic a larger fighting force than there actually was. In 2017, the Myanmar military was accused of committing atrocities against the people of the Rohingya. One of the key mechanisms that has been cited as instilling the spread of hateful anti-Rohingya content was the algorithmic systems of Facebook, thus creating an echo chamber for such views and biases to take hold, hence leading to actual physical violence against the Rohingya people. The mechanisms at work linked back to the example of Gideon could include the analogy of a night attack to a sudden appearance of viral content, in turn spreading discontent and surprise. Fear could also be used as another tactic in this instance, where such feelings are stocked through the spread of misinformation. There has also been a wealth of co-ordinated campaigns that have spread fear and confusion during the COVID-19 pandemic, most aimed at undermining the work of health professionals and the fight to bring the spread of infection under control. This has been partly linked to fear, usually on behalf of individuals who believe they are spreading information that could help friends and family prevent themselves from becoming infected with the virus.

The Modern History of Psychological Warfare

The first known use of the term "psychological warfare" has been linked to the military analyst and historian J.F.C. Fuller, who presented an academic overview of the developments during the First World War. In his exploration, he presented the idea that breaking the enemy's will to fight was more important than destroying their forces or equipment. He emphasised the need to use tactics that would disrupt the operations of opposing forces rather than engage in a war of attrition. He noted that propaganda formed an essential part of modern warfare and was keen to draw upon an analogy that was previously adopted by another writer in this domain, Oswald Spengler. Spengler suggested that the functioning of the journalistic press could be seen as a military force, where reporters assume the role of officers and the readers assume the role of soldiers. The key to this analogy is the notion that the soldier will obey the instructions of their commanding officers blindly and without question (Fuller, 1937). Indeed, Fuller details the following in a deeply prophetic way:

> In the next war, the war of the word will be waged as it never has been waged before. In short, the next world conflict will at base be far more a psychological than a physical contest, in which souls rather than bodies will be wounded and destroyed.
>
> (Fuller, 1937, p. 149)

In the context of current conflicts around the world, including the Russia–Ukraine war and the Israeli offensive on Hamas, the Gaza Strip, and Iran, such words have never been truer. Indeed, the labelling that is often used to describe such conflicts (e.g., the use of the term "special military operation" for Russia's war on Ukraine) is a clear example of how a specific narrative in the form of propaganda can be used to blind the masses against the actual intent behind actions.

Influence and Persuasion

One of the core principles that is often used in the context of psychological warfare is the tools aligned with influence and persuasion. There are several mechanisms that can be employed underneath this broad category, which we will return to again in Chapter 8 when we explore the use of social engineering. However, most of these principles are fundamentally linked to the shaping of beliefs, attitudes, and actions without them being directly aware of the manipulation. In the context of digital warfare, adversarial elements can craft situations and messages to harness our emotional vulnerabilities, conformity to social norms, or the initiation of cognitive shortcuts, which in turn result in biased decision-making processes. These tactics rely on the premise that humans are gregarious people-pleasers who like to follow rules but hate missing out on experiences that others around them might be having or things that might mean we have to do more work. We also like to be consistent in our actions, and in instances where our actions go against what we might have already done, or we fail to follow through with the plans we have made, we run the risk of damaging our standing within our social groups, as well as incurring psychological discomfort.

Normative Influence

In the context of digital psychological warfare, normative influence emerges as a subtle yet potent mechanism for shaping individual and collective behaviour. At its core, normative influence refers to the pressure individuals feel to conform to the expectations, behaviours, and beliefs of others, particularly those within their immediate social or cultural group. This influence can be dissected into three interrelated components: subjective norms, descriptive norms, and injunctive norms, each of which plays a critical role in the construction and maintenance of digital echo chambers and filter bubbles.

Subjective norms relate to the perceived social pressure an individual will experience to engage in a particular behaviour, based on the expectations of significant others or influential figures within one's social network. In digital environments, this can manifest through the amplification of certain voices (e.g., influencers, political figures, or algorithmically elevated peers) whose approval or disapproval of specific content subtly guides user behaviour. The mere belief that "people like me" endorse a particular viewpoint can be sufficient to nudge individuals towards alignment, even in the absence of direct coercion (Ajzen, 1991).

In contrast, descriptive norms are based on observations about what others are doing. In the algorithmically curated spaces of social media, these norms are often distorted through the artificial inflation of engagement metrics such as likes, shares, and retweets that can be frequently driven by bots or co-ordinated through inauthentic behaviour. This creates the illusion of consensus, where individuals come to believe that a particular opinion or behaviour is more widespread than it is. The result is a self-reinforcing cycle: perceived popularity begets actual engagement, which in turn reinforces the original perception (Nolan et al., 2008).

Finally, injunctive norms are linked to the rules or sanctions that serve to govern what is deemed acceptable or unacceptable within a group. These norms are often enforced through mechanisms of digital shaming, trolling, or reward, where deviation from the dominant narrative is met with social penalties, and conformity is rewarded with validation and inclusion. In this way, injunctive norms serve as the moral compass of the echo chamber, delineating the boundaries of acceptable discourse and reinforcing ideological homogeneity.

Together, these normative forces can contribute to the formation of online echo chambers or closed systems of belief, where dissenting views are filtered out, and filter bubbles, where algorithmic personalisation ensures that individuals are only exposed to information that aligns with their existing preferences. The interplay among subjective, descriptive, and injunctive norms ensures that users not only see more of what they already believe but also feel compelled to remain within those boundaries. In this sense, normative influence is not only a by-product of digital interaction but also a strategic asset in the arsenal of digital psychological warfare.

In the modern digital battlespace, the concept of psychological warfare has morphed into more specialised and distinct forms. Two aligned concepts, information warfare and cognitive warfare, are presented as strategic efforts to control not only emotions and the flow of information but also the underlying cognitive processes that shape our day-to-day activities, including decision-making and attention. These are associated concepts that are often subsumed by the overall concept of psychological warfare but do have some subtle nuances that deserve to be highlighted.

Information Warfare

Information warfare, as it would suggest, focuses directly on the control of information and serves to levy a strategic advantage through either the manipulation or denial of access to information. The methods that are a key feature of information warfare include the spread of disinformation and misinformation, targeted cyber-attacks on communication infrastructure, the manipulation and falsification of data, and the control of media. Examples of information warfare could include a targeted attack on a news outlet to spread false news reports, which in turn could create widespread panic and disruption. The psychological consequences of such attacks are multiple and could be linked to the undermining of trust in central sources for information as well as disrupting the credibility of such sources. Algorithmic manipulation, framing, and agenda-setting are all essential parts of the information warfare arsenal and are all related to how information is presented to the general populace in a way that serves a specific purpose or goal.

Algorithmic Manipulation

This process refers to the use of algorithms, or a precise set of instructions that a computer uses to complete a task, that are adjusted or biased to return a specific set of results back to the searcher. This technique is used more widely in digital platforms and social media that present information back to the end user and can be used to influence user behaviour, shape opinion, or intentionally distort the way in which information is presented. One of the prime examples of how algorithmic manipulation can be used is through the curation of content, where the algorithm at work will present content that is based on prior engagement, thus presenting individuals with more of the same information that they have already seen. This in turn creates an echo chamber where individuals will only see the information that they agree with, leading to a reinforcement of existing beliefs while preventing information that contradicts this position from filtering in. This can also mean that elements of disinformation could inadvertently be promoted to individuals because it has already generated a high level of engagement from users, potentially due to fake engagement using bots and fake accounts.

Framing Theory

A component of information warfare, the way in which something is framed, or how information is presented, can also serve to influence the likelihood that they will believe that information. While agenda-setting theory is concerned with what we think about, framing theory is more about how we think about that issue. The way information is "framed" in terms of whether it emphasises potential gains or losses can have a significant impact on the way in which people make decisions. To frame something is "to select some aspects of a perceived reality and make them more salient in a communicating text, in such a way as to promote a particular problem definition, causal interpretation, moral evaluation, and/or treatment recommendation" for the issue described (Entman, 1993, p. 52). Entman (1993) identified four key functions for framing, namely:

1. They define a problem: frames are useful for identifying what a particular thing or issue is doing and what the associated costs/benefits are for these actions, usually determined in terms of some cultural reference (e.g., threat to way of life and threat to dominant beliefs).
2. They diagnose a cause: frames present the basis for the forces that are creating the problem, usually in terms of some social group or scapegoat that is presented as a root cause for the problem.

3. They allow us to make moral judgements: the frames we are presented with allow us to make an evaluation of the current forces that are seen to be creating the issue and the associated effects of such action.
4. They allow us to explore remedial action: linked to the previous point, framing can give us the capacity to make an informed decision about the likely ways in which we can solve the issue with selected treatments with some level of prediction about their likely success (Entman, 1993).

One of the most important aspects of framing theory is that frames can be distorted or biased, which in turn can influence the way in which individuals process the information and in turn make decisions about the agent(s) responsible for the issues at hand. This can in turn create a bias in the responses that are being suggested, as well as where blame is directed.

Agenda-Setting Theory

This is a theory that describes how the mass media can serve to influence the positioning of a certain issue within the public agenda and is aligned very much with the concept of information warfare. This public agenda is usually the focus of the members of society and will be a primary concern for those members. So, in essence, the priorities of the news soon become the priorities of the public. The powerful effect of the mass media on the issues we prioritise cannot be under-estimated, and obviously, there are only so many issues that can be focused on by news outlets at any one time. This capacity to influence which issues or topics become the focus of daily news articles, and therefore the focus of the public, is perhaps one of the most important aspects of agenda-setting theory (McCombs et al., 2014). Importantly, agenda-setting theory makes the point that the mass media do not directly serve to tell what people should think but instead present them with a focus for what they should think about. From a psychological warfare perspective, the control of dominant narratives is a critical aspect; hence, the capacity to be able to set an agenda becomes a critical strategic tool. For example, it could mean that public attention is diverted away from a current critical issue in favour of another less critical issue that has a clear solution already in place or is something that is seen to have an element of control attached to it. It can also be used to focus attention on uncertain events, in turn amplifying fear and anxiety in the public domain, much of which we saw during the COVID-19 pandemic, where news outlets focused on increasing numbers of those infected and the death rates. In terms of other real-life examples of agenda-setting, authoritarian regimes will often use state-controlled media to present agendas that reinforce common narratives, such as reinforcing national pride and loyalty, while also serving to quell dissent.

Cognitive Warfare

Cognitive warfare, on the other hand, focuses on the essential processes humans complete on a second-by-second basis and can include aspects of memory, decision-making, and attention. The goal of these campaigns is to adjust or alter the way in which people think about topics that are presented to them, as well as how they make decisions, for example, which political party to vote for in a coming election. Disinformation campaigns, the use of behavioural nudges, the presence of deepfakes, and the manipulation of attention can all be easily weaponised in cognitive warfare. The underlying psychological elements of attention, memory, reasoning, and cognitive biases can all be employed to change the way in which people perceive an event, which can in turn be used to shift decision-making away from their primary choice. There is a clear overlap between these three core mechanisms that can be used in the pursuit of strategic dominance in cyberspace without any actual conventional movements towards conflict being made. The overlap between these elements is presented in Figure 1.1 below. At the centre of this diagram, we have the focus on the overall goal for these mechanisms, this being an integrated approach to influence the thoughts, feelings, ideas, and emotions of individuals in the targeted environment.

Memory Manipulation

Research in cognitive psychology has long demonstrated that human memory is not a flawless recording system but a fragile, reconstructive process. Memories are susceptible to fragmentation, decay, and distortion, and under certain conditions, entirely false memories can be implanted (Kaplan et al., 2016; Loftus et al., 1987; Loftus, 2019). The way information is presented can also significantly influence how it is encoded and later retrieved. Novel stimuli, such as striking visuals or emotionally charged events, are more likely to be remembered because they stand out against the background of routine experiences. Similarly, the serial position effect (primacy and recency) means that items presented at the beginning or end of a sequence are recalled more accurately than those in the middle (Rey et al., 2020; Terry, 2005).

These cognitive principles are not only the realm of academic curiosity but can also be actively weaponised in digital warfare. Adversaries exploit memory vulnerabilities to shape perceptions and behaviours through carefully engineered information flows:

1. **Primacy and recency exploitation**
   Disinformation campaigns often position key narratives at the start or end of social media threads, video sequences, or news cycles. This ensures that these messages occupy the most memorable positions in the cognitive sequence, increasing recall and influence.

2. **Novelty and emotional salience**
   Viral memes, sensational headlines, and shocking imagery are designed to capture attention and enhance memory encoding. Emotional arousal, in particular fear or outrage, can further strengthen retention, making these tactics highly effective in polarising audiences.
3. **Repetition and algorithmic reinforcement**
   Digital platforms amplify repeated content through recommendation algorithms, creating echo chambers. Repetition fosters familiarity, which in turn increases perceived truthfulness, a phenomenon known as the *illusory truth effect* (Udry & Barber, 2024; Unkelbach & Speckmann, 2021).
4. **False memory seeding**
   Deepfakes and fabricated narratives exploit the reconstructive nature of memory. When individuals encounter doctored images or videos repeatedly, they may later recall these as authentic experiences, reinforcing false beliefs.
5. **Attention hijacking and information positioning**
   By flooding feeds with emotionally charged or novel content, attackers can force accurate information into the middle of the stream where it is least likely to be remembered. This strategic positioning undermines corrective efforts and sustains misinformation.

In essence, digital warfare transforms cognitive vulnerabilities into strategic assets. By manipulating the conditions under which information is encoded and retrieved, adversaries can implant durable narratives, distort collective memory, and erode trust in authoritative sources, all without direct physical confrontation.

Cognitive Dissonance

The concept of cognitive dissonance has long been the focus in the realm of social psychology, ever since Festinger (1957) published his original theory on the topic. In his original work, Festinger suggested that cognitions, or elements of knowledge, can be grouped into pairs, with these pairs being either relevant or irrelevant to one another in an instance where two cognitions are dissonant so that they occupy different spaces within our current sphere of interests. A fundamental part of being human is the presence of dissonance in terms of our current cognitions, which does not sit well with us and creates a degree of psychological discomfort; in turn, an individual will be motivated to reduce the dissonance between competing cognitions, usually by avoiding any additional information that will lead to increasing the distance between the two dissonant cognitions. In terms of psychological warfare, cognitive dissonance is exploited in a way that either introduces information that is deliberately contradictory to the cognition we already have or presents us with troubling or unsettling information. In turn, this leads to a process of re-evaluation where an individual may begin to question their own beliefs, which may in turn lead to confusion, anxiety, and even a shift in loyalty. We will present a more focused exploration of cognitive dissonance later in Chapter 6.

Behavioural Economics and Decision-Making

At the heart of the concept, behavioural economics uses principles from behavioural science to study the ways in which individuals reason about decisions (Voyer, 2015). The approach combines elements from three core disciplines, these being psychology, cognitive science, and economics, to explore how we reach decisions where there is a high degree of uncertainty about the outcomes, where we have limited information, or where there is a strong emotional influence. Core to this approach is the notion that individuals function within the realms of "bounded rationality," which suggests that we do not always seek out the optimal decision for a solution, mainly because we do not have the time and all the relevant information, and we might be in a rush. Instead, we use a fallback mechanism that is guided by a set of mental shortcuts or rules of thumb that will mostly give us an answer that is close to a solution but is usually far from optimal. These rules, or heuristics, are often based on subjective information that we have observed and rely on our memory of similar situations to form a basis for the concurrent decision (Tversky & Kahneman, 1974). However, because of such processes, there is usually some inherent bias that can enter the equation, which is usually the result of faulty information or poor recall of relevant examples to draw upon. This means that if you can serve to influence the examples that individuals can draw upon or make the example that you want to be used as a reference point as being more memorable and thus easier to recall, you have more chance of effecting the decision-making process.

To effect change, behavioural economists argue that rather than force individuals towards a certain behaviour, they should be gently encouraged to assume more positive habits, where such a process is termed "behavioural nudging" (Thaler et al., 2012). Such nudges invite an individual to move towards a desired action based on the social norms that govern the cultural group to which the individual belongs, and the individual will follow that course of action because they do not want to be isolated from the rest of their social group (Damgaard & Nielsen, 2017). Thaler et al. (2012) presented the notion of a nudge as a way of injecting influence into the "choice architecture" of the individual, or the process through which individuals engage on the way to deciding (Congiu & Moscati, 2022). Essentially, a nudge is about gently guiding an individual's decision-making process in a way that is predictable but does not remove any of their respective options or make the decision more cognitively demanding or difficult (Thaler et al., 2012). Past research has noted that nudges are effective in situations where an individual has no clear preference or has a degree of uncertainty attached to their decisions (Venema et al., 2020). One good example of a nudge is the use of a GPS device: while the GPS device will make valid suggestions about the direction one should take on the way to their current destination, there is no specific restriction on the individual to choose the instructions. If we wanted to, we could choose not to follow the instructions of the GPS and instead follow our own intuition or knowledge (Sunstein, 2017).

Nudges are certainly an important element of cognitive warfare. Here, nudges can be used to persuade individuals to adopt a certain perspective or engage in certain behaviour without them being directly aware that they are doing so. Again, such nudges rely heavily on elements of social norms and will focus the individual's attention on what others in their social circle are doing or would approve of. Using nudges in combination with information warfare, where an individual's perception of things that are approved of and disapproved of is a key example of how such mechanisms can be used in concert.

The Overlapping Constructs

At the intersection between psychological warfare and information warfare, we see the phenomenon of cognitive–emotional manipulation of individuals, where information is used strategically to evoke a variety of emotional responses that serve to influence the behaviour of individuals, including fear and anxiety. This process relies on aspects of inductive reasoning, a process that is based more on intuition and past experiences rather than solid facts. Individuals will process this information not only in terms of its personal relevance to themselves and others around them but also in the context of the predominant trust and belief systems in play at any given time.

The overlap between psychological warfare and cognitive warfare is best viewed as the control of perception and relies heavily on emotional triggers as well as cognitive biases that are an inherent part of human decision-making. This mechanism can serve to shape how individuals interpret the world around them and can lead to misunderstanding or misinterpretation based on the extent to which the situation is emotionally charged and the material presents cognitively persuasive content.

Finally, we have the intersection between information warfare and cognitive warfare, which positions itself in the domain of strategic influence. This is where the use of deliberately curated, distorted, or targeted information serves to shape our cognitive processes, such as attention, decision-making, and memory. In turn, individuals begin to embed this material as the truth, which in turn can serve to influence what we remember and how we remember it. In contrast to the more traditional approaches to propaganda, the mechanics of strategic influence can serve to harness more advanced technologies such as AI personalisation, behavioural analytics, and deepfakes that can be used to subtly nudge individuals towards a set of specific actions or conclusions. What we must remember is that information is never just presented, particularly in the context of information warfare; it has been carefully optimised to create maximum psychological impact and serves to exploit a variety of cognitive biases and emotional triggers. In this way, the information can serve to engineer a variety of responses that can include confusion, compliance without the individual realising they have been coerced, and consent to participate in further activities that might serve to undermine society. One prime example of this is the co-ordinated spread of misleading information about vaccine safety during the COVID-19 pandemic. Most of these included the use of fear appeals and tapped into a deep-rooted distrust in the government and associated institutions. Overall, the goals for these types of attacks can be manifold but are generally aimed at undermining the efforts by public health bodies to get as many people vaccinated as possible while also increasing the likelihood that decreased vaccine uptake will lead to a more protracted, deadlier pandemic.

In Figure 1.1, the key principles of digital warfare are presented, detailing the key overlaps between the areas. There is also a discussion of the key mechanisms that can be used to elicit change as well as the target for the tactics that are employed.

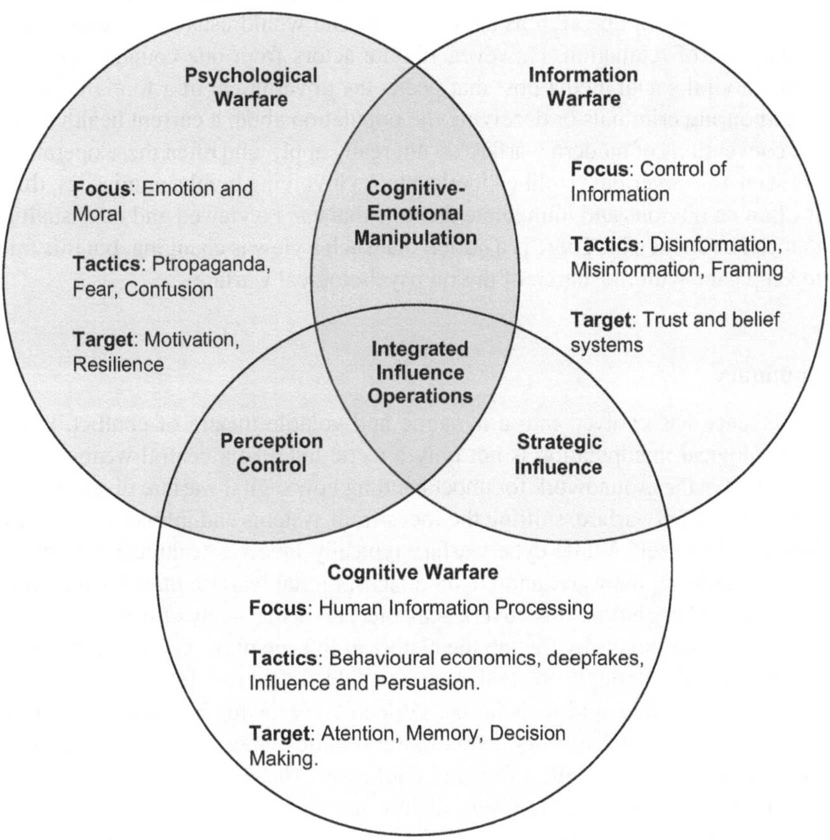

Figure 1.1 The intersection of psychological, cognitive, and information warfare in the context of digital operations.

Why Is Manipulation Central to Cyber Conflict?

This is an easy question to answer because humans are the easy target. As we will explore in Chapters 4 and 5, humans come equipped with a wide variety of vulnerabilities that make them an ideal target for psychological manipulation. They easily trust individuals and are open to persuasion and influence from techniques such as social engineering (see Chapter 8). They are also emotively driven and will respond in ways that usually serve to override rational decision-making if there is a strong feeling they should. The other good thing about psychological manipulation is that it is easy to do if you have a basic understanding of human psychology; it is relatively cheap and deployable on a large scale with the use of digital technology. Social media, the use of deepfakes, and the rollout of disinformation campaigns mean that any individual connected to the internet or digital technology is susceptible to the power of psychological manipulation.

Another key reason why psychological manipulation is so attractive relates to the conventional view of what warfare is. If a country fires a missile into another country, this would be seen as an act of war and would usually be followed by some form of retaliation. However, if state actors from one country decide to create a viral social media post that posits the government of a foreign country is harbouring criminals or deceiving the population about a current health crisis, the conventions of modern warfare do not really apply, and often these operations are seen as less serious. Unlike kinetic attacks involving bombs or missiles, there is often no obvious and immediate damage that can be viewed and no casualties that can be spoken of. There is a notion that such a view is changing, but this fails to keep pace with the march of digital psychological warfare.

Summary

Cyberspace has evolved into a dynamic and volatile theatre of conflict, where psychological manipulation is not only a tactic but also a central weapon. This chapter lays the groundwork for understanding how digital warfare diverges from traditional cyberwarfare, shifting the focus from systems and infrastructure to the human mind itself. While cyberwarfare typically involves technical disruptions such as hacking, malware, and DDoS attacks, digital warfare targets perception, emotion, and cognition. It is covert, scalable, and disturbingly effective.

The chapter begins by tracing the historical lineage of psychological warfare, from Gideon's strategic deception in the Old Testament to the modern-day deployment of bots and troll farms. Gideon's use of torches and trumpets to simulate a vast army mirrors contemporary tactics where illusion and perception are weaponised to elicit fear and confusion. These tactics have found new life in digital environments, where disinformation campaigns, such as Russian interference in the 2016 U.S. election or the algorithmic amplification of anti-Rohingya sentiment in Myanmar, demonstrate the potency of DiPsyOPs in shaping public opinion and inciting real-world consequences.

The chapter then delineates the conceptual boundaries among psychological warfare, information warfare, and cognitive warfare. Psychological warfare is framed as the strategic use of communication to influence attitudes and behaviours, often preceding or extending beyond conventional conflict. Information warfare, by contrast, focuses on controlling the flow and framing of information through mechanisms such as agenda-setting, narrative manipulation, and algorithmic bias, which are key tools here. Cognitive warfare drills deeper, targeting the mental processes that underpin decision-making, memory, and attention. These domains overlap significantly, forming a triad of influence that exploits emotional triggers and cognitive biases to engineer belief and behaviour.

Normative influence is explored as a subtle but powerful mechanism within digital psychological warfare. Subjective norms (what we think others expect of us), descriptive norms (what we see others doing), and injunctive norms (what is socially sanctioned) all contribute to the formation of echo chambers and filter bubbles. These environments reinforce ideological homogeneity and suppress dissent, making them fertile ground for manipulation.

The chapter also examines how memory can be weaponised. Techniques such as exploitation of memory, emotional salience, and repetition are used to implant durable narratives and distort collective memory. Deepfakes and fabricated content further blur the line between reality and fiction, seeding false memories that can influence future behaviour.

Cognitive dissonance is another key tool whereby, by introducing contradictory information, adversaries can destabilise belief systems and provoke psychological discomfort, leading to confusion, anxiety, and even shifts in loyalty. Behavioural economics adds another layer, showing how heuristics and bounded rationality make individuals susceptible to nudges, which act as subtle cues that guide decision-making without overt coercion.

Ultimately, I use this chapter to argue that psychological manipulation is central to cyber conflict because humans present as being replete with weaknesses that are ripe for manipulation; we are emotionally driven, cognitively biased, and socially influenced. Digital warfare serves to exploit these vulnerabilities with precision and minimal cost, and unlike kinetic warfare, these operations often go unnoticed, yet their impact can be profound and can undermine trust, polarise societies, and destabilise institutions.

Overall, this chapter highlights a compelling case for recognising cyberspace as a psychological battlefield. It makes a clear statement about the need to direct urgent attention towards the mechanisms of digital manipulation as well as the development of strategies for psychological resilience. It is the human mind, not the machine, that is the true front line in modern digital conflicts.

References

Ajzen, I. (1991). The theory of planned behavior. *Organizational Behavior and Human Decision Processes*, *50*, 179–211. https://doi.org/10.1016/0749-5978(91)90020-T

Congiu, L., & Moscati, I. (2022). A review of nudges: Definitions, justifications, effectiveness. *Journal of Economic Surveys*, *36*(1), 188–213. https://doi.org/10.1111/joes.12453

Damgaard, M. T., & Nielsen, H. S. (2017). The use of nudges and other behavioural approaches in education. *EENEE Analytical Reports*, (29).

Entman, R. M. (1993). Framing: Toward clarification of a fractured paradigm. *Journal of Communication*, *43*(4), 51–58. https://doi.org/10.1111/j.1460-2466.1993.tb01304.x

Festinger, L. (1957). *A theory of cognitive dissonance*. Stanford: Stanford University Press.

Fuller, J. F. L. (1937). Propaganda and war: The new technique of mendacity as a psychological weapon. *Army Ordnance*, *18*(105), 141–151.

Groš, S. (2024). Social engineering warfare as a tactic of information warfare. *European Integration Studies*, *20*(2), 67–86. https://doi.org/10.46941/2024.2.3

Kaplan, R. L., Van Damme, I., Levine, L. J., & Loftus, E. F. (2016). Emotion and false memory. *Emotion Review*, *8*(1), 8–13. https://doi.org/10.1177/1754073915601228

Linebarger, P. M. A. (1946). *A syllabus of psychological warfare: I*. Intelligence Division, Propaganda Branch, WDGS.

Loftus, E. F. (2019). Eyewitness testimony. *Applied Cognitive Psychology*, *33*(4), 498–503. https://doi.org/10.1002/acp.3542

Loftus, E. F., Banaji, M. R., Schooler, J. W., & Foster, R. A. (1987). Who remembers what? Gender differences in memory. *Michigan Quarterly Review*, *26*, 64–85. Retrieved from http://labs.psych.ucsb.edu/schooler/jonathan/sites/labs.psych.ucsb.edu.schooler.jonathan/files/pubs/1987_MQR.pdf

McCombs, M. E., Shaw, D. L., & Weaver, D. H. (2014). New directions in agenda-setting theory and research. *Mass Communication and Society*, *17*(6), 781–802. https://doi.org/10.1080/15205436.2014.964871

Narula, S. (2004). Psychological operations (psyops): A conceptual overview. *Strategic Analysis*, *28*(1), 177–192. https://doi.org/10.1080/09700160408450124

Nolan, J. M., Schultz, P. W., Cialdini, R. B., Goldstein, N. J., & Griskevicius, V. (2008). Normative social influence is underdetected. *Personality and Social Psychology Bulletin*, *34*(7), 913–923. https://doi.org/10.1177/0146167208316691

Rey, A., Le Goff, K., Abadie, M., & Courrieu, P. (2020). The primacy order effect in complex decision making. *Psychological Research*, *84*(6), 1739–1748. https://doi.org/10.1007/s00426-019-01178-2

Robinson, M., Jones, K., & Janicke, H. (2015). Cyber warfare: Issues and challenges. *Computers & Security*, *49*, 70–94. https://doi.org/10.1016/j.cose.2014.11.007

Sunstein, C. R. (2017). Misconceptions about nudges. *Available at SSRN 3033101*.

Terry, W. S. (2005). Serial position effects in recall of television commercials. *The Journal of General Psychology*, *132*(2), 151–163. https://doi.org/10.3200/GENP.132.2.151-164

Thaler, R. H., Sunstein, C. R., & Balz, J. P. (2012). *Choice architecture 0*, 428–439. Retrieved from http://ssrn.com/abstract=1583509

Tversky, A., & Kahneman, D. (1974). Judgment under uncertainty: Heuristics and biases. *Science (New York, N.Y.)*, *185*(4157), 1124–1131. https://doi.org/10.1126/science.185.4157.1124

Udry, J., & Barber, S. J. (2024). The illusory truth effect: A review of how repetition increases belief in misinformation. *Current Opinion in Psychology*, *56*, 101736. https://doi.org/10.1016/j.copsyc.2023.101736

Unkelbach, C., & Speckmann, F. (2021). Mere repetition increases belief in factually true COVID-19-related information. *Journal of Applied Research in Memory and Cognition*, *10*(2), 241–247. https://doi.org/10.1016/j.jarmac.2021.02.001

Venema, T. A. G., Kroese, F. M., Benjamins, J. S., & de Ridder, D. T. D. (2020). When in doubt, follow the crowd? Responsiveness to social proof nudges in the absence of clear preferences. *Frontiers in Psychology*, *11*(June), 1–13. https://doi.org/10.3389/fpsyg.2020.01385

Voyer, B. (2015). "Nudging" behaviours in healthcare: Insights from behavioural economics. *British Journal of Health Care Management*, *21*(3), 130–135. https://doi.org/10.12968/bjhc.2015.21.3.130

2 Understanding Your Digital Adversary

Introduction

For much of this text, we focus on the techniques that expose the psychological fragility of humans when targeted by digital warfare campaigns. These operations, whether subtle or overt, are not only technical exploits but also present clearly crafted, strategic psychological manoeuvres designed to destabilise, manipulate, and control. Yet, to fully grasp the scope of digital warfare, it is pertinent to also examine the adversaries who orchestrate these campaigns. The digital battlefield is populated not only by victims but also by actors: individuals whose motives, traits, and behaviours shape the nature and trajectory of cyber conflict.

While the execution of cyber-offensive operations is often assumed to be delegated to automated systems such as AI and bots, these technologies are ultimately directed by human agents. These individuals, whether state-sponsored operatives, ideological hackers, or financially motivated actors, form the core implementors of digital adversarial activity. Understanding the psychological drivers and social structures that underpin their actions is essential to developing effective counter-measures. By interrogating their motivations, we gain insight into the strategic logic behind digital warfare and open pathways to disrupt, deter, or even prevent future attacks.

This chapter begins by tracing the historical emergence of one of the most influential groups in the digital warfare landscape: the hacker subculture. Originating in the 1960s and 1970s, this community laid the groundwork for many of the offensive techniques now weaponised in cyber conflict. We then differentiate the various types of digital adversaries, such as white hat, black hat, and grey hat hackers; crackers; and cyberterrorists, each with distinct operational roles and psychological profiles. By exploring the motives that drive these actors, from curiosity and peer recognition to ideological commitment and financial gain, we situate their behaviours within the broader strategic framework of digital warfare.

DOI: 10.4324/9781003752400-2

A Brief History of Hacking

It would be impossible to detail every aspect that contributed to the development of hacking as we know it today, but Kizza (2024) presents a compelling overview of how key historical milestones gave rise to hacker culture and, by extension, to the cyber adversaries who now play a central role in digital warfare (see Table 2.1). The original term "hack" carried no deviant or malicious connotations; rather, it described a creative and efficient means of bypassing laborious programming processes. However, what began as a form of technical ingenuity has since evolved into a strategic capability, with hacking techniques now weaponised in service of ideological, political, and economic agendas. Understanding this evolution is critical to grasping how digital warfare has emerged not only from technological advancement but also from the cultural and psychological roots of hacker subcultures.

Table 2.1 Timeline: Evolution of Hacking Culture (1960s–2025)

1960s–1970s: The Birth of Hacking Culture
1960s – The term "hacker" emerges at MIT.
Late 1960s – Phone phreaking begins; John Draper uses a toy whistle to mimic AT&T tones.
1971 – The Creeper virus was created on the U.S. Department of Defence's Advanced Research Projects Agency Network (ARPANET).
1972 – Reaper antivirus developed to remove Creeper.
1980s: Hacking Goes Public
1983 – WarGames film popularised hacking.
1986 – The United States passes the Computer Fraud and Abuse Act (CFAA).
1988 – Morris Worm infects ARPANET; Robert Tappan Morris convicted under CFAA.
1990s: Rise of Cybercrime and Hacker Celebrities
1990 – U.K. hacker "Data Stream" infiltrates 200+ institutions.
1994 – Vladimir Levin steals $10 million from Citibank.
1995 – Kevin Mitnick was arrested after a two-year manhunt.
1999 – The Melissa virus causes $80 million in damages.
2000s: Hacktivism and Global Threats
2000 – The ILOVEYOU worm infects millions.
2003 – Anonymous hacker collective emerges.
2007 – Estonia suffers a massive cyber-attack.
2010s: Cyberwarfare and Mega Breaches
2010 – Stuxnet sabotages Iran's nuclear programme.
2011 – LulzSec and Anonymous attack Sony, PBS, and others.
2013 – Yahoo breach affects three billion accounts.
2017 – WannaCry ransomware exploits Windows vulnerabilities.
2020s: Sophistication and State-Sponsored Attacks
2020 – The SolarWinds hack compromises U.S. government agencies.
2021 – Colonial Pipeline ransomware halts fuel distribution.
2023 – MOVEit breach affects thousands of companies.
2024–2025 – Surge in ransomware and state-sponsored attacks; increased use of AI and targeting of critical infrastructure.

The development of hacking culture from the 1960s onwards provides a crucial backdrop for understanding the emergence, evolution, and proliferation of cyberwarfare in digital environments. What began as a technical curiosity and playful exploration seen in early MIT hacker communities and phone phreaking gradually evolved into a more complex ecosystem encompassing cybercrime, hacktivism, and digital warfare.

Each decade introduced new motivations and methods, from the playful viruses of the 1970s to the ideological campaigns of Anonymous in the 2000s and the financially driven ransomware attacks of the 2020s. These shifts reflect broader transformations in technology, geopolitics, and social dynamics. Crucially, the tools and tactics developed by hackers, such as website defacement, data breaches, and social engineering, have become instrumental in the creation and dissemination of misinformation. Understanding this historical trajectory allows us to view cyberwarfare not as an isolated phenomenon but as one deeply embedded in the evolution of digital subcultures, technological capabilities, and socio-political agendas.

The Typology of the Digital Adversary

The term "hacker" is often used as a broad label to describe a wide variety of sub-actors capable of launching digital attacks in cyberspace. However, this umbrella term encompasses individuals with diverse motives, behaviours, and operational roles. We begin with the most established typology: the hacker.

Hacking refers to the act of exploiting, modifying, or manipulating systems to achieve a specific goal. As noted earlier, the original use of the term "hack" described a method of circumventing lengthy programming processes in favour of more efficient shortcuts (Kizza, 2024). Central to the hacker ethos is the idea that such actions are not inherently malicious; rather, they are often intended to improve or streamline existing systems. Nonetheless, these activities frequently challenge societal norms and institutional rules, leading to their perception as subversive or threatening.

Hackers can be broadly categorised into three types:

- *White hat*: ethical hackers who use their skills to identify vulnerabilities within systems and assist organisations in resolving them.
- *Black hat*: malicious hackers who exploit system weaknesses for personal gain, disruption, or as agents of state-sponsored cyber operations.
- *Grey hat*: individuals who operate in a legal and moral grey area – violating laws without necessarily intending harm.

The motivations behind hacking are varied, with curiosity often cited as a primary driver. The origins of hacking lie in communities of intellectually curious individuals seeking to push the boundaries of technological capability. This curiosity manifests in a continual desire to improve, discover, and challenge systems (Kizza, 2024). Many hackers engage in research to stay abreast of developments and identify exploitable weaknesses.

Other motivations include activism, where *hacktivism* merges technical skill with ideological purpose. Hacktivists may disrupt systems that propagate messages or policies they oppose, aiming to restore what they perceive as moral balance. Financial gain and elevated status are also significant motivators, particularly among black hat hackers who seek recognition within the hacking community.

A further classification is the *cracker,* which is used to describe a more aggressive subset typically associated with attacks on security infrastructure and digital theft (Kizza, 2024). Crackers use their expertise to "crack" software or systems, enabling unauthorised access and sabotage. Common activities include

1. Removing copy protection from software for redistribution and resale.
2. Breaking encryption or password protections to steal data.
3. Modifying software to unlock premium features without payment.

These actions are often driven by monetary incentives, intellectual challenges, and the strategic aim of enabling sabotage or advancing digital warfare.

One final classification relevant to this discussion is the *cyberterrorist.* Cyberterrorists are motivated by political, economic, or religious ideologies and employ tactics rooted in intimidation, fear, and destruction to achieve their objectives (Kizza, 2024). While some scholars have argued that the threat of cyberterrorism has been overstated (Weimann, 2004, 2005), prominent incidents that have occurred in recent history suggest that such views may now be outdated. These events, often linked to state-sponsored actors, underscore the evolving and increasingly strategic role of cyberterrorism within the broader landscape of digital warfare.

The Insider Threat

It is often assumed that the threats that emerge in the context of digital conflict come from unseen, often underdetermined external sources, where adversarial actors operate outside the systems we seek to protect. However, a critical yet frequently overlooked dimension of digital warfare is that of the insider threat. While space does not permit an exhaustive treatment of this topic here, a comprehensive overview is available in other texts (e.g., see Hadlington & Ryding, 2025; Hadlington, 2018). Nonetheless, it is important to present a broad outline of the insider threat dynamic.

Any individual embedded within a context, be it an organisation, society, or social group, is typically afforded a degree of trust and privilege by those around them. In digital warfare, however, this trust can be misplaced and may become a significant vulnerability. Although insider threats are often framed within the domain of cybersecurity, their mechanisms have evolved to intersect with a wide array of cyber operations, including information warfare and digital sabotage.

Insider threats encompass a broad spectrum of behaviours, ranging from deliberate acts of espionage and sabotage to accidental data leaks and policy violations. According to the U.S. Cybersecurity and Infrastructure Security Agency (CISA), such threats may include terrorism, unauthorised disclosure, corruption, and even workplace violence. Within the context of digital warfare, these actions can be weaponised to disrupt operations, leak strategic data, or manipulate internal communications.

While the term "threat" often conjures images of malicious actors, the reality is more nuanced. Malicious insider threats (MITs) account for only around 6% of internal breaches, yet they are disproportionately costly, with some estimating they cost $4.9 million globally in 2023 (IBM, 2023). These actors may be ideologically driven, financially incentivised, or coerced by external forces, including state-sponsored entities.

Defining the Insider in a Digitally Fluid Environment

The concept of an "insider" is becoming increasingly complex. Traditional definitions often assumed that there was a clear set of organisational boundaries between what exists "inside" and what is "outside." However, with the advent of modern work environments that are characterised by remote access, subcontracting, and hybrid teams, these lines have become blurred (Hadlington & Ryding, 2025; Hadlington, 2018). Individuals with temporary credentials, external consultants, or even former employees with lingering access can all pose insider risks. Research in this area is very telling, where 83% of individuals who were questioned continued to have access to accounts from a previous employer when they left the organisation (Beyond Identity, 2021). 56% of those who still had access to digital systems of their previous organisation said that they had used them for nefarious reasons, usually to initiate some form of revenge. Such trends serve to highlight the systemic vulnerabilities that exist within the modern digital workforce, something that is ripe for digital adversaries to use to their advantage.

Early frameworks treated insider threats as binary, where an individual functioned as either a threat or not. However, later researchers challenged this position, claiming that the concept was better viewed in terms of "insiderness" (Bishop & Gates, 2008). Instead of individuals being categorised using a simple dichotomy, the concept of "insiderness" presents a continuum that accounts for motive, intent, and impact. Even individuals with no malicious intent can cause significant damage through negligence or ignorance. In the context of digital warfare, such actors may unknowingly facilitate misinformation campaigns, data breaches, or system compromise.

Privilege, Access, and Intent for Insider Threat

In the evolving theatre of digital warfare, the insider threat represents a uniquely potent and often underestimated vector and one that operates not only through technical access but also through psychological proximity, ideological alignment, and informational influence. Unlike external adversaries, insiders possess embedded trust, contextual awareness, and privileged access that make them ideal conduits for cognitive and information-based attacks. These actors may be motivated by personal grievance, ideological conviction, or external coercion, and their actions can destabilise systems from within, often without immediate detection.

Hunker and Probst (2011) emphasised that insider threats cannot be defined solely by access to IT systems. Privileged access now includes operational knowledge, residual credentials, and even indirect influence over digital infrastructure. For example, a software developer who designed a system may retain deep insight into its vulnerabilities long after leaving the organisation.

Cappelli et al. (2012) offer a widely accepted definition of a malicious insider threat:

> A current or former employee, contractor, or business partner who has or had authorised access to an organisation's network, system or data and intentionally exceeded or misused that access in a manner that negatively affected the confidentiality, integrity, or availability of the organisational information or information systems.
>
> (p. xiii)

While this definition aligns closely with the principles of information security, namely confidentiality, integrity, and availability, it also intersects directly with the strategic objectives of digital warfare. At the heart of many cyber operations is the intent not only to breach systems but also to subvert or manipulate the information those systems contain and disseminate. In this context, insider threats become more than technical risks; they are psychological and informational assets capable of distorting reality from within.

Digital warfare increasingly targets the creation and control of information itself. As we will see in later chapters of this text, both misinformation (false information shared without intent to deceive) and disinformation (deliberately false content designed to mislead) are tools that are used to erode trust, sow confusion, and destabilise institutions. Insider actors, with privileged access and contextual knowledge, are uniquely positioned to seed or amplify such content, often under the radar of conventional security protocols. Whether through deliberate sabotage or accidental exposure, insider threats represent a critical vector in the broader landscape of cyber conflict, where the manipulation of perception is as strategically significant as the compromise of infrastructure.

In the context of digital warfare, the insider threat has become increasingly weaponised by both state and non-state actors. These individuals may be ideologically radicalised, financially incentivised, or psychologically manipulated to act against their organisations. The recruitment of insiders, whether this be through coercion, blackmail, or ideological alignment, has become a valuable strategic tactic in cognitive warfare, where adversaries exploit emotional vulnerabilities and moral ambiguity to destabilise systems from within.

Shifts in technology have further complicated the detection and mitigation of insider threats. Remote work, cloud-based systems, and decentralised access models have blurred traditional boundaries of trust and control. Advanced techniques such as credential spoofing, deepfake impersonation, and AI-driven surveillance evasion make it increasingly difficult to distinguish between legitimate and malicious activity. As a result, organisations are increasingly adopting behavioural analytics and zero-trust architectures to counteract these evolving risks.

It is worth noting that the insider threat is not only an organisational concern but also a national security issue. High-profile incidents such as the Capital One breach (2019) and the SolarWinds supply chain attack (2020) underscore how internal vulnerabilities can be exploited to achieve geopolitical objectives. To view attack vectors solely as emerging from external forces, without considering what may be occurring within one's own "back yard," is to overlook the possibility that ideologically subversive messages are being planted online to disrupt societal cohesion, furthering an information war from within.

Understanding insider threats as a strategic component of digital warfare requires us to look beyond technical access and consider the human ecosystems from which these actors emerge. The capacity for internal sabotage, ideological subversion, and information manipulation is not only shaped by individual motives but also by the broader social structures and cultural norms that define hacker communities. These communities that are often hierarchically organised, reputation-driven, and ideologically diverse serve as incubators for both ethical innovation and adversarial intent. To fully grasp the psychological and operational dynamics of digital conflict, we must now turn to the social fabric of the hacking world, where identity, influence, and intent converge to shape the adversaries we face.

The Social Dynamics of the Hacking Community

Hackers are often portrayed in popular media as solitary, shadowy figures who operate in isolation, have limited social connections, and are generally depicted as socially undesirable. The prototypical view is of someone who is either "geeky" or "nerdy," with poor social skills and personality traits that predispose them to forming relationships with computers rather than people. However, this stereotype overlooks the active and complex sense of community that exists within hacker networks globally. These communities are often structured around a meritocratic ethos, where individuals are judged by their technical exploits and their ability to manipulate and innovate with technology (Holt & Kilger, 2012).

Skill distribution within the hacking community has been shown to be hierarchical. The lower ranks are typically occupied by individuals who are new to hacking and tend to rely on tools and techniques developed by more experienced members. According to Holt and Kilger (2012), the upper tiers of this hierarchy are occupied by a small number of highly skilled individuals, referred to as "makecraft hackers." These actors possess advanced technical capabilities, enabling them to identify vulnerabilities, develop new exploits, and implement sophisticated programmes. Young et al. (2007) refer to this group as "Elites," highlighting their superior knowledge of systems and coding and noting that they pose the greatest threat due to their ability to rapidly create and deploy innovative exploits.

At the other end of the spectrum is a larger population of semi-skilled individuals. While they possess some technical knowledge and can identify system weaknesses, they lack the proficiency to exploit these independently. Holt and Kilger (2012) term this group "technocrafters," as they often modify existing tools created by elite hackers to carry out their activities. Young et al. (2007) offer a less favourable characterisation, labelling them "script kiddies," a derogatory term used within the hacking community to describe inexperienced individuals who rely on prewritten scripts. Other terms such as "noobs" or "newbies" are also commonly used to describe this level of the community (Jordan & Taylor, 2017).

The hacker community is far from a monolith. It is a dynamic, stratified ecosystem in which individuals are evaluated not by formal credentials but by their technical prowess and capacity for innovation. As Holt and Kilger (2012) and Young et al. (2007) illustrate, this meritocratic structure fosters a hierarchy ranging from novice script kiddies to elite exploit developers, each with distinct roles and threat profiles. In the context of digital warfare, this hierarchy functions as a strategic map: elite hackers (or "makecraft hackers") represent high-value assets capable of developing zero-day exploits and orchestrating sophisticated attacks, while technocrafters and script kiddies may serve as foot soldiers in broader campaigns, often unknowingly amplifying misinformation or disruption.

Understanding this layered structure is essential for anticipating how cyber operations unfold. Whether state-sponsored or ideologically driven, digital warfare frequently recruits from this hierarchy, leveraging the skills and motivations of different hacker types to achieve tactical and psychological objectives. The internal dynamics of the hacker community, including its norms, reputational systems, and collaborative networks, are not merely cultural artefacts; they are operational mechanisms that shape the trajectory of cyber conflict.

The Hacker Code of Ethics

It may come as a surprise to some readers that hackers possess a shared code of ethics, originating from the foundational principles of the subculture. These ethical norms, though informal, serve as a regulatory framework within the hacking community. Transgressions against this code that may include actions deemed excessively malicious or disruptive can result in various forms of intra-community retaliation. Sanctions may include social ostracism, trolling, flaming, or other reputational consequences. In some cases, offending individuals may even become targets of counter-attacks from other members of the hacking community (Holt & Kilger, 2012).

(Levy, 1984) outlined six tenets of the hacker ethic:

1. Access to computers and systems that enable understanding of the world should be unlimited and free.
2. All information should be free.
3. Authority should be mistrusted, and decentralisation encouraged.
4. Hackers should be judged by their skills, not by credentials or demographic factors.
5. Computers can be used to create art.
6. Computers are a force for change and can improve lives.

At its core, the hacker ethic promotes freedom – freedom to explore, to express oneself through technology, and to redefine artistic boundaries. It champions open access to technology and unrestricted information flow.

Chiesa et al. (2008) later identified four key rules that once governed hacker activity:

1. Do not damage penetrated systems.
2. Do not modify information on the invaded computer.
3. Share information with others.
4. Share access to information with others.

These principles align with the original hacker ethos, which emerged from a belief in the free flow of information. While advocating for openness, this ethos also emphasised the protection of information integrity and the infrastructure on which it resides.

However, the relevance of these ethical codes has been increasingly questioned, particularly with the rise of state-sponsored actors in the digital arena. Wible (2003) argued that the hacker community is no longer unified by the ethical guidelines that once prevailed, though remnants of the original ethos persist. Javaid (2013) further contended that hacker ethics are now largely performative, used to portray hacking as socially beneficial rather than as a genuine moral framework.

The hacker ethic, as articulated by Levy (1984) and Chiesa et al. (2008), reflects a foundational philosophy rooted in openness, decentralisation, and creative exploration. These values once served as informal codes of conduct within the hacking subculture, fostering community and mutual respect. Yet the advent of digital warfare has disrupted this ethical landscape. As Wible (2003) and Javaid (2013) suggested, the cohesion of the hacker community has fractured, and the original ethos is often invoked more as rhetoric than as a guiding principle.

In the context of digital conflict, hacker motivations have diversified, ranging from ideological activism and financial gain to geopolitical manipulation. State-sponsored actors operate outside traditional hacker norms, prioritising strategic objectives over community values. This shift has redefined what it means to be a hacker in the modern era, where ethical boundaries are blurred, and tactics such as retaliation, sabotage, and misinformation are increasingly common.

Understanding the evolution of hacker ethics is essential for interpreting the behaviour of cyber actors in digital warfare. It highlights how cultural norms, community enforcement, and moral ambiguity shape the actions of individuals and groups in cyberspace, often with profound implications for security, trust, and the integrity of information.

The Psychology of the Hacker

There has been a long history of media hype surrounding the personality profiles of hackers, something that is often personified in common popular media (e.g., Mr Robot, Hackers, and Wargames). Often hackers are typified as being gifted individuals who are socially inept, usually displaying one or more psychological disorders (e.g., Asperger's syndrome, autism, and ADHD). They can be seen as a lone genius who spends most of their time huddled in a darkened room (good examples can be found in the series *Mr Robot, 2015,* or the feature film *The Matrix, 1999*) or a rebellious individual who relishes the challenge of breaking into systems (e.g., Kevin Mitnick). These stereotypes run the risk of oversimplifying the nature of cyber threats we face online and can also influence legislation and policy-making. Some police forces actively engage in trying to deter young people from engaging in a life of cybercrime but heavily focus their attention on young males rather than directing their attention to females, which again furthers the stereotype.

In terms of the interpersonal characteristics of the hacking community, many researchers have noted that the data contradict the often-held stereotype of hackers and cybercriminals as isolated loners. For example, Lieberman (2003) noted that most individuals who were questioned about aspects related to social anxiety and social avoidance reported normal romantic relationships and sex lives. Lieberman's (2003) exploratory study marked a pivotal shift in how hackers were conceptualised, not only as isolated technical experts or digital outlaws but also as individuals with complex interpersonal relationships and social motivations. By interviewing hackers and assessing their attitudes towards legality and social engagement, Lieberman revealed that many hackers operate within tight-knit communities, where trust, reputation, and shared values play a central role.

In the context of digital warfare, these interpersonal dynamics can become even more critical. Attackers can and do form temporary alliances for co-ordinated attacks, sharing exploits and vulnerabilities, or engage in social engineering that relies on a keen understanding of human behaviour. The social fabric of these communities may in turn become a strategic asset, enabling the rapid dissemination of tools, tactics, and misinformation (Jordan & Taylor, 2017).

However, some research has mentioned some negative elements in the interpersonal relationships of cybercriminals. Some noted that malicious hackers were typically loners who had low self-esteem and exhibited better interactions with technology rather than humans. Kirwan and Power (2013) also highlighted that cybercriminals often had weaker relationships with family members in comparison to non-cybercriminals, while Chiesa et al. (2008) noted that hackers often exhibited difficult relationships with their parents, often typified by the absence of a father figure.

In terms of personality traits, there is a broad set of findings, some of which serve to contradict previous findings. For example, in a small-scale study that examined the personality traits of 30 hackers, researchers noted that each subcategory of the hacking typology exhibited different dominant traits (Matulessy & Humaira, 2016). White hat hackers had the dominant personality trait of agreeableness, tending to be cooperative and empathetic as well as being motivated by strong ethical principles. For the cyberwarfare context, white hat hackers are capable defenders who can safeguard systems. Grey hat hackers exhibited higher levels of neuroticism, symptomatic of their operating in what could be seen as morally ambiguous territory in their exploits. Due to this, they may experience feelings of instability and anxiety or suffer guilt and internal turmoil when it comes to the ramifications of their actions. These are not the sort of people you want to depend upon in the context of any conflict, as their unpredictability makes them prone to exposing vulnerabilities while also being open to crossing ethical boundaries with their activities (Matulessy & Humaira, 2016). Finally, black hat hackers showed a more dominant level of openness to experience, showing a level of curiosity and inventiveness when it comes to carrying out their activities. It also means that they are perhaps more likely to transgress more conventional routes on the way to achieving their goals. This group of individuals will usually form the most aggressive element in any cyber conflict, driven by the want to explore their skill base in a live setting.

Other psychological elements that have been attached to cybercriminals include the capacity to morally disengage from their actions. Moral disengagement was an original concept that was presented by Bandura (1999), where he argued that our capacity to control our own actions is highly selective in nature. In essence, individuals can serve to "disengage" their morality filter if it allows us to assume a behaviour that we would normally deem questionable (Moore, 2015). In essence, when we choose to morally disengage from an action that is seen as being on the boundaries of our moral map, we can use several mechanisms that come under the banner of moral disengagement to do this. Researchers have noted that hackers often have higher levels of moral disengagement, meaning that they have the capacity to justify some of their actions and step aside from the repercussions that could accompany them, such as psychological harm and guilt (Young et al., 2007).

Taken together, the portrayal of hackers in popular media and the nuanced findings from psychological and sociological research reveal a complex and often contradictory picture. While the archetype of the socially isolated, morally ambiguous genius persists in cultural narratives, empirical studies suggest that hackers, whether white, grey, or black hats, are far more socially and psychologically diverse than these stereotypes allow. The interpersonal dynamics within hacking communities, ranging from collaborative alliances to fractured familial relationships, underscore the importance of understanding hackers not only as individuals but also as members of evolving digital ecosystems.

In the context of digital warfare, these insights become particularly salient. The personality traits and social behaviours of hackers can influence not only the tactics they employ but also the ethical boundaries they are willing to cross. The capacity for moral disengagement, for instance, may enable certain actors to rationalise harmful actions, while traits like openness and neuroticism can shape the unpredictability and intensity of cyber operations. As such, understanding the psychological and interpersonal profiles of hackers is not merely an academic exercise; it becomes a strategic imperative.

Ultimately, reducing hackers to simplistic stereotypes risks obscuring the real and varied threats posed by cyber actors. It can also misguide policy, enforcement, and prevention strategies, particularly when interventions are disproportionately targeted at specific demographics. A more nuanced, evidence-based understanding of hacker psychology and community dynamics is essential for crafting effective responses to cybercrime and digital conflict.

The Motivation of the Hacker

There have been numerous different attempts to explore the motives of hackers and cybercriminals, usually the perpetrators of the exploits that accompany digital warfare activities. The fruitfulness of such research, which on the surface may pay lip service to some attempt to classify and categorise cyberterrorists and other cyber operatives, has its limitations. There has been a long history in criminology and policing that has attempted to profile the criminal mind in the hope that such activities could be headed off before the perpetrator has had a chance to commit their crime (Pfleeger, 2008). Writing on the topic of insider threats, Pfleeger (2008) noted that there were some significant issues aligned with the reduction of attackers into neat psychosocial profiles with the suggestion that it might be easy to identify those individuals who are going to be responsible for an attack. Such an approach is complicated by a variety of issues, the main one being the current subject matter: cyberterrorists and attackers really do not want to be profiled in the first place, so getting access to a suitable source for relevant information is problematic, to say the least. Reducing the behaviours and motivations of an attacker to a base profile also runs the risk that new and innovative individuals break the current moulds in terms of their background and reasons for committing such exploits.

Holt and Kilger (2012) noted that there are several motives that shape an individual's willingness to engage in cyber-offensive activities:

- Feelings of addiction: this relates to the rush and the feelings of excitement that an individual can experience because of their activities, such as completing a new exploit or finding a new way of hacking a system. The main say of any behavioural addiction is the feeling of withdrawal an individual will experience once the target addictive behaviour is ceased, meaning there is always a drive to engage in more of the same activity. There is also a danger that individuals will develop a psychological resistance to the addictive behaviour, meaning that they have to engage in more extreme forms of activity in order to satisfy their needs (Griffiths, 1996; Kuss & Griffiths, 2011).
- Peer recognition: as the hacking community is heavily biased towards meritocracy, the need for peer recognition becomes an essential aspect of the motivation to engage in cyber-offensive operations. This means individuals might engage in larger, more complex attacks that target notable individuals or high-value targets.
- Ego: activities that individuals engage in are often driven by the need to enhance their self-esteem and self-worth. Individuals will seek out ways to get others in the community to like them, perhaps through the targeting of mutually disliked groups or individuals.
- Entertainment: it is hard to identify where the term came from, but "for the lulz" has often been used to capture the exploits of hackers who see themselves as doing this just for the fun of it. The term "lulz" is a derivative of the acronym "LOL" (meaning to laugh out loud in textspeak) but was often used in communities such as 4chan to denote amusement that came from causing distress or confusion. The term was often used to justify attacks that involved cyber-pranking, trolling, and cyber-attacks. Later, the term was associated with the hacking group Anonymous; individuals that emerged from the chaotic backdrop of the 4chan environment and who engaged in a variety of highly visible attacks often used the phrase to describe the motives for their actions.
- Cause: this is usually a motive that is linked to the personal beliefs and affiliations of the individual attacker and can align strongly with actions undertaken by cyberterrorists. For example, Anonymous were driven by a perception that the internet should be free for all, and they were heavily embedded in an anti-surveillance and anti-censorship agenda. Another example

is the Moses Staff, an Iranian hacker group that first came to light in 2021. The group's key target was the interests of companies based in Israel, with political and religious motivations being the main motivators in this instance.

- Money: so, there are, of course, some hacking groups and actors that focus directly on financial gain, which usually comes about because of them stealing and then selling information. A report by Mandiant (2025) noted that over 55% of threat groups identified in 2024 were financially motivated, with just a small percentage (2%) being identified as being motivated by hacktivist motives, where the focus was on disruption.

Other researchers have suggested that hackers engage in their exploits to hone their skills (Fotinger & Ziegler, 2004). Others have noted that many hackers saw website defacement as simple pranks, again something that was being done "just for lulz," with over 70% suggesting this was the case, where the remainder was down to political motivation (Woo, 2003). Others have suggested that the hacker motive is driven by a high level of intellectual challenge and a wish to learn more, where breaking the law and achieving public notoriety are of lesser desires (Lieberman, 2003).

Understanding the diverse motivations behind hacking that range from addiction, peer recognition, ego, entertainment, ideological causes, and financial gain provides a critical insight into the behavioural landscape of digital warfare. These motives do not exist in isolation; rather, they influence the nature and scope of cyber-offensive activities, especially when aligned with broader geopolitical or ideological agendas. For instance, groups like Anonymous or Moses Staff demonstrate how personal beliefs and collective identity can evolve into co-ordinated cyber campaigns targeting state infrastructure or political adversaries. Similarly, financially motivated threat actors contribute to the destabilisation of digital ecosystems by exploiting vulnerabilities for profit, often disrupting critical services in the process. The challenge of profiling cyber attackers, as noted by Pfleeger (2008), becomes even more pronounced in this context, where motivations are fluid, access to reliable data is limited, and attackers actively resist classification. As Holt and Kilger (2012) suggest, the psychological and social drivers behind cyber activity, whether this is for the "lulz" or for ideological warfare, are central to understanding how digital conflict unfolds. In this way, hacker motives are not only personal, but they are also strategic, shaping the contours of modern digital warfare and complicating efforts to predict, prevent, and respond to cyber threats.

Summary

This chapter reframes cyber conflict as a human-driven phenomenon, emphasising the psychological, social, and cultural dimensions of digital adversaries. It begins by tracing the historical development of hacker subcultures, from their origins in the 1960s to their evolution into agents of cybercrime, hacktivism, and state-sponsored operations. The typology of digital adversaries, including white hat, black hat, and grey hat hackers; crackers; and cyberterrorists, is explored to reveal the diverse motivations behind cyber-offensive behaviour, such as curiosity, ideological commitment, financial gain, and peer recognition.

The chapter then examines the insider threat, highlighting how trust and privilege within organisations can be weaponised. It challenges traditional definitions of insiders, presenting a continuum of "insiderness" shaped by motive, access, and intent. The fluidity of modern work environments and the persistence of access post-employment are shown to create systemic vulnerabilities ripe for exploitation in digital warfare.

Attention is also given to the social dynamics of the hacking community, which is revealed to be a hierarchical and meritocratic ecosystem. From elite "makecraft hackers" to novice "script kiddies," reputation and skill determine status and influence. These internal structures are not only cultural artefacts but also operational mechanisms that shape cyber operations.

The chapter explores the hacker code of ethics, originally rooted in openness, decentralisation, and creative exploration. While these principles once fostered community cohesion, the rise of financially motivated and state-sponsored actors has fractured this ethical landscape. Hacker ethics are now often invoked rhetorically rather than as guiding principles.

Psychological profiles of hackers are examined, challenging media stereotypes of socially inept loners. Empirical research reveals a spectrum of personality traits across hacker subtypes, with white hats showing agreeableness, grey hats displaying neuroticism, and black hats demonstrating openness to experience. The concept of moral disengagement is introduced to explain how some hackers rationalise harmful actions without guilt.

Finally, the chapter explores hacker motivations in the context of digital warfare. These include addiction, ego, entertainment, ideological causes, and financial gain. Such motives influence the nature and scope of cyber-offensive activities, especially when aligned with broader geopolitical agendas. The chapter concludes by asserting that understanding digital adversaries requires more than technical counter-measures, but it demands insight into the psychological and social ecosystems that shape cyber-aggression.

References

Bandura, A. (1999). Moral disengagement in the perpetration of inhumanities. *Personality and Social Psychology Review*, *3*(3), 193–209.

Beyond Identity. (2021). *1 in 4 ex-employees can login to past employers due to shared passwords*. Retrieved from https://pktech.net/blog/2021/07/1-in-4-ex-employees-can-login-to-past-employers-due-to-shared-passwords

Bishop, M., & Gates, C. (2008). Defining the insider threat. *Proceedings of the 4th Annual Workshop on Cyber Security and Information Intelligence Research*, 12–14. https://doi.org/10.1145/1413140.1413158

Cappelli, D., Moore, A., & Trzeciak, R. (2012). *The CERT guide to insider threats: How to prevent, detect, and respond to information technology crimes (theft, sabotage, fraud)*. New York: Addison-Wesley.

Chiesa, R., Ducci, S., & Ciappi, S. (2008). *Profiling hackers*. Auerbach Publications.

Fotinger, C., & Ziegler, W. (2004). Understanding a hacker's mind: A psychological insight into the hijacking of identities. *Krems, Austria: Donau-Universität Krems*, 1–48. Retrieved from http://www.donau-uni.ac.at/de/department/gpa/informatik/DanubeUniversityHackersStudy.pdf

Griffiths, M. (1996). Behavioural addiction: An issue for everybody? *Journal of Workplace Learning*, *8*(3), 19–25. https://doi.org/10.1108/13665629610116872

Hadlington, L. (2018). The "human factor" in cybersecurity. In J. Mcalaney & L. A. Frumkin (Eds.), *Psychological and behavioral examinations in cyber security* (pp. 46–63). https://doi.org/10.4018/978-1-5225-4053-3.ch003

Hadlington, L., & Ryding, C. (2025). *Human factors and cybersecurity: The psychology of online safety and security*. London, UK: Taylor and Francis Inc.

Holt, T. J., & Kilger, M. (2012). Know your enemy: The social dynamics of hacking. *The Honeynet Project*, 1–17. Retrieved from http://scholar.google.com/scholar?hl=en&btnG=Search&q=intitle:Know+Your+Enemy+:+The+Social+Dynamics+of+Hacking#0

Hunker, J., & Probst, C. (2011). Insiders and insider threats – an overview of definitions and mitigation techniques. *Journal of Wireless Mobile Networks, Ubiquitous Computing, and Dependable Applications*, *2*(1), 4–27. Retrieved from http://isyou.info/jowua/papers/jowua-v2n1-1.pdf

IBM. (2023). *Cost of a data breach report*. https://doi.org/10.1016/s1361-3723(21)00082-8

Javaid, M. A. (2013). Psychology of hackers. *SSRN Electronic Journal*, *15*(26).

Jordan, T., & Taylor, P. (2017). A sociology of hackers. *Cyberspace Crime*, 163–186. https://doi.org/10.4324/9781315199627-19

Kirwan, G., & Power, A. (2013). *Cybercrime: The psychology of online offenders*. Cambridge, UK: Cambridge University Press.

Kizza, J. M. (2024). *Cyber crimes and hackers – guide to computer network security* (J. M. Kizza, Ed.). https://doi.org/10.1007/978-3-031-47549-8_5

Kuss, D. J., & Griffiths, M. D. (2011). Online social networking and addiction: A review of the psychological literature. *International Journal of Environmental Research and Public Health*, *8*(9), 3528–3552. https://doi.org/10.3390/ijerph8093528

Levy, S. (1984). *Hackers: Heroes of the computer revolution*. Garden City, NY: Anchor Press and Doubleday.

Lieberman, B. (2003). Computer hackers: An intractable problem and what to do about it. *Research and Policy Memorandum 301.1, Pittsburgh*.

Mandiant. (2025). M-trends 2025: Supply chain attack analysis. *Mandiant/Google Cloud*.

Matulessy, A., & Humaira, N. H. (2016). Hacker personality profiles reviewed in terms of the big five personality traits. *Psychology and Behavioral Sciences*, *5*(6), 137–142. https://doi.org/10.11648/j.pbs.20160506.12

Moore, C. (2015). Moral disengagement. *Current Opinion in Psychology*, *6*, 199–204. https://doi.org/10.1016/j.copsyc.2015.07.018

Pfleeger, C. P. (2008). Reflections on the insider threat. In S. Stolfo, S. Bollovin, & S. Hershlop (Eds.), *Insider threat study: Illicit cyber activity in the banking and financial sector* (pp. 5–15). New York: Springer.

Weimann, G. (2004). Cyberterrorism how real is the threat? *United States Institute of Peace*, (Special Report 119), 1–12. https://doi.org/10.1017/CBO9781107415324.004

Weimann, G. (2005). Cyberterrorism: The sum of all fears? *Studies in Conflict and Terrorism*, *28*(2), 129–149. https://doi.org/10.1080/10576100590905110

Wible, B. (2003). A site where hackers are welcome: Using hack-in contests to shape preferences and deter computer crime. *Yale Law Journal*, *112*(6), 1577–1624. https://doi.org/10.2307/3657453

Woo, H. (2003). *The hacker mentality: Exploring the relationship between psychological variables and hacking activities*. Retrieved from http://athenaeum.libs.uga.edu/handle/10724/6624

Young, R., Zhang, L., & Prybutok, V. R. (2007). Hacking into the minds of hackers. *Information Systems Management*, *24*(4), 281–287. https://doi.org/10.1080/10580530701585823

3 Defining the Terrain

Disinformation and Misinformation

Introduction

We live in an era defined by our capacity to communicate thoughts and ideas rapidly through digital technology, granting us unprecedented global reach. The traditional gatekeepers who once served as arbiters of truth have largely disappeared, and the boundaries between truth and misinformation have become increasingly blurred. The proliferation of misinformation and disinformation has emerged as a critical challenge for many governments. Such information not only disrupts public discourse but also acts as a destabilising force against democratic processes, instilling feelings of distrust, panic, and anger. Although these mechanisms are not entirely new and have historical roots in propaganda and manipulation, the digital age presents an unprecedented array of platforms capable of spreading such content with speed and reach never witnessed.

The creation of false information is not historically new and has been a feature of the communication landscape since Roman times, to the time when Anthony met Cleopatra. Octavian, who became angered by Anthony's focus on Cleopatra and the East of the empire and Egypt, engaged in an extensive propaganda war against Anthony that was intended to result in his tarnished reputation. Octavian used slogans to describe Anthony as a serial womaniser and a useless alcoholic who had become the plaything for Cleopatra, corrupted by their affair, and being swayed by a foreign queen. In doing so, Octavian managed to sway popular public opinion and later became Emperor Augustus.

In this chapter, we engage in a journey to differentiate and define the key constructs that underpin the landscape of misinformation and offer a conceptual overview for the way in which key concepts fit into the area. As we examine the mechanisms through which information can be spread, we lay the groundwork for understanding how it can be used in digital warfare as a mechanism for disruption. While there are inherent psychological and cognitive elements attached to the proliferation of and susceptibility to misinformation, we will be exploring these in more depth later in Chapter 12, and for now, we will be focusing on creating a clear structure for understanding how the different types of

DOI: 10.4324/9781003752400-3

misinformation fit together, in turn setting the stage for a more focused exploration of one of the facets of the area, fake news, in the following chapter.

The Contagion of Misinformation

Early in the COVID-19 pandemic, General Tedros Adhanom Ghebreyesus, the then Director-General of the World Health Organization (WHO), stated at the Munich Security Conference on February 15, 2020, that

> we're not just fighting an epidemic, we're fighting an infodemic.
>
> (Zarocostas, 2020)

This quote typified the way in which information can be spread through the internet, and while cyberspace can be flooded with a wealth of information, there would also be a massive amount of disinformation and misinformation related to the COVID-19 pandemic. The spread of disinformation through cyberspace has also been likened to the spread of the COVID-19 pandemic, with Sylvie Briand, the then director of the Global Infectious Hazard Preparedness for the WHO, stating that

> But the difference now with social media is that this phenomenon is amplified, it goes faster and further, like the viruses that travel with people and go faster and further.
>
> (Zarocostas, 2020)

So the travel of misinformation is seen as a transmissible pathogen that can be passed from one person to another, and without the proper inoculation methods, it can easily infect their minds. The speed with which misinformation can be spread means that it can be created and transmitted around the world in seconds, often because of virality from likes and shares. The more sensational, fear-inducing, or attention-grabbing the misinformation is, the more likely it is to take hold, and dislodging it becomes an onerous task – mental disinfectant is not always effective.

The Architecture of Misinformation

The labels of "misinformation" and "disinformation" are often used interchangeably in everyday conversations, with each one being linked to a sense that information is being created in ways that are intended to deceive or portray a false sense of perspective in relation to current world events and current affairs. However, there are two keyways in which the concepts can be differentiated, as we illuded to in the previous chapter. *Disinformation* involves the deliberate creation and sharing of fake information that has the direct intent to harm or deceive, whereas *misinformation* is false information that is deliberately created but is often unintentionally shared and is created for purposes that are not directly intended to harm.

Wu et al. (2019) presented a group of terms that can be associated with the term of misinformation, and some of these are presented in Figure 3.1 below. In their conceptualisation, they use the term "misinformation" to include all "false or inaccurate information" (p. 2) but restrict the spread of this information to social media. Some misinformation can be spread unintentionally, and it may be shared just because the individual has a trusting relationship with the information provider (Wu et al., 2019). On the other hand, there is intentionally spread misinformation, created with a clear agenda and objective in mind. Such misinformation is where we cross over into the realm of disinformation, with conspiracies, rumours, and fake news all having the potential to be created with the intention to deceive. Each of the concepts associated with misinformation can be created with a degree of intent to harm and deliberation in its construction, meaning that each of these can be a source for offensive digital warfare operations. Propaganda is a special case, as it can cross over into misinformation and has some overlap with fake news; hence, we have presented these as having some links to each other.

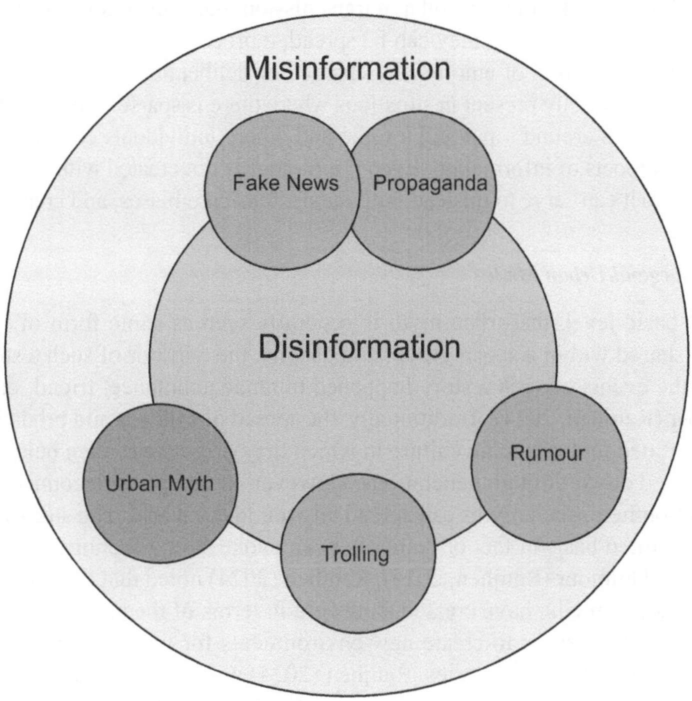

Figure 3.1 A typology for misinformation.

Fake News

This term is often used to describe various other forms of misinformation, but in essence, this category is reserved for material that is presented in a way that imitates traditional news broadcasting; this is not directly disinformation, as the intent behind the creation of such material is not done to deceive but to entertain. However, there are aspects of fake news which mean it can be unintentionally shared with others who may not understand the intent behind such material, often leading to unforeseen and undesired consequences. In the following chapter, we will pull apart the key features of fake news that make it so persuasive, as well as explore the different forms it can take.

Rumour

In its most basic form, a rumour is a piece of information that is unverified and speculative and is usually spread in a very informal way. Typically, rumours have been seen to be spread via word of mouth, but in recent years, the transmission mechanism has been enhanced by the presence of social media. Rumours have been noted to be one of the most fundamental contributors to the creation and reinforcement of false information. One of the most important characteristics of rumours that makes them so useful as a transmission mechanism for misinformation is the veracity with which they can be spread, a process that can easily be amplified with the addition of emotionally charged or deliberately sensational content. Rumours are usually present in situations where there is sparse or patchy information that exists around a particular topic and where individuals conduct searches for new snippets of information. Even if a rumour is not created with the intention to deceive, it can serve to mislead individuals, reinforce biases, and create panic.

Urban Legend/Urban Myth

At the basic level, the urban myth is generally seen as some form of folk-tale that is shared within a social group, and usually, the narrator of such a story will claim the events of such a story happened to an acquaintance, friend, or family member (Ranjhen, 2024). Traditionally, the spread of folklore and urban legends was confined to the specific culture in which they originated, often being refined and passed down through generations. However, in today's interconnected digital environment, such myths can spread all around the world. The stories usually have a limited basis in fact or reality but can evoke strong feelings such as fear, shock, and humour (Ranjhen, 2024). Ranjhen (2024) noted that digital platforms such as social media have created a new era in terms of the authorship of urban myths, and they serve to create new environments for the creation, dissemination, and editing of such stories. Ranjhen (2024) also pointed towards the speed at which new and existing urban myths can be propagated in such environments, usually due to the sensational or emotive context. These additional elements can again be seen to encourage the use of Type 1 decision-making systems, which in turn means individuals are less likely to engage in critical awareness when it comes to assessing the actual likelihood that such events took place in the first instance.

Spam

The term "spam" has been used in a variety of contexts, often to describe the presence of annoying, repetitive information, usually in the form of emails. Spamming can also be used in terms of creating repetitive, constant streams of web traffic that can be directed towards websites to overload them, resulting in a disruption of service or a DDoS attack. Spam has been seen to have a significant role in the spread of misinformation and can be seen to transcend many different platforms, defined as

> the attempt to abuse of, or manipulate, a techno-social system by producing and injected unsolicited, and/or undesired content aimed at steering the behaviour of humans or the system itself, at the current or indirect, immediate or long-term advantage of the spammer(s).
>
> (Ferrara, 2019, p. 84)

Trolling

Trolling has been used to describe a variety of online activities and is often used in the context of discussions around cyber-bullying and cyber-aggression. The activity is carried out online and generally focuses on platforms where individuals are encouraged to participate in discussion and debate as part of the cultural dynamics of that environment. Trolling involves the posting of comments or content that can be seen as being deliberately divisive in nature and will go to the extreme ends of opinion to gain some form of reaction. The goals for trolling can be multiple and diverse and include the potential to sow the seeds of discord and disharmony, enhancing the capacity for disrupting the natural flow of public debate. The action can also be used to silence the opinions of individuals who have views which go contrary to the dominant ideology within the host environment, serving to protect the stability of such and facilitating the maintenance of echo chambers in online forums. There is some evidence that trolling occurs because individuals are afforded anonymity, which comes from the use of such digital platforms and will often gain a sense of enjoyment from engaging in such activities (Centre for Strategy and Evaluation Services, 2018).

Researchers such as Hardaker (2010) noted that while the term "trolling" is often used in a singular way to describe such behaviours, it can actually be broken down into four key types:

1. Aggressive: the use of overt hostility to get a reaction from individuals, often involving the use of insults, threats, and language that is designed to offend. The

goal for this type of trolling is to generate an emotional reaction from the community or serve to intimidate others to stem the flow of discussion and debate.
2. Deceptive: the troll can sometimes pretend to be someone who they are not, pretending to be either less knowledgeable than they are or offering advice or information that is incorrect. Usually, this type of trolling will involve some form of impersonation or the use of stolen credentials, where the individual facilitates the spread of information through the manipulation of discussions. They can also generate frustration from other forum members, where they post deliberately incorrect information.
3. Disruptive: the aim of this form of trolling is to disrupt the flow of discussions by posting material that interrupts the flow of discourse or serves to distract individuals from the current focal topic. This could include the use of spam, the inclusion of completely off-topic information, or posting material that is deliberately confusing.
4. Playful: usually, this type of trolling has less of a malicious intent attached to it and is often presented as a mechanism for humorous interactions or more for satire. While it can be satirical in nature, there is always a chance that it could be misinterpreted by some, leading to unintended escalation.

Other researchers have explored the construct of misinformation according to underlying components that form the nature of the content, context, and function of the material. Zeng (2017) applied a previous framework from DiFonzo and Bordia (2007) to present a differentiation between the core elements of misinformation, these being presented in Table 3.1.

Zeng's framework, which categorises misinformation based on its content, context, and function, provides a structured lens through which to understand how misinformation operates as a tactical tool in digital warfare. In this domain, misinformation is not only accidental or incidental, but it is also often deliberately engineered to exploit cognitive biases, sow confusion, erode trust, and manipulate public perception.

- Content: in digital warfare, the nature of the misinformation (e.g., fabricated statistics, doctored images, and misleading narratives) is tailored to resonate with specific audiences. Zeng's emphasis on content helps identify the psychological hooks embedded in such material.
- Context: the situational deployment of misinformation, including the timing, platform, and socio-political climate, is crucial in digital warfare. Zeng's typology highlights how misinformation is embedded within contexts to maximise its disruptive potential.
- Function: perhaps most critical in warfare settings, the function of misinformation (e.g., to distract, deceive, destabilise, or provoke) aligns directly with strategic objectives in digital conflict. Zeng's framework allows researchers to map these functions to broader goals such as cognitive overload, polarisation, or the delegitimisation of institutions.

Table 3.1 The Seven Core Types of Information According to Content, Context, and Function

Category	*Content*	*Context*	*Function*
Misinformation	Information that is seen as inaccurate	Any situation where information is circulated among individuals	No specific function is identified for misinformation.
Gossip	Information presented as private or privileged about others	Share between individuals; presented at the level of social interaction	To improve or enhance interpersonal relations; potentially for manipulation/ malicious purposes.
Urban legend	The use of narratives to enhance societal values that relate to contemporary society	Presented as casual interactions for storytelling	To promote and strengthen core cultural and moral values.
Disinformation	The creation of deliberately incorrect information	Disseminated through social networks and widely by various state actors and non-state actors	To spread distrust and to destabilise societal cohesion.
Propaganda	Messages that are carefully curated to promote political ideologies and narratives	Creation from a top-down perspective – presented from higher officials to lower echelons of society	The promotion of political and ideological information.
Rumour	Any unofficial information that is presented by unknown or anonymous individuals	Presented in times of crisis or where information is uncertain.	To make sense of uncertainty and lack of information during ambiguous circumstances.
Conspiracy theories	Explanations for events/practices that refer to the actions of elite groups, organisations, and unseen forces.	A response to uncertainty and threats to society, constructed as alternative views or perspectives on world events.	Threat management response to uncertainty or to simplify explanations for complex events; anti-establishment narratives.

Source: adapted from Zeng (2017).

By applying Zeng's typology, analysts can better dissect the anatomy of misinformation campaigns within digital warfare, identifying not only what is being said but also why, how, and to what effect. This typological clarity is essential for developing counter-measures, resilience strategies, and educational interventions aimed at reducing susceptibility to such tactics.

On the Topic of Virality

So, at some point, we need to discuss the construct of virality, which covers many of the topics we will be discussing moving forward, including memetic warfare and the spread of misinformation. One of the key things that many influencers and advertisers aspire towards is harnessing the power of virals to spread information about their products or their channels across cyberspace, and the viral advert is seen as a highly desirable and effective process. On the other hand, for the digital adversary, gaining traction through virality can offer the opportunity to flood cyberspace with material and information that serves to align itself with current objectives or future operations. Virals are not the same as memes, but memes themselves can become viral. A meme requires some form of subtext and a wider frame of reference for it to have meaning and to be understood, while viral information can be understood as a stand-alone presentation of an image or video. Viral content is generally spread via very simple mechanisms such as liking, sharing, and retweeting. On the other hand, memes are not as responsive to such mechanics, and the process of propagation for memes relies heavily on mutations and evolution; one meme can generate many more, which in turn proliferate throughout cyberspace. In research by Beskow et al. (2020), it was noted that memes had approximately four times more links to other domains and twice as many internet domains in comparison to non-memetic information. From this standpoint, memes are seen to propagate to more areas of the internet in comparison to non-memetic material.

There have been some attempts to define what constitutes virality, with one of the most recent being presented as

> a word-of-mouth diffusion process wherein a message is actively forwarded from person to person, within and between multiple weakly linked personal networks, and marked by a period of geometric growth in the number of people who are exposed to the message.
>
> (Hemsley & Mason, 2012, p. 3930)

It is important to note that the nature of the spread is isolated as one that occurs through interpersonal communication rather than any formal channels or media. This means that at some level, within the communication process, both trust and social influence have a role to play in the distribution of viral information, where people are more likely to engage with information from people they know. This is perhaps akin to the nature of an infectious disease, and while you do not have to trust the individual who passes on a virus to you, you must have some level of interpersonal interaction with that individual for the transmission process to occur. There is also a level of agency attached to the forwarding of viral information – it is not a passive process, and individuals must choose to share that message on some conscious level. This would in turn suggest that individuals who share these types of messages see them as having some intrinsic value within their social networks, whether this is the perception of value in the message or to garner likes/social engagement.

The notion that information is transmitted from person to person shows that, rather than macrodynamic processes, such as the mass spread of information, activity is more attuned to a micro-dynamic level, which again serves to pinpoint the role social ties and interactions can play in the spread of viral information. If you can find a method of manipulating these types of interactions between individuals, you have the capacity to either amplify or suppress a viral message within social networks. Likewise, the suggestion that information is transmitted through weaker, loosely connected groups moves away from the notion that viral messages are just distributed through tightly connected networks. This allows virality to expand out from echo chambers, a critical feature of viral information, as it needs to be able to reach new audiences.

The growth of the viral is seen to be an exponential one, where the number of people who are exposed to such information increases rapidly and can often be completely unpredictable. There can be a lag in the traction for viral information, but once it reaches a critical threshold, it expands at breakneck speeds. Soon after the peak of sharing occurs, there is a steady decay of activity, which slows to nothing after a certain period. This process has been referred to as the viral *signature* (J. Hemsley, 2016) and denotes the often-critical role the internet and social networks can have in the sharing of viral content. One final point to note is that virality needs a reach – it does not necessarily need any form of interaction or conversion, as would be the case with memes.

What Causes Something to Go Viral?

This is perhaps the Holy Grail in terms of harnessing the power of the internet, both from the perspective of advertising culture and from the viewpoint of memetic warfare and the spread of misinformation. Berger and Milkman (2012, 2013) suggested that one of the key reasons for viral content spread is the emotions that are linked to viewing that information. They noted that where content was able to evoke the higher-tier emotions, such as anger or anxiety, content was more likely to go viral (Berger & Milkman, 2013).

Real-world examples illustrate this principle clearly. For instance, during the 2016 U.S. election, misinformation designed to provoke outrage and anger spread rapidly across Facebook and Twitter, demonstrating how negative high-arousal emotions can fuel virality. Similarly, during the COVID-19 pandemic, posts that triggered anxiety, such as conspiracy theories and panic-buying alerts, went viral (remember toilet rolls and antibacterial hand sanitiser!), amplifying fear and uncertainty on a global scale. Conversely, positive emotional content also drives virality. The Amyotrophic Lateral Sclerosis (ALS) Ice Bucket Challenge went viral in the summer of 2014 and became a global phenomenon, raising over $115 million for ALS research (https://www.als.org/ibc). Its success was linked to humour, excitement, and altruism, all emotions that encouraged participation and sharing. Likewise, the "Chewbacca Mom" video that went viral in 2016, which featured a woman laughing uncontrollably while wearing a Chewbacca mask, became one of Facebook's most-watched live videos, clocking 164 million views, highlighting the power of joy and amusement (https://www.bbc.co.uk/news/world-us-canada-38348401).

As we have noted earlier, other research has shown that emotional contagion can have a significant impact on the likelihood of sharing memetic information, with content that induces stronger emotional responses having the power to spread information virally (Guadagno et al., 2013). As noted by Berger and Milkman (2012, 2013), while extreme emotive content in terms of viral information can enhance the possibility of such information being shared, positively laden information tends to be shared more widely. Berger and Milkman (2012) suggested that rather than sharing of information being just about the presentation of self online, there is a deeper, more nuanced relationship. They noted that people are more inclined to share interesting and entertaining information, with the aim of helping others or serving to enhance their own current mood.

From this perspective, Berger and Milkman (2013) identified humour as a key tactic for increasing virality, noting that amusing content is more effective than relaxing content in driving engagement. Conversely, sadness appears to inhibit sharing, making its avoidance critical for viral success. This insight underscores the significant impact of emotional tone on the willingness to share information.

Psychological and Cognitive Underpinnings: A Glimpse Ahead

While this chapter has focused on the structural elements of misinformation and its definitional boundaries, it is essential to recognise that misinformation is deeply rooted in human psychology. The way we process, encode, and share information is shaped by fundamental cognitive mechanisms and personality traits. These include cognitive biases such as confirmation bias and the availability heuristic, which lead individuals to favour information that aligns with pre-existing beliefs or is easily recalled. Similarly, dual-process theories suggest that much of our engagement with online content occurs through fast, intuitive thinking (System 1), making us more vulnerable to emotionally charged or simplified narratives.

Emotions can play a pivotal role in this dynamic. Content that evokes strong emotional responses, whether it be anger, fear, or joy, can capture attention and enhance memory retention, increasing the likelihood of sharing. This emotional contagion effect is amplified in social media environments, where algorithms prioritise engagement, creating feedback loops that accelerate virality.

In a similar way, personality traits further influence susceptibility. For example, individuals who are open to a wider set of experiences may be more receptive to novel information, while those who worry a lot about things may be more reactive to anxiety-inducing content. These psychological factors are not merely incidental; they represent vulnerabilities that can be strategically exploited in digital warfare, where misinformation is weaponised to manipulate cognition and behaviour.

In the chapters ahead, we will explore these vulnerabilities in depth and examine how cognitive biases, emotional triggers, and personality profiles intersect to shape susceptibility to misinformation. By understanding this psychological terrain, we can begin to develop strategies to mitigate the risks posed by information warfare.

Summary

This chapter maps the conceptual and operational landscape of misinformation and disinformation, reframing them as strategic instruments within the broader context of digital warfare. It begins by tracing the historical lineage of deceptive information practices from ancient propaganda campaigns, such as Octavian's smear tactics against Mark Antony, to the viral dynamics of contemporary online ecosystems. The chapter differentiates misinformation (unintentional spread of falsehoods) from disinformation (deliberate deception), constructing a typology of cognitive contagions that includes fake news, rumours, urban myths, trolling, and spam. Each of these forms is examined for its capacity to exploit emotional resonance, social trust, and digital virality.

The anatomy of virality is explored in depth, revealing how emotional triggers and interpersonal networks facilitate exponential spread. Drawing on social contagion theory, the chapter explains how trust, agency, and weak social ties amplify viral content beyond echo chambers. Real-world examples such as the ALS Ice Bucket Challenge, the Chewbacca Mom video, and misinformation during the COVID-19 pandemic illustrate how emotional tone, either positive or negative, can shape the likelihood of sharing. Research by Berger and Milkman (2012, 2013) and Guadagno et al. (2013) is discussed to show how high-arousal emotions like anger and anxiety, as well as humour and joy, drive virality.

In this chapter, we have also explored Zeng's typology of misinformation, which categorises content by its nature, context, and function, providing a structured lens for understanding how misinformation operates as a tactical tool in digital warfare. This framework highlights how false information is engineered to exploit cognitive biases, erode trust, and manipulate perception.

Finally, the chapter acknowledges the psychological and cognitive underpinnings of susceptibility to misinformation such as cognitive biases, emotional triggers, and personality traits while reserving detailed analysis for later chapters. By laying this conceptual foundation, the chapter positions misinformation not as a passive phenomenon but as an active weapon capable of destabilising public discourse and influencing behaviour. The next chapter narrows the focus to one of the most culturally resonant forms of misinformation: fake news, examining its structure, intent, and persuasive power.

References

Berger, J., & Milkman, K. L. (2012). What makes online content viral? *Journal of Marketing Research, 49*(2), 192–205. https://doi.org/10.1509/jmr.10.0353

Berger, J., & Milkman, K. L. (2013). Emotion and virality: What makes online content go viral. *Insights, 5*(1), 18–23.

Beskow, D. M., Kumar, S., & Carley, K. M. (2020). The evolution of political memes: Detecting and characterizing internet memes with multi-modal deep learning. *Information Processing and Management, 57*(2), 0–3. https://doi.org/10.1016/j.ipm.2019.102170

Centre for Strategy and Evaluation Services. (2018). Rapid evidence assessment: The prevalence and impact of online trolling. *Department for Digital, Culture, Media and Sport, 44*(0). Retrieved from https://assets.publishing.service.gov.uk/government/uploads/system/uploads/attachment_data/file/811449/DCMS_REA_Online_trolling_.pdf

DiFonzo, N., & Bordia, P. (2007). Rumor, gossip and urban legends. *Diogenes, 54*(1), 19–35. https://doi.org/10.1177/0392192107073433

Ferrara, E. (2019). The history of digital spam. *Communications of the ACM, 62*(8), 82–91. https://doi.org/10.1145/3299768

Guadagno, R. E., Rempala, D. M., Murphy, S., & Okdie, B. M. (2013). What makes a video go viral? An analysis of emotional contagion and internet memes. *Computers in Human Behavior, 29*(6), 2312–2319. https://doi.org/10.1016/j.chb.2013.04.016

Hardaker, C. (2010). Trolling in asynchronous computer-mediated communication: From user discussions to academic definitions. *Journal of Politeness Research, 6*(2), 215–242. https://doi.org/10.1515/JPLR.2010.011

Hemsley, J. (2016). Studying the viral growth of a connective action network using information event signatures. *First Monday, 21*(8).

Hemsley, J., & Mason, R. M. (2012). The nature of knowledge in the social media age: Implications for knowledge management models. *45th Hawaii International Conference on System Sciences*, 3928–3937.

Ranjhen, M. (2024). Evolution of urban myths and legends in the digital age. *International Journal of Novel Research and Development (IJNRD), 9*(1), 19–27. Retrieved from https://www.ijnrd.org/papers/IJNRD2401104.pdf

Wu, L., Morstatter, F., Carley, K. M., & Liu, H. (2019). Misinformation in social media: Definition, manipulation, and detection. *ACM SIGKDD Explorations Newsletter, 21*(2), 80–90. Retrieved from https://www.public.asu.edu/~huanliu/papers/Misinformation_LiangWu2019.pdf

Zarocostas, J. (2020). How to fight an infodemic. *Lancet (London, England), 395*(10225), 676. https://doi.org/10.1016/S0140-6736(20)30461-X

Zeng, J. (2017). *Contesting rumours on social media during acute events: The 2014 Sydney Siege and 2015 Tianjin blasts*. Queensland University of Technology.

4 Exploring Minds

The Cognitive Vulnerabilities Exploited in the Digital Battlespace

Introduction

In the modern digital era, the battlefield is no longer confined to the physical landscape; it now transcends these boundaries and extends into the minds and hearts of individuals. A crucial point to understand when examining the mechanics of digital warfare is that, although the tools employed may appear highly sophisticated, they predominantly exploit inherent vulnerabilities that have evolved within the human cognitive system. These vulnerabilities, shaped by evolutionary processes, serve valuable functions in our everyday lives. Rather than viewing these traits as weaknesses or assigning blame, it is more accurate to consider them as natural by-products of human cognition and emotion. We are not perfect; indeed, we rely heavily on intuition in decision-making and are easily swayed by messages that appeal to our preferences or beliefs. The core tactics of digital warfare systematically exploit these vulnerabilities, creating an ideal environment for manipulation, persuasion, and control.

To understand how these vulnerabilities are exploited, it is essential to first consider the architecture of human cognition. Humans are not passive recipients of information; we are active information processors. This means we continuously engage with our environment, seeking out, interpreting, and responding to stimuli based on prior knowledge, goals, and emotional states. However, this dynamic processing is constrained by the limited capacity of our cognitive systems. We cannot attend to or process all available information simultaneously, and as a result, we rely on selective attention, memory shortcuts, and heuristic decision-making to navigate complex environments.

These constraints give rise to the concept of humans as "cognitive misers," a term coined to describe our tendency to conserve mental effort by relying on cognitive shortcuts rather than engaging in deep, analytical processing (Fiske & Taylor, 1991). While these shortcuts are often adaptive, they can become liabilities in digital environments where deception, distraction, and manipulation are prevalent. For example, we may accept information that aligns with our beliefs without verifying its accuracy, or we may settle for the first plausible explanation we encounter. This

DOI: 10.4324/9781003752400-4

is a process known as "satisficing," where rather than searching for the perfect solution to a problem, we settle for something that is satisfactory for the current purpose (Simon, 1957). In digital warfare, such tendencies are not only incidental aspects of human cognition, but they also become aspects that are deliberately targeted and exploited.

In this chapter, we begin to explore some of the key cognitive mechanisms that make individuals highly susceptible to the tactics employed in digital warfare. These include cognitive biases that distort decision-making, memory processes that can be manipulated to alter recall, in turn causing individuals to remember events differently, recall things that never happened, or overlook critical details and attentional systems that can be hijacked through perceptual saliency and semantic relevance. Although these mechanisms are deeply embedded in the rich literature of human cognition, they represent a crucial step in understanding how digital warfare is executed and why it is so effective. The very traits that make us efficient thinkers and socially interactive beings can also be exploited by the weapons of influence.

Humans as Active Information Processors

In the theatre of digital warfare, humans are not passive recipients of information; they are active processors, constantly interpreting, filtering, and responding to stimuli from their environment. This dynamic processing, while essential for navigating complex digital landscapes, is also riddled with vulnerabilities that adversaries can exploit. Understanding how humans process information is therefore critical to identifying the cognitive fault lines that digital warfare seeks to target.

At the core of this understanding is the notion that humans are active information processors (Wickens & Carswell, 2006). We do not simply absorb information in a passive manner; instead, we actively seek out stimuli, interpret them through the lens of prior experience, and transform them into meaningful outputs, whether that be a decision, a verbal response, or a behavioural action. This process is shaped by our goals, emotional states, and contextual awareness, making it highly dynamic but also inherently constrained.

These constraints stem from the limited capacity of our cognitive systems. We cannot attend to or process all available information simultaneously, and as a result, we rely on mechanisms such as selective attention, memory shortcuts, and heuristic decision-making to manage cognitive load. These adaptations are often efficient and necessary, but they also introduce vulnerabilities, particularly in environments saturated with competing stimuli and deceptive content.

Understanding these foundational elements of human cognition, such as our active engagement with information, the limitations of our processing systems, and our tendency to conserve cognitive resources, is an essential basis for grasping how digital warfare operates. As suggested in the opening section of this chapter, these mechanisms are not only by-products of human thought but also form the key weakness that adversaries can exploit in the manipulation of perception, the disruption of attention, and the influence on decision-making.

Humans as "Cognitive Misers"

Fiske and Taylor (1991) noted that, in most instances, humans acted to conserve as much cognitive energy as they could by placing a heavy reliance on cognitive shortcuts rather than engaging in effortful processing of information. Such processes, although not entirely bad, can mean that in more complex environments where deception and influence are commonplace, they can become a source of vulnerability.

The concept of a cognitive economy is also commonly discussed when we talk about the processing of information, and there is a finite reserve of resources we can draw upon when it comes to performing tasks (Kimball, 2015). Whenever we can prevent a substantial amount of these cognitive resources from being burnt through in the pursuit of complex or burdensome tasks, we will default to the easier, more intuitive option. This is where the notion of satisficing comes into play, where individuals will opt for a solution to a problem that is not perfect but good enough to satisfy the current parameters we are faced with. This means that instead of engaging in a mentally exhausting process of shifting through all the possible options, we will usually settle for the first option that meets the minimum threshold for the current task. This in turn leads us into another term that is also a common feature of the human information processing system, that of bounded rationality. That is to say that humans can perform rational decision-making processes within the confines of their current resources, which are usually limited by several factors (e.g., time, information availability, and limited cognitive resources).

From the perspective of digital warfare, such processes become problematic when an individual is prone to accepting information that they see without engaging in a verification process to establish the facticity of that information. This is made even more likely if such information aligns well with their current beliefs and reduces the potential for cognitive dissonance (see Chapter 6). Furthermore, individuals may be more likely to accept the first available piece of information they find on a current topic rather than engaging in a critical exploration of other alternative explanations, something that mechanics such as algorithmic manipulation can easily exploit.

The cognitive strategies discussed above, including satisficing, bounded rationality, and an inherent reliance on heuristics, are deeply intertwined with the way individuals perceive and interpret information. As we are active information processors, perception is not a passive reception of stimuli; rather, it is an interpretive process shaped by prior knowledge, expectations, and cognitive limitations. In environments saturated with digital stimuli and competing narratives, what individuals *perceive* as true or relevant is often filtered through these cognitive shortcuts.

This means that perception itself can be biased or distorted, especially when individuals are exposed to information that aligns with their existing beliefs or reduces cognitive effort. For example, the tendency to accept the first plausible explanation encountered (a satisficing strategy) can influence not only decision-making but also how one perceives the credibility or salience of information. In digital warfare, this becomes particularly dangerous: perception can be manipulated through visual framing, repetition, and algorithmic curation, all of which exploit the brain's preference for efficiency over accuracy.

Thus, understanding perception in this context requires acknowledging that it is not only about seeing or hearing but also about *interpreting,* and these interpretations are shaped by the very cognitive constraints we highlighted earlier in this chapter. In the next section, we set about exploring how perception operates within these boundaries and how it can be influenced or hijacked in digital environments to serve strategic ends.

Perception

Perception is a fundamental process in human cognition and serves as the mechanism through which individuals take in sensory input from their environment. Perception can be stimulus-driven, capturing our attention through sudden or salient events such as a loud bang, a sudden movement, or a flickering light. Conversely, our current task focus can also shape perceptual goals, directing attention towards elements of the environment that are relevant to completing the task at hand.

Prior knowledge strongly influences what we attend to, guiding our perceptual system towards information we deem important or relevant. This process is often referred to as *top-down processing*, where existing mental schemas and expectations shape how we interpret sensory input (Navalpakkam & Itti, 2005; Teufel & Nanay, 2017). For instance, when searching for a product in a supermarket, prior knowledge of the product's branding, such as its colour scheme, logo, or packaging style, can help us filter out irrelevant items and focus on those that match our expectations. This *selective attention* reduces cognitive load and speeds up decision-making.

Beyond the realm of consumer behaviour, this principle can also be applied in many other contexts. For example, an experienced driver scanning a busy road will prioritise traffic signals and vehicle movements over irrelevant details like shop signs, because prior knowledge of driving rules dictates what is critical for safety. Similarly, in digital environments, prior knowledge can bias attention towards familiar sources or formats, such as preferring information from a well-known news outlet while ignoring alternative perspectives. While this mechanism is efficient, it can also create blind spots, making individuals susceptible to confirmation bias or overlooking contradictory evidence.

It is important to note that perception represents the first and most basic stage in the information processing system. At this stage, we encode very little detail about what we perceive unless it warrants further investigation or is highly relevant to our current task.

Perceptual Saliency and Attentional Disruption in Digital Warfare

The relevance of a stimulus, particularly its semantic significance, strongly influences whether it captures attention. Semantic significance refers to how meaningful or personally relevant something is to an individual. It is not merely about visual or auditory features; it concerns what the stimulus means to the person encountering it. For instance, when scanning a crowded webpage, you might quickly notice a word like *urgent* or even your own name, despite its lack of visual prominence. This occurs because the brain is attuned to detect elements that carry personal meaning. This is semantic significance in action.

In the context of digital warfare, semantic significance becomes a powerful tool. Cyber attackers often craft messages or visuals that are personally or culturally relevant to their targets, using familiar logos, emotionally charged language, or references to current events. These elements are more likely to capture attention and influence behaviour, even if they are not the most visually striking part of the screen. While perceptual saliency refers to what stands out visually (e.g., bright colours or motion), semantic significance concerns what stands out cognitively because it connects to what we care about, know, or are currently thinking about. This is particularly relevant in digital warfare, where both perceptual saliency and semantic relevance are strategically exploited to manipulate user attention. Exogenous attentional processes, which are largely automatic and stimulus-driven, play a central role in this dynamic. These processes prioritise stimuli that stand out perceptually, often overriding the user's current task focus (Roda, 2011).

Perceptual saliency refers to the degree to which a stimulus visually or audibly stands out from its background. In digital environments, this can be influenced by features such as colour, size, shape, motion, and contrast (Roda, 2011; Rensink, 2002; Rensink et al., 2000). In the context of digital warfare, these features are often deliberately engineered to capture attention, whether through flashing alerts, animated graphics, or strategically placed keywords.

Importantly, saliency is not fixed; it can be shaped by experience. Users can learn to associate certain features with relevance, thereby lowering the threshold at which those features capture attention. For example, Roda (2011) noted that hearing one's own name in a conversation can act as a highly salient cue, instantly redirecting attention. Similarly, Lavie et al. (2003) found that the appearance of a famous face caused greater disruption in a concurrent task than an unfamiliar one, highlighting how semantic familiarity amplifies attentional capture.

In digital warfare, this principle can be exploited through targeted content designed to resonate with the user's personal relevance. For instance, a misinformation campaign that contains emotionally charged language or the name of a familiar celebrity may be more likely to draw attention and elicit interaction. These tactics rely on the interplay between perceptual saliency and endogenous (internally created) predispositions, making them particularly effective in bypassing the rational scrutiny we may normally deploy.

A key question in our exploration is whether people can be distracted from important online tasks when exposed to highly attention-grabbing content. In everyday digital environments, such distractions can lead to errors, delays, or misinterpretation of information (e.g., missing red flags while shopping online, exploring social media posts, or reading news). Understanding which types of online stimuli are most likely to divert attention is essential for creating platforms, tools, and habits that reduce cognitive vulnerability and help users stay focused.

Attention

This is a process that is closely linked to the concept of perception, but it is not the same. Attention is our way of protecting our information processing system from the potential for information overload, and it allows us to filter out the relevant from the irrelevant information in our immediate environment. One of the important things that should be noted about attention is that we do not necessarily need to have conscious awareness of something in order for that information to be processed by our attentional system. There has been a wide range of work that has demonstrated that perception can occur at a subconscious or subliminal level, which in turn has some important ramifications for information being presented in a digital warfare setting.

Researchers have agreed that attention is governed by a system that shares a similar set of limited resources with the other mechanisms of the human information processing system. This means that we can choose to select and attend to just a small number of stimuli within our current, immediate environment (Broadbent, 1957; Broadbent et al., 1982; Hahn et al., 2008). To attempt to pay attention to multiple streams of information at any one time runs the risk of important information being discarded or ignored, which can in turn result in poor memory formation and the possibility of biases in experiences and information. Attention has been seen as being fundamental in two keyways – it can act as a filter to determine what elements within the immediate environment should be attended to by the individual; secondly, it can act as a form of management system, which places certain restrictions on which tasks we can perform at the current moment in time (Hadlington, 2017; Wickens & Carswell, 2006; Wickens, 1981). There are also further ways in which attentional processes can be differentiated, particularly according to how these resources are distributed, which we will now move on to discuss.

Selective Attention

Selective attention refers to the mechanism of directing our attention towards one focal point in our current environment. This means that we will focus all our attentional resources on that point, with the trade-off being that anything else that is going on outside of that current focus will be filtered out and ignored. This has some obvious implications for digital warfare campaigns and means that if we have the capacity to capture someone's attention and direct it away from peripheral information that is still contextually important, we can manage narratives while also giving us the potential to "sneak" other information past the observer. Selective attention is useful when we are trying to complete a specific goal where it is important for us to be able to focus on the task at hand and the things that are crucial for that, while in turn allowing us to block out distracting and irrelevant information (Hadlington, 2017; Lavie et al., 2004).

Divided Attention

This is often considered the poorer cousin of selective attention and refers to the process of attending to two or more streams of information simultaneously. In effect, we divide the cognitive resources that govern attention across two or more tasks (Hadlington, 2017). The challenge is that dividing attention requires splitting already limited resources, creating a trade-off between task completion and the likelihood that each task will be performed successfully and accurately (Pashler, 2000).

There are certain parameters which determine how well an individual can attend to two tasks at the same time. For example, if the two things that we are trying to pay attention to are very similar in nature, such as trying to remember a phone number while trying to hold a telephone conversation with someone, there is going to be a high degree of certainty that some level of interference will take place (either forgetting the phone number or inadvertently not paying attention to some important information that the person on the other end of the phone is telling us). However, if the two tasks are disconnected, such as listening to music and writing, there is a much lower chance of interference occurring. Research has noted that there is a greater chance of interference in tasks where:

1. When two tasks require access to the same type of mental resources, such as language or speech, it becomes more difficult to perform them simultaneously. For example, if we try to remember a phone number while engaging in a conversation, both tasks compete for our verbal processing system: one for rehearsing the information and the other for producing speech.
2. When tasks compete for the same processing stage, such as at the point where information comes into our perceptual system (input) or where it is being processed into memory (encoding), performance can suffer, and errors start

to creep in. For example, if you are reading an important text while someone is giving you some important instructions about a new task you must do, both tasks require you to take in and encode new information. Due to the constraints of the human attentional system, it is not possible to accurately encode both streams simultaneously; there is a risk that the directions will be misremembered or that important details in the email will be overlooked.

3. The human brain uses different codes to store information, such as visual codes (pictures and images) and verbal codes (words). When two tasks rely on the same code, interference can occur, leading to confusion or merging of information. For example, if you are trying to describe something verbally while simultaneously reading text, both tasks depend on verbal codes. This overlap can make it difficult to keep the information from each task separate.
4. When two tasks rely on similar output systems, such as speaking or writing, performing them simultaneously becomes extremely difficult. If both tasks require the same physical response system, like talking or typing, it is unlikely that you can execute both effectively at the same time (unless you are an exceptionally skilled touch typist). For example, speaking on the phone while typing a report often leads to difficulties in co-ordinating attention and focus between the two tasks, which can result in errors.

(Wickens, 1984; Hadlington, 2017)

Sustained Attention (Vigilance)

This concept is generally associated with prolonged periods of focused attention, such as when we are searching for something or attempting to identify a specific item in a busy environment over an extended time. Our ability to maintain attention on a single task typically declines as time on task increases. In the context of digital warfare, prolonged and sustained disinformation campaigns exploit this limitation by gradually eroding sustained attention. Attackers often use strategies such as information flooding, repetition of narratives, and continuous exposure to emotionally charged content to wear down vigilance. As a result, individuals become more likely to overlook cues that indicate suspicious or false information, increasing susceptibility to manipulation. (Hancock & Warm, 1989; Ralph, 2014; Rose et al., 2002).

The fragility of the human attentional system creates numerous opportunities for exploitation in digital warfare. If attention can be diverted from critical information even briefly or if individuals are forced to divide their attention across multiple tasks or subjected to continual attentional overload, the likelihood of missing key information increases significantly (Hadlington, 2017). This is evident in situations where individuals might be bombarded with continuous notifications, presented with numerous clickbait headlines or presented with algorithmically curated feeds, each of which fragments attention and reduces cognitive capacity for critical evaluation. These conditions allow adversaries to carry out other actions outside the user's focus, such as embedding malicious links or spreading co-ordinated misinformation, which can often go unnoticed.

How Do We Grab Attention in Cyberspace?

Research into human attention has identified two fundamental mechanisms that influence how individuals allocate their focus: endogenous and exogenous attentional processes. These mechanisms are particularly relevant when considering how people interact with digital environments (Hadlington, 2017).

Endogenously Driven Attention

Endogenous attention refers to the internally guided allocation of focus, shaped by an individual's goals, intentions, and expectations (Rensink, 2008). For instance, when searching for a specific colour of clothing in a store, a person's attention is directed by their internal objective, rather than being passively drawn to visual stimuli. This type of attention is deliberate and reflects the cognitive prioritisation of information relevant to current tasks or desires.

A key feature of endogenous attention is its reliance on detailed knowledge of objects and scenes. This enables individuals to filter out irrelevant stimuli and concentrate on elements that align with their objectives (Rensink, 2008). In digital contexts, this has significant implications for how information is processed online. Since users bring unique goals and varying levels of expertise, the same digital content may attract different attentional responses. For example, frequent internet users may engage with online material differently than those who use it less often, due to differences in familiarity and task-driven focus.

In digital warfare, this process can play a critical role in how individuals navigate complex information landscapes. Attackers can exploit endogenous attention by designing content that aligns with users' goals or expectations, making malicious material appear relevant and trustworthy. For example, spear-phishing emails often mimic legitimate work-related tasks or urgent requests, leveraging the user's internal priorities to bypass scepticism. Similarly, disinformation campaigns frequently embed narratives within topics that audiences are already motivated to follow, such as political issues or cultural debates, ensuring that attention is voluntarily allocated to deceptive content.

Such attentional control exists before any interaction with a digital system begins. It influences how users select tools, interpret data, and prioritise actions. In warfare scenarios, this can mean the difference between identifying a threat early and missing it entirely. Importantly, individual differences such as training, experience, and cognitive predispositions can also lead to vastly different attentional responses to the same digital stimuli. This variability creates opportunities for adversaries to tailor attacks to specific user profiles, exploiting predictable patterns of goal-driven attention.

Exogenously Driven Attention

Endogenous attention is goal-driven, deliberate, and shaped by internal priorities such as tasks, intentions, and prior knowledge. It allows individuals to filter irrelevant stimuli and focus on information aligned with their objectives. For example, when shopping online for a specific item, let us say, a pair of running shoes, your attention is guided by your internal goal. You deliberately scan product listings for features like size, colour, and brand, filtering out irrelevant ads or unrelated products. This is endogenous attention in action: your focus is shaped by what you want to achieve, rather than by random visual distractions.

Exogenous attention is triggered by external stimuli and operates largely outside conscious control. It is typically fast and automatic, often redirecting focus in response to sudden or novel events (Navalpakkam & Itti, 2005; Rensink, 2008). Examples include attention being captured by a brightly coloured image, a pop-up advertisement, or a smartphone notification (Kushlev et al., 2016). This involuntary shift in attention is thought to be rooted in evolutionary mechanisms designed to detect potential threats (Roda, 2011). In digital environments, such stimuli can disrupt task-focused behaviour, pulling users away from their intended activities and potentially impacting productivity or information retention.

In digital warfare, this mechanism is often exploited to disrupt focus and redirect cognitive resources. Examples include sudden system alerts, deceptive pop-ups, or strategically timed notifications designed to interrupt critical tasks. These stimuli can override endogenous focus, leading to attentional capture, a phenomenon where attention is involuntarily redirected due to the salience or novelty of a stimulus (Franconeri & Simons, 2003; Lee Hadlington, 2017; Yantis, 2000). In hostile digital environments, adversaries may use this to their advantage, embedding attention-grabbing elements in malware, phishing emails, or disinformation campaigns that use trending hashtags or emotionally charged memes to exploit stimulus-driven attentional capture. Even irrelevant signals can divert attention if they mimic threat-like features, such as movement, novelty, or urgency.

The Interplay of Attention in Digital Warfare Operations

Attempts to disentangle the influence of endogenous and exogenous attention have proven challenging, even under controlled experimental conditions (Bacon & Egeth, 1994; Folk & Remington, 1998; Gorman et al., 2005). In the fluid and often ambiguous context of cyberspace, these challenges are magnified. Users frequently operate without clearly defined goals, such as browsing social media, scanning news feeds, or multitasking across platforms, which increases susceptibility to exogenous manipulation (Dames et al., 2019; Jenkins et al., 2025). In such circumstances, attention can switch quickly between internally guided objectives and externally triggered distractions, creating opportunities for adversaries to exploit both mechanisms simultaneously. For example, a user searching for product reviews (endogenous focus) may be interrupted by a visually salient pop-up or emotionally charged headline (exogenous trigger), redirecting cognitive resources and undermining task performance. This interplay is central to digital warfare strategies, where attackers deliberately design content to hijack attention through salience, urgency, and contextual relevance.

Semantic relevance also plays a critical role in attentional capture. For instance, an advertisement containing the word "FREE" may attract attention if the user is motivated by cost-saving, a form of endogenous attention triggered by personal relevance (Burke et al., 2005). In digital warfare, adversaries exploit this principle by crafting persuasive or misleading content that resonates with the target's psychological profile, values, or current concerns. This can include using emotionally charged language, culturally familiar symbols, or keywords aligned with personal interests. Such tactics increase the likelihood of engagement because they activate internal goals and expectations, making the content appear trustworthy or important. When combined with perceptual salience such as bold fonts, urgency-evoking colours, or pop-up formats, semantic relevance becomes a powerful mechanism for manipulating attention and influencing behaviour.

Implications for Defensive and Offensive Strategies

Understanding how attention is deployed in cyberspace has direct implications for both defensive and offensive strategies in digital warfare. System-generated alerts, status updates, and interface changes can guide attention exogenously, either to support task performance or to disrupt it. When these signals are well-designed, they can enhance situational awareness. When misused, they can degrade performance and increase vulnerability.

Relevance theory offers a useful lens for understanding this dynamic. It explains how individuals interpret communication based on expectations of relevance. A key concept, optimal relevance, suggests that when someone communicates, we expect the information to be worth our attention and represent the best the communicator can provide at that time (Javier & Pérez, 2000). Consequently, we assume that information is neither random nor trivial but conveys important details and reflects the most relevant content available. According to Sperber and Wilson (1986), individuals allocate attention to stimuli that promise the greatest cognitive benefit for the least processing effort. Information is considered relevant if it confirms existing knowledge or helps revise current beliefs.

To contextualise this for digital environments, alerts that convey clear, meaningful information aligned with user goals are perceived as highly relevant and are more likely to be acted upon. Conversely, adversaries exploit this principle by embedding semantic cues such as urgency ("Act Now"), authority ("Mandatory Update"), or personal relevance ("Your Account") into deceptive messages. These cues increase perceived relevance, override scepticism, and accelerate engagement.

Beyond semantic cues, where information forms a meaningful connection with what we might need or know, attentional capture plays a critical role in shaping how we perceive the relevance of the material we come into contact with. Features such as motion, high contrast, and semantic salience can all draw attention even before we have started to process the information we encounter, and valuation occurs. It is important to recognise which aspects of digital stimuli are most likely to capture attention, and by doing so, we can inform the design of protective systems and adversarial tactics alike. In high-stakes environments such as the digital battlefield, identifying and mitigating sources of attentional disruption is crucial for maintaining operational effectiveness, as adversaries often combine perceptual salience with relevance cues to maximise impact.

Memory

Memory is a fundamental component of the human information processing system, serving as the repository for learnt knowledge, experiences, and essential skills required for daily functioning. Like attention, memory is subject to limitations that adversaries can exploit in psychological, cognitive, and information warfare.

Memory is often conceptualised as comprising a short-term store, which retains information briefly and enables manipulation before it is either lost or consolidated into long-term memory (LTM). LTM provides more durable storage, but retrieval can be influenced by numerous factors, which we will come to shortly. Critically, what and how we remember is shaped by salience or how relevant they are to us and can be seen to come into play particularly when stimuli are paired with emotionally charged details (Brosch et al., 2013).

Furthermore, memory is not infallible. False memories can be created when post-event information biases recall, leading individuals to remember events that never occurred (Fenn et al., 2014; Sherman & Moran, 2011). This vulnerability has profound implications for offensive cognitive and information warfare campaigns aimed at subverting existing knowledge and reshaping beliefs. Because memory underpins most decision-making processes, manipulating or biasing stored information can influence future judgements and behaviours, making memory a strategic target in DiPsyOps.

Even when information is successfully stored in LTM, several processes can influence how easily it is recalled. *Proactive interference* occurs when older information blocks the acquisition or retrieval of newer information. This can be exploited in propaganda campaigns that reinforce outdated narratives, making it harder for individuals to adopt newer, more progressive ideas. Conversely, retroactive interference happens when newer information disrupts the recall of older information. A simple example is learning a new password, which makes the old one harder to remember. In the context of information warfare, misinformation campaigns can leverage retroactive interference to undermine previously accepted, accurate knowledge.

Another mechanism is *decay*, a natural process where memory traces fade over time, particularly if they are not revisited or rehearsed. This fading has been likened to an old sepia photograph losing its clarity and definition. Adversaries can exploit decay by repeatedly exposing individuals to misinformation, allowing outdated or weakened memories to be replaced with newer, incorrect information. These vulnerabilities highlight how memory, despite our assumptions about its robustness, can be systematically targeted to distort beliefs and influence future decision-making.

Decision-Making

Human decision-making is often theorised as operating through two distinct processing systems, reflecting the tendency of humans to act as cognitive misers, where we are always seeking to conserve mental effort. Type 1 processing is fast, intuitive, emotional, and largely unconscious. It is highly susceptible to bias and operates independently of cognitive ability. In contrast, Type 2 processing is slower, deliberate, and rational and is typically correlated with higher cognitive ability (Evans, 2006; Evans & Stanovich, 2013). There is a wide variety of supporting evidence from the field of neuroscience to support the existence of these two processing routes (Denton & Krebs, 2017). This dual-system architecture has profound implications for cognitive and information warfare. Adversaries often design manipulative content to trigger Type 1 processing, leveraging emotional appeals, urgency, and heuristic shortcuts to bypass rational scrutiny. By contrast, defensive strategies aim to engage Type 2 processing, encouraging reflection and critical evaluation to counter impulsive, biased responses.

One of the key vulnerabilities of Type 1 decision-making is its reliance on mental shortcuts, or heuristics or rules of thumb, that often lead to satisfactory outcomes but are not guaranteed to produce correct answers. This reflects the principle of satisficing we have introduced previously, where individuals seek "good-enough" solutions to conserve cognitive resources.

Heuristic processing is closely tied to information stored in memory, creating a critical intersection between memory and decision-making. If an adversary can influence the experiences or information that individuals draw upon, they can bias future decisions. This mechanism underpins the hybridisation of cognitive and information warfare, where strategically curated content shapes memory recalls and primes Type 1 processing. By embedding emotionally charged or salient details into misinformation, attackers can exploit intuitive reasoning, bypass reflective scrutiny, and accelerate biased judgements. We will continue our exploration of heuristics later in Chapter 9.

Cognitive Biases

Cognitive biases are an inevitable consequence of engaging in Type 1 processing, reflecting the mind's reliance on shortcuts and intuitive judgements. These biases act as unconscious influencers that exert a subtle yet powerful impact on decision-making. For example, the Dunning–Kruger effect leads individuals to overestimate their ability to perform tasks or detect threats and will continue to repeat the same pattern of overestimation even though they are presented with evidence to highlight these specific deficiencies (Ament, 2018; Schlösser et al., 2013). In the context of digital warfare, this can be dangerous when individuals believe they are highly skilled at spotting the potential threats that might exist online. Such an inflated self-assessment increases vulnerability, as overconfident users may dismiss warnings and fail to critically evaluate content, making them more likely to believe and share false information.

A wide range of cognitive biases can distort judgement, and what makes them particularly problematic is their resistance to self-awareness and mitigation. Many biases are deeply ingrained and culturally reinforced, making them difficult to neutralise (Klein et al., 2019). This creates fertile ground for adversaries to design manipulative content that exploits these unconscious tendencies, accelerating engagement and reducing rational scrutiny.

Emotion

Emotion acts as a powerful modulator of cognitive processes, shaping what we attend to, how we encode information, and the strategies we use in decision-making. Stimuli that evoke strong emotional responses are more likely to be remembered and more likely to elicit action. Emotional content also facilitates Type 1 processing, triggering intuitive, heuristic-based decisions rather than reflective analysis (Denton & Krebs, 2017).

Emotional states such as fear, anger, or sadness can narrow attentional focus to specific stimuli while suppressing peripheral information, influencing both memory formation and recall. This selective attention creates fertile ground for cognitive biases, as emotionally charged experiences are often recalled more vividly and judged as more significant. Emotional manipulation has long been a corner-stone of psychological warfare (Brooker, 2019; Chang & Park, 2025; Shen et al., 2019). In digital environments, adversaries exploit this by embedding emotionally provocative cues such as outrage, fear, or moral indignation into disinformation campaigns (Nisbet & Kamenchuk, 2019). By using these tactics, digital adversaries can bypass rational scrutiny as well as accelerate engagement in viral posts, which can in turn amplify the spread of false narratives.

Fatigue

In this, the last section of this chapter, I wanted to focus more directly on something that can directly impact how well individuals can process information. Fatigue is something that I would describe as the kryptonite of our information processing systems, undermining attention, memory, and decision-making. The experience of fatigue is quite common in the general population, with some researchers noting that at one time, about 10% of the population attended medical appointments with the symptoms associated with the concept (Pawlikowska et al., 1994). Fatigue is often viewed in subjective terms, usually in terms of how tired or drained we feel during our daily lives (Aaronson et al., 1999). However, defining the construct of fatigue is far more complex than it may first appear and could be seen as either something that individuals experience as part of everyday life activities or a more serious, pathological symptom that arises because of a chronic illness (Aaronson et al., 1999).

We have explored the concept of fatigue and the different ways it can manifest in the context of cybersecurity awareness and human factors (Hadlington & Ryding, 2025). Fatigue is not only a by-product of demanding environments, but it can also be deliberately exploited as a mechanism of influence within digital warfare. By wearing down cognitive and emotional defences, adversaries create conditions where individuals become more receptive to misinformation, propaganda, and manipulative narratives. This vulnerability emerges through three interrelated forms of fatigue: dispositional, psychological, and physiological.

Dispositional Fatigue: individual characteristics can predispose people to experience fatigue more intensely. Chronic health conditions such as insomnia or diabetes reduce cognitive resilience, making sustained attention difficult. Personality traits amplify this effect: individuals high in neuroticism may feel overwhelmed by persistent exposure to threatening or alarming content, accelerating emotional exhaustion. Those low in conscientiousness may lack the self-regulatory strategies needed to manage fatigue, leaving them more susceptible to impulsive sharing or acceptance of false information. In digital warfare, adversaries exploit these vulnerabilities by maintaining a constant stream of emotionally charged or fear-inducing content, ensuring that those predisposed to fatigue reach a breaking point more quickly (Hadlington & Ryding, 2025; Stanton et al., 2016).

Psychological Fatigue: psychological fatigue arises from sustained cognitive effort and emotional strain. Digital warfare environments often demand continuous decision-making where we are evaluating sources, verifying claims, and filtering vast amounts of information. When individuals are bombarded with conflicting narratives, urgent calls to action, and emotionally provocative messages, the cumulative cognitive load leads to mental exhaustion. This state reduces critical thinking and increases reliance on heuristics, making individuals more likely to accept simplistic or emotionally appealing narratives. Over time, psychological fatigue erodes scepticism, creating fertile ground for propaganda and disinformation campaigns (Nobles, 2022).

Physiological Fatigue: physiological fatigue, characterised by listlessness and diminished capacity to exert effort (Grandjean, 1979), further impacts our capacity to focus and pay attention. Physical tiredness often translates into

> reduced attentional control and slower cognitive processing. Empirical evidence underscores this link: 52% of individuals who fell victim to phishing attacks reported doing so because they were tired (Tessian, 2022). In the broader context of digital warfare, fatigue-driven lapses in attention make individuals more likely to skim content, overlook inconsistencies, and accept falsehoods without scrutiny. Propaganda campaigns exploit these conditions by timing releases during periods of high stress or fatigue, such as during crises where our cognitive defences are weakest.

Fatigue is not simply a passive state of diminished energy; it is a strategic vulnerability that adversaries can actively exploit to undermine cognitive resilience and decision-making. In the context of digital warfare, the deliberate actions that serve to create or amplify levels of fatigue can serve several critical objectives. In the first instance, there is the capacity to erode established cognitive defences, where fatigue weakens the mental processes required for critical evaluation of information. When individuals are fatigued, they rely more heavily on heuristics and emotional cues rather than systematic reasoning (Engle-Friedman et al., 2023). This shift makes them more susceptible to persuasive tactics embedded in misinformation and propaganda. By sustaining high levels of cognitive load through information overload, contradictory narratives, and urgent calls to action, adversaries create conditions where scepticism collapses and acceptance of falsehoods becomes more likely.

As fatigue progresses, individuals experience decision fatigue, reducing their willingness to engage in effortful thinking (Hirshleifer et al., 2019). This state can influence compliance with simple instructions, especially those framed as urgent or emotionally salient. Digital warfare campaigns often exploit this by presenting binary choices ("share or ignore," "support or oppose") that require minimal cognitive effort, which in turn nudges fatigued individuals towards behaviours that amplify the adversary's objectives.

Fatigue diminishes emotional regulation, making individuals more reactive to fear, anger, or outrage (Grillon et al., 2015; Lewczuk et al., 2022). Propaganda and disinformation campaigns leverage this vulnerability by embedding emotionally charged content within their messaging (Kadir et al., 2016; Kadir et al., 2020). Heightened emotional responses not only increase message acceptance but also drive impulsive behaviours such as rapid sharing, which accelerates the viral spread of manipulative narratives.

Finally, digital warfare is not solely about short-term influence; it seeks to degrade cognitive resilience over time. Persistent exposure to overwhelming information environments fosters chronic fatigue, which can lead to disengagement, cynicism, and a state of learnt helplessness where people accept information without interrogating it (Bawden & Robinson, 2008; Schmitt et al., 2018). In turn, this can result in reduced participation in democratic processes, weaken overall trust in societal institutions, and create fertile ground for authoritarian narratives to take hold.

Summary

This chapter explores the cognitive architecture that underpins human information processing and highlights how its inherent limitations are exploited in digital warfare. Beginning with the concept of humans as active information processors and "cognitive misers," the discussion explains how strategies such as satisficing, bounded rationality, and heuristic reliance create openings for manipulation. Perception and attention are examined as gateways for influence, with emphasis on perceptual saliency and semantic relevance as tools for hijacking focus. The chapter differentiates endogenous and exogenous attentional processes, showing how adversaries leverage both goal-driven and stimulus-driven mechanisms to disrupt task performance and redirect cognitive resources.

Memory is presented as another critical vulnerability, susceptible to distortion through false memories, interference, and decay, all mechanisms that enable adversaries to reshape beliefs and prime future decisions. Decision-making processes are conceptualised in terms of the dual-system theory, which illustrates how intuitive, Type 1 processing is targeted via emotionally charged and heuristic-laden content. Cognitive biases such as overconfidence and confirmation bias are discussed as accelerants of susceptibility.

Emotion emerges as a powerful modulator of cognition, with adversaries embedding affective triggers into disinformation campaigns to bypass rational scrutiny and amplify viral spread. The chapter concludes with an in-depth analysis of fatigue, described as the "kryptonite" of information processing. Dispositional, psychological, and physiological fatigue are explored for their role in degrading attention, memory, and decision-making, while strategic implications reveal how sustained cognitive load and emotional strain foster compliance, impulsivity, and long-term cognitive attrition. Ultimately, the chapter positions cognitive vulnerabilities as central to the operational logic of digital warfare, underscoring the need for resilience strategies to counter these weaponised weaknesses.

References

Aaronson, L. S., Teel, C. S., Cassmeyer, V., Neuberger, G. B., Pierce, J., Press, A. N., . . . Wingate, A. (1999). State of the science defining and measuring fatigue. *Journal of Nursing Scholarship*, *31*(1), 45–50.

Ament, C. (2018). The ubiquitous security expert: Overconfidence in information security. *ICIS 2017: Transforming Society with Digital Innovation*, 0–18.

Bacon, W. F., & Egeth, H. E. (1994). Overriding stimulus-driven attentional capture. *Perception & Psychophysics*, *55*(5), 485–496. https://doi.org/10.3758/BF03205306

Bawden, D., & Robinson, L. (2008). The dark side of information: Overload, anxiety and other paradoxes and pathologies. *Journal of Information Science*, *35*(2), 180–191. https://doi.org/10.1177/0165551508095781

Broadbent, D. E. (1957). A mechanical model for human attention and immediate memory. *Psychological Review*, *64*(3), 205–215.

Broadbent, D. E., Cooper, P. F., FitzGerald, P., & Parkes, K. R. (1982). The Cognitive Failures Questionnaire (CFQ) and its correlates. *The British Journal of Clinical Psychology*, *21*, 1–16. https://doi.org/10.1111/j.2044-8260.1982.tb01421.x

Brooker, C. (2019). The effectiveness of influence activities in information warfare. *Australian Army Research Centre*, 8. Retrieved from https://researchcentre.army.gov.au/sites/default/files/AARCOccasionalPaperNo8%27Effectiveness of Influence Activities in Information Warfare%27%28Brooker%29_0.pdf

Brosch, T., Scherer, K. R., Grandjean, D., & Sander, D. (2013). The impact of emotion on perception, attention, memory, and decision-making. *Swiss Medical Weekly*, *143*(May 14). https://doi.org/10.4414/smw.2013.13786

Chang, K., & Park, J. (2025). Negative emotions, projection bias, and the vote choice in South Korea. *Humanities and Social Sciences Communications*, *12*(1). https://doi.org/10.1057/s41599-025-04479-7

Dames, H., Hirschfeld, G., Sackman, T., & Thielsch, M. T. (2019). Searching vs. browsing: The influence of consumers' goal directedness on website evaluations. *Interacting with Computers*, *31*(1), 95–112.

Denton, K. K., & Krebs, D. L. (2017). Rational and emotional sources of moral decision-making: An evolutionary-developmental account. *Evolutionary Psychological Science*, *3*(1), 72–85. https://doi.org/10.1007/s40806-016-0067-3

Engle-Friedman, M., Mathew, G. M., Martinova, A., Armstrong, F., & Konstantinov, V. (2023). The role of sleep deprivation and fatigue in the perception of task difficulty and use of heuristics, *11*(2), 74–84. https://doi.org/10.5935/1984-0063.20180016

Evans, J. S. B. T. (2006). The heuristic-analytic theory of reasoning: Extension and evaluation. *Psychonomic Bulletin & Review*, *13*(3), 378–395. Retrieved from http://www.ncbi.nlm.nih.gov/pubmed/17048720

Evans, J. S. B. T., & Stanovich, K. E. (2013). Dual-process theories of higher cognition: Advancing the debate. *Perspectives on Psychological Science*, *8*(3), 223–241. https://doi.org/10.1177/1745691612460685

Fenn, K. M., Griffin, N. R., Uitvlugt, M. G., & Ravizza, S. M. (2014). The effect of Twitter exposure on false memory formation. *Psychonomic Bulletin & Review*, 1551–1556. https://doi.org/10.3758/s13423-014-0639-9

Fiske, S. T., & Taylor, S. E. (1991). *Social cognition* (2nd ed.). London: McGraw-Hill.

Folk, C. L., & Remington, R. (1998). Selectivity in distraction by irrelevant featural singletons: Evidence for two forms of attentional capture. *Journal of Experimental Psychology. Human Perception and Performance*, *24*(3), 847–858. https://doi.org/10.1037/0096-1523.24.3.847

Franconeri, S. L., & Simons, D. J. (2003). Moving and looming stimuli capture attention. *Perception and Psychophysics*, *65*(7), 999–1010. https://doi.org/10.3758/BF03194829

Gorman, N., Burke, M., Hornof, A., Nilsen, E., Hornoff, A., & Nilsen. (2005). High-cost banner blindness: Ads increase perceived workload, hinder visual search, and are forcen. *ACM Transactions on Computer-Human Interaction*, *12*(4), 423–445. Retrieved from http://dl.acm.org/citation.cfm?id=1121116

Grandjean, E. (1979). Fatigue in industry. *British Journal of Industrial Medicine*, *36*(3), 175–186. https://doi.org/10.1136/oem.36.3.175

Grillon, C., Quispe-Escudero, D., Mathur, A., & Ernst, M. (2015). Mental fatigue impairs emotion regulation. *Emotion*, *15*(3), 383–389. https://doi.org/10.1037/emo0000058

Hadlington, L. (2017). *Cybercognition: Brain, behaviour and the digital world*. London: Sage.

Hadlington, L., & Ryding, C. (2025). *Human factors and cybersecurity: The psychology of online safety and security*. London, UK: Taylor and Francis Inc.

Hahn, B., Wolkenberg, F. A., Ross, T. J., Myers, C. S., Heishman, S. J., Stein, D. J., . . . Stein, E. A. (2008). Divided versus selective attention: Evidence for common processing mechanisms. *Brain Research*, *1215*, 137–146. https://doi.org/10.1016/j.brainres.2008.03.058

Hancock, P. A., & Warm, J. S. (1989). A dynamic model of stress and sustained attention. *Human Performance in Extreme Environments: The Journal of the Society for Human Performance in Extreme Environments*, *7*(1), 15–28. Retrieved from http://www.ncbi.nlm.nih.gov/pubmed/14552346

Hirshleifer, D., Levi, Y., Lourie, B., & Hong, S. (2019). Decision fatigue and heuristic analyst forecasts. *Journal of Financial Economics*, *133*(1), 83–98. https://doi.org/10.1016/j.jfineco.2019.01.005

Javier, F., & Pérez, D. (2000). Sperber and Wilson's relevance theory and its applicability to advertising discourse: Evidence from British press advertisements. *Atlantis*, *22*(2), 37–50.

Jenkins, J. L., Denison, A., Valacich, J. S., Wilson, D., Jenkins, J. L., Denison, A., . . . Wilson, D. (2025). *Detecting goal-oriented vs. browsing users through behavior analysis*. https://doi.org/10.23919/mipro57284.2023.10159963

Kadir, S. A., Lokman, A. M., & Tsuchiya, T. (2016). *Emotion and Techniques of Propaganda in YouTube Videos*, *9*(December). https://doi.org/10.17485/ijst/2016/v9iS1/106841

Kadir, S. A., Lokman, A. M., Tsuchiya, T., & Shuhidan, S. M. (2020). Analysing implicit emotion and unity in Propaganda videos posted in social network. *Journal of Physics: Conference Series*, (1529). https://doi.org/10.1088/1742-6596/1529/2/022018

Kimball, B. M. (2015). *Cognitive Economics*, *66*(2), 167–181. https://doi.org/10.1111/jere.12070

Klein, G., Koller, T., & Lovallo, D. (2019). Premortems: Being smart at the start. *McKinsey Quarterly*, (March), 3–4. Retrieved from https://www.mckinsey.com/business-functions/strategy-and-corporate-finance/our-insights/bias-busters-premortems-being-smart-at-the-start

Kushlev, K., Proulx, J., & Dunn, E. W. (2016). "Silence your phones": Smartphone notifications increase inattention and hyperactivity symptoms. *Proc. CHI 2016*. https://doi.org/10.1145/2858036.2858359

Lavie, N., Hirst, A., de Fockert, J. W., & Viding, E. (2004). Load theory of selective attention and cognitive control. *Journal of Experimental Psychology. General*, *133*(3), 339–354. https://doi.org/10.1037/0096-3445.133.3.339

Lavie, N., Ro, T., & Russell, C. (2003). The role of perceptual load in processing distractor faces. *Psychological Science*, *14*(5), 510–515.

Lewczuk, K., Wizła, M., Oleksy, T., & Wyczesany, M. (2022). *Emotion Regulation, Effort and Fatigue: Complex Issues Worth Investigating*, *13*(February), 1–10. https://doi.org/10.3389/fpsyg.2022.742557

Navalpakkam, V., & Itti, L. (2005). Modeling the influence of task on attention. *Vision Research*, *45*(2), 205–231. https://doi.org/10.1016/j.visres.2004.07.042

Nisbet, E. C., & Kamenchuk, O. (2019). The psychology of state-sponsored disinformation campaigns and implications for public diplomacy. *The Hague Journal of Diplomacy*, *14*(1–2), 65–82. https://doi.org/10.1163/1871191X-11411019

Nobles, C. (2022). Stress, burnout, and security fatigue in cybersecurity: A human factors problem. *HOLISTICA – Journal of Business and Public Administration*, *13*(1), 49–72. https://doi.org/10.2478/hjbpa-2022-0003

Pashler, H. (2000). Task switching and multitask performance. In S. Monsell & J. Driver (Eds.), *Attention and performance XVIII: Control of mental processes* (pp. 277–307). Cambridge, MA: MIT Press.

Pawlikowska, T., Chalder, T., Hirsch, S. R., Wallace, P., Wright, D. J. M., & Wessely, S. C. (1994). Population based study of fatigue and psychological distress. *British Medical Jounrnal*, *308*(March), 763–766.

Ralph, B. (2014). Media multitasking and sustained attention. Masters Thesis; University of Waterloo, Canada. Retrieved from https://uwspace.uwaterloo.ca/handle/10012/8693
Rensink, R. A. (2002). Change detection. *Annual Review of Psychology*, *53*, 245–277. https://doi.org/10.1146/annurev.psych.53.100901.135125
Rensink, R. A. (2008). On the applications of change blindness. *Psychologia*, *51*(2), 100–106. https://doi.org/10.2117/psysoc.2008.100
Rensink, R. A., Regan, J. K. O., Clark, J. J., & Kevin O'Regan, J. (2000). On the failure to detect changes in scenes across brief interruptions. *Visual Cognition*, *7*(1–3), 127–145. https://doi.org/10.1080/135062800394720
Roda, C. (2011). *Human attention in digital environments*. Cambridge University Press.
Rose, C. L., Murphy, L. B., Byard, L., & Nikzad, K. (2002). The role of the big five personality factors in vigilance performance and workload. *European Journal of Personality*, *16*(3), 185–200. https://doi.org/10.1002/per.451
Schlösser, T., Dunning, D., Johnson, K. L., & Kruger, J. (2013). How unaware are the unskilled? Empirical tests of the "signal extraction" counterexplanation for the Dunning – Kruger effect in self-evaluation of performance, *39*, 85–100. https://doi.org/10.1016/j.joep.2013.07.004
Schmitt, J. B., Debbelt, C. A., Schneider, F. M., Schmitt, J. B., Debbelt, C. A., & Schneider, F. M. (2018). Too much information? Predictors of information overload in the context of online news exposure the context of online news exposure, *4462*. https://doi.org/10.1080/1369118X.2017.1305427
Shen, C., Kasra, M., Pan, W., Bassett, G. A., Malloch, Y., & O'Brien, J. F. (2019). Fake images: The effects of source, intermediary, and digital media literacy on contextual assessment of image credibility online. *New Media and Society*, *21*(2), 438–463. https://doi.org/10.1177/1461444818799526
Sherman, S. M., & Moran, E. J. (2011). Creating false memories for brand names. *Applied Cognitive Psychology*, *25*(2), 336–340. https://doi.org/10.1002/acp.1714
Simon, H. A. (1957). *Models of man: Social and rational*. Oxford, England: Wiley.
Sperber, D., & Wilson, D. (1986). *Relevance: Communication and cognition*. Oxford: Blackwell.
Stanton, B., Theofanos, M. F., Prettyman, S. S., & Furman, S. (2016). Security fatigue. *IT Professional*, *18*(October), 26–32. https://doi.org/10.1109/MITP.2016.84
Tessian. (2022). *Psychology of human error*. https://doi.org/10.1016/b978-0-444-42727-4.50006-2
Teufel, C., & Nanay, B. (2017). How to (and how not to) think about top-down influences on visual perception. *Consciousness and Cognition*, *47*, 17–25. https://doi.org/10.1016/j.concog.2016.05.008
Wickens, C. D. (1981). *Processing resources in attention, dual task performance, and workload assessment*. Retrieved from http://www.aviation.illinois.edu/avimain/papers/research/pub_pdfs/techreports/EPL-81-3.pdf
Wickens, C. D. (1984). Processing resources in attention. In R. Parasuraman & R. Davies (Eds.), *Varieties of attention* (pp. 63–101). New York: Academic Press.
Wickens, C. D., & Carswell, C. M. (2006). Information processing. In G. Salvendy (Ed.), *Handbook of human factors and ergonomics* (4th ed., Vol. 42, pp. 111–149). https://doi.org/10.1016/j.ipm.2006.03.005
Yantis, S. (2000). Goal-directed and stimulus-driven determinants of attentional control. *Control of Cognitive Processes: Attention and Performance Xviii*, 73–103. https://doi.org/10.2337/db11-0571

5 Hacking the Wetware

Age, Personality, and Gender in Digital Warfare

Introduction

In the previous chapter, we explored the cognitive architecture that underpins and drives the fundamental elements of human experience. We established how the limitations inherent in these systems create fertile ground for digital warfare operations. However, one crucial dimension often overlooked when examining individual vulnerabilities is the "wetware," or the biological and psychological substrate that shapes our dispositional traits.

Among the many facets of dispositional influence, personality stands out as a particularly potent force. It not only governs how individuals respond to environmental stimuli but also plays a critical role in determining susceptibility to persuasion, manipulation, and compliance. Personality traits can subtly, yet powerfully, shape our perceptions, decisions, and behaviours, making them a key target in digital warfare strategies aimed at exploiting human malleability.

Personality is an abstract construct and is conceptualised as a set of traits that individuals can possess to varying degrees. These traits help explain consistent patterns in how people think, feel, and behave. Traditional models of personality, such as the Five-Factor Model, emphasize the idea that personality traits are relatively stable across the lifespan (John & Srivastava, 1991; McCrae & Costa, 1987). This stability allows researchers and practitioners to use personality as a reliable framework for predicting behaviour and cognitive tendencies. It also means that if you know the dominant personality traits in certain cultures or environments, you can manipulate your attack vector to harness such information.

However, more recent research has shown that personality is not entirely fixed. Significant changes can occur, particularly in early adulthood. For example, Bleidorn et al. (2022) found that traits such as emotional stability and conscientiousness tend to increase with age, reflecting a maturation process that continues well into the third decade of life. These findings suggest that while personality traits are stable enough to differentiate individuals from one another, they are also dynamic and responsive to life experiences, social roles, and developmental transitions.

DOI: 10.4324/9781003752400-5

It is generally agreed that there are five core personality traits (John & Srivastava, 1991), these being the following:

1. Openness to experience: the extent to which someone is open to the challenges of new experiences or relishes an opportunity to exercise their intellectual curiosity. An individual who is high in the trait of openness to experience is someone who engages in key challenges to expand their current experience beyond their current levels and really enjoys complex, original tasks (John & Srivastava, 1991).
2. Conscientiousness: this is the extent to which an individual is goal- and task-orientated or their capacity to delay gratification and follow the accepted rules that govern their current environment. Someone who is high in conscientiousness will usually think before they act and engage in a process of planning and delayed gratification in pursuit of their daily activities. They will also prioritise current goals according to their objectives, meaning they are reliable and will usually follow the rules or instructions they are given.
3. Extraversion: the extent to which someone exhibits prosocial desires and engages in social activities. Someone who is highly extraverted is usually an individual who is keen to engage in socialising is assertive and exhibits a high degree of positivity. However, they often focus on immediate gratification at the expense of long-term planning, meaning that they are often impulsive and reckless and engage in higher levels of risk-taking behaviours.
4. Agreeableness: the extent to which someone exhibits a prosocial, conflict-avoidant nature. Someone who is highly agreeable is an individual who is eager to get on with others around them, keen to avoid interpersonal conflict, and encourages collaboration. They are also modest in their achievements and skills as well as having a trusting nature.
5. Neuroticism (or emotional stability): the extent to which an individual exhibits a stability of emotion, thought, and process. Someone who is at the higher end of the neuroticism scale is someone who exhibits higher levels of traits such as nervousness, anxiety, and negative emotionality (John & Srivastava, 1999).

Personality traits are typically conceptualised as dimensions along a continuum, where individuals fall between two poles. For instance, introversion and extraversion represent opposite ends of a spectrum, with introverts tending towards social withdrawal and extraverts towards sociability (John & Srivastava, 1999). Assessing these traits traditionally relies on psychometric instruments that ask individuals to rate their likely responses to hypothetical scenarios.

You may question how relevant personality traits might be in the context of digital warfare, as much of the relevant information that relates such traits to the individual is usually hidden from view online. However, the advent of social media means that the digital battlefield is now replete with information that can also be used to identify the potential markers, which in turn serve to differentiate individuals in terms of their personality types (Han et al., 2023; Park et al., 2015). For example, someone who frequently posts emotional content online could be highly neurotic in nature and would be ideally targeted with information that leverages a focus on emotive elements. In contrast, someone who constantly shares novel ideas and information online is likely to have a higher tendency for openness to experience and could be easily manipulated to divulge more information with the use of social engineering tactics. Consistent and structured behaviour online and conformity to rules may indicate someone who is highly conscientious, which can in turn be turned into a vulnerability. Those individuals higher in conscientiousness will be more likely to follow rules, lending them to manipulation through authoritarian messages online (Muhanad et al., 2025).

The Dark Triad

There is another set of personality traits that are often viewed as being distinct from the core five traits we have reviewed above. These have been labelled the so-called dark triad mainly because they refer to more antisocial and divisive traits associated with individuals who behave in ways that go contrary to the norms of the society or culture that they reside in (Paulhus, 2014). The dark triad of personality traits consists of three core elements:

1. Narcissism – this is viewed as a multidimensional trait that can be viewed in terms of the degree to which an individual possesses feelings of self-entitlement, their overall clamour for attention, their need to exert interpersonal dominance, and also their general disregard for the feelings of others around them (Brasher et al., 2000; Buffardi & Campbell, 2008; Cichocka et al., 2022; Paulhus, 2014). In terms of online activities, those individuals who exhibit higher levels of narcissism have been shown to engage in higher levels of social activity in online forums as well as more self-promotion on social media (Buffardi & Campbell, 2008).
2. Machiavellianism – Machiavellians have been noted to be masters at manipulation, using their social skills to engineer the environment for their own benefits (Paulhus, 2014). Some researchers have argued that internet trolls are typically those who exhibit higher levels of Machiavellianism (Buckels et al., 2014; Frischlich et al., 2021), with their capabilities lending themselves to identifying which buttons to press to get a response from their intended target.
3. Psychopathy – usually seen as the most malevolent of the dark triad personality traits, this trait is typified as an absence of empathy towards others, and they usually take a sense of enjoyment when they inflict pain or harm on others (Paulhus, 2014).

Overall, the dark triad is often more associated with the adversarial side of digital warfare, and we see that attackers who proliferate online attacks are usually those who exhibit some, if not all, of the dark triad traits (Curtis et al., 2018). One trait, that of narcissism, has been linked to a greater susceptibility to attacks, particularly in the form of phishing emails, which was in turn linked to overconfidence that is an inherent feature of that trait (Curtis et al., 2018). Often driven by a view that they are immune to coercion, given an inflated sense of self, they present an ideal target for online attacks due to this. They are also keen to blame others around them, rather than risking damage to their self-worth, which means that they are less likely to learn from their past mistakes, again making them a worthy target for repeat attacks using the same mechanism.

Risk Perception and Risk-Taking

Individuals will frequently make judgements about the risks of performing a particular action and the likely outcomes of such a behaviour. Likewise, the capacity to take risks with one's own personal safety, finances, and other linked constructs has also been linked to dispositional factors, and there has been a long history of exploring risk-taking personality types (Zuckerman & Kuhlman, 2000). People will frequently misjudge the level of risk associated with a particular decision, and the source for such misjudgements can be linked to factors associated with the situation (e.g., the way in which the risks are framed or the pressures they perceive to perform in a particular way) or a dispositional element that comes from the personality of the individual. For example, an individual might be more concerned about the physical theft of a laptop due to its monetary value while underestimating the more abstract but potentially more damaging risk of having their personal data stolen in a hacking attack. This discrepancy in risk perception is not only a cognitive bias but also something that is shaped by individual differences, particularly in what psychologists refer to as risk attitude (Blais & Weber, 2006; Weber et al., 2002).

Prospect theory (Kahneman & Tversky, 1979; Tversky & Kahneman, 1992) provides a powerful framework for understanding misjudgements in terms of risk perception, and we will focus more on aspects aligned with prospect theory in Chapters 6, 7, and 9 when we focus on cognitive biases and heuristics. Prospect theory details that rather than evaluating outcomes in absolute terms with a position of neutrality, individuals assess the potential gains and losses attached to a decision relative to a reference point. Critically, losses loom larger than equivalent gains, a phenomenon known as loss aversion. This asymmetry means that people are generally more motivated to avoid losses than to pursue gains. Adversaries in digital warfare exploit this bias by framing threats to place an emphasis on the potential losses associated with a particular course of action, such as "Your inaction will lead to dire consequences, you must act now." Such framing leverages the innate human tendency to prioritise loss avoidance, increasing compliance under conditions of uncertainty or urgency (Riet et al., 2016).

"Risk attitude" is a term that has been used to reflect how comfortable or cautious a person is when faced with uncertainty and potential loss. Traditionally, it has been viewed as a stable personality trait (Blais & Weber, 2006; Figner & Weber, 2011), meaning that an individual's approach to risk remains consistent across different situations (Weber et al., 2002). However, subsequent research has challenged this view, showing that risk attitudes can fluctuate depending on context and testing conditions (Blais & Weber, 2006).

This is particularly relevant to digital warfare, where adversaries can deliberately exploit psychological vulnerabilities to shape risk-taking behaviour. The tactics that are implemented in digital warfare often hinge on inducing rapid decisions under uncertainty, and these are the conditions where cognitive biases and personality-driven risk attitudes are seen to exert maximum influence. For example, a piece of disinformation that is labelled as breaking news during a current crisis does more than convey information; it serves to create a high-stakes scenario that amplifies perceived loss (by not paying attention to) and compresses decision time (by highlighting this is new, important information). Individuals high in neuroticism or low in openness may respond impulsively, prioritising immediate risk avoidance over rational evaluation.

Such tactics leverage principles from prospect theory and framing effects, presenting threats in ways that magnify loss aversion and trigger compliance. By manipulating both content (emotive language and authority cues) and context (urgency and scarcity), adversaries can systematically steer behaviour towards choices that benefit their objectives. Understanding these dynamics is critical for anticipating how risk attitudes interact with situational framing, enabling the design of counter-measures that reduce susceptibility to manipulation and strengthen resilience in digital ecosystems.

Locus of Control

The concept of locus of control, originally introduced by Rotter (1966), refers to the extent to which individuals believe they have control over the events and outcomes in their lives. Those with an internal locus of control tend to attribute success or failure to their own actions and decisions. For example, a person who believes that hard work and persistence lead to success exemplifies an internal orientation. In contrast, individuals with an external locus of control are more likely to view outcomes as being shaped by external forces such as luck, fate, or the actions of others.

This dispositional factor has important implications for understanding how individuals respond to influence and manipulation in the context of digital warfare. Those with an internal locus of control are more likely to resist adversarial tactics, such as disinformation campaigns or fear-based messaging, because they believe their actions can shape outcomes and mitigate risk. They may actively seek verification of information, question sources, and adopt counter-measures to maintain autonomy. Conversely, individuals with an external locus of control may perceive such threats as inevitable or beyond their personal influence, fostering passivity and acceptance of adversarial narratives. This sense of helplessness can make them particularly vulnerable to PsyOPs that exploit fatalistic beliefs, amplifying the effectiveness of tactics designed to erode trust, spread misinformation, or induce compliance. (Hadlington et al., 2019).

In the context of digital warfare, locus of control represents a critical psychological vulnerability that adversaries can strategically exploit. Individuals with an external locus of control – those who perceive outcomes as governed by luck, fate, or powerful external forces – are particularly susceptible to influence operations. Attackers may craft narratives that amplify feelings of helplessness or inevitability, such as suggesting that "data breaches are unavoidable" or "government surveillance is inescapable." These messages can erode motivation to adopt protective behaviours, fostering passivity and resignation. In contrast, individuals with an internal locus of control are more likely to resist such manipulation, as they believe their actions can meaningfully reduce risk.

Impulsivity

Impulsivity is a key psychological construct and has been included in a wide variety of personality frameworks (Whiteside & Lynam, 2001). Impulsiveness has been one trait that has been the focus of a great deal of research when it comes to aspects of online safety and security (Hadlington, 2017). In terms of a definition, impulsivity is seen as "the urge to act spontaneously without reflecting on an action and its consequences" (Coutlee et al., 2014, p. 2). Individuals who exhibit higher levels of impulsiveness are less risk adverse, and impulsiveness can also be a subcomponent of a wide variety of clinical conditions, including ADHD, personality disorders, and impulse control disorders (Hadlington, 2017). Whiteside and Lynam (2001) noted that impulsivity, while often being used as a singular term, comprises four discrete facets that include the following:

Urgency: the tendency to experience a strong impulse to do, often aligned with a situation that involves some sort of negative emotion. Those individuals who exhibit higher levels of urgency in relation to the trait impulsiveness are more likely to engage in sudden, impulsive behaviours to relieve themselves of their current negative emotional states, and this is done even though there might be significant long-term consequences for such actions (Whiteside & Lynam, 2001).

Premeditation: often linked to the lack of forethought or planning, this facet of impulsivity refers to the inability to reflect on the potential consequences of actions and take time to assess the likely positives and negatives. Individuals who exhibit lower levels of lack of premeditation will be deliberate in their actions and engage in thoughtful decision-making processes, while those high in lack of premeditation will engage in actions that are typically done without any thought about the possible future repercussions (Whiteside & Lynam, 2001).

Lack of Perseverance: an individual's ability to remain on task and see it through to the end, even though it might be tedious and uninteresting. Individuals who exhibit high levels of perseverance are those who can stay on task and complete their work while at the same time resisting the urge to engage in irrelevant, off-task stimuli. On the other hand, those who have lower levels of perseverance are usually incapable of being distracted and are often easily swayed by irrelevant, off-task information or activities that are seen as being more attractive than their current one (Whiteside & Lynam, 2001).

Sensation Seeking: this is a tendency to engage in and enjoy new activities that are exciting and often dangerous, with little direct focus on the consequences of these actions. Such an aspect crosses over with premeditation mentioned earlier, and those who score higher on sensation seeking are individuals who enjoy engaging in risks and risky activities (Whiteside & Lynam, 2001).

Impulsiveness is an important psychological construct in relation to our current focus on digital warfare. The fast-paced environment of cyberspace means that individuals are often faced with a wide variety of choices which are presented to them in a time-limited fashion, often having some form of urgency attached to them. There is also a sense of fear of missing out (FoMO) (Abel et al., 2016; Buglass et al., 2017), which can attract individuals to engage in risky behaviours in order to satisfy some element of social curiosity because they feel like others around them are having a more fulfilling social experience than they are. In essence, impulsivity plays directly into an adversary's hand quite nicely – it means that individuals exhibiting this trait will act without thinking, spend less time considering between their alternatives, and will usually share misinformation without considering the consequences of their actions.

A Digital Susceptibility Framework

Researchers have observed that by triangulating personality traits, it is possible to identify patterns that allow individuals to be grouped into distinct psychological profiles. These profiles provide insight into behavioural tendencies and susceptibility to influence. Furthermore, studies suggest subtle but meaningful links between personality dimensions and cognitive abilities, adding an additional layer of predictive power. This combined information enables a more nuanced understanding of individual differences, allowing for the development of highly tailored strategies, whether this be for targeted interventions, personalised training, or anticipating vulnerabilities in the context of digital engagement (Stanek & Ones, 2023; Kerber et al., 2021). In their research, Kerber et al. (2021) presented five personality profiles that were composites of the core personality traits of openness, conscientiousness, extraversion, agreeableness, and neuroticism, as well as including elements of risk-taking, locus of control, and impulsivity. Here, we have attempted to group the key elements of each of the emergent personality profiles from Kerber et al. (2021). Each of the classifications has several possible implications for its potential role in the context of digital warfare, which are also highlighted below.

1. Resilient

    - Big Five profile: low neuroticism; high extraversion, agreeableness, and conscientiousness.
    - Impulsivity: the individual exhibits lower levels of impulsivity, making them resilient individuals who have strong emotional regulation and self-control.
    - Risk-taking: a moderate level of risk-taking where they will engage in calculated risks but are not overly cautious.
    - Locus of control: surprisingly, this group showed the strongest association with an external locus of control, with Kerber et al. (2021) suggesting this may reflect an adaptive flexibility, not passivity. Typically, an external locus of control is associated with feelings of helplessness or reduced agency, but Kerber et al. (2021) seem to suggest a more nuanced view, and perhaps in certain contexts, being open to external influences allows individuals to better navigate complex or unpredictable environments.
    - Implications for digital vulnerabilities: due to their external locus of control, these individuals may be more prone to adopt dominant opinions and views that are presented in cyberspace. However, despite this, resilient individuals demonstrate high psychological adjustment and well-being across domains, serving to act as *stabilisers* who can help to maintain healthy discourse online.

2. Overcontroller

    - Big Five profile: high neuroticism and low extraversion and openness.
    - Impulsivity: these individuals exhibit very low levels of impulsivity and are usually emotionally restrained and rigid.
    - Risk-taking: as you would expect from the low levels of impulsivity, the overcontroller is also highly risk adverse, meaning they are less likely to engage in decisions that would serve to impact this stance.
    - Locus of control: this category of individuals has a very strong internal locus of control, with a strong sense of personal responsibility. However, this can also mean they are highly inflexible and may not be able to adapt to the dynamic environments presented online.
    - Implications for digital vulnerabilities: this group is typified by a rigid mindset that is also aligned with poor adaptability in fast-changing

environments. They can be seen as *passive resistors* who may be less likely to spread misinformation but are slow to respond to approaching threats.

3. Undercontroller

   - Big Five profile: low conscientiousness and agreeableness; high extraversion.
   - Impulsivity: a highly impulsive group of individuals who are prone to spontaneous and emotionally reactive behaviour.
   - Risk-taking: a high level of risk-taking as reflected by their similarly high levels of impulsivity, this group will engage in frequent risky or impulsive actions, often living for the moment without any thought for future consequences.
   - Locus of control: an external locus of control means that the undercontroller is more likely to attribute outcomes to luck or external forces.
   - Implications for digital vulnerabilities: most vulnerable to digital manipulation, especially via urgency or emotional triggers. This group can serve to act as *digital amplifiers* and is the group that is most likely to spread harmful or manipulative content, but perhaps without malicious intent.

4. Reserved

   - Big Five profile: low extraversion, neuroticism, and openness; above-average conscientiousness and agreeableness.
   - Impulsivity: this group exhibits moderate levels of impulsivity, suggesting a capacity for caution in decision-making. However, their choices tend to lack strategic foresight, indicating that while they may pause before acting, their decisions are often shaped by immediate circumstances rather than long-term planning.
   - Risk-taking: this group of individuals typically exhibits a low level of risk-taking, preferring familiar and predictable environments.
   - Locus of control: this group has a mixed distribution for locus of control, where individuals in this group may experience a sense of limited control over external events, which suggests an interplay between their own internal agency and the external attribution for control.
   - Implication for digital vulnerabilities: passive and disengaged individuals who may be more vulnerable to subtle manipulation. This group could be seen as *silent observers* who will internalise narratives and exhibit no intent to challenge them. They may avoid digital engagement or be passive in response to threats.

5. Vulnerable-Resilient

   - Big Five profile: this group exhibits high scores across all five of the core five personality traits.

- Impulsivity: individuals in this group present moderate to high levels of impulsivity, where aspects related to emotional instability can lead to highly reactive, spur-of-the-moment decisions.
- Risk-taking: a moderate level of risk-taking is exhibited by this group, and they are more likely to take risks when placed under emotional pressure.
- Locus of control: highly external individuals exhibit feelings of helplessness or being overwhelmed when faced with highly challenging situations because they lack the internal agency to take control.
- Implications for digital vulnerabilities: emotionally unstable and prone to cognitive overload, this group, which we could label "swing participants" (linked to their capacity to move from one state to another), exhibits reactive decision-making patterns. Their unpredictability makes them particularly susceptible to emotional manipulation, yet paradoxically, they may also resist such influence depending on their current emotional state. This volatility suggests a heightened sensitivity to environmental cues, where susceptibility is not fixed but fluctuates with affective and cognitive load.

Taken together, the five emergent personality profiles identified by Kerber et al. (2021) provide a nuanced framework for understanding individual susceptibility within digital warfare contexts. By triangulating traits such as impulsivity, locus of control, and risk-taking alongside the Big Five dimensions, these profiles offer a multilayered perspective on how psychological dispositions shape online behaviour. Crucially, vulnerability is not static; it varies in form, intensity, and expression across individuals. This variability underscores the importance of considering how personality-driven susceptibilities intersect with demographic factors such as age, which in turn introduces its own cognitive, emotional, and behavioural dynamics into the equation. While personality traits serve as a foundational lens for examining digital susceptibility, they do not operate in isolation. Age and gender add further complexity, influencing how individuals engage with digital environments and respond to manipulation. Understanding these interactions is essential for developing targeted interventions and resilience strategies that account for both dispositional and demographic influences.

Age

Age can have a variety of influences on how one approaches a wide range of decision-making processes, as well as being linked to cognitive maturity, emotional regulation, and digital literacy. All these factors can either buffer or enhance an individual's vulnerability to a wide range of digital attacks. Younger individuals may be more impulsive and digitally immersed, often linked to the development of brain systems that serve to control our impulsive nature. Prensky (2001, 2007) described younger people as "digital natives," a term that was used to describe the fact that this group was born into an era of digital technology and therefore were gifted with cognitive affordances that allowed them to multitask at speed and utilise digital technology to its full potential.

On the other side of the digital divide, we have the "digital migrants," older adults who might have taken up the use of digital technology much later in life, often exhibiting greater caution but lower adaptability to evolving digital threats (Prensky, 2001, 2007). Other researchers have noted that age can also impact an individual's susceptibility to specific persuasion techniques. It has been noted that there are significant differences between age groups according to the level of persuasion that can be elicited by different strategies. Those under 25 are more likely to respond to incentives that are offered as part of a process to get people to adopt a specific behaviour or social proof, where behavioural change is initiated through observation and imitation of the desired behaviour. Those over the age of 35 were more influenced by social comparison, where they were given the chance to compare their behaviour with other people (Abdullahi et al., 2019). We will pick up this element of our discussion in Chapter 8 when we explore aspects of influence and persuasion in the context of social engineering.

There are other tangible aspects that can be linked to the decline of cognitive abilities that comes with age. While some of our cognitive processes are generally well protected from the march of time, such as numeracy, verbal ability, and our capacity to recall general knowledge, others can begin to decline as early as middle age (Deary et al., 2009). These processes include elements of memory, processing speed, and our capacity to engage in reasoning and decision-making. Some researchers have noted that the slowing of information processing can be attributed to most of the cognitive decline we observe in individuals over the age of 30 (Deary et al., 2009; Deary et al., 2006). From this perspective, older adults may take longer to evaluate the credibility of digital content (e.g., news articles and social media posts), with this delay making them more vulnerable to misinformation, especially where it is emotionally charged or time-sensitive. In the instance of a reduced working memory capacity, older adults might find it difficult to hold and manipulate multiple pieces of information, which in turn could impair the ability to detect inconsistencies or logical flaws in persuasive messages. In the context of digital warfare, where persuasion, manipulation, and misinformation are all strategic tools, these cognitive changes could indeed make older individuals more susceptible. However, it's important to note that susceptibility is not uniform across all older adults. Factors like education, personality traits (e.g., openness and conscientiousness), and digital experience can all play a significant role.

Gender

Gender, too, plays a role, with research suggesting differences in emotional processing, risk perception, and social media engagement patterns. Abdullahi et al. (2019) noted that there were significant differences between males and females in terms of their susceptibility to pervasive strategies. Males were more likely to be susceptible to social learning, while females were more likely to be susceptible to reward and trustworthiness (motivating individuals to adopt something by enhancing their trust in that thing and the things it might offer). Research has also suggested that women may exhibit higher levels of interpersonal trust than men, making them more likely to self-disclose information and more likely to confide in people they feel close to (Qiu et al., 2022). Conversely, men are less likely to engage in aspects of self-disclosure, even in close relationships, where such behaviour could be interpreted as weakness (Qiu et al., 2022). Other research from neuropsychology studies has noted that when assessing the trustworthiness of information online, women activated more brain areas than men (Riedl et al., 2010). This is a generally accepted finding where women process information more thoroughly and more widely in comparison to men, often because women see the likelihood of uncertainty and risk as being higher (Qiu et al., 2022; Byrnes et al., 1999)

Gender plays a nuanced role in shaping how individuals respond to persuasive strategies in digital environments. Research has consistently highlighted differences in emotional processing, risk perception, and trust dynamics, all of which contribute to varying levels of susceptibility. For example, Abdullahi et al. (2019) found that males and females differ significantly in their responsiveness to persuasive cues. Males were more susceptible to social learning strategies, where behaviour is influenced by observing others. In contrast, females were more influenced by reward-based and trustworthiness-based strategies, in turn suggesting that enhancing perceived benefits and fostering trust are particularly effective in persuading women. This aligns with broader psychological findings. Women tend to exhibit higher levels of interpersonal trust, making them more likely to self-disclose and confide in others, especially within emotionally close relationships (Qiu et al., 2022). While this can foster deeper social connections, it also increases vulnerability to social engineering and phishing attacks, which often exploit trust and emotional rapport.

Neuropsychological evidence further supports these behavioural patterns. Riedl et al. (2010) demonstrated that women activate more brain regions than men when evaluating the trustworthiness of online information. This suggests that women engage in more thorough and distributed cognitive processing, potentially not only offering greater scrutiny but also increasing cognitive load, especially in complex or emotionally charged digital environments. Moreover, women generally perceive higher levels of uncertainty and risk (Byrnes et al., 1999; Qiu et al., 2022), which may lead to more cautious engagement with digital content. This heightened risk awareness can serve as a protective factor, but it may also make women more responsive to reassurance-based messaging and security framing, which can be exploited in manipulative contexts. Conversely, men are typically less inclined to self-disclose, even in close relationships, where such behaviour may be perceived as a sign of weakness (Qiu et al., 2022). This may reduce exposure to certain types of manipulation but can also limit access to corrective social feedback, which is crucial in resisting misinformation.

These gendered patterns underscore the importance of tailoring digital literacy and resilience strategies to account for differential vulnerabilities. Understanding how gender influences susceptibility can inform more effective interventions in the context of digital warfare and persuasive technologies.

Culture and Digital Susceptibility

It might come as a surprise to many readers that there is a part of this chapter devoted to exploring the role culture plays in digital warfare. Surely in cyberspace, culture is not directly apparent and easily distinguished, given the anonymity afforded to individuals by the platform. Similarly, the internet presents the capacity for individuals to transgress geopolitical divides in an instance, giving them the freedom to engage in cultural exchanges daily. However, culture can and does play a significant role in some aspects of digital warfare, but before we move on to that, we need to explore the ways in which culture has been conceptualised in the research literature. Culture can be represented on a variety of different levels, but each level can have a significant and profound impact on how an individual interprets, evaluates, and responds to digital information. In the context of digital warfare in which misinformation, manipulation, and persuasive technologies are deployed with increasing sophistication, cultural norms, values, and dominant cognitive styles can all play a pivotal role in determining susceptibility.

National culture, as conceptualised by Hofstede (1980, 2001), provides a foundational basis from which we can examine cross-cultural differences that could be relevant for digital warfare. Hofstede's dimensional model, despite its criticisms (Williamson, 2002), remains one of the most widely applied frameworks in cultural research. At its core are six bipolar dimensions: power distance, uncertainty avoidance, individualism versus collectivism, masculinity versus femininity, long-term versus short-term orientation, and indulgence versus restraint. Each dimension reflects a distinct cultural tendency that shapes how individuals relate to authority, manage ambiguity, prioritise group versus individual goals, and engage with societal norms.

For instance, cultures high in power distance tend to accept hierarchical structures and defer to authority, which can influence decision-making and communication patterns. In contrast, low power distance cultures promote egalitarianism and encourage questioning of established norms. Similarly, uncertainty avoidance reflects a society's tolerance for ambiguity; high uncertainty avoidance cultures favour structure and predictability, while low uncertainty avoidance cultures embrace flexibility and innovation. These dimensions are not only abstract constructs, but they also manifest in tangible behaviours, such as risk perception, trust formation, and compliance with social norms (Hadlington & Ryding, 2025; Khosrowjerdi, 2020).

Beyond Hofstede, alternative models such as Douglas and Wildavsky's (1983) cultural theory of risk offer a more nuanced understanding of how cultural biases shape perceptions of danger and uncertainty. In their typology, which comprises four core typologies for culture, these being hierarchical, egalitarian, individualistic, and fatalistic cultures, they suggested that individuals interpret risk through the lens of their social structures and values. For example, egalitarian cultures may perceive greater environmental or technological risks due to their emphasis on equality and collective welfare, whereas individualistic cultures may downplay such risks in favour of personal autonomy and market-driven solutions (Douglas & Wildavsky, 1983; Rippl, 2018; Tansey & O'Riordan, 1999). As such, these topics can provide a clear pathway towards leveraging attention and widespread concern if they are harnessed for offensive purposes. If we take the spread of misinformation, targeting concerns that are at the heart of an individual's culture can increase the chances of that information becoming the focus of concern and in turn being spread further afield.

In a similar vein, trust is deeply embedded within cultural frameworks. Research has shown that individuals from individualistic cultures tend to form trust based on shared group membership, while those from collectivist cultures rely more heavily on relational ties and social harmony (Williams et al., 2017; Yuki et al., 2005). These differences have profound implications for how people engage with institutions, technologies, and each other, particularly in contexts where depersonalised trust is required, so they will also have a clear impact on potential susceptibility to tactics employed in the digital warfare playbook.

Of perhaps lesser importance for the current discussion, but still worth briefly mentioning, is the concept of organisational culture. Schein's (2009) model of organisational culture presented three distinct levels that link to the concepts and constructs which make up the cultural identity of an organisation: artefacts, espoused values, and shared tacit assumptions (Schein, 2009). Artefacts are the visible expressions of culture, such as the rituals, technologies, and symbols that form the most concrete expressions of organisational culture. Espoused values represent the formal declarations of organisational priorities, usually contained in manifestos or mission statements. The deepest layer, shared tacit assumptions, comprises the unconscious beliefs that evolve through collective experience and success. These assumptions often dictate the "unwritten rules" of organisational life and can be resistant to change (Schein, 2009).

Importantly, organisational culture interacts with national culture in complex ways. Employees bring their cultural backgrounds into the workplace, which can either reinforce or challenge the prevailing organisational norms. Moreover, cultural misalignment, whether this is between national and organisational values or between espoused and actual practices, can lead to disengagement, resistance, or counterproductive behaviours (Suseno et al., 2021; Willcoxson & Millett, 2000).

This interplay can come into play when we explore some of the key tactics employed in digital warfare, where organisational culture can act as both a buffer and a vulnerability. In environments where shared tacit assumptions promote openness, innovation, and decentralised decision-making, organisations may be more agile in responding to digital threats, particularly when they come from a variety of unspecified directions. However, such cultures may also inadvertently foster risk-taking behaviours (Weber & Hsee, 1998) or overlook the importance of procedural compliance, thereby increasing susceptibility to social engineering, insider threats, or information leakage. Conversely, cultures that emphasise control, hierarchy, and rigid adherence to rules may be better positioned to enforce security protocols and resist external manipulation. Yet these same cultures may struggle with adaptability, particularly in the face of rapidly evolving digital warfare tactics that require dynamic and context-sensitive responses. The degree to which an organisation learns from past digital incidents, whether through reflective practice or post-incident analysis, also hinges on cultural norms around accountability, transparency, and institutional memory (Hadlington & Ryding, 2025).

Although perhaps not as important as national culture, organisational culture should not be seen as a backdrop to digital warfare. It can be a valuable strategic variable that shapes how threats are perceived, how defences are mobilised, and how resilience is cultivated. Understanding the cultural architecture of an organisation in terms of its visible artefacts, stated values, and underlying assumptions can also offer a critical vantage point for assessing its preparedness and responsiveness in the face of digital conflict.

Culture and Digital Warfare

There has been some previous work exploring how culture can be linked to key mechanisms employed in the digital warfare playbook. For example, there has been evidence of the use of identity propaganda or the use of narratives to target and exploit differences based on identity differences (race, class, or gender). Reddi et al. (2023) explored how racialised identity propaganda operates within digital ecosystems to reinforce disinformation and deepen social divisions, something that was evident in the U.K. Southport Riots that hit the United Kingdom in summer 2024. Their work shows that disinformation campaigns often leverage racial narratives to manipulate public opinion, particularly in contexts where race and power are historically contested. Other examples of such strategies involved the use of social media to spread misinformation related to the COVID-19 pandemic, with common posts including false information that the vaccine contained genetic material from pigs, which was designed to target individuals from religious backgrounds where the eating of pork is banned.

Establishing a level of trust is dependent upon a wide variety of factors, including shared values, beliefs, social identities, and expectations of how to interpret various interactions (Hallikainen & Laukkanen, 2018). It is no surprise then that trust and culture are invariably intertwined concepts (Hallikainen & Laukkanen,

2018). Various researchers have noted that the degree or level of trust within a particular society can influence both economic outlook and competitiveness in the global business market (Fukuyama, 1995; Saunders et al., 2014).

Cultural orientations can also significantly impact how individuals perceive and respond to risk, trust, and uncertainty, all factors that are increasingly exploited in digital warfare. For instance, studies have noted that individuals from collectivist societies (ones that value cooperation, family values, and societal cohesion) such as China tend to exhibit greater risk-seeking in financial contexts than those from individualistic cultures (favouring competition, self-promotion, and capitalism) like the United States. This difference has been attributed to the social safety nets and familial support structures prevalent in collectivist cultures, which reduce the perceived consequences of risky decisions (Hsee & Weber, 1999, 1998; Weber & Hseeet al., 1998).

Other cultural dimensions, such as power distance (the acceptance of hierarchical authority) and uncertainty avoidance (the discomfort with ambiguity), can play a critical role in shaping digital behaviour. High power distance cultures may be more susceptible to authoritarian messaging, hierarchical cues, or state-sponsored narratives, while cultures with low uncertainty tolerance may be more vulnerable to security-based persuasion, fear appeals, or information framed as definitive and risk-reducing (Bontempo et al., 1997; Hadlington & Ryding, 2025; Hofstede, 2011; Kanagaretnam et al., 2014). Conversely, cultures that score high on individualism often encourage personal autonomy and self-expression, which can make individuals more receptive to personalised content, freedom-framed messaging, and emotionally resonant appeals. These traits can be directly exploited in microtargeted disinformation campaigns, where psychological profiling is used to tailor persuasive content to cultural and individual preferences.

In the context of cyberwarfare, these cultural variables are not only passive traits but also form an active button a digital adversary can push. Manipulative actors can design digital content that aligns with culturally specific values, risk perceptions, and trust dynamics, thereby increasing its persuasive power. Understanding these cultural susceptibilities is essential for developing resilient digital ecosystems and counter-strategies that are sensitive to the diverse ways people engage with online information.

Summary

This chapter examined how individual differences rooted in personality, age, gender, and culture can shape susceptibility to digital manipulation and cyberwarfare. In the current context, the concept of "wetware" is used to describe the psychological architecture that adversaries exploit to influence behaviour, decision-making, and other such vulnerabilities in digital environments.

Personality traits, particularly those outlined in the Big Five model (openness, conscientiousness, extraversion, agreeableness, and neuroticism), can play a significant role in determining how individuals engage with digital content. Traits such as high neuroticism, low conscientiousness, and high extraversion have been reliably associated with impulsivity and emotional reactivity, which can increase the potential vulnerability to misinformation and manipulation. In addition, the dark triad traits (narcissism, Machiavellianism, and psychopathy) not only feature in the psychological makeup of adversaries but can also serve to heighten susceptibility to a wide variety of online attacks, particularly due to overconfidence and a lack of empathy.

Impulsivity, risk perception, and locus of control further shape digital vulnerability. Impulsivity undermines reflective decision-making, especially in fast-paced digital contexts where urgency and emotional triggers are common. Risk perception is influenced by both personality and situational context and can be manipulated through strategic framing. Individuals with an external locus of control are more likely to feel helpless or passive in the face of digital threats, making them easier targets for manipulation.

Age introduces cognitive and emotional dynamics that influence susceptibility. Younger individuals, often more digitally immersed, may exhibit higher impulsivity, while older adults may experience declines in processing speed and working memory. These age-related changes affect how individuals respond to persuasive strategies, with younger users more influenced by rewards and social learning and older users more responsive to social comparison.

Gender also plays a nuanced role. Women tend to exhibit higher levels of interpersonal trust and more thorough cognitive processing, which can increase their vulnerability to emotionally framed manipulation. Men, on the other hand, may be less emotionally expressive and more resistant to trust-based persuasion, but this can also limit their access to corrective feedback, making them susceptible in different ways.

Cultural values act as strategic levers in digital warfare. Dimensions such as individualism versus collectivism, power distance, and uncertainty avoidance shape how people perceive risk, trust, and authority. Identity-based propaganda and culturally tailored disinformation campaigns exploit these values to deepen division and enhance persuasive impact. For example, collectivist cultures may be more susceptible to group-based appeals, while individualist cultures may respond more strongly to personalised or emotionally resonant content.

In conclusion, susceptibility to digital warfare is not a singular trait but a multilayered construct. By triangulating psychological, demographic, and cultural elements, we can begin to build predictive models of vulnerability and resilience. These insights are essential for informing both defensive strategies and ethical considerations in the design and deployment of persuasive technologies.

References

Abdullahi, A. M., Oyibo, K., Orji, R., & Kawu, A. A. (2019). The influence of age, gender, and cognitive ability on the susceptibility to persuasive strategies. *Information (Switzerland), 10*. https://doi.org/10.3390/info10110352

Abel, J. P., Buff, C. L., & Burr, S. A. (2016). Social media and the fear of missing out: Scale development and assessment. *Journal of Business & Economics Research (JBER), 14*(1), 33. https://doi.org/10.19030/jber.v14i1.9554

Blais, A.-R., & Weber, E. U. (2006). A Domain-Specific Risk-Taking (DOSPERT) scale for adult populations. *Judgement and Decision Making, 1*(1), 33–47. https://doi.org/10.1037/t13084-000

Bleidorn, W., Schwaba, T., Zheng, A., Hopwood, C. J., Sosa, S. S., Roberts, B. W., & Briley, D. A. (2022). Personality stability and change: A meta-analysis of longitudinal studies. *Psychological Bulletin, 148*(7–8), 588–619. https://doi.org/10.1037/bul0000365

Bontempo, R. N., Bottom, W. P., & Weber, E. U. (1997). Crosscultural differences in risk perception: A model-based approach. *Risk Analysis, 17*, 479–488.

Brasher, G. R., Koester, K. L., Pickard, J. D., & Swinney, K. (2000). *Tying it together: Salience as a predictor of change blindness.*

Buckels, E. E., Trapnell, P. D., & Paulhus, D. L. (2014). Trolls just want to have fun. *Personality and Individual Differences, 67*, 97–102. https://doi.org/10.1016/j.paid.2014.01.016

Buffardi, L. E., & Campbell, W. K. (2008). Narcissism and social networking web sites. *Personality and Social Psychology Bulletin, 34*(10), 1303–1314.

Buglass, S. L., Binder, J. F., Betts, L. R., & Underwood, J. D. M. D. M. (2017). Motivators of online vulnerability: The impact of social network site use and FOMO. *Computers in Human Behavior, 66*, 248–255. https://doi.org/10.1016/j.chb.2016.09.055

Byrnes, J. P., Miller, D. C., & Schafer, W. D. (1999). Gender differences in risk taking: A meta-analysis. *Psychological Bulletin, 125*(3), 367–383. https://doi.org/10.1037/0033-2909.125.3.367

Cichocka, A., Marchlewska, M., & Biddlestone, M. (2022). Why do narcissists find conspiracy theories so appealing? *Current Opinion in Psychology, 47*, 101386. https://doi.org/10.1016/j.copsyc.2022.101386

Coutlee, C. G., Politzer, C. S., Hoyle, R. H., & Huettel, S. A. (2014). An abbreviated impulsiveness scale constructed through confirmatory factor analysis of the Barratt Impulsiveness Scale Version 11. *Archives of Scientific Psychology, 2*, 1–12. https://doi.org/10.1037/arc0000005

Curtis, S. R., Rajivan, P., Jones, D. N., & Gonzalez, C. (2018). Phishing attempts among the dark triad: Patterns of attack and vulnerability. *Computers in Human Behavior, 87*, 174–182. https://doi.org/10.1016/j.chb.2018.05.037

Deary, I. J., Corley, J., Gow, A. J., Harris, S. E., Houlihan, L. M., Marioni, R. E., . . . Starr, J. M. (2009). Age-associated cognitive decline. *British Medical Bulletin, 92*(1), 135–152. https://doi.org/10.1093/bmb/ldp033

Deary, I. J., Whalley, L. J., Batty, G. D., & Starr, J. M. (2006). Physical fitness and lifetime cognitive change. *Neurology, 67*, 1195–1200.

Douglas, M., & Wildavsky, A. (1983). *Risk and culture: An essay on the selection of technological and environmental dangers*. University of California Press.

Figner, B., & Weber, E. U. (2011). Who takes risks when and why? *Current Directions in Psychological Science, 20*(4), 211–216. https://doi.org/10.1177/0963721411415790

Frischlich, L., Schatto-Eckrodt, T., Boberg, S., & Wintterlin, F. (2021). Roots of incivility: How personality, media use, and online experiences shape uncivil participation roots of incivility: How personality, media use, and online experiences. *Media and Communication, 9*(1), 195–208. https://doi.org/10.17645/mac.v9i1.3360

Fukuyama, F. (1995). *Trust: The social virtues and the creation of prosperity*. New York: Free Press.

Hadlington, L. (2017). Human factors in cybersecurity; examining the link between internet addiction, impulsivity, attitudes towards cybersecurity, and risky cybersecurity behaviours. *Heliyon*, *3*(7), e00346. https://doi.org/10.1016/j.heliyon.2017.e00346

Hadlington, L., Popovac, M., Janicke, H., Yevseyeva, I., & Jones, K. (2019). Exploring the role of work identity and work locus of control in information security awareness. *Computers and Security*, *81*, 41–48. https://doi.org/10.1016/j.cose.2018.10.006

Hadlington, L., & Ryding, C. (2025). *Human factors and cybersecurity: The psychology of online safety and security*. London, UK: Taylor and Francis Inc.

Hallikainen, H., & Laukkanen, T. (2018). National culture and consumer trust in e-commerce. *International Journal of Information Management*, *38*(1), 97–106. https://doi.org/10.1016/j.ijinfomgt.2017.07.002

Hallikainen, H., & Laukkanen, T. (2018). National culture and consumer trust in e-commerce. *International Journal of Information Management*, *38*(1), 97–106. https://doi.org/10.1016/j.ijinfomgt.2017.07.002

Han, N., Li, S., Huang, F., Wen, Y., & Su, Y. (2023). How social media expression can reveal personality, (March), 1–12. https://doi.org/10.3389/fpsyt.2023.1052844

Hofstede, G. (1980). *Culture's consequences: International differences in work-related values*. Beverly Hills, CA: Sage Publications.

Hofstede, G. (2001). *Culture's consequences: Comparing values, behaviours, institutions and organisations across nations*. London, UK: Sage Publications.

Hofstede, G. (2011). Dimensionalizing cultures: The hofstede model in context. *Online Readings in Psychology and Culture*, *2*, 1–26.

Hsee, C. K., & Weber, E. U. (1998). Cross-cultural differences in risk perception, but cross-cultural similarities in attitudes towards perceived risk. *Management Science*, *44*(9), 1205–1217.

Hsee, C. K., & Weber, E. U. (1999). Cross-national differences in risk preference and lay predictions. *Journal of Behavioral Decision Making*, *12*(2), 165–179. https://doi.org/10.1002/(SICI)1099-0771(199906)12:2<165:AID-BDM316>3.0.CO;2-N

John, O. P., & Srivastava, S. (1991). The big five trait taxonomy: History, measurement, and theorectical perspectives. In L. A. Pervin & O. P. John (Eds.), *Handbook of personality: Theory and research* (Vol. 2, pp. 102–138). New York: Guilford Press.

John, O. P., & Srivastava, S. (1999). Big five inventory (Bfi). *Handbook of Personality: Theory and Research*, *2*, 102–138. https://doi.org/10.1525/fq.1998.51.4.04a00260

Kahneman, D., & Tversky, A. (1979). Prospect theory: An analysis of decision under risk. *Econometrica*, *47*(2), 263–292.

Kanagaretnam, K., Lim, C. Y., & Lobo, G. J. (2014). Influence of national culture on accounting conservatism and risk-taking in the banking industry. *Accounting Review*, *89*(3), 1115–1149. https://doi.org/10.2308/accr-50682

Kerber, A., Roth, M., & Herzberg, P. Y. (2021). Personality types revisited: A literature-informed and data-driven approach to an integration of prototypical and dimensional constructs of personality description. *PLoS One*, *16*(1 January), 1–27. https://doi.org/10.1371/journal.pone.0244849

Khosrowjerdi, M. (2020). National culture and trust in online health information. In *Journal of librarianship and information science* (Vol. 52). https://doi.org/10.1177/0961000619836716

McCrae, R. R., & Costa, P. T. (1987). Validation of the five-factor model of personality across instruments and observers. *Journal of Personality and Social Psychology*, *52*(1), 81–90. https://doi.org/10.1037/0022-3514.52.1.81

Muhanad, A., Abuelezz, I., Khan, K., & Ali, R. (2025). On how Cialdini's persuasion principles influence individuals in the context of social engineering: A qualitative study. *Lecture Notes in Computer Science (Including Subseries Lecture Notes in Artificial Intelligence and Lecture Notes in Bioinformatics), 15438 LNCS*(November), 373–388. https://doi.org/10.1007/978-981-96-0570-5_27

Park, G., Schwartz, A., Eichstaedt, J. C., Kern, M. L., Kosinski, M., Stillwell, D. J., . . . Seligman, M. (2015). Automatic personality assessment through social media language. *Journal of Personality and Social Psychology, 180*(6), 934–952. https://doi.org/10.1111/jopy.12674

Park, G., Schwartz, H. A., Eichstaedt, J. C., Kern, M. L., Stillwell, D. J., Ungar, L. H., . . . Stillwell, D. J. (2014). *Automatic personality assessment through social media language.*

Paulhus, D. L. (2014). Toward a taxonomy of dark personalities. *Current Directions in Psychological Science, 23*(6), 421–426. https://doi.org/10.1177/0963721414547737

Reddi, M., Kuo, R., & Kreiss, D. (2023). Identity propaganda: Racial narratives and disinformation. *New Media and Society, 25*(8), 2201–2218. https://doi.org/10.1177/14614448211029293

Riet, J. Van, Cox, A. D., Cox, D., Zimet, G. D., Bruijn, D., Putte, B. Van Den, . . . Ruiter, R. A. C. (2016). Does perceived risk influence the effects of message framing? Revisiting the link between prospect theory and message framing, *7199*. https://doi.org/10.1080/17437199.2016.1176865

Rippl, S. (2018). Cultural theory and risk perception: A proposal for a better measurement. In *The institutional dynamics of culture, volume I and II: The new durkheimians* (Vol. 1–2, pp. 251–269). https://doi.org/10.4324/9781315238975-13

Saunders, M. N. K., Dietz, G., & Thornhill, A. (2014). *Trust and distrust: Polar opposites, or independent but co-existing?* https://doi.org/10.1177/0018726713500831

Schein, E. H. (2009). *The corporate culture survival guide.* San Fransico: John Wiley & Sons.

Stanek, K., & Ones, D. S. (2023). Meta-analytic relations between personality and cognitive ability. *Proceedings of the National Academy of Sciences, 120*(23), 1–12. https://doi.org/10.1073/pnas

Suseno, Y., Chang, C., Hudik, M., Fang, E., & Liu, N. (2021). Why do employees engage in counterproductive work behaviours? Cultural values and white-collar employees in China. *Motivation and Emotion, 45*, 397–421.

Tansey, J., & O'Riordan, T. (1999). Cultural theory and risk: A review. *Health, Risk and Society, 1*(1), 71–90. https://doi.org/10.1080/13698579908407008

Tversky, A., & Kahneman, D. (1992). Advances in prospect theory: Cumulative representation of uncertainty. *Journal of Risk and Uncertainty, 5*, 297–323.

Weber, E. U., Blais, A.-R. R., & Betz, N. E. (2002). A domain-specific risk-attitude scale: Measuring risk perceptions and risk behaviors. *Journal of Behavioral Decision Making, 15*(4), 263–290. https://doi.org/10.1002/bdm.414

Weber, E. U., & Hsee, C. (1998). Cross-cultural differences in risk perception, but cross-cultural similarities in attitudes towards perceived risk. *Management Science, 44*(9), 1205–1217. https://doi.org/10.1287/mnsc.44.9.1205

Whiteside, S. P., & Lynam, D. R. (2001). The five factor model and impulsivity: Using a structural model of personality to understand impulsivity. *Personality and Individual Differences, 30*(4), 669–689. https://doi.org/10.1016/S0191-8869(00)00064-7

Willcoxson, L., & Millett, B. (2000). The management of organisational culture. *Australian Journal of Management and Organisational Behaviour, 3*(2), 91–99.

Williams, M., Nurse, J. R. C., & Creese, S. (2017). "Privacy is the boring bit": User perceptions and behaviour in the internet-of-things. *15th International Conference on Privacy, Security and Trust (PST)*. Retrieved from http://www.cs.ox.ac.uk/files/9213/2017-pst-wnc-preprint.pdf

Williamson, D. (2002). Forward from a critique of Hofstede's model of national culture. *Human Relations, 55*(11), 1373–1395. https://doi.org/10.1177/0018726702551100б

Yuki, M., Maddux, W. W., Brewer, M. B., & Takemura, K. (2005). Cross-cultural differences in relationship: And group-based trust. *Personality and Social Psychology Bulletin, 31*(1), 48–62. https://doi.org/10.1177/0146167204271305

Zuckerman, M., & Kuhlman, D. M. (2000). Personality and risk-taking: Common biosocial factors. *Journal of Personality, 68*(6), 999. https://doi.org/10.1111/1467-6494.00124

6 Cognitive Biases in Digital Warfare I

Disrupting Information Processing and Risk Perception

Introduction

Cognitive biases arise when our decisions systematically deviate from what we would expect to be the norm or a more rational, logical decision-making process. The key to almost all the cognitive biases we will be introducing in this and the following chapter is the level at which we are aware of using them. Biases, such as the confirmation bias, availability heuristic, or false consensus bias, operate automatically, shaping how we interpret information, recall memories, and make decisions, usually without our awareness. Biases form the basic tools that help us navigate a complex world, but they can also lead us astray.

Biases can come in a variety of forms, and there are literally hundreds that can be applied to almost every aspect of decision-making. To review all of these would be an impossible task, and for the purposes of our current discussion, although it might be possible to make direct links between digital warfare and every cognitive bias, the focus for the next two chapters will be on those that are inherently linked to the area. This chapter explores cognitive biases that emerge from individual information processing mechanisms, which serve to shape how we perceive, remember, and evaluate information. Unlike socially reinforced biases, which we will be exploring in the next chapter, these distortions operate largely within the individual's cognitive architecture, making them particularly susceptible to manipulation in digital environments.

Towards the end of this chapter, we explore another associated concept that is aligned with the existence of cognitive biases, that of cognitive dissonance. Cognitive dissonance is often viewed as a distinct psychological concept set apart from that of cognitive biases, but they are very much intertwined with each other. On the one hand, cognitive dissonance holds that individuals will experience a level of psychological distress when they hold conflicting beliefs or attitudes and will take steps to resolve this. On the other hand, cognitive biases are the deviations we make from a normative decision-making process. The link between the two concepts is the use of cognitive biases, which can be used to counter the dissonance individuals might be experiencing, and they might engage in biased reasoning to

DOI: 10.4324/9781003752400-6

do this. For example, if we take the confirmation bias, individuals seek out information that serves to support their existing beliefs while at the same time ignoring information that goes against their current beliefs. This process, therefore, reduces the cognitive dissonance we might be experiencing, as it removes the potential for competing viewpoints to be encountered. Framing bias acts in a similar way and allows us to reinterpret information that might threaten our current viewpoint in such a way that conforms to the beliefs that we currently have.

In the context of digital warfare, these mechanisms are not only the stuff of academic indulgence but also key strategic targets. Adversaries can exploit dissonance and bias to manipulate public opinion, spread misinformation, and destabilise trust in institutions. Whether through emotionally charged propaganda, algorithmically curated content, or co-ordinated disinformation campaigns, the digital environment is uniquely suited to triggering dissonance and reinforcing bias.

Cognitive Biases – The Impact of Heuristic Processing

Often, cognitive biases are confused or combined with the function of heuristics that can mask their true functionality and impact on decision-making. While heuristics sit as mental shortcuts that can be used to simplify decision-making, cognitive biases are seen as the systematic errors or deviations from what would be the result of a more normative decision-making process because we have relied on a heuristic (Hadlington & Ryding, 2025). While a heuristic is seen to improve efficiency in terms of releasing valuable cognitive resources from more labour-intensive processing, cognitive biases can lead to distortions in decision-making because of suboptimal processing. For example, if we take the example of the availability heuristic, it is used to make a judgement about risk or the likelihood of an event occurring, depending on how easily examples of said event come to mind. On the other hand, the availability bias is an overestimation of something occurring because we have been presented with information that makes us believe such events are more likely, such as news reports or repetitive messages. So, where the heuristic is the mechanical part of the decision-making process, the cognitive bias forms the outcome when the heuristic we are using fails. We will focus more directly on heuristics and their interactions with memory later in Chapter 9, and for the remainder of this chapter, we will move on to focusing on the biases that form the backbone for disrupting aspects of information processing. I have tried to group the most relevant biases around the core categories which underpin the most disruptive elements of information processing, and this is by no means an exhaustive list.

Framing and Narrative Construction

In the digital age, the way information is presented often holds more persuasive power than the content itself. This section explores how cognitive biases, particularly *framing bias* and *narrative bias,* interact with our innate preference for coherent stories and emotionally resonant messaging. These biases are instrumental in shaping how individuals interpret, remember, and respond to information, especially in online environments where content is rapidly consumed and shared. By manipulating the structure and emotional tone of narratives, adversaries can subtly influence public opinion, reinforce ideological divides, and obscure objective truths. Understanding these mechanisms is essential for identifying how digital warfare exploits our cognitive vulnerabilities to construct persuasive, yet potentially misleading, realities.

Framing Bias

People often make decisions based on the perceived benefits to them, drawing from the information available at the time. However, research has consistently shown that the presentation of that information can significantly influence the choices they make. This phenomenon is known as the framing effect, a cognitive bias that causes individuals to make different decisions depending on whether the same information is framed in terms of potential gains or potential losses.

The framing effect has been demonstrated in multiple ways, with perhaps the most frequently discussed method being that of the "Asian Disease" problem that was created by Tversky and Kahneman (1986), which follows the following scenario. *Imagine a scenario where the United States is preparing for an outbreak of a deadly disease that is expected to kill 600 people.* Two groups of participants are presented with two different descriptions which are identical but differ in terms of their framing. Group 1 is presented with the positive frame that presents a gain in terms of the actions taken.

Option A: 200 people will be saved.
Option B: There is a one-third chance that all 600 people will be saved, with a two-third chance that none will be saved.

Given these two options, most people will default to Option A, which presents a sure gain.

For Group 2, these are presented with a negative frame that presents a loss in terms of the actions that are taken.

Option C: 400 people will die.
Option D: a one-third chance that no one will die and a 2/3 chance that all 600 will die.

In this instance, most people will go with the riskier choice, that being Option D. In terms of the processes that underpin these decisions, the way in which they are framed, either as gains or as losses, significantly impacts an individual's preferences in terms of decision-making. Where the outcomes of a decision are framed in a positive way, with some form of gain, an individual is more likely to take the certain, safe option. On the other hand, if the outcome is framed in a negative, loss-related way, the individual is more likely to choose the option that involves a risk. This notion links back to the prospect theory we introduced earlier (see Chapter 5), which challenged the dominant theory that individuals make rational decisions. Instead, prospect theory suggests that an individual will make decisions by evaluating the outcome relevant to the current situation. In turn, there is an asymmetry between the way in which we process gains and losses – gains are seen as being more positive and rewarding, whereas losses are viewed as being more painful and intrinsically harder to deal with (Kahneman & Tversky, 1979; Tversky & Kahneman, 1974, 1986, 1992).

The framing effect can be easily weaponised to manipulate how individuals interpret news and events that go on around them. When you bias the way in which information is presented to individuals to emphasise the likely gains or losses that might come about as a result of an action (or inaction), it can significantly influence opinion, create confusion, or drive specific behaviours that align with adversarial goals and objectives. In the context of propaganda, the use of framing can be easily deployed to hide the true intention behind specific behaviours. If we take the example of Russia's "Special Military Operation" that has been used to describe the full-scale invasion of Ukraine, the optics of framing are clearly visible. Using this term removed any negative connotations that other terms such as "invasion" and "war" might have and managed public perceptions of such an attack. You can also redefine core aspects of a physical conflict using framing, such as presenting civilian infrastructure (power plants, hospitals, schools, and factories) as having dual purposes or being relevant to military objectives; states can serve to justify their attacks without running the risk of these being considered war crimes. This tactic is not something that is new, and if you look back over recent history, you can see examples where military campaigns have been conducted under the banner of "pacification" or some level of acceptance for "collateral damage."

Narrative Bias

This is captured in our inherent tendency to remember and interpret information better when it is embedded in a coherent story, even if that story is inaccurate or misleading. This is particularly prominent in the creation of conspiracy theories, where creators of such ideas provide an intuitive narrative or backstory which appears to make sense, even though it lacks the evidence to support it. An initial study by Bordiga and Nisbett (1977) demonstrated this effect quite eloquently using participants from a university campus. Participants were presented with information about the current course they were planning to enrol in in three different ways: (1) statistics on course evaluations, (2) short testimonials from students who had previously taken the course, or (3) no additional information. Participants were then asked to rate how likely they would take the relevant courses, and those who were presented with the short testimonials were more likely to choose that course. This work demonstrated that information that is presented in a narrative, coherent format that makes it more relatable and relevant to the individual has a more significant impact on choices in comparison to abstract information that lacks tangibility (Bordiga & Nisbett, 1977).

Now that the power of media has become decentralised and the traditional forms of gatekeeping information have been mostly removed, the internet gives the capacity to write and produce information in a variety of unique ways, increasing the potential for information to be falsified or for narratives to be framed in ways that serve to perform an action. The proliferation of digital media has served to create a wide variety of opportunities and challenges when it comes to the communication of information to the public. On the one hand, there is the opportunity to rapidly communicate information to a wide range of audiences. However, such rapid and widespread communication comes with relative risks, particularly when we look at how information is framed and how users attempt to assess the credibility of that information (see Chapter 10). As many researchers have noted, there has been an increasing shift from reports that use a fact-driven approach more towards the use of sensationalism and emotionally driven narratives (Singh et al., 2023; Khawar & Boukes, 2025).

Campos-Castillo and Shuster (2023) suggested that a state of diminished trust now exists between individuals and traditional media sources, which can lead to enhanced polarisation and can also serve to undermine the capacity to build consensus for support, especially where audiences see information as being biased or inaccurate. It has been generally the case that, despite widespread attempts to improve digital literacy, there is still a tendency for individuals to fall into the trap of engaging with material that aligns with their current beliefs. This can have the impact of perpetuating the spread of misinformation, as well as contributing to the growth in mistrust that exists towards formal institutions and democratic processes. Understanding how media framing can serve to influence public perception, therefore, has critical importance in the theatre of digital warfare.

The concept of framing has been explored in the media, defined as the process by which the media focuses on specific elements related to the reality of news or current affairs. This has the knock-on effect of influencing public perception and interpretation about what the current important issues are at any one time (Song, 2024). It has also been noted that framing is not only related to the delivery of the information but can also be aligned to agenda setting and the construct of narratives (Valenzuela, 2022; Valenzuela et al., 2017). Other researchers have noted that framing in political news can significantly alter public trust and voter behaviour (Boukes et al., 2015; Boukes & Hameleers, 2023; Khawar & Boukes, 2025), while others have noted that health-risk framing and the way in which risks are communicated in the media can have a significant impact on public understanding and behavioural responses (Riet et al., 2016), even more so in situations where there is a degree of ambiguity or scientific uncertainty. Mohammadi et al. (2022) also noted that misinformation framing across media platforms served to impact how audiences viewed health-related guidance, how much trust they had in the authorities, and how hesitant they were to engage in vaccination drives.

Memory and Attention Biases

Memory and attention are foundational to how individuals process and respond to information, yet both are highly susceptible to cognitive distortion. This section examines how biases such as the *misinformation effect*, *confirmation bias*, and *illusory truth effect* exploit the limitations of memory encoding, retrieval, and attentional focus. In digital environments where there is an abundance of information that is rapidly changing and often emotionally charged, such biases can be strategically manipulated to alter perceptions of truth, reinforce existing beliefs, and impair critical evaluation. Understanding how memory and attention are shaped by bias is essential for recognising the psychological mechanisms that adversaries exploit in digital warfare to influence cognition and behaviour.

The Misinformation Effect

This cognitive bias has some crossover with the concept of false memories that we explore later on in Chapter 9, but there are some distinct differences between the two. The misinformation effect is observed when information that occurs after a critical event leads to the alteration of a memory. This is one way in which false memories can be formed. However, the false memory effect is a broader construct that refers to any inaccurate memory and is seen as being the result of other factors, which could include that of the misinformation effect. Examples of this could include suggestive or leading questioning or the use of social pressure or framing.

McCloskey and Zaragoza (1985) suggested that misinformation effects are more likely to occur where the original memory traces for observed information are poorly constructed or do not exist at all. Most misinformation effects from the research in the area are noted for aspects of the environment that are in the periphery and something that is not a central component to the scene or storyline (Tousignant et al., 1986). There is also evidence to show that the impact of misinformation increases when there is a delay between the critical event and the exposure to the misleading information. This is possibly due to the action of decay in memory, where the information related to the original event has been lost or fragmented over time, meaning that the newer, misleading information has more recency (Chrobak & Zaragoza, 2012). Even in instances where participants in research settings are given explicit warnings that the information contained in post-event questions may not be entirely accurate, they still fall foul of the misinformation effect (Chroback & Zaragoza, 2013). So, from the perspective of digital misinformation and fake news, even though we may engage in active warnings to individuals as to the potential for false information to be present in online environments, there is still a real danger that they will be susceptible to its influence. Chrobak and Zaragoza (2013) suggested that this is due to faulty cognitions, insomuch as the individuals who are being warned do not have sufficient information to contradict the misleading information and so default to accepting it as true.

While much of the earlier research on the misinformation effect was conducted using face-to-face experimental testing, a substantial body of work has examined the impact of viewing traumatic events online (Sievwright et al., 2021). In studies where participants viewed realistic, viral images of traumatic events, those exposed to misinformation one week later were significantly less accurate at distinguishing false information from true information compared to a control group that had no exposure to misinformation (Sievwright et al., 2021).

The misinformation effect has profound implications for digital warfare, particularly in the context of post-event narrative manipulation. In online environments, adversaries can strategically release misleading content, such as doctored images, false eyewitness accounts, or biased commentary after a critical incident (e.g., a cyber-attack, protest, or military strike). This timing is crucial, and as Chrobak and Zaragoza (2013) noted, the delay between the original event and the introduction of misinformation increases susceptibility due to memory decay and lack of competing information.

In digital warfare, the misinformation effect can be strategically exploited to reshape public perception of events, influence emotional and moral decision-making, and erode trust in reliable sources. By flooding the information space with conflicting narratives and misleading content, often amplified through bots or viral reposting, adversaries can create a false sense of consensus and obscure the truth. This manipulation is especially potent when there is a delay between the actual event and the introduction of misinformation, allowing distorted narratives to take root in the absence of clear, competing information.

The Sievwright et al. (2021) study is particularly relevant here as it demonstrates that exposure to traumatic viral content online, followed by misinformation, significantly impairs the ability to distinguish truth from falsehood. This mirrors real-world tactics in PsyOPs, where emotive imagery is used to prime audiences before introducing distorted narratives.

Confirmation Bias

There is a tendency for individuals to search for information that serves to support their own current beliefs while ignoring information that serves to contradict them (Peters, 2022), and confirmation bias is often seen as one of the most persistent and pervasive of the cognitive biases (Nickerson, 1998). Zhou and Shen (2022) noted that confirmation bias is linked to a wider set of cognitive biases that are related to something termed *epistemic egocentrism,* where individuals are seen to project their own knowledge, beliefs, or mental states onto others with the assumption that others see things in the same way that they do. Essentially, confirmation bias presents a critical failure to engage in the processes of reflection or perspective-taking, particularly in situations where there is some form of knowledge testing. If we know the answer to a question that has been presented to us, we might make an overestimation of the extent to which such an answer is clearly obvious, particularly when that individual lacks the same level of knowledge as we do.

Confirmation bias is a multifaceted cognitive tendency that influences how individuals seek, interpret, and evaluate information. One prominent manifestation is through selective exposure and attention, where people gravitate towards information that aligns with their existing beliefs. This preference can be driven by a desire for validation, but it may also occur in the absence of conscious motivation. For instance, research has shown that when individuals are presented with two sequential visual stimuli, their sensitivity to the second stimulus increases if it supports their initial choice, which in turn suggests individuals exhibit a perceptual bias towards consistency (Talluri et al., 2018; Zhou & Shen, 2022, 2024).

Confirmation bias can also involve a process where the individual will inherently bias the weighting of information according to its importance or relevance to their current goals or objectives. Individuals tend to devote more cognitive resources to information that supports their prior decisions or attitudes, in turn processing it more efficiently and integrating it more heavily into subsequent judgements. This selective assimilation reinforces existing views and can distort decision-making processes. Furthermore, confirmation bias can influence perception, leading individuals to regard information that aligns with their existing attitudes as more credible and persuasive. This perceptual skew can lead individuals to overestimate the validity of supportive evidence while undervaluing contradictory data (Ahluwalia, 2000).

These biases in attention, processing, and perception often co-occur with another cognitive distortion known as illusory correlation, which is the mistaken belief that two unrelated events or characteristics are linked. Conversely, individuals may also fail to detect genuine associations, a phenomenon referred to as invisible correlation (Hamilton & Rose, 1980). Together, confirmation bias can serve to contribute to polarisation, as individuals become increasingly entrenched in their views. Over time, this can lead to more extreme positions and heightened societal divisions, particularly in environments where information is curated or manipulated to reinforce existing beliefs (Zhou & Shen, 2022).

Confirmation bias is inherently linked to a variety of other concepts and factors mentioned not only in this chapter but also in sections covered elsewhere in the book. It can serve to strengthen the polarisation of thoughts and ideas, particularly when it operates within socially homophilic digital environments. Social homophily refers to the tendency of individuals to associate and bond with others who are like themselves in certain attributes, such as beliefs, values, social status, interests, or demographic characteristics: in other words, *like attracts like* (McPherson et al., 2001). This concept is important in social networks because it influences how information spreads, how communities form, and how echo chambers develop online. For example, people who share similar political views are more likely to connect and interact, reinforcing shared perspectives and limiting exposure to diverse viewpoints. In such contexts, individuals can become trapped in a self-perpetuating feedback loop of ideas that strengthen their existing beliefs while preventing contradictory perspectives from breaking through. Confirmation bias is a key mechanism underlying the creation and maintenance of echo chambers and filter bubbles. Within these structures, congruent information is amplified, whereas cognitively incongruent information is filtered out and ignored.

Illusory Truth Effect

Truth, while often seen as something that is a verifiable fact or piece of information, can also be a socially constructed concept. Researchers have noted that individuals have the capacity to believe a wide range of "facts" that are not actually true. For example, Dekker et al. (2012) explored beliefs around what they termed "neuromyths" or incorrect information about learning and cognition. The researchers noted that teachers believed just under half (49%) of the neuromyths they were presented with, including information about learning styles, the processing of information and hemispheric differences in terms of dominant learning styles. It was noted that people are more influenced to believe something as being truthful based not on the factual content of that information but on their subjective experience of seeing that information (Henderson et al., 2021). The frequency with which statements or information about a particular piece of information becomes a fundamental predictor for the likelihood that someone will believe that information is true (Hassan & Barber, 2021; Henderson et al., 2021; Udry & Barber, 2024). This is referred to as the illusory truth effect (or repetition-induced truth effect; Henderson et al., 2021). As with most socially driven cognitive biases, the process of repetition serves to drive the perception that such information must be true, as well as linking into memory processes that make such information more accessible to the individual.

The illusory truth effect is another example of heuristic-based processing, where individuals judge the validity of information based on the frequency with which they have been exposed to it rather than its factual accuracy. (Dechêne et al., 2010). The effect has also been shown to exert an influence on both true and false statements and occurs irrespective of cognitive ability (Henderson et al., 2021). As Henderson et al. (2021) noted, it can exist even when individuals are warned about its potential existence or when someone has the knowledge about the actual correct information. Other researchers have noted that the illusory truth is persistent and stubborn, and while the actual size of the effect can be reduced over time, it is never fully extinguished (Henderson et al., 2021).

The illusory truth effect has been demonstrated to have a wide range of implications that are pertinent to digital warfare. For example, Pennycook et al. (2018) noted that illusory truth effects can form a corner-stone tactic in the spread and reinforcement of propaganda, enhancing the believability of spurious claims. Others have noted the impact of the illusory truth effect on the spread and believability of misinformation (Hassan & Barber, 2021; Vellani et al., 2023). Vellani et al. (2023) noted that individuals were more likely to share information that they had previously seen and that the likelihood of sharing was influenced by how accurate they saw such information to be. Repetition of information was seen to bias an individual's perception of accuracy, where repeated exposure to misinformation increased their perception of accuracy as well as the likelihood of sharing such misinformation (Vellani et al., 2023). These findings have been well supported by additional research in the area (Dechêne et al., 2010; Hassan & Barber, 2021; Henderson et al., 2021), demonstrating the persistent and potentially damaging effects repeated exposure to misinformation and disinformation can have.

Offensive digital operations can exploit the illusory truth effect, particularly when an adversary seeks to gain traction with misinformation. By ensuring that false information is repeated across multiple platforms, its perceived credibility increases, making it more likely to be accepted as fact. Strategies such as trolling, disinformation campaigns, and memetic warfare can amplify the distribution of this content within digital environments, creating an effective attack vector.

Decision-Making and Risk Perception Biases

Decision-making under uncertainty is a core component of human cognition, yet it is frequently compromised by systematic biases that distort risk perception and judgement. This section explores key biases, including *negativity bias*, *optimism bias*, *sunk-cost fallacy*, and *overconfidence bias,* that influence how individuals evaluate outcomes, assess threats, and commit to courses of action. In digital environments, where information is often incomplete, emotionally charged, or strategically manipulated, these biases can be exploited to shape behaviour, reinforce ideological commitments, and impair rational deliberation. Understanding these vulnerabilities is essential for recognising how digital warfare targets the cognitive mechanisms underpinning decision-making and risk assessment.

Negativity Bias

We generally prefer decisions that lead us to avoid losing something in comparison to gaining something of similar value. The psychological pain that we experience when we lose something is seen as a far more powerful motivator than the pleasure we experience when we gain something. This is another cognitive bias that has its roots firmly planted in prospect theory (Kahneman & Tversky, 1979), suggesting that individuals make decisions based on their perceptions of future consequences, especially where risk and uncertainty are involved. As a result, loss aversion can make individuals engage in a wide range of risk adverse behaviours and irrational decision-making processes. If you want to harness the power of loss aversion, the main way to achieve this is to frame persuasive messaging in a way that emphasises the potential negatives of not complying with the requests being made, fear-based messaging, potentially missing out on opportunities or experiences, and social exclusion.

Norris et al. (2019) observed that, when all other factors are controlled, negative information tends to exert a stronger influence across multiple domains, including attention, memory, perception, and behaviour. This is the crux of the negativity bias, where individuals will be more influenced and attracted to the negative aspects of information over the positive. In instances where individuals are presented with information about someone who has committed two morally questionable acts, individuals will choose the worst of the two acts to make an evaluative judgement for both (Amabile & Glazebrook, 1982; Birnbaum, 1972). Similarly, where someone is considering an individual for employment, interviewers have been shown to focus more directly on the negative attributes of candidates rather than the positive ones (Bolster & Springbett, 1961).

How can the negativity bias be used in digital warfare? If the goal is to influence the perception of a particular group, destabilise trust in an organisation, or initiate action for a specific cause, it can be easily exploited. The first step is to flood digital platforms with increasingly negative information through memetic images, stories, and testimonials that portray the target group in a negative light. This strategy brings the perception of threat from such a group to the forefront of individuals' attention and memory. In turn, it enhances the potential for an emotive response from wider audiences while strengthening in-group/out-group biases.

Furthermore, even when the information presented is technically and factually correct, framing bias can be used to focus attention on the negative aspects of a story or event. This might involve crafting a narrative that emphasises past failings of the target group, such as highlighting previous errors. Additionally, confirmation bias can drive individuals to seek out more information that aligns with their existing beliefs, creating a self-perpetuating cycle of negativity. When combined with algorithmic curation and echo chambers, this cycle becomes even more entrenched, amplifying the overall impact of negativity bias in digital environments.

Optimism Bias

We tend to be overly optimistic when it comes to the outcomes associated with our current decisions. This is a persistent problem, even though many of us have had considerable life experiences to demonstrate that things do not always go the way we want them to (Sharot et al., 2011). An individual can make numerous different decisions that are based on the likely outcome of a particular action. For example, we could make a judgement about how successful we might be if we carry on with a current project, how likely we might be to fall ill if we do not get a seasonal flu vaccination, or how likely we might be involved in a serious accident if we do not wear a helmet while out cycling. Bracha and Brown (2010) noted that whenever an individual is faced with assessing the likelihood of success or failure for a current course of action, they will fall foul of the optimism bias, meaning that they consistently overestimate the positives and potential successes over the negatives or the likelihood of failure.

Optimism bias has been well established in the context of personal risk, where people are generally more optimistic about the risks posed by hazards they have rarely experienced (Costa-Font et al., 2009) or where the hazards in question appear to have a degree of personal control attached to them (Weinstein, 1980). Other research has shown that the link between optimism and perceived likelihood of being involved in a road traffic accident is influenced by the length of time an individual has been driving. Furthermore, individuals consistently overestimated the degree of control they had over other causative factors. (Dejoy, 1989). More recent research also noted that individuals held a variety of unrealistic, over-optimistic views around the potential dangers and likelihood of contracting COVID-19 (McColl et al., 2022).

Optimism bias is another mechanism that can be effectively leveraged in the context of the digital battlefield. Individuals tend to place a positive spin on potential outcomes of their decisions, often ignoring the possibility of emerging threats in the digital environment, particularly when engaging in risky activities. By amplifying the positive framing of a specific outcome (e.g., "Join this action; the authorities will not intervene" or "Share this material with your friends; it will help protect them in the future"), adversaries can strengthen optimism bias and make individuals feel more confident in acting.

False narratives can also exploit optimism bias, especially when the goal is to pacify a population or divert attention from negative developments. For example, spreading claims that the economy is performing better than it is, or that an offensive operation is progressing as planned, can create a false sense of security. Additionally, adversaries can foster distrust in official sources by contrasting negative, fact-based information with fabricated optimistic narratives. These narratives, though entirely untrue, tap into the human tendency to seek reassurance and maintain a positive outlook.

Sunk-Cost Fallacy

Have you ever spent an inordinate amount of time, energy, or money on a project, a hobby, or an activity and continue to engage in the same, even though it might no longer be the right decision to do so? This is the crux of the sunk-cost fallacy, where individuals who have invested in a particular venture or activity fail to realise that adding more resources to such will not result in success (Arkes & Blumer, 1985). The critical aspect that individuals often fail to understand is that the level at which they have invested prior to deciding to continue or terminate the activity should has no direct bearing on such a decision; it is only the further costs that should be considered (Arkes & Ayton, 1999).

Daily life is littered with examples of how sunk costs can be manifested. For example, people often stay in unhealthy relationships because they have committed so much time to them. Other examples could include sitting through a particularly tedious and lengthy movie when you are almost halfway through, especially when you have spent money on the tickets, drinks, and snacks. Sunk cost is easy to see from an objective viewpoint, but individuals who have invested so much in the activities they continue to engage in are often oblivious to the fallacy. Indeed, the term "Concorde Fallacy" has been used to describe the sunk-cost fallacy, named after the supersonic aircraft that was a joint project between the UK and French governments (Arkes & Ayton, 1999). Even though there was a very poor financial outcome for the project, with this information being known a long time before the aircraft was constructed, the project continued, given that too much had been invested already (Arkes & Ayton, 1999).

The sunk-cost fallacy can manifest in digital environments in several ways. Users may persist in using ineffective platforms or spend additional money on upgrades, hoping these actions will enhance functionality and improve their overall experience, primarily because they have already invested heavily in the initial product. Similarly, subscriptions to premium streaming services often remain active for long periods, as individuals resist cancellation. This resistance is frequently driven by the lure of new, upcoming shows, even when the quality of new content is comparable to or worse than previously viewed programmes.

On social media platforms, sunk-cost behaviour is evident when users continue engaging with toxic communities or forums because they have invested significant time building their profile, followers, or reputation. For example, individuals may remain active in polarising Facebook groups or Reddit threads despite recognising the negative impact on their mental well-being, simply because leaving would mean abandoning years of effort and social capital. Likewise, influencers on Instagram or TikTok often persist in producing content for declining audiences because of prior investments in branding and follower acquisition. Another manifestation occurs when users refuse to delete old Twitter accounts or migrate to new platforms, even when the current platform no longer meets their needs, due to the perceived loss of historical posts and engagement.

The sunk-cost fallacy can also drive the continued adoption of beliefs that are objectively false or rooted in conspiracy theories. In such cases, individuals may perceive abandoning these beliefs as psychologically damaging, motivating them to maintain and defend these values despite contrary evidence, especially when their identity and online social connections are tied to these narratives.

Sunk cost has some considerable overlaps with the concept of commitment and consistency that we discuss in Chapter 11. However, commitment and consistency are processes that are driven by the individual's subjective expectations of how others around them will view them if they fail to behave in a consistent way. On the other hand, sunk cost is linked to a core process of loss aversion, where we will do anything to avoid admitting that we have made a mistake, choosing instead to continue with our current course of action. Both mechanisms are fundamentally driven by the same desire to avoid psychological distress. However, they differ in terms of where the sources of discomfort come from. With commitment and consistency, the pressure is socially driven and external to the individual. In contrast, the sunk cost effect is driven internally. It comes from our own evaluation of how much effort we have already invested in an activity, the current status of that activity, and whether we believe continuing with that action will eventually pay off. With the sunk cost, the threat to psychological stability comes from within the individual.

Overconfidence Bias

Overconfidence bias is the tendency to overestimate one's abilities, knowledge, or judgement. People often believe they are more competent or accurate than they are, particularly in areas where they lack expertise (Moore & Healy, 2008; Nascimento, 2025). Researchers have noted that overconfidence can emerge in three distinct ways, according to the focus of the overconfidence judgement. The first aspect of overconfidence is that of *overestimation* and can be related to an overestimation of skill level, level of control over events, or the chance to complete an activity successfully. Secondly, we have overconfidence that arises when an individual believes that they are better than others at something, a concept that Moore and Healy (2008) labelled as *overplacement*. The third form of overconfidence is that of *over-precision* and is related to the misplaced certainty that one's own beliefs are accurate and without reproach (Moore & Healy, 2008).

Overconfidence bias is part of a broader set of biases that serve to reinforce it, particularly those aligned with self-protection and the need to maintain a self-identity untarnished by admitting shortcomings (Nascimento, 2025). Biases such as the Dunning–Kruger effect (Schlösser et al., 2013) exemplify how related biases can compound overconfidence, creating a self-serving cycle of illusions that reinforce the belief that we are more competent than we actually are. Individuals with partial or incomplete knowledge of a topic can often overestimate their understanding of topics that might be complex and offer incorrect opinions, something that could further the spread of misinformation (Nascimento, 2025). Similarly, people may also be more resistant to correction because they have a misplaced view that they are more knowledgeable, and this could be elevated due to the presence of the over-precision, precision, and overplacement elements of the overconfidence bias.

The potential for the overconfidence bias to emerge as a tactic in digital warfare is not something that is completely inescapable. Firstly, individuals will have an overwhelming belief that they are more capable and more able to detect the potential for influence and persuasion online than they are. This is something that has been noted in other aspects of online safety, particularly from the perspective of cybersecurity, where individuals have a misplaced overconfidence in their capabilities (Hadlington & Ryding, 2025). In terms of getting people to fall into the use of the overconfidence bias, adversaries can seed platforms with emotionally charged narratives that appeal directly to non-experts but in a way that serves to simplify arguments or perspectives that allow them to believe they have a full grasp of the situation. Once you have a hold, a gentle nudge towards allowing overconfident users to create their own interpretations of such material can serve to stoke the fires of virality and misinformation spread.

Cognitive Dissonance: The Hidden Engine Behind Biases

In the final section for this chapter, I wanted to briefly explore a concept that exerts a constant influence on many of the biases we have discussed here, that of cognitive dissonance. Cognitive dissonance refers to the psychological discomfort experienced when an individual holds two or more contradictory beliefs, values, or attitudes simultaneously, or when their behaviour conflicts with their beliefs. First introduced by Festinger (1957), the theory posits that individuals are motivated to reduce this discomfort by altering their cognitions or behaviours to restore internal consistency. Although cognitive dissonance is not classified as a cognitive bias itself, it is seen to interact with a broad spectrum of biases that we have discussed in the current chapter, including confirmation bias, framing, sunk cost, and overconfidence bias, making it a key driver in many skewed judgements.

In digital environments, cognitive dissonance is not only a theoretical construct but can also be leveraged as a key vulnerability. The discomfort caused by presenting individuals with conflicting information can be weaponised by adversarial actors to manipulate beliefs, reinforce biases, and drive behavioural change. For example, when individuals encounter information that contradicts their political or ideological stance, they may experience dissonance. To resolve this, they often engage in biased reasoning: dismissing the source, reinterpreting the facts, or seeking out confirmatory content. This process is frequently unconscious and serves to protect the self from psychological discomfort (Nascimento, 2025). Put very simply, we do not want to change the views and opinions we already have, so we are going to seek out ways to justify those views even in the face of contradictory viewpoints and evidence – enter the use of cognitive biases.

Accordingly, Nascimento (2025) argued that cognitive dissonance is amplified in digital environments due to the heightened visibility of individuals and their opinions. Public corrections of long-held beliefs can feel like personal attacks, triggering defensive reactions and fear of social isolation or ridicule. Digital platforms intensify these dynamics through algorithmic curation, echo chambers, and emotionally charged content. While repeated exposure to congruent information minimises dissonance and reinforces belief systems, the introduction of dissonant information, such as fact-checking or counter-narratives, can often provoke denial, hostility, or deeper entrenchment of existing views.

This dynamic can be particularly potent in disinformation campaigns, and by deliberately introducing conflicting narratives, adversaries can induce dissonance and then guide resolution through biased content. For example, presenting emotionally evocative misinformation alongside contradictory official statements can create confusion and discomfort. The individual, seeking resolution, may gravitate towards the emotionally resonant (but false) narrative, especially if it aligns with their pre-existing world-view.

As we will discuss later in Chapter 13, cognitive dissonance can play a critical role in radicalisation and the commitment to ideological content presented in propaganda. As individuals invest more time and identity into a belief system, the psychological cost of abandoning it increases. Dissonance arising from contradictory evidence is resolved not by changing beliefs but by rejecting the evidence and doubling down on the ideology (Garcet, 2021). This mechanism underpins the persistence of conspiracy theories, extremist views, and misinformation adherence in digital spaces.

Summary

In this chapter, we have examined some of the core cognitive biases that act as critical mechanisms for distorting information processing and memory, as well as highlighting their exploitation in digital warfare. Beginning with an overview of biases as systematic deviations from rational decision-making, the discussion explores how these distortions emerge from heuristic-driven processing and interact with memory and attention systems. Key biases such as framing, confirmation bias, the illusory truth effect, negativity bias, optimism bias, the sunk-cost fallacy, and overconfidence are analysed for their role in shaping perception, reinforcing false narratives, and amplifying susceptibility to manipulation. Each bias is contextualised within digital environments, illustrating how adversaries weaponise these tendencies through tactics such as algorithmic curation, echo chambers, and emotionally charged content.

The chapter also introduces cognitive dissonance as a foundational concept that, while not a bias itself, acts as a catalyst for biased reasoning. Dissonance reduction strategies, such as selectively exposing oneself to information that supports existing perspectives or reframing material to align with prior beliefs, underpin many of the biases discussed in this chapter. These mechanisms create a self-reinforcing cycle of belief persistence and resistance to corrective information. By mapping these processes, the chapter demonstrates how cognitive biases and dissonance operate as strategic vulnerabilities in the digital battlespace, enabling adversaries to manipulate perception, erode trust, and influence behaviour. Understanding these mechanisms is essential for developing resilience strategies that counteract bias-driven distortions and strengthen cognitive integrity in hostile information environments.

References

Ahluwalia, R. (2000). Examination of psychological processes underlying resistance to persuasion. *Journal of Consumer Research*, *27*(2), 217–232. https://doi.org/10.1086/314321

Amabile, T. M., & Glazebrook, A. H. (1982). A negativity bias in interpersonal evaluation. *Journal of Experimental Psychology*, *18*, 1–22.

Arkes, H. R., & Ayton, P. (1999). The sunk cost and concorde effects: Are humans less rational than lower animals? *Psychological Bulletin*, *125*(5), 591–600. https://doi.org/10.1037/0033-2909.125.5.591

Arkes, H. R., & Blumer, C. (1985). The psychology of Sunk cost. *Organizational Behaviour and Human Decision-Making Processes*, *35*, 124–140.

Birnbaum, M. H. (1972). Morality judgments: Tests of an averaging model. *Journal of Experimental Psychology*, *93*(1), 35–42.

Bolster, B. I., & Springbett, B. M. (1961). The reaction of interviewers to favorable and unfavorable information. *Journal of Applied Psychology*, *45*(2), 97–103.

Bordiga, E., & Nisbett, R. E. (1977). The differential impact of abstract vs, concrete information on decisions. *Journal of Applied Social Psychology*, *7*(3), 258–271.

Boukes, M., Boomgaarden, H. G., Moorman, M., & Vreese, C. H. De. (2015). Political news with a personal touch: How human interest framing indirectly affects policy attitudes. *Journalism & Mass Communication Quarterly*, *92*(1), 121–141. https://doi.org/10.1177/1077699014558554

Boukes, M., & Hameleers, M. (2023). Fighting lies with facts or humor: Comparing the effectiveness of satirical and regular fact-checks in response to misinformation and disinformation fighting lies with facts or humor: Comparing the, *7751*. https://doi.org/10.1080/03637751.2022.2097284

Bracha, A., & Brown, D. J. (2010). *Affective decision making: A theory of optimism bias affective decision making: A theory of optimism bias*, Working Papers, No. 10-16, Federal Reserve Bank of Boston, Boston, MA.

Campos-Castillo, C., & Shuster, S. M. (2023). So what if they're lying to us? Comparing rhetorical strategies for discrediting sources of disinformation and misinformation using an affect-based credibility rating. *American Behavioral Scientist*, *67*(2), 201–223. https://doi.org/10.1177/00027642211066058

Chrobak, Q. M., & Zaragoza, M. S. (2012). The Misinformation Effect: Past Research and Recent Advances. *Suggestibility in Legal Contexts: Psychological Research and Forensic Implications*, 21–44. https://doi.org/10.1002/9781118432907.ch2

Costa-Font, J., Mossialos, E., Rudisill, C., Costa, J., Mossialos, E., & Rudisill, C. (2009). Optimism and the perceptions of new risks, *9877*. https://doi.org/10.1080/13669870802445800

Dechêne, A., Stahl, C., Hansen, J., & Wänke, M. (2010). The truth about the truth: A meta-analytic review of the truth effect. *Personality and Social Psychology Review*, *14*(2), 238–257. https://doi.org/10.1177/1088868309352251

Dejoy, D. M. (1989). The optimism bias and traffic accident risk perception. *Accident Analysis and Prevention, 21*(4), 333–340.

Dekker, S., Lee, N. C., Howard-Jones, P., & Jolles, J. (2012). Neuromyths in education: Prevalence and predictors of misconceptions among teachers. *Frontiers in Psychology, 3*. https://doi.org/10.3389/fpsyg.2012.00429

Festinger, L. (1957). *A theory of cognitive dissonance*. Stanford: Stanford University Press.

Garcet, S. (2021). Understanding the psychological aspects of the radicalisation process: A sociocognitive approach. *Forensic Sciences Research, 6*(2), 115–123. https://doi.org/10.1080/20961790.2020.1869883

Hadlington, L., & Ryding, C. (2025). *Human factors and cybersecurity: The psychology of online safety and security*. Taylor & Francis.

Hamilton, D. L., & Rose, T. L. (1980). Illusory correlation and the maintenance of stereotypic beliefs. *Journal of Personality & Social Psychology, 39*(5), 832–845.

Hassan, A., & Barber, S. J. (2021). The effects of repetition frequency on the illusory truth effect. *Cognitive Research: Principles and Implications, 6*(1). https://doi.org/10.1186/s41235-021-00301-5

Henderson, E. L., Simons, D. J., & Barr, D. J. (2021). The trajectory of truth: A longitudinal study of the illusory truth effect. *Journal of Cognition, 4*(1), 1–23. https://doi.org/10.5334/JOC.161

Kahneman, D., & Tversky, A. (1979). Prospect theory: An analysis of decision under risk. *Econometrica: Journal of the Econometric Society*. Retrieved from http://www.jstor.org/stable/1914185

Khawar, S., & Boukes, M. (2025). Analyzing sensationalism in news on twitter (X): Clickbait journalism by legacy vs. online-native outlets and the consequences for user engagement. *Digital Journalism, 13*(8), 1482–1502. https://doi.org/10.1080/21670811.2024.2394764

McCloskey, M., & Zaragoza, M. S. (1985). Misleading postevent information and memory for events: Arguments and evidence against memory impairment hypotheses. *Jounral of Experimental Psychology: General, 114*(1), 1–16.

McColl, K., Debin, M., Souty, C., Guerrisi, C., Turbelin, C., Falchi, A., . . . Raude, J. (2022). Are people optimistically biased about the risk of covid-19 infection? Lessons from the first wave of the pandemic in Europe. *International Journal of Environmental Research and Public Health, 19*(1). https://doi.org/10.3390/ijerph19010436

McPherson, M., Smith-Lovin, L., & Cook, J. M. (2001). Fuzzy homophily in social networks. *Annual Review of Sociology, 27*, 415–444. https://doi.org/10.1109/CFIS.2015.7391644

Mohammadi, E., Tahamtan, I., Mansourian, Y., & Overton, H. (2022). *Identifying Frames of the COVID-19 Infodemic: Thematic Analysis of Misinformation Stories across Media Corresponding Author, 2*(1). https://doi.org/10.2196/33827

Moore, D. A., & Healy, P. J. (2008). *The Trouble with Overconfidence, 115*(2), 502–517. https://doi.org/10.1037/0033-295X.115.2.502

Nascimento, I. (2025). The psychological cycle of misinformation: An integrative model of legitimation perception in social networks. *Frontiers in Social Psychology*, (August). https://doi.org/10.3389/frsps.2025.1621794

Nickerson, R. S. (1998). Confirmation bias: A ubiquitous phenomenon in many guises. *Review of General Psychology, 2*(2), 175–220.

Norris, C. J., Leaf, P. T., Fenn, K. M., Norris, C. J., Leaf, P. T., & Negativity, K. M. F. (2019). Negativity bias in false memory: Moderation by neuroticism after a delay, *9931*. https://doi.org/10.1080/02699931.2018.1496068

Pennycook, G., Cannon, T. D., & Rand, D. G. (2018). Prior exposure increases percieved accuracy of fake news. *Journal of Experimental Psychology: General, 147*(12), 1865–1880.

Peters, U. (2022). What is the function of confirmation bias? *Erkenntnis, 87*, 1351–1376.

Riet, J. Van, Cox, A. D., Cox, D., Zimet, G. D., Bruijn, D., Putte, B. Van Den, . . . Ruiter, R. A. C. (2016). Does perceived risk influence the effects of message framing? Revisiting the link between prospect theory and message framing, *7199*. https://doi.org/10.1080/17437199.2016.1176865

Schlösser, T., Dunning, D., Johnson, K. L., & Kruger, J. (2013). How unaware are the unskilled? Empirical tests of the "signal extraction" counterexplanation for the Dunning – Kruger effect in self-evaluation of performance, *39*, 85–100. https://doi.org/10.1016/j.joep.2013.07.004

Sharot, T., Korn, C. W., & Dolan, R. J. (2011). How unrealistic optimism is maintained in the face of reality. *Nature Neuroscience, 14*, 1475–1479. https://doi.org/10.1176/appi.ap.30.3.218

Sievwright, O., Philipp, M., Drummond, A., Knapp, K., & Ross, K. (2021). Misinformation effects in an online sample: Results of an experimental study with a five day retention interval. *PeerJ*, 1–19. https://doi.org/10.7717/peerj.12299

Singh, V. V., Gupta, S. S., Singh, V. V., & Basera, J. (2023). An analysis of sensationalism in news. *Journal of the Asiatic Society of Mumbai, XCV*(45), 168–177. Retrieved from https://www.researchgate.net/publication/374812735

Song, Q. (2024). Framing in media and communication studies: A bibliometric analysis. *Insight – News Media, 7*(1), 674. https://doi.org/10.18282/inm674

Talluri, B. C., Urai, A. E., Tsetsos, K., Usher, M., Donner, T. H., Talluri, B. C., . . . Donner, T. H. (2018). Confirmation bias through selective overweighting of choice-consistent evidence report confirmation bias through selective overweighting of choice-consistent evidence. *Current Biology, 28*(19), 3128–3135.e8. https://doi.org/10.1016/j.cub.2018.07.052

Tousignant, J. P., Hall, D., & Loftus, E. F. (1986). Discrepancy detection and vulnerability to misleading postevent information. *Memory & Cognition, 14*(4), 329–338. https://doi.org/10.3758/BF03202511

Tversky, A., & Kahneman, D. (1974). Judgment under uncertainty: Heuristics and biases. *Science (New York, N.Y.), 185*(4157), 1124–1131. https://doi.org/10.1126/science.185.4157.1124

Tversky, A., & Kahneman, D. (1986). Rational choice and the framing of decisions. *Journal of Business, 59*(4), 251–278.

Tversky, A., & Kahneman, D. (1992). Advances in prospect theory: Cumulative representation of uncertainty. *Journal of Risk and Uncertainty, 5*, 297–323.

Udry, J., & Barber, S. J. (2024). The illusory truth effect: A review of how repetition increases belief in misinformation. *Current Opinion in Psychology, 56*, 101736. https://doi.org/10.1016/j.copsyc.2023.101736

Valenzuela, S. (2022). *A Downward Spiral? A Panel Study of Misinformation and Media Trust in Chile*. https://doi.org/10.1177/19401612211025238

Valenzuela, S., Piña, M., & Ramírez, J. (2017). *Behavioral Effects of Framing on Social Media Users: How Conflict, Economic, Human Interest, and Morality Frames Drive News, 67*, 803–826. https://doi.org/10.1111/jcom.12325

Vellani, V., Zheng, S., Ercelik, D., & Sharot, T. (2023). The illusory truth effect leads to the spread of misinformation. *Cognition, 236*(March), 105421. https://doi.org/10.1016/j.cognition.2023.105421

Weinstein, N. D. (1980). Unrealistic optimism about future life events. *Journal of Personality and Social Psychology, 39*(5), 806–820. https://doi.org/10.1037/0022-3514.39.5.806

Zhou, Y., & Shen, L. (2022). Confirmation bias and the persistence of misinformation on climate change. *Communication Research, 49*(4), 500–523. https://doi.org/10.1177/00936502211028049

Zhou, Y., & Shen, L. (2024). Processing of misinformation as motivational and cognitive biases. *Frontiers in Psychology, 15*. https://doi.org/10.3389/fpsyg.2024.1430953

7 Cognitive Biases II

Social and Emotional Biases in Digital Warfare

Introduction

In the previous chapter, we focused on cognitive biases that can serve to directly influence information processing and linked these to their impact on decision-making, perception, and evaluation. These biases act in various ways that can severely impact our capacity to engage in rational judgements while largely operating on an intrapersonal, individualistic level. However, there are other cognitive biases that can be amplified and reinforced within social environments, particularly where there is a capacity to make comparisons to others, or where the behaviours of others are plainly visible. The power of social comparison in terms of the trigger of cognitive biases cannot be underestimated in platforms that encourage individuals to engage in social comparison and the sharing of ideas. Social drivers can be seen as one of the critical ways in which cognitive biases can be triggered, particularly when it means we do not have to assess the entirety of knowledge that is encapsulated in an online environment, or we do not have to analyse every single instance of a particular social group.

There is another associated mechanism that can also be used to effectively trigger the use of cognitive biases, and it is something that remains at the forefront of our discussions throughout this book, that being emotion. Anything that is presented to us as emotionally charged has the capacity to trigger a variety of heuristic processes (e.g., the affect heuristic; see Chapter 9), which in turn can also influence the capacity for cognitive biases to kick in as well. Researchers have noted that experiences of negative emotions during an election because of scandals can lead individuals to distance themselves from the ideological standpoint of the person at the centre of such events (Chang & Park, 2025). This can be linked to a negativity bias where individuals attach more weight to the detrimental aspects of an event or individual, rather than taking everything into consideration. Emotion has been shown to have a detrimental impact on a wide range of cognitive processes, including memory, decision-making, perception, and attention (Chang & Park, 2025), so it is not surprising that it is so closely intertwined with the main tactics that are employed in digital warfare.

DOI: 10.4324/9781003752400-7

Social and Group Identity-Based Biases

Social identity plays a pivotal role in shaping cognitive biases, particularly within digital environments where group affiliations and ideological boundaries are often amplified. These biases emerge from our tendency to categorise ourselves and others into social groups, leading to distorted perceptions and judgements that favour in-group members while marginalising out-groups. In the context of digital warfare, such biases are not only prevalent but also actively weaponised to deepen divisions, reinforce tribalism, and manipulate public sentiment. This section explores key social identity-based biases, including in-group bias and out-group homogeneity bias, and examines how they are exploited to influence behaviour and belief systems in online spaces.

In-Group Bias

Sherif et al. (1961) demonstrated the existence of the in-group bias in a seminal study, the so-called Robbers Cave experiment, named after the summer camp, where the boys were attending. In the initial stages of the study, the boys were split into two groups, and the existence of the other group was hidden from them. Soon enough, the two groups established themselves as self-identified groups and identified themselves as the Rattlers and the Eagles. After this, the groups were introduced to each other in settings that created an element of intergroup conflict, such as competitive games that offered prizes for the winning team. Initially, the intergroup conflict was restricted to simple name-calling or the creation and singing of songs that served to ridicule the opposing group (Sherif et al., 1961). Even when attempts were made to reduce the intergroup frictions, such as organising a meal where both groups attended, the event was marred by a food fight that broke out. Only when there was a goal that superseded group identity and was seen to be beneficial to both groups were antagonistic tendencies removed, and cooperation between the two groups flourished. Generating an in-group bias does not have to be as involved as this, with other researchers noting that simply assigning people to one group based on arbitrary distinctions can serve to create the same effect (Tajfel, 1982; Tajfel & Turner, 2004; Turner et al., 1979).

It is a fact of life that we tend to form close relationships or social contacts with people who are like us, where similarity can be built around various dimensions (e.g., interests and hobbies, religion, and culture) (Currarini & Mengel, 2016; Gillani et al., 2018). The concept of *social homophily,* as we saw in the previous chapter, is one of the driving forces in the creation and maintenance of echo chambers in online forums and can lead to other cognitive misjudgements (Gillani et al., 2018). A variety of studies have been conducted to explore how social media platforms can serve to increase the perception of social divides between groups. For example, posts on Twitter were shown to generate more replies when they shared a similar set of views to those of the audience in comparison to counter-perspectives (Yardi & Boyd, 2010).

In-group bias can also lead individuals to bias their perceptions of the behaviours they have observed by other members of the same group. In original research by Hastorf and Cantril (1954), two opposing football teams were asked to describe what they had seen during a highly competitive and controversial match. While the in-group team blamed most of the negative behaviour on the opposing (out-group) team, the out-group team served to highlight that both teams were equally to blame. Even when watching a video of the game, the two teams differed significantly in terms of their interpretation of the events that unfolded. One of the teams that came from Princeton University suggested that members of the opposing team, Dartmouth, were overly aggressive and were responsible for the most infringements. However, the Dartmouth Group suggested that both teams were equally rough, demonstrating in-group loyalty, rationalising the aggressive actions of individuals within their group. This shows that in some instances, perception is not an objective process but can be driven by an individual's existing group affiliations, which in turn leads to a biased representation of events that we might observe.

Such in-group bias can be used in several ways in the context of digital warfare. In a report published by Brooker (2019), which presented a case study exploring the use of ISIS's online propaganda and radicalisation material, the role of in-group bias was demonstrated as a mechanism that was used to reinforce ideological messages and enhance the tribal dynamics of the group. This was perpetuated using a feedback loop that consistently fed narrative information linked to "us versus them" messaging, as well as using other methods, such as social contagion (the rapid spread of ideas, emotions, or behaviours through social networks without any critical evaluation). In-group bias can therefore be seen as a way of deepening the divisions between different social groups as well as enhancing the creation of ideological silos that exist. Such a bias is easily weaponised using misinformation and emotionally charged narratives that feed into in-group identities, often using the idea that members of an out-group present a threat or are morally inferior to the in-group. Again, reflecting on the events that followed the Southport attacks in 2024, such mechanisms were observed on various social media platforms, where the Islamic extremist out-group was presented as being a clear threat to the safety and security of the dominant British in-group.

Out-Group Homogeneity Bias

Out-group homogeneity bias refers to the tendency to perceive members of an out-group as more like one another than members of one's own group. This bias manifests in statements like "they all look the same to me" and reflects a cognitive shortcut that simplifies social categorisation. As Ackerman et al. (2006)

suggested, this bias is a functional response to limited cognitive resources; grouping individuals together based on perceived similarities allows for quicker, albeit less accurate, judgements about others' beliefs, attitudes, and behaviours.

In the context of digital warfare, this bias can become a potent psychological tool. Adversaries can exploit it to reinforce stereotypes, justify hostility, and simplify complex social dynamics. Online environments such as social media platforms that are driven by algorithmic content delivery provide a fertile ground for such manipulation. By portraying out-groups as monolithic, extreme, or irrational, digital actors can mobilise in-group support by creating an emotionally charged narrative that establishes the boundaries between the in-group (us) and the out-group (them). It could also be used to suppress support and empathy for the members of the out-group, which in turn can allow adversarial elements to justify aggressive actions towards them. The methods that are utilised to achieve these goals are multiple, with the use of memetic messages and visual information that can be created to exaggerate key features of the out-group. Such a process can make stereotypes more engrained and engaging and can also make the out-group appear more homogeneous as well as more threatening. Co-ordinated online campaigns involving the use of bots and troll networks can also flood digital platforms with repetitive messages that serve to reinforce dominant stereotypes and can interact with other biases (e.g., confirmation bias, negativity bias, and the illusory truth effect).

There are many real-world examples of how such a process has already been used. Far-right campaigns, such as those that emerged during the aftermath of the Southport 2024 attacks, serve to depict immigrants and those individuals who are Islamic as a cohesive, uniform threat to national security while serving to brush over the diverse cultural differences that exist among these groups. Russian disinformation campaigns and propaganda serve to portray Western societies as being morally corrupt and having a uniformly negative attitude towards Russia, which in turn is used to reinforce ultra-nationalistic views, as well as serving as a pretext for the current invasion of Ukraine. Indeed, the invasion of Ukraine was presented as a need to eradicate the neo-Nazism that was seen as an inherent part of the out-group (the Ukrainian people).

The Bandwagon Effect

This is something that we will mention again in Chapter 10 when we explore the key tactics related to social engineering, but we will discuss it here in more depth and detail. The bandwagon effect is generally seen as the tendency for an individual to assume the perspective of the majority even though they might have a different personal perspective (Bindra et al., 2022). The bandwagon effect is often also referred to in the research literature as either herding or conformity bias (Knyazev & Oosterhuis, 2022). The bandwagon effect is particularly evident in instances where individuals follow the ratings or opinions of others, and in instances where people are told that a particular item has gained a high number of positive ratings, individuals will follow suit (Knyazev & Oosterhuis, 2022).

The bandwagon effect has been shown to influence a wide range of behaviours. For example, when individuals were presented with information about the most popular choices for election votes, this had the effect of increasing the votes for the options that the majority had chosen by 7% (Farjam, 2021). Similar effects have also been noted for aspirations to purchase luxury goods (Niesiobędzka, 2018; Shaikh et al., 2017), tourism travel choices (Boto-García & Baños-Pino, 2022), and social networking site use (Fu et al., 2012).

In digital warfare, this bias can be exploited to rapidly spread misinformation or propaganda by creating the illusion of widespread agreement or popularity. Tactics such as artificially inflating likes, shares, or comments, often through bots or co-ordinated networks, can trigger this effect, leading users to accept and propagate false or biased narratives without critical evaluation. The bandwagon effect also interacts with social contagion and in-group bias, reinforcing echo chambers and suppressing dissent. By leveraging this bias, digital actors can manipulate public opinion, shape discourse, and influence collective decision-making at scale.

False Consensus Bias

Individuals frequently overestimate how widely their own beliefs, opinions, and attitudes are shared by others, a cognitive distortion known as the false consensus bias (Luzsa & Mayr, 2021). This bias is closely linked to the egocentric bias, wherein people use their own perspective as a reference point for judging others' attitudes. Such a tendency leads to a skewed perception that others think similarly, reinforcing a sense of social validation. This validation, in turn, bolsters confidence in one's views, even in the absence of objective evidence that such support exists.

Luzsa and Mayr (2021) investigated how false consensus bias manifests in digital environments, particularly on social media platforms. In their study, participants were exposed to news feeds containing either attitudinally congruent (agreeing) or incongruent (disagreeing) content. Exposure to predominantly congruent information increased the perception that one's views were widely shared, demonstrating a clear false consensus effect. Interestingly, the level of endorsement (e.g., number of likes) played a nuanced role in shaping this bias. When congruent messages received low endorsement, the false consensus bias was stronger. In contrast, highly endorsed congruent messages led to greater scepticism, possibly because they appeared overly agreeable, prompting suspicion of artificial manipulation or astroturfing. Astroturfing is a form of deceptive online practice where messages are crafted to appear as though they represent genuine grassroots opinions or widespread public support, but they are strategically manufactured to promote specific agendas. The term draws from the idea of "fake grass," symbolising an artificial grassroots movement. In digital environments, astroturfing often involves co-ordinated efforts such as creating fake accounts, deploying bots, or amplifying certain narratives to make them seem organically popular or widely endorsed. This tactic is commonly used in political campaigns, disinformation operations, and marketing strategies to manipulate perceptions of consensus and legitimacy (Zhang et al., 2013).

In the context of cognitive biases, astroturfing interacts strongly with the false consensus effect, where individuals overestimate how widely their own beliefs are shared. When people encounter content that appears to align with their views and seems broadly supported, they may assume their perspective is mainstream, reinforcing confidence in those beliefs. This illusion of consensus can be further amplified by engagement metrics like likes, shares, and comments, even if these are artificially inflated. Interestingly, research suggests that low levels of endorsement can sometimes be more persuasive than high levels, as heavily endorsed content may trigger suspicion of manipulation (e.g., astroturfing). From this regard, Luzsa and Mayr (2021) proposed that individuals may become wary of information that aligns too neatly with their views when it is heavily endorsed, perceiving it as potentially fabricated or strategically amplified.

These dynamics reveal how false consensus bias can be weaponised through deliberate manipulation of digital content. By flooding social media platforms with attitudinally congruent messages that appear with limited objective endorsement, adversarial actors can create the illusion that certain views are more mainstream than they truly are. This tactic is particularly potent in information warfare, propaganda, and PsyOPs. For instance, politically motivated campaigns might deploy bots or co-ordinated accounts to amplify fringe ideologies, making them appear widely accepted. This can sway undecided voters or encourage individuals to promote misinformation, such as conspiracy theories, by reinforcing the illusion of widespread belief. Crucially, as Luzsa and Mayr (2021) suggest, endorsement levels must be carefully calibrated. To maximise persuasive impact, low endorsement may be more effective than high, as it avoids triggering scepticism and maintains the illusion of organic consensus.

Pluralistic Ignorance

This is a bias where individuals within a group or society will personally reject a belief or an opinion or disengage in a particular activity but will believe that everyone else in that group privately accepts it. This means that while the individual might dismiss such a norm or belief, they will publicly conform to it because they believe others actively believe it. This can in turn result in a false consensus or the perpetuation of beliefs that on the surface may appear to be well supported, but on a more individualistic level, people reject such norms (Prentice & Miller, 1996). Pluralistic ignorance again plays on the need for individuals to conform to social norms, which are an inherent part of any group of individuals.

As Prentice and Miller (1996) note, such norms do not have to be explicitly stated but can be very subtle rules that tell individuals how they should behave to conform to the rest of the group.

Pluralistic ignorance has been demonstrated to be a key feature of social situations or group interactions. Prentice and Miller (1996) point to work that has been conducted exploring the way in which people interact during emergency situations and noted that pluralistic ignorance is evident in bystander situations. In work by Latané and Darley (1970), it was noted that individuals would often hesitate to intervene in an emergency because they feared they would be seen to be overreacting. When individuals observed other people not rushing to help, having a calm outward experience, they assumed that the emergency was not as critical as they first thought and therefore resisted the internal urge to get involved. However, as Latané and Darley (1970) noted, the other individuals within the same situation could have also been experiencing the same levels of fear and uncertainty. One other example, which is something that I have observed in a classroom environment, is the tendency for students not to ask questions in open-group sessions because they have the fear that they will be seen to be foolish. When students view other students being silent, they make the erroneous assumption that everyone else in the room has understood the material, even though other students may be equally confused (Prentice & Miller, 1996).

It is argued that there is a fundamental process at work for pluralistic ignorance to occur and that is referred to as mutual observability (Miller, 2021). When we can observe the behaviours of others, we can engage in a process of social comparison, which in turn leads them to conclude that the inaction they are observing comes from a genuine indifference to the current situation rather than shared uncertainty about what to do. If this visibility is removed, people are much more likely to assume that the internal concerns that they have would be shared by others if they were present, which fits into the work that has been done on the false consensus effect (Marks & Miller, 1987). In online communities, the capacity for us to observe the behaviours of others in the group is greatly reduced, leading to low mutual observability (Miller, 2023). In this instance, individuals are forced to make an inference about what others in that group would do based on a scant review of what a smaller number of members might do (Miller, 2023). However, as this information itself could be biased, perhaps because the information has been taken from extreme examples within the group, it in turn leads to the potential for the group norms being misinterpreted.

In digital environments, pluralistic ignorance is another bias that can be widely exploited in digital warfare. As noted above, in digital environments, the capacity for individuals to observe the behaviour of others is vastly reduced. This in turn means there is a tendency to rely on visible markers, such as the number of likes, shares, comments, or indeed the type of topics that are trending within that group. This process can be harnessed if your aim is to control the dominant narratives and behaviours within a group. This might include presenting a perspective on a current topic, making a particular political movement more prominent than another, or encouraging the reinforcement of misinformation. If you can amplify the visibility of views that might otherwise sit in the periphery of the social group, you can control the dynamic of the group, where individuals will happily conform to the dominant social norms. Using bots, co-ordinated misinformation campaigns or manipulating engagement statistics can create an overall illusion of widespread support for a particular thing, while also controlling the possibility for dissenting views and opposing perspectives to emerge. Low visibility of disagreement combined with a fear that individuals will suffer harm to their social standing within the current group can fuel the existence of pluralistic ignorance, which in turn can give the perfect environment for misinformation and extremist views to persist.

Pluralistic ignorance can also be seen to interact with other biases mentioned in this chapter, such as the false consensus effect, bandwagon bias, and in-group bias, creating a complex web of social distortion. In echo chambers, users may see only congruent views, reinforcing the belief that their silence is justified or that dissent is futile. The result is a digitally engineered conformity that stifles critical thinking and facilitates ideological manipulation.

Temporal and Emotional State Biases

Human cognition is not static; it fluctuates with emotional states and temporal contexts, often leading to systematic misjudgements. In digital warfare, these fluctuations are strategically exploited to manipulate perceptions, decisions, and behaviours. Biases such as projection bias, the hot–cold empathy gap, and authority bias reveal how transient emotions and visceral states can distort future expectations, suppress rational evaluation, and increase susceptibility to persuasive messaging. This section explores how these biases operate, interact, and are amplified in online environments, particularly during emotionally charged events, and how they contribute to the entrenchment of ideologies and the mobilisation of individuals in digital conflict.

Projection Bias

Projection bias occurs when individuals assume that their current cognitive, emotional, or ideological state will persist into the future (Loewenstein et al., 2000). This misjudgement can lead to flawed decision-making and heightened susceptibility to influence and persuasion. In the context of digital warfare, this bias can be strategically exploited. For example, adversarial actors may reinforce transient emotional states such as anger, fear, or patriotic fervour by using targeted messaging and digital stimuli. By amplifying these emotions, they create an illusion of permanence, encouraging individuals to make decisions or adopt beliefs that align with their current state, regardless of its temporary nature.

This manipulation can contribute to the entrenchment of ideologies and cognitive frameworks that become resistant to change, particularly when individuals later shift into different emotional or cognitive states. Projection bias thus plays a pivotal role in the formation and maintenance of echo chambers, where individuals are repeatedly exposed to content that validates their current beliefs and emotions (Arce, 2024; Luzsa & Mayr, 2021). These echo chambers can be further reinforced through memetic warfare, which, as we will see later in Chapter 14, is the strategic use of culturally resonant symbols, narratives, and ideas. This process can provide a very powerful mechanism in the process of radicalisation and seeding dissent in populations, especially when combined with algorithmic reinforcement and social validation (Hancock, 2010; Munk et al., 2025).

During emotionally charged events, such as general elections, referenda, or crises, projection bias can be strategically manipulated to sway individuals towards supporting extreme policies (e.g., enforced deportation, stricter laws, or curtailments of civil liberties). This bias leads to individuals overestimating the permanence of their current emotional states, believing that how they feel in the present will endure into the future. By amplifying transient emotional reactions, such as fear, anger, or anxiety, actors can create a false sense of long-term conviction. This illusion of emotional permanence makes calls for immediate and drastic action appear more justified and urgent. In effect, projection bias transforms short-lived emotional responses into perceived enduring beliefs, thereby facilitating support for policies that might otherwise be rejected under more neutral conditions.

Hot and Cold Empathy Gap

The hot and cold empathy gap is a bias where an individual will make a prediction about something based on their current visceral state (Helton & Register, 2023). An example of this could be something as simple as trying to establish how hungry someone else might be, where we make a prediction based on how hungry we currently feel (Helton & Register, 2023). This effect can also act in an intrapersonal way when the individual is making relevant predictions about their future behaviour, and they tend to underestimate the influence emotional states will have on their own actions. Neutral or "cold" states are characterised by minimal visceral stimulus, and hot states are seen as being a heightened state of stimulation, whether this be emotional or some other physiological response. Individuals often engage in the consumption of information on a wide range of topics online while we are in relatively neutral, cold states, often ignoring the potential for such information to be viewed in a different way when we switch to hot states. However, once an individual becomes emotionally triggered, perhaps through the implementation of memetic measures or false narratives, they may in turn act in ways that override more rational, normative processing of that information. This in turn could motivate the individual to share such information or create a situation where they see the potential benefits from engaging in real-world actions that they otherwise would not have considered while being in their neutral, cold state.

Disinformation campaigns can also utilise this hot–cold empathy gap with digital adversaries targeting the release of emotionally charged information. Individuals who are occupying concurrent hot states are more ready to accept such information, even though in a more rational state, they would ignore it. Campaigns could also target individuals who are occupying current hot states to influence decisions that could have long-term ramifications, such as voting behaviours. Individuals in hot states may be more likely to misjudge their future feelings while being emotionally stimulated, in contrast to a more relaxed, neutral state. Fear-based messaging about immigration could lead to an individual being more accepting of draconian measures being adopted or a more vitriolic outpouring against minority groups or government officials.

Authority Bias

Authority is something that we will discuss in Chapter 10 in terms of social engineering. While that aspect explores how authority can be constructed and weaponised in the context of digital warfare, authority bias explains the cognitive foundations as to why these tactics are so effective. Authority bias often emerges when individuals make a faulty assertion that those who occupy a position of authority are also endowed with better expertise and knowledge, in turn allowing them to make better decisions (Okushko, 2022). In turn, this means individuals can devolve a great deal of their own decision-making processes to those in authority, which can lead to obedience.

People have an innate susceptibility to comply with the demands of authority figures, often overriding personal judgements or ethical concerns (Miller et al., 1995). This is amplified when the individual believes that the individual in authority can exert some form of psychological or physical pressure on them, such as an aggressive action or engaging in some form of punitive actions against those individuals who have been seen to fail to comply with their commands (Okushko, 2022). This again links to the central tenet of cognitive economy, with individuals willing to devolve aspects of their decision-making to authority figures whom they assume have a greater grasp of the current situation and are much better informed to make decisions. While authority as a tactic involves the deliberate use or construction of authoritative personas, authority bias is the psychological mechanism that makes such tactics effective. The former is strategic; the latter is cognitive.

The extent to which authority bias can influence decision-making has been questioned. For example, Kembau et al. (2024) noted that the impact of the authority bias on the decision of Gen Z students (born between 1995 and 2010) to take an online course was limited, and instead, they appeared to be more guided by peer reviews when evaluating the course content and likelihood to enrol.

In the context of digital warfare, authority bias becomes a potent psychological lever for manipulation. Malicious actors can exploit this bias by crafting messages that appear to originate from trusted institutions, experts, or government bodies, often using spoofed emails, deepfakes, or cloned websites (Horowitz, 2019; Paterson et al., 2020). These tactics are particularly effective in phishing campaigns, disinformation operations, and influence campaigns, where the mere appearance of authority can override critical thinking and prompt compliance (Milhazes-Cunha & Oliveira, 2023). The digital environment amplifies this effect by obscuring traditional cues of legitimacy, making it easier for adversaries to fabricate authority and harder for individuals to verify authenticity. As such, authority bias not only explains why individuals fall for these tactics but also underscores the importance of digital literacy and critical evaluation in resisting manipulation.

The Amplification of Cognitive Biases

There are various ways in which the effects of cognitive biases can be enhanced or influenced through simple yet highly efficient methods. Some researchers have noted that digital environments themselves can serve as a key mechanism for the amplification of cognitive biases, mainly because of the wealth of concentrated information that they contain. Ecker (2025) noted that aspects of confirmation bias and projection bias are often amplified in digital environments, possibly due to the ease with which information can be accessed and discounted and the relative anonymity that is afforded by the internet.

Digital spaces can also amplify the potential use of cognitive biases, usually through the action of two core mechanisms: emotional contagion and social contagion. Emotional contagion refers to the rapid spread of affective states such as fear, anger, or enthusiasm through networks, often triggered by emotionally charged content. This phenomenon is intensified by algorithms that prioritise engagement, ensuring that high-arousal emotions propagate widely. On the other hand, social contagion involves the diffusion of behaviours, attitudes, and norms within online communities, where individuals adopt actions or beliefs modelled by others. Both processes can interact with cognitive biases, creating feedback loops that reinforce polarised thinking, accelerate misinformation, and heighten susceptibility to manipulative tactics in digital warfare. We will move on to exploring each of these mechanisms in more detail in the following section.

Emotional Contagion

One form of amplification is linked to something termed *emotional contagion* (Hatfield et al., 1993; Hatfield & Rapson, 2010), which has been described as the tendency for individuals to mimic the emotional states of others around them. The notion of “contagion” heavily implies that individuals can catch emotional states much as they would catch a cold. There is a wide variety of research that demonstrates individuals can indeed catch other people's emotions and that this can occur on large scales (Hatfield & Rapson, 2010).

There has been some work that demonstrates emotional contagion can extend to the digital environment, where essential non-verbal cues that can be used to elicit emotion from others are largely removed. A controversial study by Kramer et al. (2014) explored the potential for emotional contagion to be elicited through social networks, in which they used Facebook as their testing ground. In their study, they manipulated emotional contagion by reducing the overall amount of emotional content that individuals viewed within their news feeds. In instances where the amount of positive information was reduced, people were seen to produce fewer positive posts while at the same time increasing the frequency with which they posted negative comments. The opposite trend was observed for negative posts, with people posting fewer negative posts and more positive posts (Kramer et al., 2014). The authors of this study also noted that there was another significant impact from viewing less emotional posts in their feeds; for the day after, they were generally less expressive, in turn demonstrating that emotional content does have a significant detrimental impact on social engagement online. Goldenberg and Gross (2020) made an insightful observation directly relevant to this effect: if the goal is to keep users engaged in digital environments, particularly on social media, then it is essential to "upregulate" the emotions users encounter. This means engaging in a process of deliberately increasing the presence, intensity, and frequency of emotional stimuli within the digital environment. This principle has important implications for digital warfare. To gain traction with information, especially misinformation, or to sustain outrage and dissent, online environments must be saturated with emotive content. Recalling the example from the previous chapter on the Southport attacks of 2024, we see a perfect storm in which highly charged emotional material was persistently circulated online. This led to a reciprocal amplification of negative emotional content, creating a feedback loop that intensified the overall emotional climate.

However, as Goldenberg and Gross (2020) note, there is an important distinction according to the traction gained by emotional content within online environments. Research indicates that positively valenced material is more likely to be shared and retweeted compared to negative information, perhaps because individuals perceive greater social rewards for expressing positivity online on social media (Tsugawa & Ohsaki, 2017; Ferrara & Yang, 2015). Regardless of the underlying reasons, this demonstrates that emotional contagion significantly influences how individuals experience emotions online, and this process can be directly shaped by the content appearing in their social media feeds. Further evidence has also suggested that individuals who engage extensively with digital devices are more susceptible to emotional contagion in online spaces, with digital emotional contagion also being linked to heightened feelings of anxiety (Gardner, 2022; Goldenberg & Gross, 2020; Prikhidko et al., 2020).

Emotional contagion can readily amplify existing cognitive biases, which can then be exploited for offensive digital warfare operations. For instance, the presence of information that triggers fear or outrage can serve to activate the availability heuristic, with emotionally charged information about current events being more easily recalled. Similarly, aligning content with the prevailing emotions of dominant reference groups can strengthen in-group bias and confirmation bias, reinforcing group identity and perpetuating echo chambers. Moreover, viral content with strong emotional elements can intensify both the affect heuristic and the hot–cold empathy gap, increasing the likelihood of impulsive, in-the-moment decisions or leading individuals to misjudge the risks associated with a given choice.

Social Contagion

Similar to emotional contagion, the concept of *social contagion* draws on the analogy that information can spread through social networks much like a pathogen moves through a population (Hodas & Lerman, 2012, 2014). Social contagion refers to the rapid dissemination of ideas, emotions, or behaviours across networks, often occurring without critical evaluation. Within social media environments, this phenomenon takes on a new level of virulence, as platforms provide fertile ground for the seeding and propagation of ideas and misinformation. Individuals not only passively encounter information but also actively seek it out and become conscious agents in its spread (Hodas & Lerman, 2012, 2014).

One of the most widely used models for examining the spread of social contagion is the *independent cascade model* (ICM) (Hodas & Lerman, 2014). This model posits that each time an individual sees a friend share a piece of information, such as a meme or news article, there is a certain probability that they will share it as well. The likelihood of sharing increases as more friends share the same content, creating the conditions for virality. However, empirical research on social media behaviour indicates that this pattern does not always hold consistently. While repeated exposure can increase the probability of sharing, there is a threshold beyond which additional exposure reduces engagement. To address these limitations, alternative models have been proposed. For example, the *complex contagion model* suggests that individuals may require exposure from multiple trusted sources before engaging, whereas the *linear threshold model* argues that adoption occurs only after a specific proportion of one's network has embraced the information (Hodas & Lerman, 2014). Other factors, such as the novelty and persistence of content and competition within an already crowded information space, also influence diffusion dynamics, which in turn can increase the spread of information. Interestingly, research has shown that individuals typically limit their online interactions to approximately 150 contacts (Gonçalves et al., 2011), highlighting that cognitive constraints on information processing continue to shape digital behaviour.

In the context of digital warfare, social contagion can be weaponised to amplify misinformation, incite panic, or mobilise collective action. When emotionally charged or ideologically resonant content is introduced into a network, particularly by trusted in-group sources, it can trigger cascades of sharing and endorsement, reinforcing false narratives and deepening polarisation. The viral architecture of digital platforms accelerates this process, enabling adversaries to manipulate public sentiment and decision-making at scale. Through the mechanics of algorithmic amplification, individuals are more likely to come into contact with information that generates strong reactions, serving to create loops of virality (Milli et al., 2025; Rathje et al., 2024). Also, the design of online platforms affords individuals a highly intuitive, effortless process for sharing information, which means it can be shared both within and across multiple platforms at speed (Gordon-Tapiero et al., 2023; Jahn et al., 2023; Ruiz et al., 2024). Moreover, social contagion interacts with cognitive biases such as in-group bias, confirmation bias, and the illusory truth effect, making individuals increasingly vulnerable to repeated, emotionally salient misinformation.

Case Study: QAnon – The Perfect Storm for Bias Exploitation

So it might be useful to contextualise all these biases and frame them in a real-world example. The rise and persistence of the QAnon conspiracy movement offer a compelling illustration of how multiple cognitive, social, and emotional biases can be weaponised in digital warfare. The movement emerged in 2017 because of anonymous posts on 4chan, and QAnon quickly evolved into a sprawling belief system that claimed a secret cabal of elites was engaged in nefarious activities, with former President Donald Trump positioned as a saviour figure. QAnon as a group is something that we will return to in Chapter 8, but for now, we will focus on how the functioning of key biases served to help the rise to prominence of the movement.

1. In-group bias
   QAnon created a strong sense of community among its followers, who often referred to themselves as "patriots" fighting against a corrupt elite. This identity fostered intense in-group loyalty and out-group hostility, particularly towards political opponents, journalists, and scientists. The movement's tribal dynamics were reinforced through shared symbols, slogans ("Where We Go One, We Go All"), and rituals, deepening ideological silos.
2. Out-group homogeneity bias
   Opponents of QAnon were frequently portrayed as uniformly evil, corrupt, or brainwashed. This simplification allowed adherents of the movement the capacity to dismiss more nuanced perspectives and justified hostility towards perceived (out-group) enemies. The portrayal of the "deep state" as a monolithic threat serves to exemplify this bias.

3. Bandwagon effect
   The growth of QAnon was no doubt accelerated by the illusion of widespread support. Co-ordinated sharing of "Q drops" (information that appeared to come from the mysterious individual Q), memes, and hashtags created a feedback loop that made the movement appear more popular and credible than it was. Social media algorithms further amplified this effect by promoting content with high engagement.
4. False consensus bias
   Followers often believed their views were widely shared, especially within echo chambers on platforms like Facebook, Telegram, and Parler. This illusion of consensus reinforced belief in the movement's legitimacy and discouraged dissent, often leading to individuals being overtly ridiculed online.
5. Pluralistic ignorance
   Many individuals may have privately doubted QAnon's claims but remained silent due to perceived group norms. The fear of social ostracism or being labelled a "traitor" led to public conformity, even among some of those who may have been more sceptical about some of the claims being made.
6. Projection bias and hot–cold empathy gap
   During emotionally charged events, such as the COVID-19 pandemic, Black Lives Matter protests, and the 2020 U.S. election, QAnon content exploited fear, uncertainty, and anger. Followers projected their current emotional states into the future, believing drastic action was justified. The January 6th Capitol riot is a prime example of how hot emotional states can override rational judgement, and many individuals overrode more rational decision-making processes that would have been evident in cold states.
7. Authority bias
   QAnon leveraged perceived authority figures, both real and constructed. "Q" was framed as a high-level government insider, and influencers within the movement gained credibility through repetition and engagement. Followers deferred judgement to these figures, often ignoring contradictory evidence.
8. Amplification through emotional and social contagion
   QAnon's success hinged directly on its ability to spread emotionally charged content, such as the fear of child trafficking, anger at political corruption, and hope for a coming "Great Awakening." These emotions were contagious, especially in digital environments where algorithms prioritised engagement. Memes, videos, and viral posts acted as vectors for both emotional and social contagion, rapidly expanding the movement's reach.

This example documenting the rise and proliferation of the QAnon conspiracy network demonstrates very clearly how digital warfare can exploit a whole network of interconnected biases and heuristics. In turn, the processes can be seen to undermine trust in established institutions and present a counter-perspective to dominant views that could endanger lives and lead to civil unrest. They can also enhance the polarisation of communities, as well as lead to the large-scale mobilisation of like-minded individuals, taking the influence from the online to the offline in quite dramatic ways. Much of this mobilisation is based around the proliferation of misinformation, created in ideologically resilient echo chambers that are incredibly resistant to correction. The movement's persistence, despite widespread debunking, underscores the power of bias-driven manipulation in online environments. It also highlights the need for countermeasures that address not only misinformation but also the psychological mechanisms that make individuals susceptible to it.

Summary

This chapter has examined the intricate web of social and emotional cognitive biases that underpin human behaviour and how these biases are systematically exploited within digital warfare environments. Unlike the intrapersonal biases discussed in the previous chapter, the biases explored here, including in-group bias, out-group homogeneity bias, bandwagon effect, false consensus bias, pluralistic ignorance, projection bias, hot–cold empathy gap, and authority bias, are all deeply embedded in social contexts and emotional states. These biases do not operate in isolation; rather, they interact dynamically, creating fertile ground for manipulation, misinformation, and ideological entrenchment.

Digital warfare thrives on the amplification of these biases. Social media platforms, algorithmic content delivery systems, and online communities provide the infrastructure for adversarial actors to weaponise cognitive distortions. In-group bias fosters tribalism and ideological silos, while out-group homogeneity bias simplifies complex identities into threatening caricatures. The bandwagon effect and false consensus bias create illusions of widespread agreement, encouraging individuals to adopt and propagate views without critical scrutiny. Pluralistic ignorance further compounds this by suppressing dissent and reinforcing conformity, even when individuals privately disagree with dominant narratives.

Emotional states play a pivotal role in this manipulation. Projection bias and the hot–cold empathy gap reveal how transient emotions, such as fear, anger, or anxiety, can be misinterpreted as enduring convictions, leading individuals to make decisions that feel justified in the moment but may not withstand rational reflection. Emotional contagion and social contagion serve as accelerants, spreading affective and behavioural responses across networks with viral efficiency. These mechanisms are not incidental; they are deliberately harnessed to shape public opinion, incite action, and destabilise social cohesion.

The chapter also highlighted how authority bias can be exploited to lend credibility to misinformation, particularly when authoritative personas are constructed or strategically positioned within digital ecosystems. This bias reinforces obedience and deference, allowing adversaries to bypass critical thinking and embed persuasive narratives more deeply. The case study of QAnon served as a powerful illustration of how these biases converge in real-world scenarios. The movement's rise and persistence demonstrate how digital warfare can exploit psychological vulnerabilities to create resilient belief systems, mobilise collective action, and undermine democratic institutions. Despite widespread debunking, QAnon's ideological grip persisted, underscoring the formidable influence of bias-driven manipulation.

Ultimately, this chapter underscores the necessity of understanding the psychological architecture of digital warfare. The exploitation of social and emotional biases is not a peripheral tactic, but it is central to the success of disinformation campaigns and PsyOPs. Counter-measures must therefore go beyond fact-checking and content moderation; they must address the cognitive and emotional mechanisms that make individuals susceptible to manipulation. Only by recognising and mitigating these biases can we begin to build digital resilience and safeguard the integrity of online discourse.

References

Ackerman, J. M., Shapiro, J. R., Neuberg, S. L., Kenrick, D. T., Becker, D. V., Griskevicius, V., . . . Schaller, M. (2006). They all look the same to me (unless they're angry): From out-group homogeneity to out-group heterogeneity. *Psychological Science*, *17*(10), 836–840. https://doi.org/10.1111/j.1467-9280.2006.01790.x

Arce, D. (2024). Disinformation strategies. *Defence and Peace Economics*, *35*(6), 659–672. https://doi.org/10.1080/10242694.2024.2302236

Bindra, S., Sharma, D., Parameswar, N., Dhir, S., & Paul, J. (2022). Bandwagon effect revisited: A systematic review to develop future research agenda. *Journal of Business Research*, *143*(February), 305–317. https://doi.org/10.1016/j.jbusres.2022.01.085

Boto-García, D., & Baños-Pino, J. F. (2022). Social influence and bandwagon effects in tourism travel. *Annals of Tourism Research*, *93*. https://doi.org/10.1016/j.annals.2022.103366

Brooker, C. (2019). The effectiveness of influence activities in information warfare. *Australian Army Research Centre*, (8). Retrieved from https://researchcentre.army.gov.au/sites/default/files/AARCOccasionalPaperNo8%27EffectivenessofInfluenceActivitiesinInformationWarfare%27%28Brooker%29_0.pdf

Chang, K., & Park, J. (2025). Negative emotions, projection bias, and the vote choice in South Korea. *Humanities and Social Sciences Communications*, *12*, 164. https://doi.org/10.1057/s41599-025-04479-7

Currarini, S., & Mengel, F. (2016). Identity, homophily and in-group bias. *European Economic Review*, *90*, 40–55. https://doi.org/10.1016/j.euroecorev.2016.02.015

Ecker, U. K. H. (2025). Misinformation: Current directions and new insights. *Journal of Applied Research in Memory and Cognition*, *14*(2), 149–153.

Farjam, M. (2021). The bandwagon effect in an online voting experiment with real political organizations. *International Journal of Public Opinion Research*, *33*(2), 412–421. https://doi.org/10.1093/ijpor/edaa008

Ferrara, E., & Yang, Z. (2015). Quantifying the effect of sentiment on information diffusion in social media. *PeerJ Computer Science*, *2015*(9), 1–15. https://doi.org/10.7717/peerj-cs.26

Fu, W., Teo, J., & Seng, S. (2012). The bandwagon effect on participation in and use of a social networking site. *First Monday*, *17*(5).

Gardner, M. (2022). *The relations among digital emotion contagion, emotion regulation, and anxiety*. Edwardsville: Southern Illinois University.
Gillani, N., Yuan, A., Saveski, M., Vosoughi, S., & Roy, D. (2018). Me, my echo chamber, and i: Introspection on social media polarization. *The Web Conference 2018 – Proceedings of the World Wide Web Conference, WWW 2018*, 823–831. https://doi.org/10.1145/3178876.3186130
Goldenberg, A., & Gross, J. J. (2020). Published in trends in cognitive science. *Digital Emotion Contagion*, 1–36.
Gonçalves, B., Perra, N., & Vespignani, A. (2011). Modelling users' activity on twitter networks: Validation of Dunbar's number. *PLoS One*, *6*(8). https://doi.org/10.1371/journal.pone.0022656
Gordon-Tapiero, A., Ohm, P., & Ramaswami, A. (2023). Fact and friction: A case study in the fight against false news. *UC Davis Law Review*, *57*, 171–251.
Hancock, B. J. (2010). Memetic war. *Intelligence*, *36*(2), 41–46.
Hastorf, A. H., & Cantril, H. (1954). They saw a game: A case study. *Journal of Abnormal and Social Psychology*, *49*(1), 129–134. https://doi.org/10.1037/h0057880
Hatfield, E., Cacioppo, J. T., & Rapson, R. L. (1993). Emotional contagion. *Current Directions in Psychological Science*, *2*(3), 96–99. https://doi.org/10.1007/978-3-319-19650-3_301425
Hatfield, E., & Rapson, R. L. (2010). Emotional contagion. In I. B. Weiner & W. Craighead (Eds.), *Encyclopaedia of psychology* (4th ed.). Hoboken, NJ: John Wiley and Sons Inc.
Helton, G., & Register, C. (2023). Hot-cold empathy gaps and the grounds of authenticity. *Synthese*, *202*(5), 1–24. https://doi.org/10.1007/s11229-023-04311-2
Hodas, N. O., & Lerman, K. (2012). How visibility and divided attention constrain social contagion. *Proceedings – 2012 ASE/IEEE International Conference on Privacy, Security, Risk and Trust and 2012 ASE/IEEE International Conference on Social Computing, SocialCom/PASSAT 2012*, 249–257. https://doi.org/10.1109/SocialCom-PASSAT.2012.129
Hodas, N. O., & Lerman, K. (2014). The simple rules of social contagion. *Scientific Reports*, *4*. https://doi.org/10.1038/srep04343
Horowitz, M. A. (2019). Disinformation as warfare in the digital age: Dimensions, dilemmas, and solutions. *Journal of Vincentian Social Action*, *4*(2), 5–21.
Jahn, L., Rendsvig, R. K., Flammini, A., Menczer, F., & Hendricks, V. F. (2023). *Friction interventions to curb the spread of misinformation on social media*, 1–17. Retrieved from http://arxiv.org/abs/2307.11498
Kembau, A. S., Tarigan, A., & Pangaribuan, C. H. (2024). *Influencing Gen-Z consumer perception of online course participation: The impact of Freebies, social proof, and authority bias in social media promotion captions* (Vol. 2023). https://doi.org/10.2991/978-94-6463-508-9_21
Knyazev, N., & Oosterhuis, H. (2022). The bandwagon effect: Not just another bias. *ICTIR 2022 – Proceedings of the 2022 ACM SIGIR International Conference on the Theory of Information Retrieval*, 243–253. https://doi.org/10.1145/3539813.3545142
Kramer, A. D. I., Guillory, J. E., & Hancock, J. T. (2014). Experimental evidence of massive-scale emotional contagion through social networks. *Proceedings of the National Academy of Sciences of the United States of America*, *111*(24), 8788–8790. https://doi.org/10.1073/pnas.1320040111
Latané, B., & Darley, J. M. (1970). *The unresponsive bystander: Why doesn't he help?* New York, NY: Appleton-Century Crofts.
Loewenstein, G., O'Donoghue, T., & Rabin, M. (2000). Projection bias in predicting future utility. *Quarterly Journal of Economics*, *118*, 1209–1248.

Luzsa, R., & Mayr, S. (2021). False consensus in the echo chamber: Exposure to favorably biased social media news feeds leads to increased perception of public support for own opinions. *Cyberpsychology*, *15*(1), 1. https://doi.org/10.5817/CP2021-1-3

Marks, G., & Miller, N. (1987). Ten years of research on the false-consensus effect: An empirical and theoretical review. *Psychological Bulletin*, *102*(1), 72–90. https://doi.org/10.1037/0033-2909.102.1.72

Milhazes-Cunha, J., & Oliveira, L. (2023). Doctors for the truth: Echo chambers of disinformation, hate speech, and authority bias on social media. *Societies*, *13*. https://doi.org/10.3390/soc13100226

Miller, D. T. (2023). A century of pluralistic ignorance: What we have learned about its origins, forms, and consequences. *Frontiers in Social Psychology*, *1*. https://doi.org/10.3389/frsps.2023.1260896

Miller, A. G., Collins, B. E., & Brief, D. E. (1995). Perspectives on obedience to authority: The legacy of the milgram experiments. *Journal of Social Issues*, *51*(3), 1–19. https://doi.org/10.1111/j.1540-4560.1995.tb01331.x

Milli, S., Carroll, M., Wang, Y., Pandey, S., Zhao, S., & Dragan, A. D. (2025). Engagement, user satisfaction, and the amplification of divisive content on social media. *PNAS Nexus*, *4*. https://doi.org/10.1093/pnasnexus/pgaf062

Munk, T., Mahoney, I., & Monastryrska, K. (2025). *The complex web in memetic warfare: A comprehensive analysis of societal dynamics, interactions and impact*. Nottingham: Nottingham Trent University.

Niesiobędzka, M. (2018). An experimental study of the bandwagon effect in conspicuous consumption. *Current Issues in Personality Psychology*, *6*(1), 26–33.

Okushko, E. (2022). *Influence of social forces in the form of authority bias and conformity bias on the degree of individuals' risk -aversion*. Radbound University.

Paterson, T., Hanley, L., & Paterson, T. (2020). *Political warfare in the digital age: Cyber subversion, information operations and 'deep fakes'*, *7718*. https://doi.org/10.1080/10357718.2020.1734772

Prentice, D. A., & Miller, D. T. (1996). Pluralistic ignorance and the perpetuation of social norms by unwitting actors. *Advances in Experimental Social Psychology*, *28*, 161–209. https://doi.org/10.1016/S0065-2601(08)60238-5

Prikhidko, A., Long, H., & Wheaton, M. G. (2020). The effect of concerns about COVID-19 on anxiety, stress, parental burnout, and emotion regulation: The role of susceptibility to digital emotion contagion. *Frontiers in Public Health*, *8*(December), 1–10. https://doi.org/10.3389/fpubh.2020.567250

Rathje, S., Robertson, C., Brady, W. J., & Van Bavel, J. J. (2024). People think that social media platforms do (but should not) amplify divisive content. *Perspectives on Psychological Science*, *19*(5), 781–795. https://doi.org/10.1177/17456916231190392

Ruiz, N., Molina León, G., & Heuer, H. (2024). Design frictions on social media: Balancing reduced mindless scrolling and user satisfaction. In *ACM international conference proceeding series* (Vol. 1). https://doi.org/10.1145/3670653.3677495

Shaikh, S., Malik, A., Akram, M. S., & Chakrabarti, R. (2017). Do luxury brands successfully entice consumers? The role of bandwagon effect. *International Marketing Review*, *34*(4), 498–513. https://doi.org/10.1108/IMR-09-2014-0302

Sherif, M., Harvey, O. J., White, B. J., Hood, W. R., & Sherif, C. W. (1961). Intergroup conflict and cooperation: The Robbers Cave experiment. *American Sociological Review*, *4*(Stage 3), 229.

Tajfel, H. (1982). Social psychology of intergroup relations. *Annual Review of Psychology*, *33*, 1–39.

Tajfel, H., & Turner, J. (2004). An inegrative theory of intergroup conflict. In M. J. Hatch & M. Schultz (Eds.), *Organizational identity: A reader* (pp. 56–65). London, UK: Oxford University Press.

Tsugawa, S., & Ohsaki, H. (2017). On the relation between message sentiment and its virality on social media. *Social Network Analysis and Mining*, *7*(1), 1–14. https://doi.org/10.1007/s13278-017-0439-0

Turner, J. C., Brown, R. J., & Tajfel, H. (1979). Social comparison and group interest in ingroup favouritism. *European Journal of Social Psychology*, *9*, 187–204. https://doi.org/10.1002/ejsp.2420090207

Yardi, S., & Boyd, D. (2010). Dynamic debates: An analysis of group polarization over time on twitter. *Bulletin of Science, Technology & Society*, *30*(5), 316–327. https://doi.org/10.1177/0270467610380011

Zhang, J., Carpenter, D., & Ko, M. (2013). Online astroturfing: A theoretical perspective. *19th Americas Conference on Information Systems, AMCIS 2013 – Hyperconnected World: Anything, Anywhere, Anytime* (Vol. 4), 2559–2565.

8 Weaponising Influence: Social Engineering in Digital Warfare

What Is Social Engineering?

The term "social engineering" is used to describe the use of a variety of psychological tactics to leverage influence over others, usually without them realising that they are being manipulated (Hadlington & Ryding, 2025). There are several key mechanisms through which social engineers can craft exploits that can serve to act in a variety of different ways, depending on the target and the net goal of the exploit in question. In contrast to more traditional ways of hacking a system, such as using code or password hacking to gain access, the use of social engineering is seen as a way of hacking the human mind. Irrespective of the way in which many individuals would like to view the realm of social engineering, it is not magic; it is not some sort of illusion – it is firmly based in human psychology and links to many concepts that we have already reviewed in this book. Although much of the work around social engineering has been linked to aspects of cybersecurity, there are some clear crossovers to the realm of digital warfare, of which cybersecurity is a key aspect.

In terms of the actual way in which a social engineer will attack a system, there have been some attempts to categorise the pathway through which these will happen. There are generally thought to be four key phases associated with a social engineering attack, these being the following:

1. Collect information: in this stage, the attacker will set about doing their research about the potential environment or target in which they are going to conduct their attacks. This could be scoping out information on social media about a particular individual, group, or organisation to explore any of the inherent weaknesses that might be evident; individuals are more than willing to divulge detailed information about themselves, their workplaces, and indeed other people that they might know on social media, as well as being over trusting of people that they meet online. Hence, social media becomes the surveillance capital of many social engineering operations. The concept of self-disclosure, through which individuals present information

DOI: 10.4324/9781003752400-8

about themselves and others online, is a core aspect of the social media environment, with many people exhibiting what has been termed "online disinhibition," making them more likely to give out information that they perhaps would not normally share in person. Part of this links into the anonymity offered by social media, as well as the perception that everyone you meet online is who they say they are.
2. Build trust: creating a rapport with your intended target is an essential part of the social engineer's toolkit and acts as a key part of facilitating the trust process that can enhance how much people are willing to tell you (Butavicius et al., 2015; Calic et al., 2016). Individuals who have a greater level of trust established with someone are far more likely to give out sensitive information that might include material that could be leveraged for a later attack (Tait & Jeske, 2015).
3. The exploit: once the social engineer has created an air of trust with their target, they will then go about their business; this is the manipulation element of the attack where the social engineer will use inherent cognitive biases and heuristic processing to get individuals to release information or perform tasks that in turn lead to some form of breach, compromise, or release of data. This could be limited to an individual being asked to send money or gifts as part of an online fraud exploit, or it could be someone leaking sensitive, classified information to someone they have shared intimate information with or formed a romantic relationship with over the internet.
4. The exit: in this stage, the damage has been done, the attacker has got what they wanted, and they will usually leave without a trace (Hadlington & Ryding, 2025). There is usually little that the victim can do at this point, other than engage in feelings of remorse, guilt, and self-doubt.

This four-phase model of information gathering, trust-building, exploitation, and exit provides a foundational lens through which to view the anatomy of a social engineering attack. However, to fully grasp the strategic significance of these tactics, it is essential to move beyond the individual-level mechanics and consider their broader implications within the digital battlespace. Social engineering is not just a tool that is isolated to being used by cybercriminals; it is increasingly being adopted as a core tactic in digital warfare, where psychological manipulation is deployed at scale to compromise systems, influence populations, and destabilise institutions. The following section explores how these techniques are leveraged in offensive cyber operations, highlighting their scalability, subtlety, and capacity to bypass traditional security measures by targeting the human element at the heart of digital ecosystems.

Why Is Social Engineering Relevant to Cyberwarfare?

This is an interesting question, and I would like to point out that this topic has not just been shoehorned into the book for the sake of it; the inclusion of social engineering needs some further explanation to contextualise it. For the most part, social engineering has been seen as the mainstay of cyber attackers who focus their efforts on leveraging information from susceptible individuals within an organisation. Social engineering has been highlighted as one of the key tactics used in a wide range of cyber-attacks on organisations that have led to wide-scale breaches, loss of revenue, and loss of reputation. For example, Twitter was the target of social engineering attacks in 2020 that led to the attackers gaining access to their internal systems via leaked passwords, resulting in high-profile accounts being taken over and a substantial amount of bitcoin being stolen. More recently, in 2025, the U.K. retailers Marks and Spencer were the target of another attack, where the attack vector was believed to be a phishing attack, where individuals who were working for a third-party supplier were duped into resetting their login credentials (https://www.blackfog.com/marks-and-spencer-ransomware-attack/). Members of the Scattered Spider ransomware group who claimed responsibility for the attack impersonated members of the internal IT team and managed to get login credentials for the system, which in turn allowed them to gain access to the internal systems of the organisation. As a result, the attackers then deployed ransomware within the system, resulting in what has been estimated to be around £300 million in lost revenue, along with the untold impact on its reputation among its customers.

This is usually the main way in which we see the use of social engineering in the realm of offensive cyber operations, and while many of these attacks are seen as small scale (compared to the wider battlefield of cyberspace), they can still have severe, detrimental impacts on a wide variety of services and individuals. However, there is more to social engineering than just attacks on businesses and well-crafted phishing emails. While technical exploits that use social engineering often dominate the discourse in cybersecurity, the use of social engineering can also be exploited at both the psychological and cognitive levels and can be used to influence behaviour or sow disharmony in society. There are many ways in which social engineering is relevant to the realm of digital warfare, including the following:

1. Penetrating the wetware: you do not need to expend massive amounts of time and effort on targeting technical systems with social engineering, and you can bypass most of the protection that is put in place by system designers if you access the cognitive architecture of the human brain; it is not encrypted, very rarely gets patched, and you can exploit it by using fear, emotion, and social norms to get what you want.
2. Scalable and subtle: the use of social engineering tactics offers a relatively simple, cheap, and scalable solution to targeting different groups across a wide range of platforms and populations. Phishing attacks can be rolled out on a massive scale, and in doing so, the attackers create the potential for

success through sheer numbers. You only need a small percentage of the people you target to respond for key information or login credentials to be taken and used later. You can also use techniques such as priming to make people behave in a more predictable way if you present individuals with specific information. Priming is a concept from the area of social cognition which details that presenting specific information to an individual prior to some later response can serve to act as a facilitator for that later response. Such mechanisms are widely used in everyday life; have you ever seen a lot of advertisements for a particular soft drink and then, when faced with a choice between two competing products, chosen the advertised one? You may do this even though you cannot consciously remember seeing the ad; such are the subtle effects of priming. If you take an example where individuals are repeatedly presented with emotionally charged information prior to a significant event (say, e.g., an election), you can prime a population to make specific choices without them realising they have done so based on false information.

3. Weaponising social networks: social engineers will often utilise existing trust structures to help them elicit a response to a request that people would otherwise dismiss. By exploiting existing trust structures, they do not have to set about spending time and effort creating trust themselves; they can simply inherit it. So, in the instance of the Marks and Spencer attack above, you can inherit trust and credibility through impersonation of relevant team members – they are part of your "team," so you trust them! Social media offers social engineers a whole new playing field in which they can impersonate people that you might know, clone accounts, or garner your trust because "they are a friend of a friend."
4. Integrate with memetic warfare: leveraging the tactics of social engineering, one can enhance your delivery mechanism for memetic payloads. Through the exploitation of existing narratives, stereotypes, and emotionally charged themes, memetic payloads can be loaded with frames that tap into these, in turn making them both more persuasive and harder to detect. When you layer in emotive elements to memes, you can introduce a very powerful mechanism for societal destabilisation and polarisation, as well as serve to amplify existing cultural divides.

It is from these perspectives that social engineering is included as a cornerstone mechanism for digital incursions in the cyberwarfare sphere. Not only is social engineering a subtle and often overlooked tool in the arsenal of the digital adversary, but it is also extremely hard to inoculate against, given the many forms it can come in. In the following sections, we will explore the basis for the mechanics of social engineering and the ways it could be used in the digital battlespace.

The World of Fixed Action Patterns

The background to the realm of influence lies in something that is termed "fixed action patterns" (FAPs) (Schleidt, 1974). These are automatic, unlearned behaviours that are triggered in animals as a response to a particular stimulus. There are several examples that can be gleaned from the animal world, with the most common one being that of the Greylag goose, which will instinctively crane its neck out of its nest to retrieve eggs that roll away. However, it has been observed that even when the egg is removed while the goose is in mid-crane, the goose will still complete the action until it is completed. FAPs mean that animals are generally slaves to their instinctual behaviours, and even in the absence of the physical trigger for this behaviour, they can be fooled into completing it.

The extent to which humans possess FAPs is somewhat questionable. Humans do have some close approximations to FAPs that are hardwired into our DNA, such as the sucking reflex in infants or the grasping reaction when something is placed within the palm of their hand. Other elements, such as facial expressions, are also automatic and generally universal, often triggered by emotional stimuli and are hard to suppress. However, because human behaviour is directly influenced by our cognitive processes, through social norms and learning, we can often override many aspects related to what could be termed "FAPs," preventing them from reaching their conclusion. There is another set of processes that can serve to act as close approximations to FAPs, and these are inherently hard to prevent and even harder to detect.

Humans can be triggered to behave in certain ways that serve to be predictable given the right background stimulus. For example, imagine you are on a busy, crowded street and you see someone fall over, but you see that no one has rushed to help that individual. Often, people will ignore this incident and carry on about their daily lives, assuming that the individual is not seriously hurt, as other people around are not helping. However, there is more at work than us just looking at the behaviour of other people; we have learnt from past experiences that in instances where someone is seriously injured, and there are other people around, we can usually sit by and let them get on with it. This is known as the bystander effect, and when we are in situations where we can divert responsibility away from us to other people, we feel less personally responsible to act. Another way of looking at this is the fear that we might be seen to be getting involved in someone else's business without direct need, and our concern is unnecessary. The bystander effect has been demonstrated to be a key process in online communities, especially in the presence of fake news; people often assume that because these communities are full of other individuals, they do not have to call out the fake news and the person posting it (Gimpel et al., 2021). The bystander effect is just one example of many ways in which we can, given certain parameters, predict how an individual will act (Attrill-Smith & Wesson, 2020). However, there is a downside to these processes, and they are not perfect; while they work a lot of the time, they can often lead to faulty decisions (Jansson & von Solms, 2013). As humans conform to the need for cognitive economy, given the sheer volume of decisions we have to make on a daily basis, we really need some way of streamlining these processes. By doing so, we open ourselves up to a myriad of potential issues that can and do impact our ability to make clear and realistic decisions, especially when we are faced with an uncertain outcome.

In past research, there have been some dramatic examples of how you can get someone to do something without them realising it. This was demonstrated very clearly in research by Langer et al. (1978), who conducted an experiment to show how easy it is to manipulate a social situation to elicit compliance. In the experiment, a person who is part of the experiment, the confederate, made a request to someone who was waiting in the queue for a photocopier, asking to take their place in line. They would present three reasons for asking to do this, with these being:

1. May I use the photocopier?
2. May I use the photocopier because I am in a rush?
3. May I use the photocopier because I have copies to make?

It may come as a surprise, but the latter two statements resulted in similar levels of compliance in those people who were waiting in the queue, with the confederate successfully being allowed to push into the queue around 94% of the time. The researchers suggested that this was an example of how individuals can demonstrate mindless conformity, and individuals become susceptible to this due to the actions *because* of heuristics. Most of the time, we ignore the actual reason someone presents for us to comply with their demands, as we fall into the trap of making a very big assumption that anything which follows the word "*because*" will be an honest reason for the individual wanting to push into the queue. Most of the time, people are also quicker to comply with the request when the individual wanting to push into the queue uses the "because" heuristic, and this is contrasted with a longer decision-making process when they refuse to comply with the demands (Scott Key et al., 2009). This would tend to suggest that people who are agreeing to the demand being made by the individual who wants to push in are engaging in the faster, Type 1 process route for decision-making, while those who are assessing the legitimacy of the reason for moving in front of them in the queue are more likely to engage in a rationale, Type 2 processing route.

The Weapons of Persuasion and Influence

Much has been made of the processes aligned with persuasion and influence in the context of cybercrime, where attackers will leverage these principles to harvest personal information and login credentials. However, these methods are also key in the way attackers can influence large swathes of the population to engage in actions and behaviours that could undermine societal stability or, in the very least, share misinformation and disinformation within their social circles. If you want to engage in psychological manipulation, there are six core principles of influence and persuasion, each of which forms clear strategies that could be used in both cognitive and psychological warfare. (Cialdini, 2009; Cialdini & Goldstein, 2004; Ferreira et al., 2015).

Authority

There has been a lengthy history of research exploring the role of authority and its capacity to influence people to comply with specific demands (Burger, 2009). Authority and its role in persuasion have been linked to source credibility theory, which states that when an individual perceives someone as having a higher level of authority, they will in turn see them as also being more credible (Algarni et al., 2016). We can create the notion of credibility based on two different elements, these being expertise or position within a hierarchy, whether this be social or organisational (Uebelacker & Quiel, 2014). Expertise is usually an obvious way of assuming authority, and individuals can display this in any number of ways, including subject expertise, academic qualifications, and level of experience in a particular field; all of these could be used as a metric for establishing credibility. However, in today's modern digital age and the world of deepfakes, forged qualifications, pseudo-experts, and influencers, the capacity to create an illusion of authority is easy to accomplish. All you need is a platform for your voice to be heard and a healthy number of people to buy into your narrative, and you have your authority. As we will see in Chapter 10, authority and credibility are often taken as being one and the same concept for many people who are searching for information online, so harnessing the power of authority can also serve to make people believe that something is more credible and therefore trustworthy.

In the context of digital warfare, there is a wide variety of opportunities to use authority as a weapon of influence. Perhaps the most prominent mechanism for this technique to be used is through propaganda, where the use of authority can be harnessed to validate dominant ideological messages. We have seen such examples of this in the context of the Russia–Ukraine conflict, where pro-Russian bloggers and prominent members of the state-sponsored media have been keen to parrot the narratives being presented by Kremlin officials. Such a mechanism can also link to the creation of echo chambers, where the narratives being controlled and spouted by those in authority are maintained and reinforced.

Using authority can also be a mechanism that can be harnessed through impersonation or cloning, particularly as the sophistication of deepfake technology and AI-generated images continues to accelerate at speed. One prominent example of this happening was the use of an AI-generated voice of the Secretary of State for the United States, Marco Rubio. The impersonator used this technique to contact three foreign ministers, as well as a U.S. governor and another member of the U.S. Congress. It is not known exactly what was discussed in these communications, but at the time it was noted that such a move was seen as a direct attempt to disrupt the U.S. elections (https://www.bbc.co.uk/news/articles/crrqkyyjewno). Other examples include a deepfake video that allegedly showed U.S. President Donald Trump calling Ukrainian President Volodymyr Zelensky a "total cokehead" during a press conference. The deepfake used footage from a previous press conference, with the content being quickly debunked by fact-checkers. However, the combination of an easy-to-digest format (video) portraying someone in authority disparaging the president of an embattled nation is a powerful weapon in any attacker's arsenal, especially if you want to sow the seed of dissent and disharmony among countries (https://www.aap.com.au/factcheck/trump-cokehead-attack-on-zelenskiy-is-a-deepfake/).

How Does Obedience Link to Authority?

One of the most well-known and unsettling studies from the history of psychology is Milgram's (1963) experiment that explored how far individuals would go in obeying authority, even when it conflicted with their moral judgement (Burger, 2009; Miller et al., 1995). Participants were led to believe they were part of a learning experiment involving electric shocks. They were assigned the role of "teacher," while a confederate always played the "learner." Another confederate, dressed in a lab coat to convey the vestiges of authority, acted as the experimenter. The teacher was instructed to administer increasingly severe electric shocks to the learner for each incorrect answer in a word-pair memory task. Although no real shocks were given, the set-up was convincing: the learner was placed in a mock electric chair, and the shock generator ranged from mild to potentially lethal voltages. As the learner deliberately gave wrong answers, the experimenter prompted the teacher to continue, using scripted commands like "You must go on." The results were striking: all participants administered shocks up to 300 volts, and over 65% continued to the maximum 450 volts, despite hearing distress or eventually silence from the learner. The study revealed the powerful influence of perceived authority on obedience, even when actions could cause serious harm (Burger, 2009; Miller et al., 1995).

The important takeaway from this study is that you can get people to do a lot of things they believe might be morally wrong if you can manipulate authority and obedience. In the realm of cyberwarfare, you can use this to get people to comply with a wide selection of demands if they perceive them coming from people in authority. We have seen this tactic used a great deal in cybercrime, where individuals will impersonate individuals in authority and leverage this to get a victim to carry out a task which may be questionable. For example, in the CEO fraud exploit, an individual will be duped into believing they are being contacted by a senior member of their organisation who usually asks them to access a system or send them money as they are currently unable to access the relevant information at that time (Hadlington & Ryding, 2025). Such a technique can be used in conjunction with other social engineering mechanisms, such as urgency, which serves to enhance the utility of obedience by overriding the more logical and systematic Type 2 processing route.

The psychological mechanisms uncovered by Milgram's obedience study are deeply embedded in the architecture of digital warfare. Propaganda and fake news campaigns frequently exploit perceived authority to bypass critical scrutiny, much like the lab-coated experimenter in Milgram's set-up. Whether through impersonated experts, fabricated institutional endorsements, or algorithmically amplified messages, digital actors leverage authority to manipulate belief and behaviour. When urgency is added to the mix, such as in breaking news alerts or crisis narratives, individuals are pushed towards automatic, Type 1 processing, reducing their capacity for rational evaluation. From this perspective, obedience to perceived authority becomes a powerful tool in the arsenal of digital warfare, enabling the spread of disinformation and the erosion of truth.

We Do What Others Do; Normative Influence and Social Proof

Normative influence refers to the way we conduct ourselves based on our assumptions about what others think we should be doing. By observing the behaviour of others, we can assess whether certain actions are appropriate for us in any given situation. The power of normative influence on an individual's behaviour cannot be underestimated, as people often witness the actions of others and subsequently modify their own behaviour (Asch, 1956; Cialdini & Goldstein, 2004). Normative influence operates through social norms, impacting behaviour when individuals conform to these norms to gain approval from their social circle or to avoid disapproval. Consequently, normative influence is often regarded as the effect that underlying norms have on behaviour (Rimal & Real, 2005). Researchers have noted that the strength of normative information can influence individuals' decisions to engage in certain behaviours even more than having specific information about the behaviour itself (Nolan et al., 2008).

Humans are inherently predisposed to function within social norms and pay close attention to the behaviour of others in their social circle (McDonald & Crandall, 2015). Others have noted that directly viewing a behaviour is not necessary for normative influence to take its desired effect; instead, communicating a norm in written information can also induce levels of conformity comparable to that of a directly observed behaviour (Nolan et al., 2008; Parks et al., 2001).

Normative influence is built around the core ways in which norms exert their influence on the individual.

1. Descriptive norms: are those that align with what most people are seen to be doing within the individual's immediate sphere of influence. These norms are often seen as what is perceived as being normal and form the behaviours that

people engage in, given a specific situation or context (Cialdini et al., 1990). Some examples of descriptive norms would include statements that relate the behaviours of a reference group to the current desired behaviour, such as "Most people in the neighbourhood recycle their waste" or "Most drivers slowdown in this area."

2. Injunctive norms: while descriptive norms are seen as the preferred or ideal, injunctive norms are seen to communicate what is appropriate or inappropriate behaviour in each situation. Rather than being what is preferred, these are the norms that are accepted practice and therefore what should be done by the individual (Cialdini et al., 1990).
3. Subjective norms: this is the perceived social pressure to perform or not perform a particular behaviour. Social norms are based on an individual's perception of whether important people in their life (like family, friends, or colleagues) think they should engage in behaviour. For example, if your friends believe that doing something is important, you might feel pressured to engage in this behaviour too.

Social norms are an effective mechanism for encouraging conformity to desired behaviours while simultaneously isolating and neutralising dissent. Research by Asch (1956) demonstrated that people will often group their views and responses that align with the majority of the groups, even though they knew that such a decision was incorrect (Mori & Arai, 2010). People frequently adjust their beliefs about what is right or wrong to match what they perceive as group approval. The drive for social acceptance is a critical determinant of behaviour, and this dynamic can be strategically leveraged in the digital battlefield. Online platforms such as X (formerly Twitter), TikTok, and Facebook frequently present dominant narratives or trending opinions. Even when individuals privately disagree with these narratives, they may publicly align with them to avoid backlash, criticism, or potential abuse. The desire to avoid psychological distress associated with ostracism or trolling is powerful enough to compel conformity. This dynamic facilitates control over digital narratives and reduces the visibility of dissenting viewpoints that could disrupt the status quo. Consequently, conformity becomes a key strategic tool in digital warfare, enabling both the control of narratives and the manufacturing of perceived consensus, whether this be for political manipulation or ideological influence.

There is an aligned concept that is very closely linked to normative influence, this being *social proof* (Cialdini et al., 1999; Muscanell et al., 2014). When we talk about social proof, we are examining the way in which people make their decisions about what is acceptable to do, and to achieve this, they make observations on people around them. Social proof is often used in situations where an individual may be unsure as to the correct or most appropriate action to take, so it can act to inform someone; if we see someone acting in a certain way, we might assume that they know something we do not, so we imitate this action.

In the context of digital warfare, this can be a potent method for spreading misinformation. If a news story is widely shared, it might appear to be more credible and not necessarily associated with its content. As other people have shared this information, it might appear that they are endorsing it as correct, even though they themselves may have made the same assumption about the content of the new story. We make an erroneous assessment that those who have shared it have done so because they have a better understanding of the information contained within it, rather than it being shared based on the number of likes or shares it already has. This links back to the use of the bandwagon effect, which we explored back in the previous chapter (Chapter 7). Just to revisit this effect briefly, this is where individuals engage in a particular pattern of behaviour not because they believe it is the right action to take but because people in their immediate social circle have started to do the same thing (Schmitt-Beck, 2015). As more people engage with the same behaviour, whether that be sharing a piece of information or liking a particular trend, there is an increasing likelihood that more people will follow suit, which in turn serves to reinforce the dominant narratives. This process can in turn serve to create an echo chamber where any information that goes contrary to the message being bandwagoned is simply crushed by the groundswell of support.

Being Someone You Can Depend upon; Commitment and Consistency

Within the context of societal cohesion, most individuals strive to be perceived as someone who is trustworthy and dependable, as well as fair in their interactions. This represents another pillar of influence: the human drive for consistency and commitment to prior decisions. Consistency is a fundamental principle in persuasion, as people generally seek to align their behaviour with their previous commitments. Conversely, when an individual behaves inconsistently, it can raise concerns and potentially lead others to initiate processes that isolate the person from their in-group (Muscanell et al., 2014). Being committed to something can also mean that an individual becomes bound to a particular set of behaviours or a set of beliefs, which is a clear way in which consistency can also be observed (Isenberg & Brauer, 2022).

How does this play out in the context of digital warfare? Well, much of the work that has explored how commitment and consistency are used in social engineering has framed it in terms of the *foot-in-the-door* (FITD) method (Burger, 1999; Burger & Caldwell, 2003). The process follows a pattern where an individual will be approached with a relatively small and innocuous request, perhaps something like giving out their email address or sending a small amount of money (Anesa, 2020). If the target responds to the initial request, the attacker will start to follow up with additional requests, usually increasing in magnitude. Although this process is often used as a method in online fraud, it has other functionality that extends across the cyber battlespace. One area in which commitment and consistency could be demonstrated is in online radicalisation. At the beginning of their journey into radicalisation, individuals could start at a lower level of engagement, maybe by liking or sharing videos that have strong links to extremism. As they are doing so, they are making a commitment to an extremist ideology, where repeated online engagement results in reinforcement of these beliefs. Rather than being someone who backtracks on their views, such an individual would maintain consistency by continuing engagement with these beliefs and perhaps even escalating them to actual acts (Mutton et al., 2023). This premise has been supported in other worlds, where radicalisation reflects a growing involvement as well as a commitment to extremism (Silber & Bhat, 2007; Wilner & Dubouloz, 2011). A similar pattern would apply to other forms of ideological manipulation and could be evident in individuals who share conspiracy theories and/or other forms of misinformation, where an individual, rather than compromising their consistency and commitment, continues to support a preferred position.

A similar process operates in the facilitation of propaganda, where individuals who make a public commitment to a cause are more likely to act in accordance with that commitment to maintain a consistent self-image. Online radicalisation often begins with small, incremental steps towards commitment, and propaganda follows the same pattern. For example, an individual might initially agree to low-level actions, such as liking a post or sharing an image. Over time, however, they may adopt more extreme beliefs and behaviours to preserve consistency. Digital platforms amplify this effect significantly. Rather than making a commitment within a small social network, individuals display their stance to a much larger audience that monitors their consistency. This amplification through digital visibility gives propaganda a more persuasive and resilient platform. As individuals become increasingly invested in their public position, they take greater steps to maintain it, even though doing so overrides their current ethical or moral standards.

The Lure of Similarity – We Like to Be Liked

There has been an extensive amount of research in social psychology exploring the way in which individuals prefer people who they see as belonging to their current social group (Sherif et al., 1961; Turner et al., 1979). In-group favouritism is seen as any tendency for an individual to favour their in-group as opposed to their out-group in terms of behaviours, attitudes, preferences, or perceptions (Turner et al., 1979). There is a potential where such a favourable view of the in-group can also lead to a potential for bias to creep in, particularly where such a view could override what is fair or justified and is seen to go beyond the objective evidence (Turner et al., 1979). Such a process is not only isolated to situations in which aspects of in-group and out-group conflict start to emerge, but it has also been the most studied element of this field.

Harnessing the power of in-group identity has some clear applications to the digital battlefield. It is very easy to create the position of an in-group in the digital space, especially where individuals coalesce into interest groups, forums, and online communities. One obvious example of where such a mechanism could be evidenced is the presence and maintenance of echo chambers online, where individuals express a desire to remain within the current in-group due to their beliefs and opinions. In contrast, they are quick to dismiss potential outsiders and any potential perspective that could serve to undermine the current in-group cohesion. Similarly, even though objective evidence may be present to support a contradictory position to the dominant ideology being circulated within the in-group, the presence of in-group bias means that this is soon quashed and cancelled out.

Humans are generally viewed as being inherently gregarious and naturally inclined towards sociability, seeking to form close relationships with those they like. From this perspective, individuals are generally more likely to engage in behaviours that enhance relationship formation, such as agreeing to requests for help. (Cialdini & Goldstein, 2004). Cialdini's (2009) research has demonstrated that influence can also be manipulated through likeability. Studies show that individuals perceived as more likeable are often rated as more influential, with physical attractiveness and perceived similarity being key contributing factors. Liking has also been identified as a significant predictor of phishing susceptibility, providing relevant evidence for its application in the context of cyberwarfare. Attackers frequently exploit this principle by crafting messages that appear friendly, familiar, or personally tailored, thereby increasing compliance and reducing scepticism. (Parsons et al., 2019).

The extent to which you like someone does not necessarily mean you have a close relationship or bond with that individual. Indeed, many of the relationships we form within cyberspace can be very superficial. Burger and colleagues (Burger et al., 2004; Burger et al., 2001), in a series of studies, demonstrated that similarity and compliance can be created in highly incidental ways. For example, researchers found that even brief interactions with a stranger that lasted no more than two minutes significantly increased compliance with a subsequent request compared with conditions where there was no direct interaction. Individuals who engaged in a short conversation about university classes were twice as likely to comply with a request as those who merely shared the same space without interaction (Burger et al., 2001). In a further study, researchers manipulated incidental similarity and examined its effect on compliance with later requests. Participants who believed they shared a birthday, a first name, or even fingerprint similarities with a stranger were more likely to comply with a request to donate money to a charitable organisation.

The psychological mechanisms of in-group favouritism, liking, and perceived similarity are not only passive social tendencies, but they can also be turned into active tools that can be weaponised in the digital battlefield. Online environments make it remarkably easy to simulate social closeness, shared identity, and group cohesion even in the absence of genuine interpersonal relationships. This creates fertile ground for influence operations, where hostile actors manipulate group dynamics to foster trust, suppress dissent, and amplify ideological narratives. Digital platforms can further enhance this effect through algorithmic personalisation, echo chambers, and recommendation systems that reinforce perceived similarity and in-group identity. By exploiting these biases, digital propaganda can bypass rational scrutiny and embed itself within the social fabric of online communities, making it both persuasive and resilient. In practice, this means that operations can manufacture consensus, create the illusion of majority opinion, and pressure individuals into conformity. Taken together, all of these serve as strategic levers in digital warfare to destabilise societies, polarise populations, and advance ideological or political objectives.

Scarcity

Humans, in general, dislike missing out on opportunities. Consider offers that are only available to select customers for a limited time or the lure of heavily discounted prices on specific days of the year. Events such as Cyber Monday and Black Friday have become synonymous with exclusive deals for a short period, prompting consumers to act quickly and often impulsively. This FoMO (Przybylski et al., 2013) drives individuals to make hasty decisions under time pressure. In the digital battlefield, this principle is weaponised through urgency-based influence tactics. Cybercriminals and propagandists frequently use time-limited offers, countdown timers, or messages such as "Act now before it's too late" to override rational decision-making. Phishing emails, fake donation campaigns, and fraudulent investment schemes often exploit this urgency, compelling individuals to comply without verifying authenticity. By leveraging scarcity and time pressure, hostile actors can manipulate behaviour at scale, making urgency a powerful psychological lever in digital warfare (Bullée et al., 2018). We rush to make decisions on a wide variety of topics without any real thought for the repercussions of such, just because there is a time limit attached to the offer. Individuals tend to perceive greater value in something that is rare or has a limited supply, a trend that should be obvious to anyone who has tried to buy something that has been produced in limited quantities (new game consoles, new smartphones, or concert tickets).

The scarcity principle works to override the more labour-intensive Type 2 processing mechanism and can automatically trigger the heuristic processes, which are less reliable. Time-sensitive offers or the need to act urgently is something that is often used in the context of phishing emails, where people are threatened with the removal of access to a critical account if they do not respond in a specific time frame (Hadlington & Ryding, 2025). For digital warfare operations, the use of scarcity and urgency can be harnessed in several ways. For example, creating fake news stories that are presented as breaking news can offer individuals information that is new and important for a short period of time. As one of the key drivers for individuals to share fake news has been seen to be the need to protect others from harm (Hadlington et al., 2022), many individuals will act to share such information quickly, without taking the time to fact-check this information. This can also be used as a manipulation tactic in times of crisis, where the capacity to check information is limited and decisions need to be made quickly. Couple this with high levels of emotionally charged content, and you have the perfect environment to release information that could lead to massive behavioural shifts, ones that could go in contradiction to the requirements of officials trying to tackle the current crisis.

The digital environment can only serve to act as an amplification mechanism for scarcity and urgency, particularly in social media networks where trending topics are at the forefront of people's feeds. Due to algorithmic curation, individuals are often presented with trending or time-sensitive information or topics that can serve to reinforce the illusion of scarcity (Liu, 2024). Add to this the possibility of using disinformation campaigns or bots to enhance the perception that something is currently time-sensitive, and you have the perfect vector for creating panic and disarray in a population (Tomassi et al., 2024).

Reciprocation

If you do something for someone, you usually expect something in return – this is the basic law of reciprocity. The exchange does not have to involve equivalent actions; for example, you might receive a gift and later be asked to aid. According to Cialdini, this response is deeply embedded in societal norms, and even minimal interactions can create a transactional bond where we feel obligated to reciprocate. Individuals are also susceptible to manipulation regarding the magnitude of the reciprocal action, as demonstrated by the door-in-the-face technique (Cialdini et al., 1975). This phenomenon suggests that people are more likely to agree to a smaller request after refusing a larger one. For instance, if you ask someone for a large sum of money and then follow up with a significantly smaller amount, they are more likely to agree to the latter request.

It may be hard to see how this mechanic could be used in the context of digital warfare, but there are some less-than-overt ways in which it could be used. If you want to build trust in people, increase engagement and lower the threshold for acceptance of ideological principles, then you can offer incentives at the very start of the process. This might be the chance to gain a valuable insight into the inner workings of an organisation or group, often a thinly veiled attempt to present propaganda or misinformation. Even though the information is probably heavily biased and has limited objective rigour, the offensive actor can serve to create a sense of indebtedness. This means the individuals who have received the special information are now more likely to share or support the narrative as they feel that they need to return the favour. A potential real-world example of this could be encapsulated by the QAnon movement. The movement first rose to prominence in the autumn of 2017 on the message board 4chan as a result of two moderators and one YouTube creator deciding to focus on one conspiracy theory that was posted (Zadrozny & Collins, 2018; Kaplan, 2023). A person posting as "Q" claimed to have high-level security clearance (or "Q Clearance") that allowed them to access the deepest secrets held by the U.S. government. In turn, the messages that were posted on 4Chan became known as "Q drops," presented as cryptic details about various conspiracy theories. Such drops became framed as privileged information that in turn created a sense of getting a gift from a trusted source. In return, following the law of reciprocation, the followers of "Q" perhaps felt compelled to spread the messages, defend the narrative that was being popularised, and engage more deeply with the community. Such a dynamic is probably the key mechanism through which QAnon was able to grow into such a large-scale movement, where users are the key amplifiers of conspiracy theories, serving to act without verifying the information. This sense of being chosen served to create a powerful bond between the source of the information and the audience, creating a self-replicating reciprocation loop.

Summary

In this chapter, we explored the strategic deployment of social engineering as a core mechanism in digital warfare, reframing it as a cognitive intrusion that targets human psychology rather than technical systems. Unlike conventional cyber-attacks, social engineering exploits the "wetware" of human cognition, leveraging psychological principles such as trust, authority, urgency, and emotional manipulation to bypass rational scrutiny and elicit compliance. The chapter introduced a four-phase model (information gathering, trust-building, exploitation, and exit) that outlines the anatomy of a social engineering attack, demonstrating how adversaries manipulate cognitive vulnerabilities to achieve their goals.

Social engineering is positioned not only as a cybersecurity concern but also as a scalable and subtle weapon in digital warfare. It bypasses technical defences by penetrating cognitive architecture, exploiting biases and heuristics to manipulate behaviour. Techniques such as priming, impersonation, and trust inheritance are examined for their capacity to influence individuals and groups at scale. The chapter also highlights how social engineering integrates with memetic warfare, using emotionally charged narratives and stereotypes to amplify ideological manipulation and societal polarisation.

Drawing on Cialdini's six principles of influence – authority, social proof, commitment and consistency, liking, scarcity, and reciprocation – the chapter demonstrates how these psychological levers are weaponised in digital environments. Each principle is explored in depth, with real-world examples illustrating their use in phishing, fraud, propaganda, and disinformation campaigns. The manipulation of authority through deepfakes, the exploitation of normative influence in echo chambers, and the use of urgency to override rational decision-making are shown to be central tactics in cognitive warfare.

The chapter also examined the psychological foundations of obedience, linking Milgram's classic experiments to modern digital tactics that exploit perceived authority to elicit compliance. It discusses how social proof and the bandwagon effect can create illusions of consensus, serving to reinforce dominant narratives and suppressing dissent. Commitment and consistency are explored as mechanisms for ideological entrenchment, particularly in radicalisation and propaganda. Liking and perceived similarity are shown to facilitate trust and compliance, even in superficial online interactions, while scarcity and urgency are used to trigger impulsive decisions under time pressure.

Finally, the principle of reciprocation is analysed as a subtle but powerful tool for building trust and fostering ideological alignment. The chapter uses the QAnon movement as a case study to illustrate how these principles converge to create resilient belief systems and mobilise collective action. It argues that social engineering is a corner-stone tactic in digital warfare, capable of undermining societal trust, destabilising institutions, and influencing populations at scale. The chapter concludes by emphasising the need for psychological resilience and awareness as critical defences against cognitive manipulation in the digital battlespace.

References

Algarni, A., Xu, Y., & Chan, T. (2016). Measuring source credibility of social engineering attackers on Facebook. *Proceedings of the Annual Hawaii International Conference on System Sciences*, March, 3686–3695. https://doi.org/10.1109/HICSS.2016.460

Anesa, P. (2020). Lovextortion: Persuasion strategies in romance cybercrime. *Discourse, Context and Media, 35*, 100398. https://doi.org/10.1016/j.dcm.2020.100398

Asch, S. E. (1956). Studies of independence and conformity: I. A minority of one against a unanimous majority. *Psychological Monographs: General and Applied, 70*(9), 1–70. https://doi.org/10.1037/h0093718

Attrill-Smith, A., & Wesson, C. (2020). The psychology of cybercrime. *The Palgrave Handbook of International Cybercrime and Cyberdeviance*, 653–678. https://doi.org/10.1007/978-3-319-78440-3_25

Bullée, J. W. H., Montoya, L., Pieters, W., Junger, M., & Hartel, P. (2018). On the anatomy of social engineering attacks: A literature-based dissection of successful attacks. *Journal of Investigative Psychology and Offender Profiling, 15*(1), 20–45. https://doi.org/10.1002/jip.1482

Burger, J. M. (1999). The foot-in-the-door compliance procedure: A multiple-process analysis and review. *Personality and Social Psychology Review, 3*(4), 303–325. https://doi.org/10.1207/s15327957pspr0304_2

Burger, J. M. (2009). Replicating milgram: Would people still obey today? *American Psychologist, 64*(1), 1–11.

Burger, J. M., & Caldwell, D. F. (2003). The effects of monetary incentives and labeling on the foot-in-the-door effect: Evidence for a self-perception process. *Basic and Applied Social Psychology, 25*(3), 235–241. https://doi.org/10.1207/S15324834BASP2503_06

Burger, J. M., Messian, N., Patel, S., Del Prado, A., & Anderson, C. (2004). What a coincidence! The effects of incidental similarity on compliance. *Personality and Social Psychology Bulletin, 30*(1), 35–43. https://doi.org/10.1177/0146167203258838

Burger, J. M., Soroka, S., Gonzago, K., Murphy, E., & Somervell, E. (2001). The effect of fleeting attraction on compliance to requests. *Personality and Social Psychology Bulletin, 27*(12), 1578–1586. https://doi.org/10.1177/01461672012712002

Butavicius, M., Parsons, K., Pattinson, M., & McCormac, A. (2015). Breaching the human firewall: Social engineering in phishing and spear-phishing emails. *26th Australasian Conference on Information Systems (ACIS)*, 1–10. Retrieved from http://arxiv.org/abs/1606.00887

Calic, D., Pattinson, M., Parsons, K., Butavicius, M., & McCormac, A. (2016). Naïve and accidental behaviours that compromise information security: What the experts think. In S. M. Furnell & N. L. Clarke (Eds.), *Proceedings of the 10th international symposium of human aspects of information security and assurance*. Frankfurt, Germany: HAISA.

Cialdini, R. B. (2009). *Influence: Science and practice* (5th ed.). Boston, MA: Allyn & Bacon.

Cialdini, R. B., & Goldstein, N. J. (2004). Social influence: Compliance and conformity. *Annual Review of Psychology, 55*(1974), 591–621. https://doi.org/10.1146/annurev.psych.55.090902.142015

Cialdini, R. B., Reno, R. R., & Kallgren, C. A. (1990). A focus theory of normative conduct: Recycling the concept of norms to reduce littering in public places. *Journal of Personality and Social Psychology, 58*(6), 1015–1026. https://doi.org/10.1037/0022-3514.58.6.1015

Cialdini, R. B, Vincent, J. E., Lewis, S. K., Catalan, J., Wheeler, D., & Darby, B. L. (1975). Reciprocal concessions procedure for inducing compliance: The door-in-the-face technique. *Journal of personality and social psychology*, 31(2), 206–215. https://doi.org/10.1037/h0076284

Cialdini, R. B., Wosinska, W., Barrett, D. W., Butner, J., & Gornik-Durose, M. (1999). Compliance with a request in two cultures: The differential influence of social proof and commitment/consistency on collectivists and individualists. *Personality and Social Psychology Bulletin, 25*(10), 1242–1253. https://doi.org/10.1177/0146167299258006

Ferreira, A., Coventry, L., & Lenzini, G. (2015). Principles of persuasion in social engineering and their use in phishing. *Lecture Notes in Computer Science (Including Subseries Lecture Notes in Artificial Intelligence and Lecture Notes in Bioinformatics), 9190*, 36–47. https://doi.org/10.1007/978-3-319-20376-8_4

Gimpel, H., Heger, S., Olenberger, C., & Utz, L. (2021). The effectiveness of social norms in fighting fake news on social media. *Journal of Management Information Systems, 38*(1), 196–221. https://doi.org/10.1080/07421222.2021.1870389

Hadlington, L., Harkin, L. J., Kuss, D., Newman, K., & Ryding, F. C. (2022). Perceptions of fake news, misinformation, and disinformation amid the COVID-19 pandemic: A qualitative exploration. *Psychology of Popular Media*. https://doi.org/10.1037/ppm0000387

Hadlington, L., & Ryding, C. (2025). *Human factors and cybersecurity: The psychology of online safety and security.* London, UK: Taylor and Francis Inc.

Isenberg, N., & Brauer, M. (2022). Commitment and consistency. *Commitment and Consistency*, 1–7. https://doi.org/10.4324/9780367198459-reprw126-1

Jansson, K., & von Solms, R. (2013). Phishing for phishing awareness. *Behaviour and Information Technology, 32*(6), 584–593. https://doi.org/10.1080/0144929X.2011.632650

Kaplan, T. (2023). Qanon and social media. In M. K. Miller (Ed.), *The social science of Qanon: A new social and political phenomenon* (pp. 195–214). Cambridge, UK: Cambridge University Press.

Langer, E. J., Blank, A., & Chanowitz, B. (1978). The mindlessness of ostensibly thoughtful action: The role of "placebic" information in interpersonal interaction. *Journal of Personality and Social Psychology*, *36*(6), 635–642. https://doi.org/10.1037//0022-3514.36.6.635

Liu, J. (2024). Research on trending algorithms of digital platforms: A case study of little red book and Instagram. *Media and Communication Research*, *5*(4), 58–68. https://doi.org/10.23977/mediacr.2024.050409

McDonald, R. I., & Crandall, C. S. (2015). Social norms and social influence. *Current Opinion in Behavioral Sciences*, *3*, 147–151. https://doi.org/10.1016/j.cobeha.2015.04.006

Milgram, S. (1963). Behavioral study of obedience. *Journal of Abnormal and Social Psychology*, *67*, 371–378.

Miller, A. G., Collins, B. E., & Brief, D. E. (1995). Perspectives on obedience to authority: The legacy of the milgram experiments. *Journal of Social Issues*, *51*(3), 1–19. https://doi.org/10.1111/j.1540-4560.1995.tb01331.x

Mori, K., & Arai, M. (2010). No need to fake it: Reproduction of the Asch experiment without confederates. *International Journal of Psychology*, *45*(5), 390–397. https://doi.org/10.1080/00207591003774485

Muscanell, N. L., Guadagno, R. E., & Murphy, S. (2014). Weapons of influence misused: A social influence analysis of why people fall prey to internet scams. *Social and Personality Psychology Compass*, *8*(7), 388–396. https://doi.org/10.1111/spc3.12115

Mutton, R., Lewis, J., & Marsden, S. (2023). *Full report online radicalisation: A rapid review of the literature full report July 2023*. (July). Retrieved from www.crestresearch.ac.uk/projects/contest

Nolan, J. M., Schultz, P. W., Cialdini, R. B., Goldstein, N. J., & Griskevicius, V. (2008). Normative social influence is underdetected. *Personality and Social Psychology Bulletin*, *34*(7), 913–923. https://doi.org/10.1177/0146167208316691

Parks, C. D., Sanna, L. J., & Berel, S. R. (2001). Actions of similar others as inducements to cooperate in social dilemmas. *Personality and Social Psychology Bulletin*, *27*(3), 345–354. https://doi.org/10.1177/0146167201273008

Parsons, K., Butavicius, M., Delfabbro, P., & Lillie, M. (2019). Predicting susceptibility to social influence in phishing emails. *International Journal of Human Computer Studies*, *128*, 17–26. https://doi.org/10.1016/j.ijhcs.2019.02.007

Przybylski, A. K., Murayama, K., Dehaan, C. R., & Gladwell, V. (2013). Motivational, emotional, and behavioral correlates of fear of missing out. *Computers in Human Behavior*, *29*(4), 1841–1848. https://doi.org/10.1016/j.chb.2013.02.014

Rimal, R. N., & Real, K. (2005). How behaviors are influenced by perceived norms a test of the theory of normative social ehaviour. *Communication Research*, *32*(3), 389–414. https://doi.org/10.1177/0093650205275385

Schleidt, W. M. (1974). How "fixed" is the fixed action pattern? *Zeitschrift Für Tierpsychologie*, *36*(1–5), 184–211. https://doi.org/10.1111/j.1439-0310.1974.tb02131.x

Schmitt-Beck, R. (2015). Bandwagon effect. In G. Mazzoleni (Ed.), *The international encyclopedia of political communication* (1st ed., pp. 23–24). https://doi.org/10.1002/9781118541555.wbiepc015

Scott Key, M., Edlund, J. E., Sagarin, B. J., & Bizer, G. Y. (2009). Individual differences in susceptibility to mindlessness. *Personality and Individual Differences*, *46*(3), 261–264. https://doi.org/10.1016/j.paid.2008.10.001

Sherif, M., Harvey, O. J., White, B. J., Hood, W. R., & Sherif, C. W. (1961). Intergroup conflict and cooperation: The Robbers Cave experiment. *American Sociological Review*, *4*(Stage 3), 229.

Silber, M. D., & Bhat, A. (2007). *Radicalization in the West: The homegrown threat (The NYPD jihadist report)*, 1–90. Retrieved from https://www.brennancenter.org/sites/default/files/legacy/Justice/20070816.NYPD.Radicalization.in.the.West.pdf

Tait, S. E., & Jeske, D. (2015). Hello stranger! Trust and self-disclosure effects on online information sharing. *International Journal of Cyber Behavior, Psychology and Learning*, *5*(1), 42–55. https://doi.org/10.4018/ijcbpl.2015010104

Tomassi, A., Falegnami, A., & Romano, E. (2024). Mapping automatic social media information disorder: The role of bots and AI in spreading misleading information in society. *PloS One*, *19*. https://doi.org/10.1371/journal.pone.0303183

Turner, J. C., Brown, R. J., & Tajfel, H. (1979). Social comparison and group interest in ingroup favouritism. *European Journal of Social Psychology*, *9*, 187–204. https://doi.org/10.1002/ejsp.2420090207

Uebelacker, S., & Quiel, S. (2014). The social engineering personality framework. *2014 Workshop on Socio-Technical Aspects in Security and Trust*, 24–30. https://doi.org/10.1109/STAST.2014.12

Wilner, A. S., & Dubouloz, C. J. (2011). Transformative radicalization: Applying learning theory to Islamist radicalization. *Studies in Conflict and Terrorism*, *34*(5), 418–438. https://doi.org/10.1080/1057610X.2011.561472

Zadrozny, B., & Collins, B. (2018). *How three conspiracy theorists took "Q" and sparked Qanon*. Retrieved from NBC News website https://www.nbcnews.com/tech/tech-news/how-three-conspiracy-theorists-took-q-sparked-qanon-n900531

9 The Battle for Decisions: The Role of Memory and Heuristics

Introduction

There are numerous ways in which human decision-making processing can be influenced, often without their direct knowledge that these things are taking place. Digital warfare offers the perfect environment to deploy a variety of focused and co-ordinated methods that can be used to lay the basis for manipulating the decisions we make, particularly because so many of us spend so much time online. What we must remember is that humans are not the most reliable when it comes to being able to systematically explore information and then use a logical approach to come to a solid conclusion. We are heavily influenced by information from past events, as well as being subject to the pressures of social norms and the opinions of others around us. As we highlighted in the early chapters of this book, we have limited cognitive resources that can be deployed at any one time. As decision-making is an inherent part of cognition, it is also bound by the laws of cognitive economy, and it is also controlled and restricted by the limitations that are associated with human information processing.

When an individual is placed into a situation where a decision is littered with uncertainty, this can serve to challenge our judgement. This is more evident when individuals are faced with novel decisions that they may not have encountered previously, meaning that they have no prior experience upon which to make an informed decision. It is at this point that individuals will start to use heuristic processing, something that we introduced way back in Chapter 4. Heuristics are seen as a set of rules that are based on intuition, past experiences, and the ease with which we can bring relevant examples of similar, past events to mind. Heuristic processing falls, as we noted in Chapter 4, serve to present the individual with a solution to a problem that satisfies our current needs and aims without needing to engage in lengthy, protracted research or deliberation. However, as we also noted earlier, these rules are not perfect, and there are some key pitfalls when it comes to their use. As heuristic rules are based on our own experiences, anything that serves to shape our memory of past events or enhances our perception of a particular salient piece of information can in turn influence the later use

DOI: 10.4324/9781003752400-9

of such rules. If you experience bad customer service at a particular shop, you might be less inclined to use that shop in the future and be more negative towards that brand in the future. However, you have based your conclusion that the bad customer service is representative of all other examples of that brand of shops, which in turn has biased your judgement and willingness to shop there again.

Dual-Process Theories and Decision-Making

As we posited back in Chapter 4, researchers have theorised that humans have two distinct pathways when it comes to problem-solving and decision-making. These processes have been captured in what have been labelled *dual-process theories that* have their basis firmly rooted in social cognition. Much of what we have discussed in this text relates directly to the functioning of these dual-process theories, and they frame the way in which individuals make decisions in the realm of digital warfare extremely well. Of the models proposed, the heuristic–systematic model (HSM) (Chaiken & Trope, 1999; Todorov et al., 2002) is perhaps one of the most relevant to our current discussions. This framework has been demonstrated to be highly applicable where individuals are confronted with complex, high-stakes information environments, including those found in cyberspace (Hadlington, 2017; Wirth et al., 2009).

The HSM proposes two distinct modes of cognitive processing: heuristic (Type 1) and systematic (Type 2). Systematic processing involves a deliberate, analytical approach in which individuals scrutinise available information, compare it against prior knowledge, and make decisions based on logical evaluation. This mode is resource-intensive and often constrained by cognitive capacity and situational demands. In contrast, heuristic processing is fast, intuitive, and relies on mental shortcuts, drawing on prior experience, salient cues, or emotionally charged content.

In digital warfare contexts where information overload and psychological manipulation are common, individuals frequently default to heuristic processing due to limited cognitive resources or time pressure. Importantly, these two modes can operate concurrently. Depending on the nature of the digital threat or manipulation tactic, they may interact in additive or competitive ways. For example, exposure to a familiar meme or narrative (a heuristic cue) may be reinforced by a systematic review of corroborating sources, strengthening belief and decision-making. Conversely, when systematic analysis contradicts heuristic impressions, such as when a trusted source is revealed to be compromised, the influence of the heuristic may be attenuated, allowing more rational evaluation to dominate (Hadlington, 2017).

This dynamic is particularly salient in information operations, where adversaries exploit cognitive vulnerabilities to shape perception and behaviour. Zarro (2012) extended dual-process theory to online information-seeking behaviour, noting that users often begin with limited domain knowledge and adapt their search strategies based on feedback. In digital warfare, this adaptive process can be weaponised: individuals may be nudged towards heuristic processing using emotionally resonant content, misinformation, or cognitive overload, thereby bypassing critical scrutiny (Baum et al., 2024; Lee et al., 2021). Where situations relate to scenarios involving health misinformation, political propaganda, or PsyOPs, users motivated to seek truth may still fall prey to biased or incomplete information if they rely too heavily on heuristic cues (van der Linden et al., 2023; Wilson & Wiysonge, 2020). These cues, including familiarity with the information source, the visual salience of the information, and alignment with pre-existing beliefs, can all serve to distort judgement, especially when systematic processing is impaired or discouraged.

While Zarro's work remains largely descriptive, it underscores the need for empirical research into how individuals transition between processing modes in digital conflict environments. Given the automatic nature of heuristic reasoning and its susceptibility to manipulation, understanding these cognitive mechanisms is crucial for developing resilience against digital threats.

On the Role of Memory

Memory has an inherent and undeniable link to the deployment and use of heuristics. Primarily, heuristics are governed by cognitive schemas (or scripts) stored in LTM (Meylani, 2024. This means we maintain a repository of heuristic mechanisms that are readily available and primed for use in a wide range of situations. These schemas typically function as pre-learnt decision-making frameworks, activated when individuals encounter familiar or high-pressure scenarios online. Accordingly, Todorov et al. (2002) identified three key dimensions that influence the deployment of heuristic strategies:

Availability: for a heuristic to be used, it must first exist in the individual's memory. This implies prior exposure to similar situations where the heuristic was learnt and encoded into LTM. In digital warfare, repeated exposure to certain online patterns, such as the structure of search engine results or the framing of persuasive content, can lead to the formation of these heuristics.

Accessibility: even if a heuristic is stored in memory, it must be retrievable at the moment of decision-making. Accessibility is influenced by the salience and emotional impact of previous experiences. For example, if a user vividly remembers a successful interaction with a top search result, that memory may bias future decisions towards similar behaviour. Conversely, if the memory is weak or disrupted (e.g., due to misinformation or cognitive overload), the heuristic may not be activated.

Application: the relevance of a heuristic to the current context determines its use. In digital warfare, this means that heuristics are more likely to be applied when the situation closely resembles past experiences. For instance, a user may rely on the heuristic that "top search results are most trustworthy" if they've consistently found useful information in that position.

In the online digital domain, these mechanisms manifest clearly: individuals often rely on heuristic processes when navigating digital environments, a tendency that is particularly evident in how users interact with search engines (Wirth et al., 2009). Research has shown that users instinctively focus on the top-left portion of the results page, often referred to as the "golden triangle" (Cutrell & Guan, 2007; Granka et al., 2004). This pattern reflects a learnt heuristic that equates higher placement with higher credibility. Lorigo et al. (2008) provided further support for this, noting that users tend to ignore lower-ranked search results, even when they may be more accurate or relevant. In the context of digital warfare, these heuristic patterns can be exploited easily. Adversaries can act to manipulate search engine optimisation (SEO) (King, 2008), social media algorithms, or interface design to ensure that misleading or manipulative content appears in positions of high visibility. High visibility often equates to high credibility for many users, allowing them to rely on this heuristic as a shortcut and reduce the need for individual evidence evaluation.

Primacy–Recency Effects in Memory

There are other aspects of memory that can come into play when we start to look at decision-making processes, particularly in relation to the order in which we experience things. A prime example is that of the primacy–recency effect that emerged from research in cognitive psychology, showing that items that are presented at the start of a list are remembered much better than those that come in the middle or later in a list (Crowder, 1976). The primacy effect, where information at the start of the list has an advantage, is seen as the result of this information having to compete less for resources to be processed (Waugh & Norman, 1965). Items that appear later in a list are also seen to be better recalled (the recency effect) as they are still very fresh in short-term memory, hence less likely to decay or suffer from interference from older items. Such memory processes have a clear relevance to a wide variety of different elements that could be used in offensive digital operations, from the position of information in search results to the formation of memories that will later be used as a basis for further decision-making. Researchers have noticed that primacy can also have a direct impact on complex decisions. Rey et al. (2020) elegantly demonstrated this in a study where participants were presented with information about four cars, each characterised by 12 key attributes. After reading the sentences describing the cars, participants were asked to choose which one they would prefer to buy. However, two of the cars shared identical descriptive information in terms of positive and negative attributes. The only difference was the order of presentation: for one car, the positive attributes appeared at the beginning of the list, while for the other, they appeared at the end. The results revealed that participants demonstrated a clear preference for the car whose positive information was presented first, and participants were unaware that two cars shared the same attributes. (Rey et al., 2020).

There has also been some considerable effort placed into research that explores the impact of primacy on our formation of an attitude towards someone. The adage "first impressions count" is perhaps more relevant than we realise when we consider the research in this area. Original research in this area came from Asch (1946), who showed that when participants were presented with two identical lists of adjectives that described a person, but the order of these was changed, participants formed different attitudes towards that person. For example, someone described as "fun, witty, and vicious" was rated more positively compared to someone who was described as "vicious, witty, and fun." In digital warfare, this tactic can be used to build trust and rapport with individuals or to present fake profiles and influencer bios that appear more appealing. By front-loading a profile with positive personality traits and those reflecting a high level of morality, digital adversaries can lure people into accepting the information they present, information that is often persuasive and potentially disruptive in nature.

Primacy–recency effects have also been noted to occur in the context of persuasion, noting a very subtle interaction between the presentation of opposing arguments and the influence on opinion. In situations where two opposing arguments are presented with a long period of time between them, the second, more recent argument is more likely to have a stronger impact on opinions if they are gathered straight away (Haugtvedt & Wegener, 1994). However, if you delay the measurement of opinions after the second communication has been presented, this recency effect becomes diminished (Insko, 1964; Miller & Campbell, 1959). However, if you present two opposing arguments in close temporal proximity to each other, there is a clear primacy effect for the earlier presented information when opinion is measured later (Insko, 1964). Therefore, timing plays a critical role in the effectiveness of pervasive content.

In terms of the impact primacy–recency effects have upon our behaviour in the online environment, there has been some research to suggest that this phenomenon can extend to how we see information. For example, it has been observed that there is a clear effect of link order on the likelihood of a user clicking a link: the higher a link appeared in search results, the greater the probability that an individual would click on it (Ansari & Mela, 2003; Drèze & Zufryden, 1997; Murphy et al., 2006). Other studies have noted the impact of position bias, where the probability of a link being clicked on relates not to its relevance for the search process but to its position in the results page (Craswell et al., 2008). There is also the possibility that the relevance of information can intensify primacy–recency effects, with high message relevance leading to increased primacy effects and low relevance leading to increased recency effects (Murphy et al., 2006).

Primacy–recency effects can offer a clear vulnerability that could be strategically exploited in the context of digital warfare, being used to shape perceptions and attitudes and manipulate memory. As we will see in the following section, the capacity to manipulate search engine results can provide the ideal opportunity to influence decision-making by making the desired information appear at the top of the search results. Similarly, social media feeds can also be used to flood platforms with fresh information, therefore influencing the potential for recency effects to override earlier presented narratives.

False Memory

During the 1990s, there was a sudden upsurge in research related to a phenomenon known as false memories, where individuals were seen to remember events that never actually happened, or they remembered them in a very different way than how they occurred (Loftus & Zanni, 1975; McNally & Geraerts, 2009; Roediger & McDermott, 1995). One of the motivations for this research was a sudden uptick in the number of legal cases where individuals recalled historical events surrounding childhood trauma and abuse, usually under therapeutic conditions (Roediger & McDermott, 1995). In a popular and well-known paradigm named after the researchers who developed it, the Deese–Roediger–McDermott (DRM) paradigm, this effect is well demonstrated. The researchers present participants with a list of words that are grouped together by a key thematic category and are related to a word that is not presented in the list but becomes the "critical lure." For example, presenting the words *bed, pillow, duvet, and dream* would make participants more likely to recall the critical lure of sleep, even though it was not presented in the list (Roediger & McDermott, 1995; Storbeck & Clore, 2005). Another commonly used approach gets participants to watch an event, after which they are presented with some form of misinformation, usually something that is incorrect but related to the event in question. When the participants are later tested on their memory recall for the event, they demonstrate the capacity to incorporate aspects of the misinformation into the memory of the original event, remembering them as though they were real (Nichols & Loftus, 2019). For example, participants watched a short video in which a burglar picked up a hammer to gain access to a building; later, participants were given conflicting information that the burglar had been handing a screwdriver. In a later test of recall, when participants were asked what tool the burglar had been handed, most participants (66%) claimed it was the screwdriver, not the hammer, as had been originally portrayed in the video (Nichols & Loftus, 2019). Nichols and Loftus (2019) also established that the susceptibility to such false information was a ubiquitous phenomenon, and it did not rely on individual differences, an important facet when we consider the wider implications for the theatre of digital warfare.

There is also evidence to suggest that the way in which individuals are questioned after they have seen an event can also influence their recall of events. For example, in a classic study by Loftus and Zanni (1975), the researchers manipulated the wording of a question that related to the events of a car accident. Participants were asked either "Did you see *a* broken headlight?" or "Did you see *the* broken headlight?" In the conditions where participants were presented with "the" in the question text, they were more likely to falsely recall a headlight being broken in the video that they had seen. In turn, when participants were presented with the question about the speed with which the two cars were travelling, participants were more likely to judge speed to be faster in conditions where the word "smashed" was included in the question rather than "hit" (Loftus & Zanni, 1975).

Research has also noted that individuals are far more susceptible to forming false memories when they are presented in context with events that are compatible with their beliefs (Murphy et al., 2019). Murphy et al. (2019) also noted that half of the participants who took part in their study during the Irish referendum on abortion reported a false memory for at least one fictitious event. Yes, voters who were in favour of legalising abortion were more likely to remember a fictional scandal that implicated the campaign to vote no to legalising abortion. The opposite result was found for no voters, where warnings related to the warning of potential misinformation and its effect failed to eliminate this effect. This demonstrates the real-world capacity to create false memories in individuals based on the presentation of false information, something that has clear and direct implications for digital warfare.

On the Role of Emotion in Memory

Emotion has been shown to have a key interaction with memory, particularly in terms of false memory formation. According to Kaplan et al. (2016), emotional arousal can significantly impair an individual's memory and increase their susceptibility to misinformation. The extent to which such emotional states impair or enhance memory depends largely on the personal significance of the information. When emotional arousal increases, attention tends to narrow towards the most salient and important details, often at the expense of peripheral information. As a result, other critical cues such as indicators that information is false may be overlooked. This phenomenon is commonly referred to as *emotional memory narrowing* (Kaplan et al., 2016). Events that evoke high stress or extreme emotional arousal can make individuals more vulnerable to misleading post-event information, which may distort their recall of the original event. Laney and Loftus (2008) demonstrated that this effect can occur even in seemingly trivial situations, such as an overnight hospital stay or witnessing a parental argument.

Emotions can be closely tied to our current goals and motivations when completing a task, and these, in turn, can influence memory formation – potentially increasing susceptibility to false memories. Goal-related emotions can be classified into two distinct categories: pregoal and postgoal. Pregoal emotions occur when approaching a task and include feelings such as hope, fear, desire, or anger. Although these emotions may have positive or negative aspects, they are generally characterised by high intensity and, consequently, a strong motivational force (Kaplan et al., 2016). For example, anger may act as a precursor to behaviours that remove barriers to achieving a goal, while fear may help an individual avoid potential threats that could hinder progress (Kaplan et al., 2016). Kaplan et al. (2016) found that pregoal emotions tend to narrow attention towards elements directly related to the goal, effectively filtering out irrelevant information. In contrast, postgoal emotions, or those experienced after completing the objective (e.g., sadness, happiness, regret, and denial), can serve to broaden attention and increase resilience to manipulation by misinformation.

Emotionally charged information has also been seen to influence moral judgements being made by individuals (Denton & Krebs, 2017). Research has also shown that people are more likely to make harsher moral judgements when presented with scenarios in a dirty room filled with discarded food, empty pizza boxes, and used tissues (Denton & Krebs, 2017; Schnall et al., 2008). Other research has noted that individuals were more likely to recommend harsher punishments for crimes that were relatively minor in nature if they watched a film that induced a high emotive state (anger) before they made that decision (Denton & Krebs, 2017; Lerner et al., 1998). In most cases, individuals are more likely to make harsher moral judgements against those acts that are related to commission (e.g., lying, harming someone, and stealing) versus acts of omission (withholding the truth or allowing someone to steal).

So, as we have seen, emotion can play a pivotal role in shaping memory, often enhancing the vividness of recollections while simultaneously increasing susceptibility to distortion. Research shows that emotionally arousing experiences, particularly those tied to personal significance or goal pursuit, can serve to narrow attentional focus, leading individuals to overlook peripheral details, including cues that might signal misinformation (Kaplan et al., 2016; Laney & Loftus, 2008). This phenomenon, known as emotional memory narrowing, becomes especially relevant in the context of digital warfare, where adversaries can exploit emotional triggers to impair critical thinking and implant false memories. Moreover, emotionally charged environments can skew moral judgement, making individuals more punitive or reactive, especially when exposed to anger-inducing stimuli (Schnall et al., 2008; Lerner et al., 1998). In the digital battlespace, such emotional manipulation can be weaponised to polarise public opinion, distort collective memory, and erode social cohesion, turning emotion into both a target and a tool of cognitive warfare.

Assessing the Impact of Memory in Decision-Making

It is often hard to pull together a picture of how memory can be manipulated in the realm of digital warfare when looking at all the disparate pieces of research, but there are some key findings that have relevance here. Being able to flood digital spaces with information is a key tactic that can leverage dividends, particularly if you want to influence the decision-making processes of individuals. Hitting people with information that you want them to use and integrate into their memories seems like a key strategy, most likely to be relevant if there is less chance of this material being overwritten later. If you are looking to leverage recency in your strategy, then you need to make sure the gap between the initial injection of information and your pitch is delayed, but the measurement of the effect, which may be a public vote, must come immediately afterwards. False memories offer another opportunity to manipulate opinions, and you need to craft material in such a way that it is linked to previously viewed information or aligns well with the beliefs of those whom you are trying to sway. By using keywords or phrases, you can enhance the perception of an event being more serious than others may see it (e.g., a special military campaign sounds less dramatic than an invasion or war). The ability to implant memories into an individual's mind, particularly in a way that they are not aware of, offers another possible attack vector, and that relates to the use of heuristic processes, as we will explore in the next section of this chapter.

Heuristics and Digital Warfare

There are a variety of heuristic mechanisms that could be applicable to the realm of digital warfare, and it would be impossible to cover each of the possible dimensions along which they could be used. However, there are some common heuristic processes that have been widely referred to in the literature on decision-making that have a clear relevance to our current discussion, and in the next section, these are introduced alongside an exploration of how they could be harnessed in a digital conflict situation. In the context of information warfare and influence operations, it has been proposed that the three most relevant heuristics are the availability heuristic, the representative heuristic, the anchoring heuristic, and the affect heuristic (Lin & Kerr, 2021). It is these that we will focus on in this next section.

The Availability Heuristic

The availability heuristic is a key mechanism that individuals will use when faced with decisions related to how likely or how frequent an event might be to occur. Rather than engaging in a very protracted process of calculating probabilities or consulting data, we tend to base our decisions on how easily relevant examples related to the space in which the decision must be made come to mind (Tversky & Kahneman, 1974). In the context of digital warfare, the availability heuristic can form a key vulnerability. As the availability heuristic relies heavily on the ease with which we can retrieve relevant information, if you can influence the perception of something being more frequent or more common than it is, you can also influence decision-making. Adversarial elements can serve to exploit this process by flooding the information environment with emotionally charged, memorable, or repetitive content. The goal here is to make certain narratives or threats more "available" in the minds of targets, whether this is individuals, groups, or entire populations. When people are repeatedly exposed to specific claims (e.g., misinformation about election fraud, health risks, or geopolitical threats), those claims become easier to recall and are therefore judged as more likely or true, regardless of their factual accuracy (Tversky & Kahneman, 1974).

Such a tactic is central to information operations, where the manipulation of perception is seen as a more effective approach than direct confrontation. By amplifying certain stories through bots, influencers, or algorithmic targeting, hostile actors can shape public opinion, sow distrust, or provoke action, all by leveraging the cognitive tendency to judge likelihood based on ease of recall. The search engine manipulation effect (SEME) has been noted as a key mechanic for influencing an individual's decision-making, often without them directly realising it. For example, Epstein and Robertson (2015) noted that biased search results served to have a significant impact on voter preferences, with 20% of undecided voters moving their decisions following viewing biased search results. They also noted that the impact of such biased search results could be hidden from the individuals viewing them so that they had no direct knowledge of such manipulation taking place. Others have noted that SEME has been used to spread pro-Kremlin propaganda with the use of bots and trolls to manipulate recommendation algorithms on social media platforms (Williams & Carley, 2023).

The Representativeness Heuristic

This heuristic relates to individual assessments on how likely something is based on a set of preceding events. This can also be related to predictions about someone's behaviour in the absence of any reliable information about that individual. The functionality of this heuristic has been reliably demonstrated in a wide range of circumstances, such as the famous piece of research by Tversky and Kahneman (1974). In their original study, participants were presented with a description of someone who was shy and socially withdrawn, and who was very helpful but not very outgoing. He was also described as tidy and someone who prefers a routine and order in his daily life. Participants were then presented with a choice: was the description more likely to be that of a librarian or an engineer? In most cases, participants will make a judgement that the description matches that of a librarian, mainly because (based on past experiences) the description fits with what we believe is more representative of a librarian. Importantly, even when individuals are told that the population from which the described person comes contains more engineers than librarians, they still choose to pick a librarian. This is something called the *base-rate fallacy* and demonstrates the powerful drive that heuristics can have. Even when individuals are given detailed statistical information about the occurrence of an event, they are still more likely to default to the representativeness heuristic.

The inherent danger here lies in how this heuristic serves to bypass analytical thinking. Just as people overlook base rates when judging the profession of the individual described in the study by Tversky and Kahneman, users in digital environments may ignore statistical likelihoods, source credibility, or contextual cues if something "looks right." This makes representativeness a powerful tool for shaping perception and manipulating judgement. It can lead individuals to assess the likelihood or authenticity of something based on how closely it matches a familiar stereotype or mental prototype, and this is often at the expense of a more rational analysis. Adversarial actors can exploit this by crafting online personas that align with stereotypical images of certain social or political categories, such as "terrorist," "activist," "sympathiser," or "whistleblower." These fabricated identities are designed to look and sound like what people already expect from such figures. When a persona fits the mental image, someone holds of a whistleblower, perhaps by using technical jargon, a notion of anonymity, and a tone of urgency, it is more likely to be perceived as credible, even if the source is entirely fabricated. This tactic not only reinforces existing stereotypes but also guides the interpretation of content and intent. For example, a social media account that mimics the language and aesthetics of a radical group may be more readily accepted as authentic, prompting emotional reactions, fear, or even support depending on the audience. Similarly, content that resembles known propaganda or disinformation formats may be dismissed too quickly, even if it contains legitimate information, simply because it does not "look right."

By leveraging the representativeness heuristic, information warfare operations can bypass critical thinking and steer audiences towards conclusions that feel intuitively correct but are not necessarily grounded in fact. Such processes serve to highlight the importance of cognitive awareness in digital environments, where perception can be shaped as much by form as by content.

The Anchoring Heuristic

This heuristic refers to a process where an individual will choose an initial reference point (or the anchor) upon which to base a further decision. Individuals will rely too heavily on this initial reference point when making later decisions, even if that anchor is irrelevant or is simply an arbitrary value. This can in turn influence subsequent decisions in a disproportionate way, meaning that estimates or evaluations are heavily biased (Tversky & Kahneman, 1974; Epley & Gilovich, 2006). Anchoring is powerful because it affects not only what people believe but also how they *process* new information. In digital warfare, the aim is to control the information upon which the initial anchor is based, therefore placing direct control in the frame of reference from which individuals then make further decisions. This could be presenting extremely inflated statistics that serve to demonstrate a relevant viewpoint, such as a high percentage of a given population being in favour of a new policy. In turn, this information can serve to anchor individual expectations and influence how people analyse new information later. This is a crucial tactic that is used in propaganda campaigns where a strong narrative is presented early on, such as the amount of support citizens give to a current operation or their ruling regime. This can serve to set a clear benchmark that influences how individuals will interpret information that comes afterwards, but people are more likely to dismiss contradictory information because the anchor remains so powerful.

The Affect Heuristic

Individuals will often rely heavily on affective responses or their immediate emotional reactions to help them make decisions. This is especially true where individuals are placed under time pressure, or there is some form of uncertainty attached to the outcome of the decision-making process. This is embodied in another heuristic, known as the affect heuristic, which allows people the capacity to bypass complex analysis by substituting feelings for facts. If a person feels positively about a technology, platform, or action, they are likely to perceive it as less risky, regardless of objective evidence. Conversely, negative feelings can inflate perceived risk (Finucane et al., 2016; Slovic et al., 2007; Slovic & Peters, 2006).

Early research into risk perception revealed that emotions such as dread were strongly associated with heightened perceptions of hazard (Slovic, 1987; Slovic & Peters, 2006). Importantly, Slovic also found that perceived benefits and risks are often inversely related, so as the perceived benefit of an action increases, its perceived risk tends to decrease. This dynamic is tightly linked to the emotional valence attached to the activity (Alhakami & Slovic, 1994). In other words, people's judgements about risk are not purely rational calculations but are shaped by affective responses; activities viewed positively evoke lower risk perceptions, whereas those associated with negative emotions amplify perceived danger. This insight is a foundational element for the "affect heuristic," which suggests that individuals rely on their emotional impressions when evaluating both risks and benefits, influencing decision-making in contexts ranging from health behaviours to technology adoption.

In the context of cyberwarfare, this has profound implications. For example, individuals may underestimate the risks of using unsecured digital tools or platforms if they associate them with convenience, familiarity, or positive outcomes. Slovic and Peters (2006) emphasised that people judge technologies not only by what they know about them but also by how they feel about them, an insight that is particularly relevant to cybersecurity behaviours, where emotional associations with digital tools can override rational risk assessments. Moreover, when decisions must be made quickly, such as during a cyber-attack or disinformation surge, the reliance on affect becomes even more pronounced. Under time pressure, individuals are more likely to default to emotion-driven judgements, further strengthening the inverse relationship between perceived risk and benefit (Finucane et al., 2000). This makes affect a strategic vulnerability in digital conflict, where adversaries can manipulate emotional responses to influence risk perception and decision-making.

Recognition Heuristic

This heuristic leads an individual to favour options that they are familiar with (or recognise) over others that they do not, irrespective of the actual evidence to support that choice or the relevance to their specific goal. When an individual is faced with a choice between two alternatives, they will assume that the one that they are most familiar with is the one that is more valid (Gigerenzer & Goldstein, 2011; Pachur et al., 2011). This bias is rooted in cognitive fluency or the ease with which familiar information is processed, which the brain interprets as a marker of truth. Evolutionarily, familiarity often indicated safety, but in digital environments, this shortcut can be exploited.

A classic example of the recognition heuristic involves judgements about city size: when asked whether London or an unfamiliar city is larger, most people choose London simply because they recognise it (Tversky & Kahneman, 1974). In online spaces, this same principle applies, where familiarity often breeds credibility. Repeated exposure to a name, phrase, or image, even if false, enhances perceived legitimacy through the illusory truth effect. Social media algorithms amplify this by prioritising content that users engage with, creating echo chambers where familiar narratives dominate. Recognition can override scepticism, especially when content aligns with pre-existing beliefs or evokes strong emotions. Adversaries exploit this bias in influence operations by mimicking trusted sources (e.g., fake news sites with familiar branding) or using repetition to increase visibility and perceived authenticity. Bots can artificially inflate engagement, making content appear popular and therefore credible.

The recognition heuristic can also interact with other biases, such as the availability heuristic (judging likelihood based on ease of recall) and authority bias (trusting perceived experts), creating a potent mix for misinformation spread.

Case Study – The 2025 Southport Riots

I want to round this chapter off by exploring how some of the components could be used in the context of a real-world example and pull apart some of the techniques that have served to destabilise and polarise to extreme levels. Such an exploration is not intended to trivialise or diminish the seriousness of such events but instead highlights how heuristic processes and memory can be weaponised very easily and effectively.

On the morning of July 29, 2024, at 11:45 am, a masked attacker entered Hart Space, a dance studio in Southport, where a Taylor Swift-themed children's group was happening. Once in, the attacker began to attack adults and children indiscriminately, resulting in the death of three girls aged 6, 7, and 9. Ten others were injured, including two adults. The horrific attack was widely covered by numerous media sources, and many scrambled to find more information about the attack, particularly the motives and the identity of the attacker.

Soon after the attack, a variety of different pieces of misinformation started to circulate on social media and other platforms, including X and Telegram, claiming to have inside information about the identity of the attacker. The widely shared information suggested that the attacker was a Muslim immigrant who was an asylum seeker who had arrived illegally by boat into the United Kingdom. Soon after, specific misinformation presented the name of the attacker as Ali Al-Shakati, which soon went viral on multiple different platforms. https://news.sky.com/story/southport-attack-misinformation-fuels-far-right-discourse-on-social-media-13188274.

This information was added to an already tense environment within a hotbed of tensions related to anti-government, anti-migration, and anti-Islam sentiment. Many extreme far-right groups began to mobilise the outrage, anger, and grief that were circulating online, in turn amplifying misinformation about the attacker and calling for a series of "Protests" that were seen to target mosques not only in Southport but also across the United Kingdom. In cases where information was presented to show that the evidence to support such conclusions about the attacker was false, far-right groups were still keen to promote anti-Muslim sentiments (Venkataramakrishnan, 2025). Even when reporting restrictions were lifted, and the police reported that the attacker was of Rwandan origins, had been born and raised in Wales, and was a Christian, disinformation and misinformation were circulated to subdue this information. Many commentators from accounts associated with far-right sentiments even went as far as suggesting that such information was misinformation that had been created by the authorities to cover up the identity of the attacker (Venkataramakrishnan, 2025).

The U.K. government was keen to highlight the potential for state-backed actors to be fuelling the content of online disinformation and misinformation campaigns that occurred at the time, with the aim of increasing polarisation and creating societal destabilisation (Morley-Davies et al., 2024). While the presence of state actors in the context of the spread and creation of misinformation during this time is highly likely, the ensuing violence and riots that came in the aftermath of the Southport attacks were seen as a combination of events that had been years in the making. Commentators suggested that while the Kremlin had a hand in the amplification of misinformation in this case, it was not directly involved in the creation of material (Morley-Davies et al., 2024). Using bots and trolling activities in channels that were relaying misinformation and disinformation about the riots, the anti-Islamic sentiment could be enhanced and shared widely. One of the sources for the misinformation surrounding the racial identity of the attacker was purported to be Channel3Now, which has been linked to Kremlin-based disinformation and misinformation campaigns (Morley-Davies et al., 2024). While this theory has been widely disputed, and the site's main aim is to gain revenue through clickbait articles, it was noted that the Kremlin-backed media sources were keen to repeat the information about the riots that appeared on there (Morley-Davies et al., 2024).

The events that came in the aftermath of the July 29 attacks were, as noted earlier, years in the making. For years prior to the attack, there had been a growth in anti-Muslim and anti-Islam feelings, with the mass media and social media covering the growing concern related to illegal immigration and the erosion of the British way of life. Far-right groups such as the English Defence League had been at the forefront of presenting such issues as being a fundamental threat to Britishness, often disguising this as a patriotic desire to retain the essential values of what is seen to be "British." The polarisation of society had already started way before the attacks in Southport, but the attacks themselves served as a catalyst through which individuals with extremist views could gain legitimacy.

Let us look at the heuristic processes that could be at work in this scenario. Being prepared with information about immigration and the growing "Small boat" crisis served to enhance the prominence of this information. This serves to do two critical things in terms of heuristic and memorial processing. First, it makes information more available to individuals, as they have been bombarded with information on this topic for months, if not years, from numerous sources, including social media, the mass media, and the tabloid press. Second, linking back to the processes we explored in terms of memory formation, the recency effect comes into play, where information that has been more recently viewed and encoded prior to the Southport attack will be more salient and relevant. Coupled with the presence of emotive tweets, posts, and memes that served to highlight the threat from Islamic terrorists to innocent children, you have the perfect environment for such information to be remembered.

Representativeness was also at work in the context of the following riots and online rhetoric. Many of the ways in which the attacker was described served to fulfil the existing stereotypes that individuals had, where misinformation and disinformation used to describe the attacker were designed to fit into existing schemas that described a terrorist (e.g., Muslim, illegal immigrant, and the use of a foreign-sounding name). By doing this, disinformation and misinformation were able to bypass more analytical thinking and could be quickly integrated into the decision-making processes of individuals. This meant they were more likely to align with the perspective that the attacker was indeed a terrorist, and in turn they needed to take action to protect themselves, their loved ones, and the British way of life.

The anchoring heuristic was also at play in the context of the misinformation and disinformation that was being circulated during the aftermath of the attacks.

Initial misinformation established the identity of the attacker as a Muslim immigrant named Ali Al-Shakati, which in turn created a powerful cognitive anchor. Far-right groups sought to exploit this by reinforcing the anchor through mechanisms such as memetic bombardment, flooding of social media with aligned false information, and emotionally charged material, all of which made it impossible for the information to be processed. Despite this new information emerging about the real identity of the attacker, the anchor had created such a powerful draw that many individuals insisted on aligning themselves with this initial piece of information, resisting the assimilation of new material.

Affect was also a key factor in the processes aligned to both the spread of misinformation and disinformation, as well as a motivating factor for much of the civil unrest that was seen in the weeks after the attack. As the attack involved young, innocent children who were seen to be enjoying a holiday activity, emotive elements of fear, anger, and grief were all symptomatic of the public feelings at the time. Not only did this serve to enhance the memory trace for this information, but also the use of emotionally framed images and language that was used in the misinformation and disinformation at the time. Many of the memes and images that were being circulated on social media at the time they were created were very emotionally charged and included the notion that innocent lives had been taken away by Islamic extremists. Such emotional cues served to enhance the chances of System 1 thinking overriding a more systematic exploration of the evidence, as well as an exploration of the credibility of the individuals posting information (see Chapter 10).

Summary

In this chapter, we have explored how memory and heuristic processes form critical fault lines in human cognition that adversaries exploit within digital warfare. Beginning with dual-process theories, it explains how decision-making oscillates between fast, intuitive (Type 1) modes and slow, analytical (Type 2) modes, with heuristic shortcuts dominating under conditions of uncertainty, time pressure, or emotional strain. These key heuristics, that of availability, representativeness, anchoring, affect, and recognition, are presented as efficient yet error-prone mechanisms that adversaries weaponise through algorithmic curation, repetition, and emotionally charged narratives.

Memory is positioned as both a foundation for understanding the use of heuristics and the source of vulnerability. The chapter explored how primacy–recency effects, false memory formation, and emotional memory narrowing distort recall and amplify susceptibility to misinformation. Emotional triggers are shown to narrow attentional focus, heighten salience, and override rational scrutiny, creating fertile ground for manipulation. The discussion highlights how adversaries exploit these dynamics through tactics such as search engine manipulation, social media flooding, and framing strategies that align with pre-existing beliefs.

The detailed case study, the 2024 Southport Riots, serves to illustrate these principles in action. Following a tragic attack, misinformation anchored early and reinforced through emotive content leveraged multiple heuristics and memory biases, sustaining false narratives despite corrective information. This example underscores how cognitive shortcuts and distorted memory can escalate societal polarisation and civil unrest.

Ultimately, the chapter argues that digital warfare is not only technological but also fundamentally cognitive. By mapping the mechanisms through which memory and heuristics shape perception and judgement, it calls for resilience strategies that counteract these vulnerabilities and strengthen critical thinking in information-rich environments.

References

Alhakami, A. S., & Slovic, P. (1994). A psychological study of the inverse relationship between percieved risk and percieved benefit. *Risk Analysis*, *14*(6), 721–736.

Ansari, A., & Mela, C. F. (2003). E-Customization. *Journal of Marketing Research*, *XL*(May 2003), 131–145.

Asch, S. E. (1946). Forming impressions of personality. *The Journal of Abnormal and Social Psychology*, *41*(3), 258–290.

Baum, J., Frömer, R., & Rahman, R. A. (2024). Emotional content reduces the cognitive effort invested in processing the credibility of social (mis)information. *Emotion*, *24*(6), 1468–1480. https://doi.org/10.1037/emo0001355

Chaiken, S., & Trope, Y. (1999). *Dual-process theories in social psychology*. Retrieved from http://books.google.it/books?id=5X_auIBx99EC

Craswell, N., Zoeter, O., & Ramsey, B. (2008). An experimental comparison of click position-bias models. *WSDM '08*, 11–12. Retrieved from papers://c0f50874-1acc-4627–879e-caecd2247efe/Paper/p10

Crowder, R. G. (1976). *Principles of learning and memory*. Hillsdale, NJ: Erlbaum.

Cutrell, E., & Guan, Z. (2007). An eye-tracking study of information usage in Web search: Variations in target position and contextual snippet length. *In Proceedings of the SIGCHI Conference on Human Factors in Computing Systems*, 407–416. Retrieved from http://www.divinewrite.com.au/downloads/MS_eye_tracking_study.pdf

Denton, K. K., & Krebs, D. L. (2017). Rational and emotional sources of moral decision-making: An evolutionary-developmental account. *Evolutionary Psychological Science*, *3*(1), 72–85. https://doi.org/10.1007/s40806-016-0067-3

Drèze, X., & Zufryden, F. (1997). Testing web site design and promotional content. *Journal of Advertising Research*, *37*(2), 77–91. https://doi.org/10.1080/00218499.1997.12466663

Epley, N., & Gilovich, T. (2006). The anchoring-and-adjustment heuristic: Why the adjustments are insufficient. *Psychological Science*, *17*(4), 311–318. https://doi.org/10.1111/j.1467-9280.2006.01704.x

Epstein, R., & Robertson, R. E. (2015). The search engine manipulation effect (SEME) and its possible impact on the outcomes of elections. *Proceedings of the National Academy of Sciences of the United States of America*, *112*(33), E4512–E4521. https://doi.org/10.1073/pnas.1419828112

Finucane, M. L., Alhakami, A., Slovic, P., & Johnson, S. M. (2016). The affect heuristic in judgments of risks and benefits. *Journal of Behavioral Decision Making*, *13*, 413–429.

Gigerenzer, G., & Goldstein, D. G. (2011). The recognition heuristic: A decade of research. *Judgment and Decision Making*, *6*(February), 100–121. https://doi.org/10.1017/s1930297500002126

Granka, L. A., Joachims, T., & Gay, G. (2004). Eye-tracking analysis of user behavior in WWW search. *Proceedings of the 27th Annual International ACM SIGIR Conference on Research and Development in Information Retrieval*, 478–479. https://doi.org/10.1145/1008992.1009079

Hadlington, L. (2017). *Cybercognition: Brain, behaviour and the digital world*. London: Sage.

Haugtvedt, C. P., & Wegener, D. T. (1994). Message order effects in persuasion: An attitude strength perspective. *Journal of Consumer Research*, *21*(1), 205. https://doi.org/10.1086/209393

Insko, C. A. (1964). Primacy versus recency in persuasion as a function of the timing of arguments and measures. *Journal of Abnormal and Social Psychology*, *69*(4), 381–391. https://doi.org/10.1037/h0042765

Kaplan, R. L., Van Damme, I., Levine, L. J., & Loftus, E. F. (2016). Emotion and false memory. *Emotion Review*, *8*(1), 8–13. https://doi.org/10.1177/1754073915601228

King, A. B. (2008). Website optimization. *Website Optimization*. https://doi.org/http://proquestcombo.safaribooksonline.com.ezproxy.uws.edu.au/book/web-development/9780596515089?bookview=overview

Laney, C., & Loftus, E. F. (2008). Emotional content of true and false memories. *Memory*, *16*(5), 500–516. https://doi.org/10.1080/09658210802065939

Lee, J., Ott, T., & Deavours, D. (2021). Emotional appeal in false beliefs. *Combating Misinformation in Risk*, 17. Retrieved from https://www.taylorfrancis.com/chapters/edit/10.4324/9781003008828-12/combating-misinformation-risk-jiyoung-lee-tanya-ott-danielle-deavours?context=ubx

Lerner, J. S., Goldberg, J. H., & Tetlock, P. E. (1998). Sober second thought: The effects of accountability, anger, and authoritarianism on attributions of responsibility. *Personality and Social Psychology Bulletin*, *24*(6), 563–574. https://doi.org/10.1177/0146167298246001

Lin, H., & Kerr, J. (2021). On cyber-enabled information warfare and information operations. *The Oxford Handbook of Cyber Security*, (May), 251–272. https://doi.org/10.1093/oxfordhb/9780198800682.013.15

Loftus, E. F., & Zanni, G. (1975). Eyewitness testimony. *Bulletin of the Psychonomic Society*, *5*(1), 86–88. https://doi.org/10.1002/acp.3542

Lorigo, L., Haridasan, M., Brynjarsdottir, H., Xia, L., Joachims, T., Gay, G., . . . Pan, B. (2008). Eye tracking and online search: Lessons learned and challenges ahead. *Journal of the American Society for Information Science and Technology*, *59*(7), 1041–1052. https://doi.org/10.1002/asi

McNally, R. J., & Geraerts, E. (2009). A new solution to the recovered memory debate. *Perspectives on Psychological Science*, *4*(2), 126–134. Retrieved from http://myaccess.library.utoronto.ca/login?url=http://search.ebscohost.com/login.aspx?direct=true&db=rzh&AN=105509800&site=ehost-live

Meylani, R. (2024). Innovations with schema theory: Modern implications for learning, memory, and academic achievement. *International Journal for Multidisciplinary Research*, *6*(1), 1–33. https://doi.org/10.36948/ijfmr.2024.v06i01.13785

Miller, N., & Campbell, D. T. (1959). Recency and primacy in persuasion as a function of the timing of speeches and measurements. *Journal of Abnormal and Social Psychology*, *59*(1), 1–9. https://doi.org/10.1037/h0049330

Morley-Davies, J., Thomas, J., & Baines, G. (2024). *Russian information operations outside of the Western information environment*. NATO Strategic Communications Centre of Excellence.

Murphy, G., Loftus, E. F., Grady, R. H., Levine, L. J., & Greene, C. M. (2019). False memories for fake news during Ireland's abortion referendum. *Psychological Science*, *30*(10), 1449–1459. https://doi.org/10.1177/0956797619864887

Murphy, J., Hofacker, C., & Mizerski, R. (2006). Primacy and recency effects on clicking behavior. *Journal of Computer-Mediated Communication, 11*(2), 522–535. https://doi.org/10.1111/j.1083-6101.2006.00025.x

Nichols, R. M., & Loftus, E. F. (2019). Who is susceptible in three false memory tasks? *Memory, 27*(7), 962–984. https://doi.org/10.1080/09658211.2019.1611862

Pachur, T., Todd, P. M., Gigerenzer, G., Schooler, L. J., & Goldstein, D. G. (2011). The recognition heuristic: A review of theory and tests. *Frontiers in Psychology, 2*(July). https://doi.org/10.3389/fpsyg.2011.00147

Rey, A., Le Goff, K., Abadie, M., & Courrieu, P. (2020). The primacy order effect in complex decision making. *Psychological Research, 84*(6), 1739–1748. https://doi.org/10.1007/s00426-019-01178-2

Roediger III, H. L., & Mcdermott, K. B. (1995). Roediger McDermott 1995 creating false memories.pdf. *Journal of Experimental Psychology: Learning, Memory, and Cognition, 21*, 803–814.

Schnall, S., Haidt, J., Clore, G. L., & Jordan, A. H. (2008). Disgust as embodied moral judgment. *Personality and Social Psychology Bulletin, 34*(8), 1096–1109. https://doi.org/10.1177/0146167208317771

Slovic, P. (1987). Perception of risk. *Science, 236*, 280–285.

Slovic, P., Finucane, M. L., Peters, E., & MacGregor, D. G. (2007). The affect heuristic. *European Journal of Operational Research, 177*(3), 1333–1352. https://doi.org/10.1016/j.ejor.2005.04.006

Slovic, P., & Peters, E. (2006). Risk perception and affect. *Current Directions in Psychological Science, 15*(6), 322–325. https://doi.org/10.1111/j.1467-8721.2006.00461.x

Storbeck, J., & Clore, G. L. (2005). With sadness comes accuracy; with happiness, false memory: Mood and the false memory effect. *Psychological Science, 16*(10), 785–791. https://doi.org/10.1111/j.1467-9280.2005.01615.x

Todorov, A., Chaiken, S., & Henderson, M. D. (2002). The heuristic-systematic model of social information processing. In *The persuasion handbook: DDevelopments in Theory and Practice* (pp. 195–211). Thousand Oaks, CA: Sage.

Tversky, A., & Kahneman, D. (1974). Judgment under uncertainty: Heuristics and biases. *Science (New York, N.Y.), 185*(4157), 1124–1131. https://doi.org/10.1126/science.185.4157.1124

van der Linden, S., Albarracín, D., Fazio, L. K., Freelon, D., Roozenbeek, J., Swire-Thompson, B., & Van Bavel, J. (2023). Using psychological science to understand and fight health misinformation. *American Psychological Association*, (November). Retrieved from https://www.apa.org/pubs/reports/misinformation-consensus-statement.pdf

Venkataramakrishnan, S. (2025). From disinformation to violence: The UK far right and 2024 riots the UK far right and 2024 riots. *Counter Terrorist Trends and Analyses, 17*(2), 8–15. Retrieved from https://www.jstor.org/stable/48815455

Waugh, N., & Norman, D. (1965). Primary memory. *Psychological Review, 72*(2).

Williams, E. M., & Carley, K. M. (2023). Search engine manipulation to spread pro-Kremlin propaganda. *Harvard Kennedy School Misinformation Review, 4*(1), 1–13. https://doi.org/10.37016/mr-2020-112

Wilson, S. L., & Wiysonge, C. (2020). Social media and vaccine hesitancy. *BMJ Global Health, 5*(10), 1–7. https://doi.org/10.1136/bmjgh-2020-004206

Wirth, W., Böcking, T., Karnowski, V., & Von Pape, T. (2009). The WEBNAS analysis method: A holistic approach to the analysis of web navigating and searching behavior. *Communication Methods and Measures, 3*(3), 115–146.

Zarro, M. (2012). Developing a dual-process information seeking model for exploratory search. *Mikezarro.Com*. Retrieved from http://www.mikezarro.com/docs/Zarro_HCIR2012_FINAL.pdf

10 Manipulation of Credibility Online

Introduction

The internet has rapidly evolved into one of the primary reference points for individuals seeking information to guide decisions, actions, and purchases, supplanting many traditional modes of information gathering. To illustrate this shift, research conducted by Horrigan and Rainie (2006) found that 45% of U.S. internet users had relied on online information to make a major life decision, a figure that underscores the internet's growing influence in shaping personal and societal outcomes (Hadlington, 2017). However, this blind reliance on internet-based sources introduces a critical vulnerability, especially when individuals misplace trust in online sources. In high-stakes contexts, the consequences of devolving decisions to content and material that is found online can be profound. In the digital battlefield, credibility itself becomes a weapon and can be used to sway opinions, distort debates, and influence behaviour. As such, understanding how credibility is constructed and perceived is central to any analysis of digital warfare. Credibility, as defined by Fogg (2003), refers to the believability of a source, often assessed through dimensions such as trustworthiness and expertise. These judgements are not made in isolation; they are shaped by prior exposure, perceived authority, and contextual cues, linking back to the use of heuristic processing we explored in the previous chapter. For example, readers may be more inclined to trust this book based on their familiarity with the author's previous work or academic credentials. This reflects a broader cognitive tendency: when a source is perceived as expert, the information it provides is often judged as more trustworthy (Hilligoss & Rieh, 2008). In digital warfare, this mechanism is frequently exploited. Adversarial actors may simulate expertise, manipulate trust signals, or embed persuasive content within seemingly credible platforms. As such, the study of credibility is not merely about information quality; it is about strategic influence, psychological manipulation, and the architecture of trust in contested digital spaces.

Understanding credibility in digital environments requires a multidimensional approach that accounts for both psychological processes and technological

DOI: 10.4324/9781003752400-10

design. Three influential frameworks, Fogg's prominence–interpretation theory, Metzger et al.'s heuristic model, and Sundar's MAIN model, offer complementary perspectives on how trust is constructed, perceived, and manipulated online.

In Fogg's prominence–interpretation theory (Fogg, 2003; Fogg et al., 2001, 2003), there is an emphasis on the sequential nature of credibility assessment: users must first notice a cue (prominence) and then interpret its relevance (interpretation). Prominence is shaped by factors such as user involvement, task orientation, topic, prior experience, and individual differences, while interpretation reflects subjective judgements influenced by assumptions, skills, and situational context. This model underscores that credibility is not inherent in content but emerges through user interaction and cognitive processing. In digital warfare, adversarial actors exploit these mechanisms by designing content that captures attention and aligns with user expectations, thereby reducing scrutiny and increasing susceptibility to manipulation.

Meanwhile, Metzger et al.'s (Flanagin & Metzger, 2000; Metzger, 2007; Metzger & Flanagin, 2013) heuristic model complements Fogg's theory by identifying five key heuristics, these being reputation, endorsement, consistency, expectancy violation, and persuasive intent, that users employ to simplify credibility judgements. These heuristics operate under conditions of cognitive load and time pressure, making them efficient but vulnerable to exploitation. For instance, co-ordinated bot networks can simulate endorsement, while a polished design can mask persuasive intent. In adversarial contexts, these shortcuts become strategic targets, enabling actors to engineer trust through repetition, consensus, and aesthetic cues rather than substantive accuracy.

While Fogg and Metzger focus on cognitive strategies, Sundar's MAIN model (Sundar, 2008) introduces a technological dimension, highlighting how interface design and digital affordances shape credibility perceptions. MAIN stands for modality, agency, interactivity, and navigability, all features that activate specific heuristics influencing trust. Modality affects judgements through realism and immersion, with multimedia formats often perceived as more authentic than text. Agency relates to perceived authorship, where cues such as verified accounts or platform familiarity trigger authority and bandwagon heuristics. Interactivity and navigability enhance credibility by fostering user control and seamless engagement, signalling professionalism and reliability. In digital warfare, adversaries exploit these affordances by deploying high-fidelity visuals, simulating consensus, and designing intuitive interfaces to mask manipulative intent.

Taken together, these frameworks highlight the concept of something that is not static credibility but a dynamic construct that can be shaped by the interplay of heuristics and technological affordances. Fogg's model explains how users notice and interpret cues, Metzger's heuristics show the shortcuts that guide evaluation, and Sundar's affordances demonstrate how interface features trigger these processes. Integrating these perspectives provides a holistic understanding of credibility as both a psychological judgement and a strategic battleground, one where adversarial actors weaponise trust through a fusion of persuasive design and cognitive exploitation. This synthesis underscores the need for interventions that address not only user cognition but also the structural and technological conditions under which credibility is assessed.

The Disintermediation of Gatekeeping

In a traditional, non-digital information search process, an individual would go through a variety of different options to look for the material that they needed. For example, you could go to a library and look through textbooks and journal articles from reputable sources. You could also look for documentary evidence that has been produced by a mainstream television network, or search for discussion points around your topic in offline databases. When we engage in such a process, we assume that the information we are gathering is legitimate, and in a predigital era, there were various mechanisms that served to sanction the facticity of information. There were only a few accepted routes to publishing material, and these routes were governed by a variety of different processes that would serve to establish the expertise of the respective author and the verification of the information being presented. For example, journal articles go through extensive peer review processes to garner the opinion of other experts in the field according to the accuracy and relevance of the information contained in them. Suler (2002, 2005) suggested that the internet has created a net democracy, levelling the playing field for publishing information. No longer do individuals need to have relevant expertise or experience in a field, and their opinions can be heard irrespective of their qualifications (Hadlington, 2017).

However, the speed at which digital media has proliferated has not seen a similar change in the cognitive processes that we might use to assess credibility. As Flanagin and Metzger (2007, 2000) noted, the core strategies that we use to assess credibility online are still the same as those we use to assess credibility offline; however, because the internet contains such a wealth of information that can change in such a fluid and dynamic way, the propensity for individuals to adapt these mechanisms has increased exponentially. In the digital environment, the demand for individuals to actively digest information and distinguish between what is credible and what is misleading has intensified. This process places significant cognitive strain on already limited information processing capacities, often leading users to default to heuristic strategies rather than engaging in deeper, systematic evaluation. However, other researchers have presented a different perspective on the processes that we use to assess credibility online. For example, Burbules (2001) contended that credibility judgements in cyberspace should be seen as being qualitatively distinct from those made in traditional, offline contexts. Burbules noted that there are specific features related to interface design, hyperlink architecture, and loading speeds that serve to introduce novel cues that influence trustworthiness assessments. These elements are not typically present in offline interactions, suggesting that the digital domain requires a recalibration of credibility heuristics.

Crucially, the rise of digital platforms has disrupted conventional information hierarchies. Metzger and Flanagin (2013) described this phenomenon as *disintermediation*, a process whereby individuals must independently seek, evaluate, and synthesise information without the guidance of traditional gatekeepers such as experts, salespeople, or institutional authorities. Originally conceptualised by Eysenbach (2007), disintermediation reflects a broader shift in information consumption, where users, whether patients researching medical conditions or consumers making purchasing decisions, are increasingly reliant on their own judgement in the absence of expert mediation (Hadlington, 2017). Such a transformation has profound implications for digital warfare, where the perceived credibility of information can be weaponised. In such contexts, understanding how individuals assess trustworthiness online becomes not only an academic concern but also a strategic one, central to both the dissemination and defence against manipulative content.

The Search for Credibility

There have been a variety of attempts in the past to understand the way in which individuals search for credible information online. There has been somewhat of a resurgence in the interest in these theories over the past few years, mainly due to the voracious spread of misinformation and fake news during the COVID-19 pandemic and the use of propaganda and disinformation in the Russia–Ukraine conflict. It is easy to underestimate the power credibility can have on our decision-making processes when it comes to digesting information, but such an underestimation is a dangerous one. If you can understand the ways in which credibility judgements are made, you can easily manipulate them, therefore making people more susceptible to the information you want them to believe.

The Signals of Trust: Prominence and Interpretation in Digital Warfare

Fogg (2003) presented one of the first frameworks for exploring the ways in which people use digital technologies to search for information. In this conceptual framework, there are four main ways in which an individual can establish the quality of information and, in turn, assess the credibility of the same.

1. *Presumed credibility*: rather than an individual making a judgement about the credibility of a source, they will often default to a heuristic-type process, meaning they will use an assumption of trustworthiness. This is the type of credibility judgement that utilises our past experiences about markers for

credibility, such as a brand name or domain name, and we use this as a basis for credibility rather than a deeper verification process.

2. *Surface credibility*: appearances are everything in the realm of credibility assessments, and individuals will often judge websites and sources that are presented professionally as being more trustworthy. This can be easily linked to the tactics that are often used in the context of fake news and misinformation, where actors will serve to mimic the appearance of formal news outlets to inherently surface credibility.
3. *Earned credibility*: this is a process that takes time to establish, and an individual will attribute trustworthiness to websites or information sources over several visits. The process at work here is linked to how easy the individual finds the information source to access and use, where poor useability will be associated with poor quality of information, in turn leading to a perception of reduced credibility.
4. *Report credibility*: this is a more rigorous assessment of credibility that is formed around the perception of professional feedback or uses a method of triangulation that compares the qualifications of the individual and their expertise in the field.

Fogg's framework for assessing credibility makes an important contribution to our understanding of how individuals make decisions about who and what to trust. Predominantly, users will place a heavy emphasis on the visual aesthetic of an information source and make a direct assessment of credibility based on this (Hadlington, 2017). Others have noted this, with researchers highlighting that a professional-looking website has been linked to higher credibility ratings from users (McKnight & Kacmar, 2007).

Linked to this initial exploration of credibility judgements, Fogg's framework suggested that two processes must occur before they can assess credibility in the digital world. Firstly, they must notice something within the digital environment; it must have prominence. This concept links back to the initial discussions we had around attention back in Chapter 4. Secondly, the user must then go deeper into that stimulus and make a judgement about its relevance to their current situation and needs, and it must be interpreted. Both these processes form the cornerstone of Fogg's (2003) prominence–interpretation framework.

Prominence

Prominence is very similar to the construct of selective attention (Chapter 4), where an individual will pay attention to something that stands out in their current environment. Fogg suggested that prominence is linked to the likelihood that an element of a website or information source will be noticed and, in turn, perceived by the individual. Remember that the first stage in the attentional process is the key mechanism of perception, so this must happen before any further action can be taken to explore the information source further. Fogg suggested that there are five fundamental aspects of information that will serve to enhance the prominence of information, these being the following:

1. *Involvement*: the degree of user involvement in an information search plays a pivotal role in shaping which elements of a digital environment become prominent. According to Fogg's framework, prominence is not a fixed attribute of a website or digital source; it is dynamically influenced by the user's engagement level and the context in which the information is encountered. Individual differences, such as motivation, cognitive capacity, and situational relevance, determine how attentively users interact with digital content. For instance, a highly motivated user seeking critical health information may scrutinise source credibility more rigorously than a casually browsing user. In digital warfare contexts, this variability in involvement becomes strategically significant: adversarial actors may exploit low-involvement scenarios to seed misinformation, knowing that users are less likely to critically evaluate content when their engagement is minimal.
2. *Topic*: the thematic domain in which an information source is situated, be it news, entertainment, education, or commerce, can play a critical role in shaping how users interpret credibility cues. Each topic area carries its own set of expectations and heuristics that influence what users notice and how they evaluate it. For instance, users may expect higher factual accuracy and source transparency in educational or news contexts, while entertainment platforms may be judged more on aesthetic appeal or user engagement. In the realm of digital warfare, this contextual framing becomes a strategic tool: adversarial actors may embed persuasive content within seemingly benign topic areas to bypass critical scrutiny. Understanding how topic influences prominence and interpretation is essential for decoding how credibility is constructed and potentially manipulated within digital conflict environments.
3. *Task*: this links to the user's objective during an information search, whether it is goal-directed (they are searching for specific information) or exploratory (randomly browsing the internet) and can serve to significantly influence which elements of a digital environment become prominent. In goal-directed searches, users typically engage with content more deliberately, scanning for specific cues that align with their informational needs. This focused engagement can enhance the salience of credibility cues such as source reputation, clarity, and relevance. Conversely, general or free browsing often involves lower cognitive investment, allowing peripheral features like visual design or interactivity to disproportionately shape perceptions of trustworthiness. Within the context of digital warfare, understanding task orientation is critical: adversarial actors may tailor content to exploit low-effort browsing behaviours, embedding persuasive or misleading elements that gain prominence precisely because users are not actively scrutinising them.

4. *User experience*: the user's prior experience associated with both digital environments and the specific topic at hand can serve to shape how credibility cues are perceived and interpreted. Experienced users may be more adept at navigating digital interfaces, recognising manipulative design patterns, and identifying trustworthy sources. Similarly, familiarity with the subject matter enhances the user's ability to detect inconsistencies or misinformation. In contrast, individuals with limited digital literacy or topic-specific knowledge may rely more heavily on superficial cues such as visual appeal or domain familiarity, increasing their vulnerability to deceptive content. Within the context of digital warfare, this disparity in user experience becomes a tactical consideration: adversarial actors often target less experienced users with tailored misinformation campaigns, exploiting gaps in digital fluency and subject expertise to distort perceptions and influence behaviour.
5. *Individual differences*: differences in cognitive and perceptual capacities (e.g., learning styles, literacy levels, and information processing preferences) can play a significant role in how users engage with and interpret digital content. These differences influence not only what becomes prominent in a digital interface but also how that information is evaluated for credibility. For example, users with higher digital literacy may focus on structural and source-based cues, while those with lower literacy may rely more on visual or emotional appeal. Similarly, individuals with a preference for visual learning may be more influenced by imagery and layout than by textual depth. In the context of digital warfare, these variations become exploitable vulnerabilities: hostile actors can tailor content to resonate with specific cognitive profiles, increasing the likelihood of persuasive impact and misinformation uptake. Recognising these individual-level factors is essential for understanding how credibility is constructed and manipulated across diverse user populations.

Fogg (2003) identified user involvement as a central determinant in the prominence of digital elements during an information search. When individuals approach a website with high motivation driven by a clear goal or personal relevance, they are more cognitively engaged and thus more likely to notice and process a greater number of features within the digital environment. This heightened perceptual sensitivity increases the salience of credibility cues, making users more discerning in their evaluations. Fogg's model aligns closely with the elaboration likelihood model (ELM) proposed by Petty and Cacioppo (1986), which posits that both motivation and ability jointly influence the depth of information processing. When both are elevated, users are more likely to engage in central route processing, critically evaluating content rather than relying on superficial heuristics. In the context of digital warfare, this interaction becomes strategically significant: adversaries may attempt to suppress user motivation or overwhelm cognitive capacity to reduce scrutiny, thereby increasing the effectiveness of manipulative or deceptive content.

Interpretation

Fogg (2003) defined interpretation as the user's personal judgement about a specific element encountered during an online interaction. This evaluative process is inherently subjective, shaped by a constellation of factors that influence how credibility is assigned. Unlike prominence, which determines what is noticed, interpretation governs how those noticed elements are understood and valued.

Fogg noted that there are some key contributing factors associated with interpretation; these include the following:

1. Assumptions: these are internalised beliefs and prior experiences that shape how users perceive digital content. For example, a user who has previously encountered misinformation on a certain platform may interpret similar content with heightened scepticism.
2. Skills and knowledge: a user's domain expertise and digital literacy directly affect their ability to critically assess content. Those with greater familiarity are more likely to identify inaccuracies or manipulative design features.
3. Context: the situational environment and user expectations at the time of the search play a crucial role. A user seeking urgent health information may interpret content differently from one casually browsing for entertainment.

Fogg emphasises that interpretation is not uniform across users. Cultural background, personal values, and situational relevance all contribute to divergent credibility assessments. For instance, a website featuring religious content may be interpreted as trustworthy and meaningful by some users, while others may view it as irrelevant or even manipulative, depending on their cultural and ideological standpoint.

In the context of digital warfare, this variability in interpretation becomes a strategic vulnerability. Adversarial actors can craft content that resonates with specific cultural or ideological groups, enhancing perceived credibility and increasing the likelihood of influence. Understanding the mechanics of interpretation is therefore essential for both defending against and deploying persuasive digital content in contested information environments.

Technological Affordances and the Mechanics of Credibility Judgement

Sundar (2008) introduced the concept of technological affordances as a foundational element in understanding how users make credibility judgements in digital environments. In essence, an *affordance* refers to the functional capabilities that a digital medium offers or features that serve to shape and guide user interaction. These affordances are not merely technical attributes; they serve as triggers that influence how users perceive and evaluate information. One illustrative example is the affordance of hypermedia, which enables users to interact dynamically with content through hyperlinks, embedded media, and navigational structures. This interactivity can activate a range of heuristics that users employ to assess credibility. For instance, a well-structured site with intuitive navigation and responsive design may be interpreted as more trustworthy, while broken links or poor grammar may undermine perceived credibility. In the context of digital warfare, technological affordances become strategic tools. Manipulative actors can design environments that exploit these affordances to either enhance perceived legitimacy or obscure deceptive intent. Understanding how affordances shape credibility judgements is therefore essential for both defending against and deploying persuasive digital content in contested information spaces.

In his exploration of digital media credibility, Sundar (2008) identifies four core technological affordances that significantly influence how individuals assess the trustworthiness of online content: *modality* (M), *agency* (A), *interactivity* (I), and *navigability* (N). These affordances are embedded across most digital platforms and serve as functional cues that shape user experience and cognitive processing. Taken together, these affordances form the basis for the MAIN model of credibility assessment.

- Modality refers to the format in which information is presented, such as text, video, audio, or multimedia combinations. Different modalities can trigger distinct heuristics; for example, professionally produced video content may be perceived as more credible than plain text.
- Agency concerns the perceived source of the information, whether it is user-generated, algorithmically curated, or institutionally authored. This affects judgements about authenticity and bias.
- Interactivity reflects the user's ability to engage with the content, such as commenting, liking, or navigating through hyperlinks. Higher interactivity can enhance perceived credibility by fostering a sense of control and engagement.
- Navigability pertains to the ease with which users can move through the digital environment. A well-organised and intuitive interface often signals professionalism and reliability.

These affordances act as cognitive triggers, activating heuristics that guide credibility assessments. In the context of digital warfare, understanding how these affordances are manipulated becomes critical. Adversarial actors may design content that exploits these cues such as using slick multimedia to mask misinformation or simulating agency to create false consensus, in turn shaping perception and influencing behaviour in contested information spaces.

Modality

Among the four key affordances identified by Sundar (2008), modality stands out as the most structurally visible and immediately perceptible element of digital content. It refers to the format through which information is delivered – textual, visual, auditory, or multimedia – and plays a central role in shaping users' initial impressions and credibility judgements. Digital devices typically support multiple output modalities, each of which engages users differently and activates distinct cognitive heuristics.

Sundar argued that text-based modalities are often perceived as less credible than visual or auditory formats. This is partly due to the interpretive complexity involved in textual communication: the sender must translate their experience into written language, and the receiver must decode that message, a process that introduces opportunities for ambiguity, irrelevance, or even deception. In contrast, visual and auditory modalities are often seen as more direct and immersive, reducing interpretive friction and enhancing perceived authenticity.

In the context of digital warfare, modality becomes a strategic design choice. Adversarial actors may deliberately employ high-fidelity visual or auditory content to enhance perceived credibility and emotional resonance, even when the underlying message is misleading or manipulative. Understanding how modality influences credibility perception is therefore essential for both evaluating digital content and anticipating how it may be weaponised in information conflict.

Sundar (2008) identified several key heuristics that are activated through the modality of digital content. Each of these serves to shape how users interpret credibility based on the format and sensory engagement of the media. These heuristics are particularly relevant in the context of digital warfare, where the strategic use of modality can influence perception and trust.

- *Realism heuristic*: this heuristic suggests that users are more likely to trust information that mimics real-world sensory experiences. Audio-visual content, for example, is often perceived as more credible than text alone because it aligns more closely with how individuals encounter information in everyday life. Seeing and hearing content creates a stronger sense of authenticity and immediacy.
- *Old-media heuristic*: information presented in formats reminiscent of traditional media, such as newspaper-style layouts or broadcast-style video, has a tendency to be viewed as being more credible. This stems from users' associations with legacy media institutions, which are perceived to uphold higher editorial standards and gatekeeping practices.
- *Being-there heuristic*: this heuristic emerges from immersive digital experiences, particularly those involving rich multimodal environments. The more intense and engaging the interaction, the more likely users are to perceive the content as credible. The sensation of "presence" in a virtual space can blur the line between simulation and reality, enhancing trust in the presented information.
- *Distraction heuristic*: paradoxically, high levels of multimodal stimulation can reduce critical scrutiny. When users are cognitively overwhelmed by interactive or sensory-rich environments, they may allocate fewer resources to evaluating

credibility. This heuristic highlights vulnerability in digital warfare: immersive content can distract users from questioning the validity of the message.

These mechanisms demonstrate that modality is not only a technical attribute of digital content but also a psychological lever that shapes trust perceptions. High-fidelity visuals, immersive audio, and multimedia formats serve to activate heuristics such as realism and old-media associations, making content appear more authentic and authoritative. In adversarial contexts, these features are deliberately engineered to create a false sense of credibility, masking manipulative intent behind professional aesthetics. By targeting modality, actors in digital warfare exploit cognitive shortcuts, leveraging sensory engagement to override critical scrutiny and foster belief in misleading narratives.

Agency

Sundar (2008) introduces the concept of agency as a key affordance in digital media, referring to the way users assign authorship or origin to the information they encounter. In digital environments, this attribution process is often ambiguous, as users may associate credibility not only with the content itself but also with the perceived entity delivering it. Sundar highlights the notion of the "front-end box" or the output device through which information is accessed, such as a computer, tablet, or television, which can act as a potential source of perceived agency. This attribution can influence credibility judgements, especially when users conflate the trustworthiness of the device or platform with the reliability of the content.

In the context of digital warfare, agency becomes a critical point of manipulation. Adversarial actors may obscure or falsify the origin of content, leveraging platform familiarity or interface design to create a false sense of legitimacy. For example, misinformation presented through a polished app or a familiar social media feed may be interpreted as more credible simply because of the perceived authority of the delivery mechanism. Understanding how users assign agency and how this affects credibility is essential for decoding the psychological strategies embedded in digital conflict.

Sundar's (2008) exploration of agency highlighted several key heuristics, some of which we have already encountered in previous chapters, that shape how users assign credibility. These heuristics reflect cognitive shortcuts that individuals use to evaluate trustworthiness based on cues about who (or what) is delivering the message.

- *Bandwagon heuristic*: this is one of the effects that we have frequently returned to throughout this book and is an incredibly powerful heuristic process. This heuristic reflects a tendency to equate popularity with credibility. Users are more likely to trust content that appears widely endorsed, such as posts with high engagement metrics or trending topics, regardless of its factual accuracy. In digital warfare, this can be exploited through co-ordinated amplification strategies, where false or manipulative content is made to appear popular to enhance its perceived legitimacy.

- *Authority heuristic*: another heuristic that has featured elsewhere in this text and is one of the most robust credibility cues. Generally, this heuristic is activated when users perceive the source as having expertise or institutional legitimacy. Content attributed to official bodies, experts, or verified accounts is more likely to be trusted. Adversarial actors often mimic authoritative formats or impersonate credible entities to exploit this heuristic.
- *Social presence heuristic*: this heuristic is triggered when users perceive a human-like presence in their digital interaction. Sundar and Nass (2000) demonstrated that users tend to anthropomorphise digital interfaces, meaning that they attribute greater credibility to systems that simulate human traits. For example, automated help for clients or chatbots that appear conversational and responsive can enhance trust, even when no actual human is involved. In digital warfare, this heuristic can be manipulated using AI-generated personas or interactive bots designed to simulate authenticity and build rapport.

Interactivity

Sundar (2008) draws a clear distinction between traditional analogue media and digital interfaces, emphasising the latter's capacity to foster deeper user interaction. This interactivity affordance, or the degree to which users can engage with and influence their digital environment, can play a significant role in shaping credibility judgements. The more interactive the interface, the more the users feel in control of their experience, which in turn enhances the perceived relevance and trustworthiness of the information presented.

Several heuristics are activated through interactivity:

- *Interaction heuristic*: this heuristic suggests that higher levels of user–system interaction led to greater credibility. When users can tailor their experience – by filtering content, navigating freely, or engaging with features – they perceive the information as more aligned with their needs and therefore more trustworthy.
- *Choice heuristic*: the availability of meaningful choices within a digital environment also influences credibility. Users are more likely to trust sources that offer flexible navigation, detailed content, and clear options. Conversely, limited choice or poor information architecture can undermine credibility by creating frustration or ambiguity.

- *Flow heuristic*: derived from Csikszentmihalyi's (1990) concept of flow, this heuristic reflects the importance of seamless, frictionless interaction. When the pace and responsiveness of a system match the user's expectations, it fosters immersion and satisfaction. Interruptions such as lag, poor design, or broken links can serve to disrupt this flow and negatively impact credibility perceptions.

In the context of digital warfare, interactivity becomes a tactical asset. Manipulative actors may design highly engaging interfaces to distract users from critically evaluating content or, conversely, create friction in credible sources to reduce trust. Understanding how interactivity shapes heuristic activation is essential for decoding the psychological mechanisms behind digital influence operations. The other element that comes into play here is the concept of frictionless design, where the capacity to interact with digital platforms and the information provided within them is offered with minimum cognitive effort (Gordon-Tapiero et al., 2023; Jahn et al., 2023). This means individuals are more likely to experience elements of the flow heuristic, in turn bolstering their perceptions of credibility in such environments.

Navigability

Sundar (2008) makes the contrast between the static, linear nature of traditional print media and the dynamic, non-linear structure of digital environments, highlighting navigability as a key affordance that shapes credibility judgements. Unlike analogue formats, digital interfaces allow users to engage in parallel processing, moving fluidly between content areas without the constraints of sequential progression. This mirrors the associative structure of human memory, enabling users to follow intuitive paths through information and reinforcing the perception of coherence and trustworthiness. The credibility of a digital source, therefore, is closely tied to its navigational design, specifically its flexibility, intuitiveness, and support for exploratory behaviour. Sundar identifies two key heuristics linked to navigability:

- *Browsing heuristic*: this heuristic is activated when users are free to explore content without restriction. A site that encourages skimming, link following, and open access fosters a sense of transparency and user empowerment. Conversely, barriers to browsing, such as gated content or limited navigation, may signal bias or concealment, undermining credibility.
- *Scaffolding heuristic*: when users encounter difficulty navigating a site, well-designed structural aids (e.g., site maps, hierarchical menus, and visual landmarks) can guide their experience and restore confidence. These scaffolding elements help users maintain orientation and focus, enhancing their perception of the site's professionalism and reliability.

Sundar's work offered a practical and realistic framework for understanding how individuals assess credibility in digital environments. His identification of four core affordances, modality, agency, interactivity, and navigability, alongside their associated heuristics, reveals that credibility is dynamically shaped by user interaction, heuristics, and interface design. Importantly, these processes differ markedly from those used to evaluate traditional media. In the digital domain, users engage in complex, interactive, and heuristic-driven assessments, reflecting the evolving nature of media consumption in the age of digital warfare. This shift underscores the need to understand credibility not only as a psychological judgement but also as a strategic battleground, where interface design, user traits, and technological affordances converge to influence belief, trust, and susceptibility.

While Sundar's (2008) model offers a nuanced understanding of how technological affordances shape credibility judgements through interface design and user interaction, it is equally important to consider the broader cognitive strategies individuals employ when evaluating digital content. Building on this foundation, Metzger et al. (2010) distilled a set of five core heuristics that reflect the mental shortcuts users rely on when assessing the credibility of online information. These heuristics operate independently of specific interface features and instead capture the generalised evaluative tendencies that emerge across digital contexts. Together, Sundar's affordance-based cues and Metzger's heuristic framework provide a comprehensive lens through which to understand the psychological mechanisms underpinning credibility in the digital age, particularly in environments shaped by strategic manipulation and information warfare.

From Affordances to Heuristics: Expanding the Lens on Credibility Assessment

Sundar's (2008) model provided a foundational understanding of how technological affordances serve to shape the conditions under which users engage with digital content and form credibility judgements. As we noted, these affordances activate specific heuristics that guide perception and evaluation at a mostly subconscious level and are deeply embedded in the design and structure of digital media. However, credibility assessment is not solely a product of interface design. It also involves broader cognitive strategies that users employ across digital contexts, regardless of platform or modality (Hadlington, 2017). Building on this perspective, Metzger et al. (2010) identified a set of five core heuristics that reflect the mental shortcuts individuals use when evaluating the trustworthiness of online information. These heuristics, reputation, endorsement, consistency, expectancy violation, and persuasive intent, offer a complementary framework that captures the psychological mechanisms underpinning credibility judgements in the digital age.

- *The reputation heuristic*: this heuristic reflects a tendency to trust sources based on perceived reputation rather than direct evaluation. In digital warfare, adversarial actors may mimic the branding or visual identity of reputable organisations to exploit this shortcut. Users often transfer credibility from a known entity to its digital representation, assuming legitimacy based on familiarity. This reduces cognitive effort but increases susceptibility to spoofing and impersonation tactics.

- *The endorsement heuristic*: credibility is frequently conferred through perceived consensus. If others endorse a source via reviews, shares, or ratings, users are more likely to trust it. This heuristic is closely tied to information cascades, where early endorsements influence subsequent users, creating a feedback loop that amplifies popularity. In digital warfare, co-ordinated bot networks and manipulated engagement metrics can simulate endorsement, manufacturing credibility through artificial consensus. Such a concept is very closely linked to the bandwagon heuristic.
- *The consistency heuristic*: users often engage in superficial cross-referencing, checking a few sources to confirm information. While this may appear rigorous, it typically involves minimal scrutiny. In adversarial contexts, narrative repetition across multiple platforms can simulate consistency, reinforcing falsehoods through strategic duplication. This heuristic is particularly vulnerable to echo chamber effects, where co-ordinated messaging creates the illusion of widespread agreement.
- *The expectancy violation heuristic*: credibility is influenced by whether a digital source meets user expectations in terms of design, structure, and content quality. Violations such as poor grammar, broken links, or disjointed layouts are interpreted as signs of unreliability. In digital warfare, actors may deliberately design content to appear polished and professional, masking manipulative intent behind a façade of legitimacy. Conversely, credible sources may be undermined through visual disruption tactics that erode trust.
- *The persuasive intent heuristic*: users are sensitive to overt attempts at persuasion, particularly commercial or ideological messaging. When content appears to have an ulterior motive, such as advertising or political bias, it is often judged as less credible. In digital warfare, subtle framing and emotionally charged language can bypass this heuristic, embedding persuasive intent in ways that feel organic or user-driven. Pop-up ads, unsolicited promotions, and aggressive calls to action are common triggers that reduce perceived trustworthiness.

These heuristics, while serving to optimise cognitive efficiency and reduce the potential for the expenditure of precious mental resources, expose users to credibility manipulation in digital warfare contexts. By gaining an understanding of how reputation, endorsement, consistency, expectancy, and persuasive intent shape perception, we can better anticipate how adversarial actors engineer trust and influence. The convergence of interface design (Sundar's affordances) and cognitive shortcuts (Metzger's heuristics) reveals a complex landscape where credibility is not just evaluated; it is actively constructed, contested, and weaponised.

How Do We Identify the Good Bits from the Bad?

Being able to assess the credibility of information online has been seen as one of the most focused on aspects of digital literacy (Leu et al., 2007). Many researchers have discussed the widespread issues when it comes to vast swathes of the population being out of touch with digital literacy, not just those who have limited access or experience of using digital technologies (Hargittai et al., 2010; Hargittai, 2001). Such problems are associated with failures in digital literacy that can in turn lead to a wider spectrum of issues, particularly with things such as missing the telltale signs that a website is fake or hints that information might be fake news and misinformation (Schwarz & Morris, 2011). Some researchers have explored how best to facilitate better credibility judgements in people with the addition of supplementary features as part of the information searching process. Including a capacity to highlight how experts searching for the same information behaved in terms of the results from a search enquiry yielded some improvements in assessing the credibility of the search results. However, such improvements failed to be passed on to a similar credibility assessment of individual websites (Schwarz & Morris, 2011). The authors of this research suggested that such a finding is not a surprise given the nature of webpages, and in line with Fogg's prominence–interpretation model, these environments offer a great deal of competition for information that all crave for attention, so the implementation of subtle cues for highlighting credibility information is lost.

Other researchers have focused on the implementation of media literacy interventions and the resulting contribution to identifying fake news. In a review of the literature in the field, Lu et al. (2024) noted that media literacy significantly improved fake news credibility assessments, with those interventions that used gamified strategies being seen as the most effective. However, a great deal of this work has focused very narrowly on engaging critical judgement skills in young adults and those aged under 18 (Boler et al., 2025). Researchers have subsequently noted that older adults are more likely to share disinformation in comparison to younger age groups, suggesting there is a real gap in information and media literacy (Guess et al., 2019). Boler et al. (2025) noted that many of the techniques they had reviewed were focused on how individuals should deploy critical thinking skills in the context of source information or when locating accurate, reliable sources. Further, they noted that neither of these options offers a comprehensive and effective approach to enhancing the credibility judgements of individuals, given the wide range of information they could encounter.

Boler et al. (2025) noted that interventions to improve credibility judgements for fake news and misinformation fell into several key categories, these being:

- *Course-based interventions*: these are based around a traditional didactic method of disseminating information with some inclusion of practical hands-on exercises, such as exploring examples of fake news.

- *Public-based events*: these included the provision of invited speakers and experts in the field to discuss the importance of being able to spot the telltale signs of misinformation. Participants were allowed to pose questions to the experts, and while the participants expressed an appreciation for having the experts present, there was a limited indication as to how effective such sessions were overall.
- *Web-based interventions*: like the mechanics explored in the work by Schwarz & Morris (2011), these interventions seek to aid web-based literacy through the provision of ad hoc information about the potential for exposure to misinformation (Tully et al., 2022). Tully et al. (2022) noted that individuals who simply noticed these messages failed to exhibit any improvement in their capacity to identify credible information. In view of the work by Schwarz and Morris (2011), this is not surprising, and often such information fails to reach a level of salience that results in deeper processing; therefore, the relevance of such information is lost.
- *Game-based interventions*: some have harnessed the functionality of games to gamify the process of identifying credible information with some mixed results. Games that focus on getting individuals to spot reliable and valid information showed that there was a positive impact on the capacity to critically assess web-based information. However, there was no additional impact on overall scepticism for web-based material, and there was no provision for an objective measure of participants' willingness to believe the information that they had seen (Boler et al., 2025).
- *Visual resources*: Boler et al. (2025) noted that recent efforts to improve credibility judgements have increasingly incorporated visual aids, such as infographics and video-based materials. Domgaard and Park (2021) provided empirical evidence showing that adults who viewed infographics outlining steps to identify fake news were significantly better at spotting such signs compared to those who received only text-based information. Similarly, Lewandowsky & Yesilada (2021) demonstrated that short videos shown to participants prior to exposure to radicalised misinformation reduced both the perceived reliability of the content and the participants' willingness to share it. However, Vraga and colleagues (Vraga & Tully, 2021; Vraga et al., 2021) cautioned that while video presentations can enhance fact-checking behaviours, their effectiveness is limited. They argued that source credibility plays a more substantial role in influencing individuals' willingness to revise their beliefs.

Can We Teach Mindfulness to Help with Credibility Judgements?

This is a very good question, and while a great deal of the research into improving credibility judgements has focused on heuristic processes or adding functionality to aid with such processes, others have focused more on the psychological and emotional elements related to engaging in digital content. As we have noted elsewhere in this text, one of the critical triggers utilised in misinformation is the use of emotion, which can serve to increase the possibility that such material will engage heuristic processing (Boler et al., 2025; Jaeger & Taylor, 2021; Larraz et al., 2024; Serrano-Puche, 2021). Emotionally charged information and narratives are not created accidentally, and they can be easily tailored to an individual through algorithmic biases, heightening the resonance they have with the identity, beliefs, and emotional states of the audience (Boler et al., 2025; Milli et al., 2025). Understanding how emotionally laden data can be gleaned from the internet and used in this way is seen as a critical mechanism for the prevention of individuals being manipulated by rogue credibility judgements, with Boler et al. (2025) noting that to do so, people must:

1. Be able to recognise the presence of emotionally charged information, whether this be in terms of the language being used or the images being presented.
2. Engage in a reflective thinking process to understand how their emotional state could influence their decision-making processes and in turn their interpretation of such information, as well as their willingness to share such material.
3. Understand how identity-focused appeals could serve to increase polarisation and reduce the potential for critical thinking.

Boler et al. (2025) noted that being able to teach individuals how to achieve a state of mindfulness when it comes to making credibility judgements online offered a promising approach. Such strategies can serve to counteract the potential for reactive and impulsive responses that are often symptomatic of emotionally charged misinformation. Researchers have noted that mindfulness-related media training could target key elements related to credibility judgements (Boler, 2019; Currie Sivek, 2018), such as:

1. Click restraint: giving individuals the power to pause their actions before they engage with content or share it more widely.
2. Slow reading: slowing down the processes that govern decision-making and encouraging a deeper-level analysis of information. By doing this, researchers suggest that individuals will be more likely to engage in Type 2 reasoning, removing the potential pitfalls of using more heuristic-based processes.
3. Emotional journaling: using the capacity to write down an individual's emotional response to stimuli that they see so that they can reflect on how it makes them feel and, in turn, be able to deal with it more effectively in the future.
4. Schedule news consumption: setting aside a specific time in the day to avoid any periods where they might be feeling anxious or emotionally charged. Through gaining an understanding of the trigger impact of news, individuals can serve to limit their exposure to such information.

While these strategies offer some attractive approaches to the question of how we enhance the credibility judgements of individuals, transferring them into practical, large-scale initiatives is questionable.

Summary

This chapter examined how credibility has become a contested resource in digital environments, functioning as both a strategic asset and vulnerability in the context of information warfare. It began by tracing the erosion of traditional gatekeeping mechanisms and the rise of disintermediation, which forces individuals to evaluate information independently in an environment saturated with competing cues. This shift amplifies cognitive strain and increases reliance on heuristic shortcuts, creating exploitable weaknesses for adversarial actors.

Three foundational frameworks were introduced to unpack the psychology and mechanics of credibility assessment. Fogg's prominence–interpretation theory explains how users notice and interpret credibility cues based on factors such as involvement, task orientation, and prior experience, highlighting how adversaries manipulate attention and interpretation to embed persuasive content. Metzger et al.'s heuristic model identifies five shortcuts, these being reputation, endorsement, consistency, expectancy violation, and persuasive intent, that streamline judgement but expose users to engineered trust signals like simulated consensus and polished design. Sundar's MAIN model adds a technological dimension, showing how affordances such as modality, agency, interactivity, and navigability activate heuristics that shape perceptions of authenticity and authority. Together, these frameworks reveal credibility as a dynamic construct shaped by cognitive processes and interface design, rather than a fixed property of information.

The chapter also reviewed interventions aimed at strengthening credibility judgements, including media literacy programmes, gamified learning, and visual resources, while noting their limitations, particularly among older adults who remain highly susceptible to misinformation. Emerging approaches such as mindfulness-based strategies were explored as potential tools for counteracting impulsive, emotion-driven responses to manipulative content, though their scalability remains uncertain.

Ultimately, the discussion underscores that credibility in digital spaces is not only about information quality but also about the architecture of trust, a terrain actively weaponised in digital warfare. By mapping the interplay among psychological heuristics, technological affordances, and adversarial tactics, the chapter calls for resilience strategies that address both cognitive and structural vulnerabilities in the information domain.

References

Boler, M. (2019). Digital disinformation and the targeting of affect. *Research in the Teaching of English*, *54*(2), 187–191.

Boler, M., Gharib, H., Kweon, Y. J., Trigiani, A., & Perry, B. (2025). Promoting mis/disinformation literacy among adults: A scoping review of interventions and recommendations. *Communication Research*, 1–33. https://doi.org/10.1177/00936502251318630

Burbules, N. C. (2001). Paradoxes of the web: The ethical dimensions of credibility. *Library Trends*, *49*(3), 441–453.

Csikszentmihalyi, M. (1990). Flow: The psychology of optimal performance. In *Optimal experience: Psychological studies of flow in consciousness*. New York: Cambridge University Press.

Currie Sivek, S. (2018). Both facts and feelings: Emotion and news literacy. *Journal of Media Literacy Education*, *10*(2), 123–138. https://doi.org/10.23860/jmle-2018-10-2-7

Domgaard, S., & Park, M. (2021). Combating misinformation: The effects of infographics in verifying false vaccine news. *Health Education Journal*, *80*(8), 974–986. https://doi.org/10.1177/00178969211038750

Eysenbach, G. (2007). From intermediation to disintermediation and apomediation: New models for consumers to access and assess the credibility of health information in the age of Web2.0. *Studies in Health Technology and Informatics*, *129*(1), 162.

Flanagin, A. J., & Metzger, M. J. (2000). Perceptions of Internet information credibility. *Journalism & Mass Communication Quarterly*, *77*(3), 515–540. Retrieved from http://jmq.sagepub.com/content/77/3/515.short

Flanagin, A. J., & Metzger, M. J. (2007). The role of site features, user attributes, and information verification behaviors on the perceived credibility of web-based information. *New Media & Society*, *9*(2), 319–342. https://doi.org/10.1177/1461444807075015

Fogg, B. J. (2003). Prominence-interpretation theory: Explaining how people assess credibility online. *CHI'03 Extended Abstracts on Human Factors in Computing Systems*, 722–723. Retrieved from http://dl.acm.org/citation.cfm?id=765951

Fogg, B. J., Marshall, J., Kameda, T., Solomon, J., Rangnekar, A., Boyd, J., & Brown, B. (2001). Web credibility research: A method for online experiments and early study results. *CHI '01 Extended Abstracts on Human Factors in Computing Systems*, 295–296. https://doi.org/10.1145/634067.634242

Fogg, B. J., Soohoo, C., Danielson, D. R., Marable, L., Stanford, J., & Tauber, E. R. (2003). How do users evaluate the credibility of web sites? *Proceedings of the 2003 Conference on Designing for User Experiences*, 1–15. https://doi.org/10.1145/997078.997097

Gordon-Tapiero, A., Ohm, P., & Ramaswami, A. (2023). Fact and friction: A case study in the fight against false news. *UC Davis Law Review*, *57*, 171–251.

Guess, A., Nagler, J., & Tucker, J. (2019). Less than you think: Prevalence and predictors of fake news dissemination on Facebook. *Asian-Australasian Journal of Animal Sciences*, *32*(2), 1–8. https://doi.org/10.1126/sciadv.aau4586

Hadlington, L. (2017). *Cybercognition: Brain, behaviour and the digital world*. London: Sage.

Hargittai, E. (2001). Second-level digital divide: Differences in people's online skills. *First Monday*, *7*(4), v7i4.942.

Hargittai, E., Fullerton, L., Menchen-Trevino, E., & Thomas, K. (2010). Trust online: Young adults' evaluation of web content. *International Journal of Communication*, *4*, 468–494. Retrieved from http://megafotos.ru/-NZaWpvYy5vcmc.ZN-ojs/index.php/ijoc/article/viewPDFInterstitial/636/423

Hilligoss, B., & Rieh, S. Y. (2008). Developing a unifying framework of credibility assessment: Construct, heuristics, and interaction in context. *Information Processing & Management*, *44*(4), 1467–1484. https://doi.org/10.1016/j.ipm.2007.10.001

Horrigan, J., & Rainie, L. (2006). The internet's growing role in life's major moments. *Pew Internet & American Life Project*, (April), 1–11.

Jaeger, P. T., & Taylor, N. G. (2021). Paul T. Jaeger and Natalie Greene Taylor. *Library Quarterly: Information, Community, Policy*, *91*(1), 19–31.

Jahn, L., Rendsvig, R. K., Flammini, A., Menczer, F., & Hendricks, V. F. (2023). *Friction interventions to curb the spread of misinformation on social media*, 1–17. Retrieved from http://arxiv.org/abs/2307.11498

Larraz, I., Salaverría, R., & Serrano-Puche, J. (2024). Combating repeated lies: The impact of fact-checking on persistent falsehoods by politicians. *Media and Communication*, *12*, 1–17. https://doi.org/10.17645/mac.8642

Leu, D. J., Zawilinski, L., Castek, J., Banerjee, M., Housand, B., Liu, Y., & O'Neil, M. (2007). What is new about the new literacies of online reading comprehension. *Secondary School Literacy: What Research Reveals for Classroom Practices*, 37–68. Retrieved from http://www.newliteracies.uconn.edu/pub_files/What_is_new_about_new_literacies_of_online_reading.pdf

Lewandowsky, S., & Yesilada, M. (2021). Inoculating against the spread of Islamophobic and radical-Islamist disinformation. *Cognitive Research: Principles and Implications*, *6*. https://doi.org/10.1186/s41235-021-00323-z

Lu, C., Hu, B., Bao, M. M., Wang, C., Bi, C., & Ju, X. D. (2024). Can media literacy intervention improve fake news credibility assessment? A meta-analysis. *Cyberpsychology, Behavior, and Social Networking*, *27*(4), 240–252. https://doi.org/10.1089/cyber.2023.0324

McKnight, D. H., & Kacmar, C. J. (2007). Factors and effects of information credibility. *Proceedings of the Ninth International Conference on Electronic Commerce*, 423–432. https://doi.org/10.1145/1282100.1282180

Metzger, M. J. (2007). Making sense of credibility on the web: Models for evaluating online information and recommendations for future research. *Journal of the American Society for Information . . .*, *58*(13), 2078–2091. https://doi.org/10.1002/asi

Metzger, M. J., & Flanagin, A. J. (2013). Credibility and trust of information in online environments: The use of cognitive heuristics. *Journal of Pragmatics*, *59*, 210–220. https://doi.org/10.1016/j.pragma.2013.07.012

Metzger, M. J., Flanagin, A. J., & Medders, R. B. (2010). Social and heuristic approaches to credibility evaluation online. *Journal of Communication*, *60*(3), 413–439. https://doi.org/10.1111/j.1460-2466.2010.01488.x

Milli, S., Carroll, M., Wang, Y., Pandey, S., Zhao, S., & Dragan, A. D. (2025). Engagement, user satisfaction, and the amplification of divisive content on social media. *PNAS Nexus*, *4*. https://doi.org/10.1093/pnasnexus/pgaf062

Petty, R. E., & Cacioppo, J. T. (1986). The elaboration likelihood model of persuasion. *Advances in Experimental Social Psychology*, *19*, 123–192.

Schwarz, J., & Morris, M. (2011). Augmenting web pages and search results to help people find trustworthy information online. *Proceedings of the Annual SIGCHI Conference . . . .* Retrieved from http://www.notjulie.com/research/web_credibility/paper.pdf

Serrano-Puche, J. (2021). Digital disinformation and emotions: Exploring the social risks of affective polarization. *International Review of Sociology*, *31*(2), 231–245. https://doi.org/10.1080/03906701.2021.1947953

Suler, J. (2002). Identity management in cyberspace. *Journal of Applied Psychoanalytic Studies*, *4*(4), 455–459. https://doi.org/10.1023/A

Suler, J. (2005). The basic psychological features of the cyberspace. In *The psychology of cyberspace*. Retrieved from http://truecenterpublishing.com/psycyber/basicfeat.html

Sundar, S. S. (2008). The MAIN model: A heuristic approach to understanding technology effects on credibility. *Digital Media, Youth, and Credibility*, 73–100. https://doi.org/10.1162/dmal.9780262562324.073

Sundar, S. S., & Nass, C. (2000). Source orientation in human-computer interaction. *Communication Research*, *27*(6), 683–703.

Tully, M., Madrid-Morales, D., Wasserman, H., Gondwe, G., & Ireri, K. (2022). Who is responsible for stopping the spread of misinformation? Examining audience perceptions of responsibilities and responses in six sub-saharan African countries. *Digital Journalism*, *10*(5), 679–697. https://doi.org/10.1080/21670811.2021.1965491

Vraga, E. K., & Tully, M. (2021). News literacy, social media behaviors, and skepticism toward information on social media. *Information Communication and Society*, *24*(2), 150–166. https://doi.org/10.1080/1369118X.2019.1637445

Vraga, E. K., Tully, M., Maksl, A., Craft, S., & Ashley, S. (2021). Theorizing news literacy behaviors. *Communication Theory*, *31*(1), 1–21. https://doi.org/10.1093/ct/qtaa005

11 Fake News and Information Warfare

Introduction

We introduced the concept of fake news back in Chapter 3 when we began to explore the landscape of misinformation. In this chapter, we begin a deep dive into the area, exploring the key concepts and constructs that have been associated with this construct. There have been numerous attempts to define what constitutes fake news. For example, Allcott and Gentzkow (2017) described the concept as "a news article that is intentionally and verifiably false," and Golbeck et al. (2018) suggested that it related to "information presented as a news story that is factually incorrect and designed to deceive the consumer into believing it is true." However, other researchers have noted that such definitions are narrowly focused and are restrictive in that they focus on one or two forms of information and are also not entirely clear about the intent that sits behind the deception. For instance, Sharma et al. (2019) noted that some fake news stories are created for non-malicious purposes, something that is often omitted in definitions related to the topic. Sharma et al. (2019) suggested a more user-friendly, ubiquitous working definition for fake news as "a news article or message published and propagated through media, carrying false information regardless the means and motives behind it" (p. 111:4). This definition allows the capacity for different forms of fake news to be classified and differentiated according to the way in which the information is conveyed, as well as the motive that sits behind its creation.

In the following section, we start to explore the typology for fake news that has been presented, and as we will see, the unidimensional view of "fake news" is often an oversimplification of the area.

The Typology of Fake News

The term "fake news" is often used to describe a wide variety of mechanisms that can be used to convey false information. Fake news can be presented in numerous different ways, each of which has a distinct set of characteristics as well as subtle differences in terms of the intent and motive behind its creation (Tandoc

DOI: 10.4324/9781003752400-11

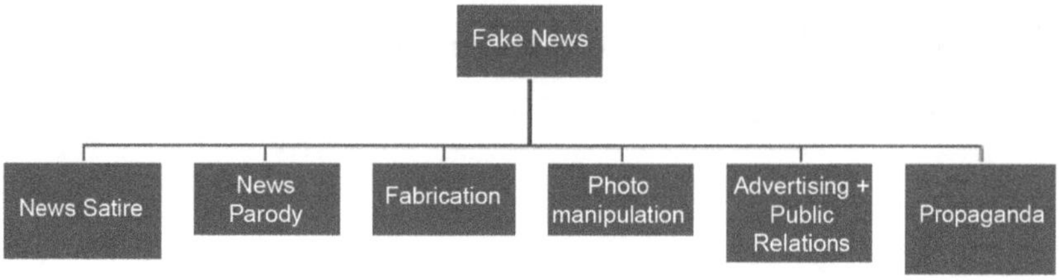

Figure 11.1 The typology of fake news.

Source: (Adapted from Tandoc et al., 2018)

et al., 2018). Tandoc et al. (2018) presented a detailed review of the ways in which different types of fake news can be classified, with the key components of this framework being presented in Figure 11.1.

News Satire

News satire is one of the most popular forms of fake news in the realms of entertainment, and the format will usually include the presentation in the form of a mock news programme that focuses on topics from current affairs (Tandoc et al., 2018). The point of this type of presentation mechanism for fake news is usually to exaggerate the key features of the current events that are the focus of the programme to the point where elements become absurd or ridiculous, in turn generating the humorous element. These programmes will emulate the appearance of more traditional and official news stories with the use of talking head presenters, flashy graphical presentations, and mock interviews with the public and slick presentation. The key difference between the "actual" news and fake news delivered through satire is the clear focus on entertainment, rather than any real mechanism for the dissemination of information. Such an aim is usually an implicit part of the creation and delivery of such news satire programmes, with the clear assumption that audiences are aware that the content included in such programmes is intended for entertainment only. However, there is always a chance that a small group of individuals may believe the information presented in such programmes to be a true reflection of current affairs, so the potential for the proliferation of misinformation is always a possibility. The professional way in which satire programmes can be presented, and the mimicry involved in the creation of backdrops and details surrounding the news stories, can be very realistic; hence, it is no surprise some people often mistake such programmes for the "real" news. Key examples of such news satire programmes include Brass Eye, which aired on Channel Four in the 1990s, The Daily Show, Last Week Tonight, and Saturday Night Live. One notable example of where fake news satire was mistaken for a real thing is *The Cake Hoax*, from a 1997 episode of Brass Eye.

The programme, created by Chris Morris, introduced a completely fictional drug called "Cake," which had originated in Prague, and while some of the actual effects of the drug were very weakly specified, one of the stories detailed an incident where one addicted "cried all of the water out of his body." There were also other side effects attached to it, including water retention on the neck because of one of the dyes used in the production process. However, even though the claims that we attached to the existence of this new drug were completely over the top, they led to several celebrities and even an MP endorsing an anti-cake campaign. The potential for digital warfare here should be clear – with the right staging and with the right level of emotiveness, authority, and urgency attached to it – people can be easily manipulated into spreading misinformation, even if it has been intended for entertainment purposes.

News Parody

News parody shares a core similarity with news satire, which is the creation of the material for the purposes of entertainment and humour. However, the key difference lies in the fact that news parody focuses on the creation of completely fictional information that has a very limited connection to current affairs. Instead of providing any real direct commentary on current topical issues, news parody takes things to an extreme and over-emphasises the extreme ends of the fake news spectrum. One element that news parody plays upon is the very remote possibility that the focus for the stories portrayed as real could be real, rather than being completely fictitious. This is one of the inherent problems with news parody, where the danger comes from the possibility that individuals may mistake information contained within it as a real news story. In one such example, a fake news story appeared on *The Onion,* a satirical news outlet, claiming that the leader of North Korea, Kim Jong Un, has been named the sexiest man alive. While the rhetoric contained within the article was clearly aimed at parody, the story was later picked up by North Korea's official communist newspaper, *The People's Daily*, which in turn printed a 55-page special edition to celebrate this notable achievement.

News Fabrication

This category of fake news is characterised by the complete absence of factual content. The material is entirely fabricated and designed to mimic the appearance and stylistic conventions of legitimate news reporting. Unlike satirical or entertainment-based fake news, news fabrication does not signal its fictitious nature, there are no implicit cues to suggest that the information is false or humorous. Instead, its objective lies at the opposite end of the fake news spectrum: to deceive, mislead, or manipulate. By adopting the visual and rhetorical markers of mainstream journalism, fabricated news seeks to exploit the credibility associated with traditional media formats. As Tandoc et al. (2018) note, this form of fake news often overlaps with the broader domain of misinformation, particularly when its dissemination is not accompanied by a clear intent to harm but nonetheless contributes to the distortion of public understanding.

One of the ways in which news fabrication can generate so much interest and can pass off as real news stories is the use of professional-looking websites and the presentation of material as though they are real news stories. Information seekers, when they are searching for information online, will rely on a variety of heuristic processes to identify material that is reliable. Researchers have noted that individuals use several such heuristic processes in a drive to establish the credibility of information (Flanagin & Metzger, 2000; Metzger et al., 2010), something that we explored in the previous chapter (see Chapter 10).

Photo Manipulation

In today's modern digital environment, the adage that an image can speak 1000 words is more salient than ever. Individuals will often pay more attention to visual elements accompanying a story than to the text itself (Wang et al., 2021). Researchers have noted that images can play a central role in driving the perception of issues (Zillman et al., 1999) or choosing which of the articles to read in more depth (Zillman et al., 2001). The term "fauxtography" (Wang et al., 2021) has often been used to describe the use of images that are manipulated or misappropriated to change the originally intended meaning or purpose, often with the proliferation of misinformation at the heart of such an action. Wang et al. (2021) noted that social media posts containing elements of fauxtography were more likely to have a higher level of engagement from users, as measured through the number of likes, number of reshares, and number of comments. Images that are created for fauxtography will also be used further in memes, therefore proliferating this information further and potentially feeding into the memetic battleground.

There are a wide variety of ways in which photo manipulation can take place, and according to Thomson et al. (2020), these can take the following forms:

- Saturation or desaturation: this process could involve the lightening or darkening of certain aspects of an image, such as darkening the appearance of someone's skin, perhaps to tap into current tensions related to racial tension or immigration issues.
- Artificial blurring: the blurring of certain words or parts of an image is used to disguise distinguishing features that could give away the actual real identity of the image in question or could serve to hide other information such as dates, uniforms, or other insignia.
- Copying, moving, or splicing images: this method is often employed in the creation of composite images, where elements from multiple different contexts are combined to create one specific image. Such a process presents an

image that never actually occurred, but such images can be highly emotive in nature and tap into current feelings around contemporary issues.

- Retouching or airbrushing: removing imperfections in images to present an ideal, such as the removal of blemishes on the skin or removing wrinkles from the face. Such retouching could be used in the context of propaganda, where images of leaders are retouched to make them look more virile and younger than they are.
- Misattribution: the use of material from other news stories in another context, with the direct intention to misattribute the origin of the image, usually with the intent to spread misinformation.
- Cropping: like artificial blurring, this process serves to remove aspects of the image that could serve as a direct link back to the original events from which the current image has been taken, or to show an image from another perspective/angle to show a different view.

Advertising and Public Relations

This is generally a mechanic that is used to get something sold, often a product or service. They are often encapsulated in video releases, prepackaged and ready to go, and produced by public relations media firms. Often, such presentations will give the impression of journalism or someone who has journalistic rigour presenting claims about the product in question, usually with an emphasis on the product and less on the rigour. The emulation of the "real news" report style in many forms of presentation can trigger inherent biases in individuals and tap into our existing metrics for credibility such as authority. One of the staples for advertising and public engagement is the much-maligned "infomercial," usually seen as a combination of information transmission about the product and an overhyped, energetic presentation about the same (Johnson, 2017). While not always the case, such presentations can present outlandish claims for the performance of the product and will often draw in the use of "real" users to give their honest feedback about their experiences with the product in question. These types of presentations can also be used to extend the reach of propaganda, with information being presented to individuals in the form of contextually relevant programmes that portray a well-researched, well-constructed argument that relies heavily on material that is historically incorrect or biased.

So, What Is Fake News?

So there appear to be differences in these classifications for fake news, and it would also seem that there is no clear way of isolating the common elements. However, Tandoc et al. (2018) suggested that the common element all these categories share is that they portray false information in a way that uses both the look and feel of real news. In doing so, the information gains credibility by appearing to be real news, which in turn increases its overall legitimacy. Tandoc et al. (2018) went on to argue that fake news has two underlying dimensions on which it can be viewed:

1. Facticity: this is the extent to which the fake news relies on real facts or relates to current affairs. For example, news satire relies on information, but the format in which they are presented can divert the reality of such facts towards more humorous content.
2. Intention: this is the degree to which the information presented in fake news is intended to mislead the audience and relates to the motives the creator of such information has for creating that information. With news satire and news parody, there is a degree of mutual understanding that this is the case; however, with fabricated or manipulated information, such as photo manipulations, there is a direct intent to deceive with no aspect of mutual understanding.

Going forward, this is how we will position fake news and set it aside from disinformation, which we will focus on later in Chapter 12. In the next section of this chapter, I want to change the focus away from *what* fake news is and concentrate more directly on the *who* and the *how* of how individuals fall foul of the charms offered by this type of misinformation. Predominantly, this is more focused on fake news that is produced for more nefarious purposes rather than the more satirical types we have reviewed above.

The Role of the Individual in Fake News

There has been a wide variety of work exploring the role of the individual and how they can serve to enhance the spread of fake news, particularly because of the rise of the spread of misinformation through such pathways. Allcott and Gentzkow (2017) suggested that the average U.S. adult may have viewed and remembered the details of one fake news story during the 2016 U.S. election. The actual capacity for individuals to distinguish fake news from real news has been the subject of much discussion in the research literature, with some ambivalent results. For example, Sharma et al. (2019) noted that individuals find it really challenging to identify fake news from real news and noted that only 4% of U.K. participants were able to identify real news stories from fake ones. However, others have noted that there is very little evidence to support a difference between the detection of fake news and real news. Some researchers have noted that the capacity for individuals to detect fake news from real news is only just above the threshold of detecting them by random choice (Bryanov & Vziatysheva, 2021; Moravec et al., 2019). However, in a review of studies that explored the capacity for individuals to detect fake news, Bryanov and Vziatysheva (2021) suggested that an individual's capacity to detect fake news from real news was better than if they were reliant on just random choices. This is partially good news from a misinformation warfare perspective, but there are many other factors which can serve to influence how susceptible an individual can be to believing and proliferating fake news.

Susceptibility to Fake News

I thought it might prove useful to explore some of the research that has been conducted into understanding why some individuals are more vulnerable to fake news. Much of this research is also applicable to the concept of misinformation, which we will examine in more depth later in Chapter 12, so rather than repeat the same information twice, we will cover most of the material here. In terms of the key areas into which susceptibility can be categorised, researchers have noted that there are typically three broad factors that serve to drive it, these being the situational (elements that are associated with the way in which the news message is presented or features of the environment where exposure to fake news occurs), trait- or psychological-based individual differences, and cognitive factors linked to the use of heuristic processing (Bryanov & Vziatysheva, 2021; Sindermann et al., 2020). We will delve further into each of these in more detail now:

Cognitive Influences

People who are more reflective are less likely to believe in false news content and are generally better at identifying information that is fake, irrespective of how it fits into their current ideological beliefs (Pennycook & Rand, 2021; Sindermann et al., 2020). When individuals are deciding on whether to believe fake news, both motivational and cognitive elements come into play (Piksa et al., 2022). This can include the capacity to decide whether something is fake or true, which is mostly reliant on the more protracted analytical reasoning process that is occupied by Type 2 decision-making. It has been noted that those individuals who engage in more purposeful thinking, such as deliberating the facticity of information, are those who are less likely to fall foul of fake news (Bago et al., 2020; Krysińska et al., 2021; Pennycook & Rand, 2021). This process is inherently linked back to the functioning of Type 1, heuristic-based processing, where individuals spend less time exploring the information they have been presented and fall into the trap of going down the more gut-based decision.

Horne and Adali's (2017) work noted that heuristics are most often used more widely by individuals who persist in believing fake news. They suggested that fake news is subjected to the more intuitive Type 1 processing route, allowing the reader to employ simple heuristic processes to establish the facticity of the information they are reading. A heavy reliance on the contextual elements of fake news to establish if it is true, such as the headline, would suggest that individuals are not engaging in fuller, deeper processing of the information they are presented with, but instead choose to take surface information as an indication of truthfulness.

Many of the heuristic processes that can be linked to an individual's susceptibility to fake news have been discussed previously, so a repetition of these would perhaps be rather self-indulgent. However, as a quick recap, the following heuristics and associated biases can be seen to have a direct impact on susceptibility to fake news:

Availability heuristic → Illusory truth effect

- Repeated exposure increases perceived truth due to familiarity and cognitive ease.

Representativeness heuristic → Prototype/format familiarity bias

- Judging credibility based on similarity to what we expect "real news" to look like, such as layout, tone, and stylistic elements.

Affect heuristic → Negativity bias

- Strong emotional content that focuses on the negative such as fear, anger, and outrage can serve to override analytical thinking.

Confirmation heuristic → Confirmation bias

- Anything that feeds into our pre-existing beliefs is more likely to be accepted as being true.

Authority heuristic → Authority bias

- Trusting claims endorsed by perceived experts or official-looking sources.

Social proof heuristic → Bandwagon effect

- Popularity signals truthfulness, and high engagement reduces scepticism.

To focus on one aspect of fake news consumption, let us take confirmation bias. Confirmation bias has been typically viewed as the commitment of the individual to their own perspective and knowledge over the presence of other information (Zhou & Shen, 2022). Individuals may pay more attention to information that directly relates to prior beliefs and experiences and will also process information that is consistent with their beliefs in a more detailed and efficient manner (Zhou & Shen, 2022). In their study that explored the impact of confirmation bias on misinformation related to climate change, Zhou and Shen (2022) noted that individuals judged messages that were consistent with their current views as being more credible versus information deemed to be inconsistent with their current ideology. Alongside this, information that is directly relevant to their current attitudes was perceived as being more factually accurate, and individuals were more likely to have greater levels of empathy for these messages (Zhou & Shen, 2022). This can have a powerful effect on the acceptance of fake news stories, where individuals are more likely to align with misinformation that can be aligned with their current beliefs and attitudes. This is particularly relevant in the context of politically charged information, such as that which might float around online during elections. Grinberg et al. (2019), in their exploration of fake news during the 2016 presidential election, noted that individuals were more likely to share information that was congruent with their current beliefs and political alignment, choosing to engage in more critical evaluation of incongruent information and therefore sharing this less. Other researchers have noted that there is a strong link between brain activity and the assessment of fake news. Moravec et al. (2019) noted that confirmation bias was a strong determinant of an individual's capacity to detect fake news. Social media users were more likely to engage in greater levels of processing with information that aligned with their current political beliefs and in turn were more likely to see it as true. Even when visual information was presented to participants indicating that the information they were seeing was fake, confirmation bias served to override this, and they were more likely to believe that the information was true.

Ross and Ward (1995) noted that another concept, that of naive realism, serves as a core cognitive bias where individuals make the erroneous assumption that they are seeing the world objectively and that they are creating their views based on a direct, unfiltered access to reality. Due to this, they assume that anyone who takes an opposing view to them or sees things in a different way is irrational, does not have the correct information, or is biased themselves. In this way, the presence of naive realism is not linked to the misinterpretation of existing information, but to the fact that individuals consistently under-estimate the role interpretation has altogether. So they fail to recognise that their own perceptions can be shaped by prior beliefs and knowledge, which can have other detrimental effects. For example, they may assume an overconfidence in their own beliefs and perspectives on a topic and in turn will be quick to dismiss opposing beliefs as being flawed themselves. They will also be resistant to accepting new information that serves to contradict their own beliefs, in turn sowing the seeds for the creation of new filter bubbles.

The implications for fake news susceptibility are significant. For example, the false consensus effect is a cognitive bias that leads individuals to overestimate the extent to which others share their beliefs and attitudes (Ross & Ward, 1995). Individuals will assume that the beliefs they have are more commonly shared than they are. In turn, as they assume that everyone agrees with this belief, this belief must be true. This perceived consensus creates a powerful validation loop: if "everyone agrees," the information must be true. In practice, naïve realism makes corrective interventions less effective because individuals dismiss fact-checks as biased while continuing to propagate misinformation within echo chambers. Thus, naïve realism does not merely coexist with confirmation bias; it amplifies it, creating fertile ground for fake news to spread unchecked.

Personality and Susceptibility

Piksa et al. (2022) presented a detailed exploration of four distinct categories along which individuals can be positioned in terms of their overall susceptibility to fake news. Much of this work aligns individuals with individual personality traits, such as the Big Five we explored back in Chapter 5. These four types are

1. The doubter: individuals in this category tend to have higher levels of anxiety and lower emotional stability. They also exhibit lower optimism, which often leads them to disengage from news consumption. Doubters are typically less narcissistic and more concerned with the views and opinions of others rather than pursuing personal goals.
2. The knower: this group is characterised by a sense of confidence in their knowledge. They are more anxious than the next category (the duffer) but lean towards optimism when faced with uncertainty or ambiguous cues. Knowers also tend to be less agreeable, which may make them more critical of the information they encounter.
3. The duffer: these are generally seen as being less anxious than the knowers but have a higher level of pessimism when it comes to interpreting information that is ambiguous. They are also more agreeable, so they are less likely to question the information that they see in news articles and information online.
4. The consumer: a combination of high levels of motivation, high levels of narcissism and a vastly inflated sense of self, they offer the perfect storm in terms of susceptibility to fake news. They are probably overconfident in their self-diagnosed capacity to spot misinformation, are more optimistic, and are generally unconcerned by the feedback they receive from others (Piksa et al., 2022).

In terms of what these classifications mean, Piksa et al. (2022) noted two dimensions: one between the consumer and the doubter, reflecting overall susceptibility to information, with consumers being highly influenced by the material they view, and another dimension relating to susceptibility to fake information, where knowers are highly resilient, while duffers are more likely to fall victim to misinformation.

Other researchers have suggested that there is a link between susceptibility to fake news and our motivations. For example, the concept of motivated social cognition (Kruglanski, 1996) proposes that individuals are motivated to accept or reject fake news based on how closely it aligns with their existing beliefs (Faragó et al., 2020). This means people do not simply evaluate information for accuracy; they interpret and accept information that supports their goals, such as protecting self-esteem or affirming identity. Rejecting such information would create cognitive dissonance. This is why confirmation bias and naïve realism (see Chapter 6) are powerful information-processing biases. People often perceive fake news as credible if it supports their ideological stance or group identity, even when contradictory evidence exists.

Research by Von Hippel et al. (2005) illustrates this principle. They found that participants rated tasks they performed well on more positively than tasks they performed poorly on, a classic example of motivated reasoning, where information is processed to maintain a positive self-image. Those who exhibited this pattern were also more likely to cheat on a maths test, but only when they could rationalise the cheating with a plausible justification. This behaviour served to protect their self-concept while supporting self-interest. These findings reveal a link between biased evaluation and motivated reasoning, suggesting that such processes do not occur in isolation. Subtle individual differences in socially motivated cognition may help explain why susceptibility to fake news varies across people.

Other researchers have focused more directly on the personality traits that can be used to differentiate between believers and non-believers in fake news. Peter et al. (2024) used a simple verification task where participants had to choose between fake and real news headlines. They found that individuals who engaged in more risk-taking behaviours online, such as freely disclosing personal information, interacting with strangers, and exhibiting low suspicion towards others, were generally less able to discern real from fake headlines. Furthermore, these individuals tended to score lower on conscientiousness, openness, and honesty, making them more likely to believe fake news. The Dark Triad traits (Machiavellianism, narcissism, and psychopathy) also emerged as strong predictors of susceptibility, with higher scores correlating with greater vulnerability to fake news.

Context and Situational Factors

Some of this content links back to the heuristic processes people use when they are trying to establish the credibility of information online (see Chapter 10). For example, the underlying premise we have presented here is that audiences are fooled into believing the veracity of fake news because it emulates the look and feel of real news. However, researchers have questioned this, with Horne and Adali (2017) presenting a detailed comparison of both real and fake news stories. They noted there were significant differences between the overall content of fake and real news stories, where real news stories were longer. On the other hand, the fake news stories they reviewed included fewer technical words and higher levels of verbosity, as well as requiring a lower education level to process. Taken objectively, it is clear that there are some key quantitative and qualitative differences between fake and real news stories, both in terms of the overall complexity of the composition as well as the way in which it is presented (Horne & Adali, 2017). Furthermore, the researchers noted that the most influential factor when determining fake from real news stories was the headline itself. They noted that fake news stories were often longer, and as with the content of the fake news stories, they were often less complex and contained fewer technical words. In turn, fake news headlines included more random capitalisation of words. The authors of this research suggested that such a finding is perhaps symptomatic of fake news creators attempting to force as much information into the headlines as possible (Horne & Adali, 2017).

Normative influence theory is another concept that is linked to the sharing and acceptance of misinformation and relates to the social environment in which the individual is sharing that information. The premise of this theory is that individuals witnessing the behaviour of others will have a significant impact on their own behaviour (Nolan et al., 2008). Research has noted that normative influence can have a significant impact on the ways in which people can act and include people agreeing with information that they know not to be true or failing to respond to a threat (Nolan et al., 2008). We have already introduced the core pillars of normative influence back in Chapter 8 when we explored its role in shaping the way in which influence and persuasion can work on an individual. However, for now, we assume that individuals are more likely to engage in behaviours that are aligned with what they believe their referent social group would approve of (injunctive norms) and what they view as being typically done (descriptive norms). While this theory extends outside elements related to the sharing and belief in misinformation, there is a very clear link to the use of normative influence here.

Social media can play a central and amplifying role in the relationship between normative influence and cyberwarfare, particularly in the spread and acceptance of misinformation. Firstly, social media is inherently designed around aspects of visibility and engagement; we are visible to everyone, and we are free to engage with our friends and wider social groups. They provide a fertile ground for descriptive norms to be applied, especially where the core beliefs and ideals of that group are evident in comments and posts. Where misinformation is present, likes, shares, and group comments can encourage individuals to believe that information is true and therefore perpetuate the idea that such material is approved of by the wider community. It is not hard to see how the creation of fake profiles and fake likes and comments can create a receptive environment for normative influence to take hold, creating the basis for an echo chamber. Normative influence can also explain why users may actively avoid the tendency to challenge misinformation, as they may fear themselves being the target for trolling, ridicule, or exclusion from their online community, instead favouring a position of passive agreement (Gimpel et al., 2021).

On the Creation of Echo Chambers and Filter Bubbles

In cyberspace, there is a great deal of choice in terms of the type of media that individuals can choose from to access a wide variety of information (Dubois & Blank, 2018). While this diverse information diet could allow individuals to garner a wide range of perspectives on a particular topic, there is also the danger that they may become overloaded with information and instead contrast their views on things that align with their current beliefs. Some have noted that the actual reality of echo chambers is overstated and that individuals are more capable of consuming a wide variety of media even if it does contradict their current perspective (Dubois & Blank, 2018).

Researchers have theorised that there are ways in which other processes linked to the consequences of naive realism, confirmation bias, and normative influence can help to create the ideal situation for echo chambers and filter bubbles to emerge (Garimella et al., 2017). While the two terms are often used interchangeably, there are subtle differences between the concepts that deserve to be highlighted. In the first instance, an echo chamber is defined as "a bounded, enclosed media space that has the potential to both magnify the messages delivered within it and insulate them from rebuttal" (Jamieson & Cappella, 2008, p. 76). Here, the basic operating principle is the reflection of information from the individual to the environment in which they are, and vice versa, and the individual in question has some relevant control over the creation of such (Arguedas et al., 2022). A key process in the formation of echo chambers is a concept termed "homophily." It has been noted that individuals were more likely to create social bonds with people who shared similar values or status to themselves (Currarini et al., 2016; Currarini & Mengel, 2016). They identified two forms of homophily, these being status homophily, which is based on socio-demographic dimensions that serve to stratify society, such as race, education, or age. On the other hand, value homophily is linked to the extent to which we share beliefs, values, and attitudes with others, with individuals being more likely to form social bonds with individuals who share such ideas. In the age of the internet, it has been noted that status homophily tends to be less relevant when individuals are forming social bonds online – the main reason is that the actual indicators of status are harder to disseminate in cyberspace. Online status can easily be manipulated and amplified using the internet, and many times people will hide their real identity and status or serve to inflate it for personal and social gain (Bisgin et al., 2010b, 2010a).

Homophily in online social networks can have some interesting repercussions that may not be that obvious. For example, researchers have noted that individuals who search for news on social media and then engage in discussions about that news with politically homogeneous groups increase their level of political anger (Cheng et al., 2024). Using social media as a news source and political anger were directly linked to political homophily on social media; individuals who had low levels of social media political homophily were shown to be less likely to exhibit political anger (Cheng et al., 2024). It is easy to see how such methods could be used for offensive campaigns in the context of cyberwarfare. All you really need to do is seed social media with a good amount of politically charged news information and then present an arena for like-minded individuals to congregate on social media to discuss such information. By adding in some trolling by relevant state actors to stir the pot a little bit more, you can easily evoke feelings of anger that can spill over into other people who sit outside of the echo chamber.

Pariser (2011) noted that a filter bubble takes the form of a personalised information ecosystem, which is often created using algorithmic curation. This in turn limits an individual's exposure to perspectives that might go contrary to their previous or current ideological approach, meaning that this information is filtered out. The main concern that was raised by Pariser (2011) is that such a situation is created without the person in question knowing it is happening, and often recommender systems engage in the use of algorithms that many individuals have limited detailed knowledge of. Part of this process links to the concept of algorithmic personalisation, a method of systematically filtering out information and attitudes that go contrary to our own ideas. Pariser (2011) suggested that this was like an "invisible auto-propaganda indoctrinating us with our own ideas" (p. 15). It should be noted that such algorithmic processes do not have to be seen as a negative aspect of information searching online. Researchers have noted that such mechanisms can be tailored to suit the needs of the environment in which they are used and can be used to expose individuals to information that cuts across their current ideology (Evans et al., 2023). However, in their research, Evans et al. (2023) noted that there was little evidence to support the notion of algorithmic personalisation and found that users in the United Kingdom were exposed to a wide variety of different sides of the political story.

The Echo Chamber in Practice: A Case Study of the "Microchip in Vaccines" Fake News Narrative

During the global rollout of COVID-19 vaccines, a widely circulated fake news narrative alleged that vaccines contained microchips designed for governmental surveillance. The rumours appeared to be linked to an interview with Bill Gates, who mentioned the possibility of having "some digital certificates" that could be used to identify people who had recovered from the virus after being vaccinated. The website Biohackinfo.com shared the news article headline "Bill Gates will use microchip implants to fight coronavirus," in which they claimed Gates was going to use the vaccination programme to deploy millions of microchips that could be used to monitor people, and it was presented in a way that emulated mainstream news stories (Ball & Maxmen, 2020). Soon after, Roger Stone, a prominent advisor to Donald Trump, was interviewed on a radio show, with the interview being picked up by The New York Post. In the interview, Stone expressed the view that he would never accept a vaccine that had been created by Gates, with the hint that the microchip idea was a reality. The New York Post story did little to dispel the notion as fake news, and it was soon across social media platforms and became entrenched within certain online communities. The persistence and amplification of this narrative can be understood through a convergence of psychological and sociotechnical mechanisms.

The communities in which such misinformation took hold were filled with individuals who often exhibited *naive realism* and believed that their perceptions of reality were inherently objective and that those who disagreed were either uninformed or deliberately misled. This cognitive stance fostered a dismissive attitude towards scientific rebuttals and institutional messaging, reinforcing the perceived legitimacy of the fake news. Users actively sought to find information that aligned with their pre-existing mistrust of government organisations and big pharmaceutical companies, both often targets for conspiracy theories posited to suggest some form of cohesive relationship that exists between the two, often seeking to control the population. The further action of *confirmation bias* meant that individuals actively disregarded any evidence that served to contradict their current perspective. This in turn further cemented their position and contributed to a resistance to other narratives.

Echo chambers were soon created in which normative influence took hold; individuals maintained that there was indeed a clear attempt by the government and a "ruling elite" to engage in large-scale tracking of individuals using microchips implanted through the vaccination programme. Within these echo chambers, anyone questioning the theory or offering a dissenting voice was shut down quickly by other members, usually with hostility or outright exclusion; this process served to deter people from making critical judgements about the theory while serving to reinforce the overall group consensus – the government and big pharma were in league to control their minds.

Obviously, the echo chamber is characterised by the presence of social homophily, where like-minded individuals share a mistrust of the government and big corporations, as well as being open to the presence of conspiracy theories that present the notion that the public is being lied to. Such homophily created a perfect breeding ground for the microchip theory, as well as other similar bizarre theories, with individuals establishing a level of trust with the community, meaning that they were not afraid to share their ideas and beliefs. Adding into the mix an element of algorithmic personalisation in searching for information and being presented with details on social media, material is curated for the individual based on their past interactions, serving to reinforce their existing beliefs. This creates a feedback loop in terms of only presenting an individual with ideologically consistent information, in turn creating a filter bubble.

Fake News and Digital Warfare

I wanted to round off this chapter by bringing the focus back to the current discussion related to digital warfare. We can see that fake news is not only a by-product of the digital age, but it can also be used as a potent instrument in the arsenal of digital warfare. Its power lies in its ability to exploit both technological affordances and human cognitive vulnerabilities. Drawing from the typologies and mechanisms discussed throughout this chapter, we can conceptualise fake news as a multifaceted tool that operates across several strategic dimensions:

1. Mimicry and legitimacy

Fake news gains traction by mimicking the aesthetic and rhetorical style of legitimate journalism. Whether through satire, parody, or outright fabrication, it leverages the credibility of traditional media formats to deceive or entertain. This mimicry is central to its effectiveness in warfare contexts, where the goal is often to sow confusion, erode trust, or manipulate public sentiment.

2. Psychological exploitation
   Cognitive biases such as naïve realism, confirmation bias, and normative influence are not incidental occurrences but are the very mechanisms that fake news exploits. These biases create fertile ground for misinformation to take root, especially when individuals are unaware of their own interpretive filters. In warfare, this means that populations can be subtly nudged towards ideological polarisation, mistrust of institutions, or even civil unrest.
3. Sociotechnical amplification
   Social media platforms act as accelerants in the spread of fake news. Echo chambers and filter bubbles, which are driven by homophily and algorithmic personalisation, help to ensure that misinformation is not only disseminated rapidly but also reinforced through repeated exposure and social validation. This creates a self-sustaining ecosystem where false narratives can thrive unchecked.
4. Strategic deployment
   Fake news can be weaponised in both offensive and defensive cyber operations. Offensively, it can be used to destabilise political systems, influence elections, or incite social division. Defensively, it can be used to obscure truth, deflect criticism, or delegitimise opposition. The case study of the "microchip in vaccines" narrative illustrates how a single falsehood, strategically seeded and amplified, can evolve into a widespread belief with real-world consequences.
5. Emotional resonance and virality
   The emotional charge of fake news, whether it be fear, anger, or moral outrage, enhances its virality. This emotional resonance is often more influential than factual accuracy, making fake news a powerful tool for shaping public discourse and behaviour in times of conflict or crisis.

Summary

In this chapter, we explored fake news as a strategic instrument in digital warfare, examining its typologies, psychological underpinnings, and sociotechnical amplification. Beginning with definitional debates, the discussion highlighted the limitations of narrow interpretations that focus solely on intent or factuality, advocating instead for a multidimensional view incorporating both motive and format. Tandoc et al.'s typology was introduced to classify fake news into categories such as satire, parody, fabrication, photo manipulation, and advertising-based content, each exploiting the aesthetic and rhetorical markers of legitimate journalism to enhance perceived credibility.

The chapter then shifted to the cognitive and psychological mechanisms that make individuals vulnerable to fake news. Susceptibility was framed across three domains: situational factors, cognitive influences, and personality traits. Cognitive biases such as confirmation bias, naïve realism, and the illusory truth effect were shown to play a pivotal role, alongside heuristic shortcuts like authority, social proof, and affect-based judgements. These processes were linked to Type 1 intuitive reasoning, which prioritises speed and emotional resonance over analytical scrutiny, creating fertile ground for misinformation uptake. Personality-based classifications, including Piksa et al.'s four susceptibility profiles (doubter, knower, duffer, and consumer), were discussed alongside traits such as low conscientiousness, risk-taking, and Dark Triad characteristics, which correlate strongly with vulnerability.

Beyond individual cognition, the chapter examined sociotechnical dynamics that amplify fake news. Normative influence theory was applied to explain how social approval signals and descriptive norms drive sharing behaviour, particularly within algorithmically curated environments. Echo chambers and filter bubbles were analysed as reinforcing structures, shaped by homophily and personalisation, which insulate users from corrective information and magnify ideological polarisation. A case study of the "microchip in vaccines" narrative illustrated how these mechanisms converge, using emotional framing, confirmation bias, and algorithmic curation combined to transform a fringe conspiracy into a mainstream belief within certain online communities.

Finally, the chapter positioned fake news within the broader context of digital warfare, identifying its strategic dimensions: mimicry and legitimacy, psychological exploitation, sociotechnical amplification, and emotional resonance. Fake news operates not as incidental misinformation but as a deliberate weapon capable of destabilising political systems, eroding institutional trust, and inciting social division. By leveraging cognitive vulnerabilities and technological affordances, adversarial actors can seed narratives that achieve virality and persistence, even in the face of factual rebuttal. The discussion underscores that combating fake news requires interventions that address both the psychological biases and structural conditions that enable its spread, situating resilience strategies at the intersection of cognition, technology, and social influence.

References

Allcott, H., & Gentzkow, M. (2017). Social media and fake news in the 2016 election. *Journal of Economic Perspectives*, *31*(2), 211–236. https://doi.org/10.1257/jep.31.2.211

Arguedas, A. R., Robertson, C. T., Fletcher, R., & Nielsen, R. K. (2022). Echo chambers, filter bubbles, and polarisation: A literature review | Reuters institute for the study of journalism. *University of Oxford*, 3–42. https://doi.org/10.60625/risj-etxj-7k60

Bago, B., Rand, D., & Pennycook, G. (2020). Fake news, fast and slow: Deliberation reduces belief in false (but not true) news headlines. *Journal of Experimental Psychology: General, 129*(8), 1–18.
Ball, P., & Maxmen, A. (2020). Battle the infodemic. *Nature, 581*(1), 371–374.
Bisgin, H., Agarwal, N., & Xu, X. (2010a). Does similarity breed connection? An investigation in blogcatalog and last.fm communities. *Proceedings – SocialCom 2010: 2nd IEEE International Conference on Social Computing, PASSAT 2010: 2nd IEEE International Conference on Privacy, Security, Risk and Trust*, 570–575. https://doi.org/10.1109/SocialCom.2010.90
Bisgin, H., Agarwal, N., & Xu, X. (2010b). Investigating homophily in online social networks. *Proceedings – 2010 IEEE/WIC/ACM International Conference on Web Intelligence, WI 2010, 1*, 533–536. https://doi.org/10.1109/WI-IAT.2010.61
Bryanov, K., & Vziatysheva, V. (2021). Determinants of individuals' belief in fake news: A scoping review determinants of belief in fake news. *PLoS One, 16*(6 June), 1–25. https://doi.org/10.1371/journal.pone.0253717
Cheng, Z., Marcos-Marne, H., & Gil de Zúñiga, H. (2024). Birds of a feather get angrier together: Social media news use and social media political homophily as antecedents of political anger. *Political Behavior, 46*(2), 1171–1187. https://doi.org/10.1007/s11109-023-09864-z
Currarini, S., Matheson, J., & Vega-Redondo, F. (2016). A simple model of homophily in social networks. *European Economic Review, 90*, 18–39. https://doi.org/10.1016/j.euroecorev.2016.03.011
Currarini, S., & Mengel, F. (2016). Identity, homophily and in-group bias. *European Economic Review, 90*, 40–55. https://doi.org/10.1016/j.euroecorev.2016.02.015
Dubois, E., & Blank, G. (2018). The echo chamber is overstated: The moderating effect of political interest and diverse media. *Information Communication and Society, 21*(5), 729–745. https://doi.org/10.1080/1369118X.2018.1428656
Evans, R., Jackson, D., & Murphy, J. (2023). Google news and machine gatekeepers: Algorithmic personalisation and news diversity in online news search. *Digital Journalism, 11*(9), 1682–1700. https://doi.org/10.1080/21670811.2022.2055596
Faragó, L., Kende, A., & Krekó, P. (2020). We only believe in news that we doctored ourselves. *Social Psychology, 51*(2), 77–90. https://doi.org/10.1027/1864-9335/a000391
Flanagin, A., & Metzger, M. (2000). Perceptions of Internet information credibility. *Journalism & Mass Communication Quarterly, 77*(3), 515–540. Retrieved from http://jmq.sagepub.com/content/77/3/515.short
Garimella, K., Gionis, A., Parotsidis, N., & Tatti, N. (2017). Balancing information exposure in social networks. *Advances in Neural Information Processing Systems*, December(Nips), 4664–4672.
Gimpel, H., Heger, S., Olenberger, C., & Utz, L. (2021). The effectiveness of social norms in fighting fake news on social media. *Journal of Management Information Systems, 38*(1), 196–221. https://doi.org/10.1080/07421222.2021.1870389
Golbeck, J., Mauriello, M., Auxier, B., Bhanushali, K. H., Bonk, C., Amine, M., . . . Everett, J. B. (2018). Fake news vs satire: A dataset and analysis. *In Proceedings Ofthe 10th ACM Conference on Web Science*, 17–21.
Grinberg, N., Joseph, K., Friedland, L., Swire-Thompson, B., & Lazer, D. (2019). Political science: Fake news on Twitter during the 2016 U.S. presidential election. *Science, 363*(6425), 374–378. https://doi.org/10.1126/science.aau2706
Horne, B., & Adali, S. (2017). This just in: Fake news packs a lot in title, uses simpler, repetitive content in text body, more similar to satire than real news. *Proceedings of the International AAAI Conference on Web and Social Media, 11*(1), 759–766. https://doi.org/10.1609/icwsm.v11i1.14976

Jamieson, K. H., & Cappella, J. N. (2008). *Echo chamber: Rush Limbaugh and the conservative media establishment*. Oxford UK: Oxford University Press.

Johnson, R. (2017). The appeal of the infomercial. *Political Economy of Communication, 5*(1), 51–76.

Kruglanski, A. W. (1996). Motivated social cognition: Principles of the interface. In E. T. Higgins & A. W. Kruglanski (Eds.), *Social psychology: Handbook of basic principles* (pp. 493–520). The Guilford Press.

Krysińska, I., Wójtowicz, T., Olejniuk, A., Morzy, M., & Piasecki, J. (2021). Be careful who you follow: The impact of the initial set of friends on COVID-19 vaccine tweets. *OASIS 2021 – Proceedings of the 2021 Workshop on Open Challenges in Online Social Networks*, 1–8. https://doi.org/10.1145/3472720.3483619

Metzger, M. J., Flanagin, A. J., & Medders, R. B. (2010). Social and heuristic approaches to credibility evaluation online. *Journal of Communication, 60*(3), 413–439. https://doi.org/10.1111/j.1460-2466.2010.01488.x

Moravec, P. L., Minas, R. K., & Dennis, A. R. (2019). Fake news on social media: People believe what they want to believe when it makes no sense at all. *MIS Quarterly: Management Information Systems, 43*(4), 1343–1360. https://doi.org/10.25300/MISQ/2019/15505

Nolan, J. M., Schultz, P. W., Cialdini, R. B., Goldstein, N. J., & Griskevicius, V. (2008). Normative social influence is underdetected. *Personality and Social Psychology Bulletin, 34*(7), 913–923. https://doi.org/10.1177/0146167208316691

Pariser, E. (2011). *The filter bubble: What the internet is hiding from you (kindle-edition)*. Retrieved from http://www.amazon.de/dp/1594203008

Pennycook, G., & Rand, D. G. (2021). The psychology of fake news. *Trends in Cognitive Sciences, 25*(5), 388–402. https://doi.org/10.1016/j.tics.2021.02.007

Peter, E. L., Kwantes, P. J., D'Agata, M. T., & Vallikanthan, J. (2024). The role of personality traits and online behavior in belief in fake news. *Humanities and Social Sciences Communications, 11*(1), 1–10. https://doi.org/10.1057/s41599-024-03573-6

Piksa, M., Noworyta, K., Piasecki, J., Gwiazdzinski, P., Gundersen, A. B., Kunst, J., & Rygula, R. (2022). Cognitive processes and personality traits underlying four phenotypes of susceptibility to (mis)information. *Frontiers in Psychiatry, 13*(June), 1–16. https://doi.org/10.3389/fpsyt.2022.912397

Ross, L., & Ward, A. (1995). Naive realism in everyday life: Implications for social conflict and misunderstanding. In E. S. Reed, E. Turiel, & T. Brown (Eds.), *Values and knowledge* (pp. 103–135). Mahwah, NJ: Lawrence Erlbaum Associates.

Sharma, K., Qian, F., Jiang, H., Ruchansky, N., Zhang, M., & Liu, Y. (2019). Combating fake news: A survey on identification and mitigation techniques. *ArXiv, 37*(4).

Sindermann, C., Cooper, A., & Montag, C. (2020). A short review on susceptibility to falling for fake political news. *Current Opinion in Psychology, 36*, 44–48. https://doi.org/10.1016/j.copsyc.2020.03.014

Tandoc, E. C., Lim, Z. W., & Ling, R. (2018). Defining "fake news": A typology of scholarly definitions. *Digital Journalism, 6*(2), 137–153. https://doi.org/10.1080/21670811.2017.1360143

Thomson, T. J., Angus, D., Dootson, P., Hurcombe, E., & Smith, A. (2020). Visual mis/disinformation in journalism and public communications: Current verification practices, challenges, and future opportunities. *Journalism Practice, 0*(0), 1–25. https://doi.org/10.1080/17512786.2020.1832139

Von Hippel, W., Lakin, J. L., & Shakarchi, R. J. (2005). Individual differences in motivated social cognition: The case of self-serving information processing. *Personality and Social Psychology Bulletin, 31*(10), 1347–1357. https://doi.org/10.1177/0146167205274899

Wang, Y., Tahmasbi, F., Blackburn, J., Bradlyn, B., De Cristofaro, E., Magerman, D., . . . Stringhini, G. (2021). Understanding the use of fauxtography on social media. *Proceedings of the International AAAI Conference on Web and Social Media*, *15*, 776–786. https://doi.org/10.1609/icwsm.v15i1.18102

Zhou, Y., & Shen, L. (2022). Confirmation bias and the persistence of misinformation on climate change. *Communication Research*, *49*(4), 500–523. https://doi.org/10.1177/00936502211028049

Zillmann, D., Gibson, R., & Sargent, S. L. (1999). Effects of photographs in news-magazine reports on issue perception. *Media Psychology*, *1*(3), 207–228.

Zillmann, D., Knobloch, S., & Yu, H. S. (2001). Effects of photographs on the selective reading of news reports. *Media Psychology*, *3*(4), 301–324.

12 Disinformation and Information Warfare

Introduction

In this chapter, we delve into one of the most pervasive and consequential aspects of digital warfare: disinformation. Disinformation is treated as a distinct sub-entity of misinformation but has distinct features that differentiate it from other aspects in the category, not only in terms of content but also in intent and strategic deployment. The spread of belief in misinformation is typified by an error in judgement, often the result of cognitive shortcuts or lack of verification. Disinformation is the deliberate creation and dissemination of manipulated information designed to deceive, sow dissent, deepen divisions, and destabilise societies (Zhou & Shen, 2022, 2024). While misinformation may arise organically, disinformation is engineered, often drawing upon misinformation as raw material to be weaponised. For example, a viral fake news story may begin as misinformation but be co-opted and amplified by actors with malicious intent, transforming it into a tool of disinformation.

As discussed in Chapter 3, not all misinformation is disinformation; some content may lack a direct link to intentional manipulation and instead reflect broader issues of media literacy, cognitive bias, and information overload. Disinformation campaigns are rarely the product of a single tactic. Instead, they employ a sophisticated blend of psychological strategies, including emotional manipulation, repetition, and the exploitation of cognitive biases, to maximise reach and impact. These tactics are often deployed in combination, amplifying their effectiveness and making them harder to counter. Moreover, individual differences such as age, education, political orientation, and cognitive style play a significant role in determining susceptibility.

The Strategic Aims of Disinformation

The content and presentation methods for digital disinformation vary broadly according to the platform on which they are deployed and the topic matter they relate to. However, despite this diversity of content and context, the mechanisms and objectives

DOI: 10.4324/9781003752400-12

of disinformation campaigns are remarkably consistent. Building off the research that has been conducted in the area (Filatova & Bolgov, 2018; Unver & Arhan, 2023), the strategic aims of disinformation appear to align with four key themes:

1. Destabilisation
   Disinformation is frequently used to undermine trust in institutions, erode social cohesion, and create uncertainty. By spreading conflicting narratives or amplifying crises (real or fabricated), adversaries can weaken the perceived legitimacy of governments, electoral processes, or public health responses. For example, during elections, disinformation may target the integrity of voting systems to reduce public confidence and increase apathy or unrest.
2. Division
   A core aim of disinformation is to deepen existing social, political, or cultural divides. Campaigns often exploit contentious issues such as immigration, race, or public health to polarise communities and pit groups against each other. To achieve this, there may be a process where extreme viewpoints are amplified through the creation of echo chambers or the deliberate targeting of vulnerable or marginalised groups.
3. Deception
   At its heart, disinformation is all about deception: presenting falsehoods as facts, fabricating evidence, or impersonating trusted sources. Modern campaigns may use deepfakes, forged documents, or fake expert networks to lend credibility to false narratives. The goal is to confuse audiences, obscure the truth, and make it difficult to distinguish reality from fiction. Whaley (1982) noted that deception can involve a process of hiding real information from the end user while presenting information that is false. So not all the strategies that are involved in disinformation campaigns are aligned with the presentation of misleading information but are designed to mask the truth (Arce, 2024). This can create an asymmetry in the information landscape where the individual(s) who have created the disinformation know what is true and what is false, but the target does not (Arce, 2024). Such a position of power means that the creator of the disinformation can control the dominant narrative for as long as the audience receiving that information is unable to establish the facticity of the material they are seeing.
4. Influence operations and geopolitical manipulation
   Disinformation is a powerful tool for influence operations, enabling state and non-state actors to shape public opinion, manipulate policy debates, and achieve strategic geopolitical objectives. These operations may be long term, seeking to shift the ideological landscape of a target society, or short term, aiming to influence specific events such as referenda or international crises.

The most widely accepted purpose of disinformation in both domestic and international politics is to distract, confuse, and demobilise adversaries. Its effects often persist long after the content has been exposed as false or discredited (Gelfert, 2018; Unver & Arhan, 2023). Disinformation's strategic value is closely tied to timing. It is most effective in the short term, particularly when there is insufficient time to formulate and disseminate counter-narratives. In time-sensitive contexts, such as elections, crises, or emergencies, the absence of reliable information creates fertile ground for disinformation to spread rapidly and influence public perception before factual corrections can take hold. For longer-term campaigns, disinformation must be refreshed and repackaged to maintain relevance. This involves retaining the overarching narrative while subtly altering the content to make it appear new and attention-worthy. Such tactics ensure continued engagement and prevent audiences from dismissing the information as outdated or irrelevant.

The Mechanics of Disinformation

Arce (2024) presented an overview of the mechanisms that can be used to present disinformation, each of which is dependent on the extent to which the source of such information is identifiable.

Lying

Is it seen as a clear example of disinformation from a recognised source? In 2027, reports emerged on social media that Syrian fighter jets had dropped nerve gas agents on the small town of Khan Sheikhoun in north-west Syria using the hashtag *#SyrianGasAttack*. Soon after, Russian and Syrian state actors responded quickly by flooding social media with an alternative hashtag, *#SyrianHoax* (Arce, 2024). Such an action presented a clearly co-ordinated attempt to instil doubt in the original reports while also attempting to neutralise international outrage at the event. Such a process highlighted how disinformation can be deployed quickly and easily to counteract potentially damaging narratives as well as control the flow of information (Arce, 2024).

Leaks

These present a unique challenge and opportunity within the broader landscape of disinformation. Unlike fabricated content, leaks typically involve the release of truthful information from a known or traceable source, often through whistleblowing or doxing. Arce (2024) highlights this process as unusual in the field of disinformation, precisely because it can produce asymmetric impacts: damaging the credibility of the source while simultaneously empowering the target audience. When disinformation is exposed, especially when the information is verified, the source of the false information may suffer credibility erosion. This is particularly acute when the debunking is conducted by an authoritative or official body. Once a source is publicly discredited, its future communications are likely to be met with scepticism, and its influence may diminish. This erosion of trust is a central concern in digital warfare, where source credibility is a key vector of influence.

Conversely, the target audience of disinformation may experience a positive shift when leaks reveal hidden truths. This can manifest in several ways:

- Empowerment through transparency: access to previously concealed information can foster a sense of agency and awareness.
- Increased group cohesion: when disinformation targets specific communities, the exposure of manipulation can galvanise solidarity and reinforce shared identity.
- Legitimisation of grievances: leaked information may validate concerns that were previously dismissed or marginalised, strengthening the perceived legitimacy of a cause.

In the case of leaks, attribution plays a critical role. Whether the source is a whistle-blower (e.g., Chelsea Manning, Edward Snowden, or Julian Assange) or an anonymous actor, the ability to trace the origin of the information allows for independent verification. This process enhances the authenticity and impact of the leaked material. Attribution also enables audiences to distinguish between truthful leaks and fabricated lies, which is essential in an environment saturated with manipulated content. For disinformation, attribution serves a different but equally important function. Identifying the origin of false information can help debunk it, but only if the source is exposed and publicly discredited. Arce (2024) noted that from the perspective of an adversary, revealing the source of disinformation can be strategically beneficial. It not only undermines the spread of the lie but also disrupts its effectiveness, especially when the source is perceived as untrustworthy.

Such a dynamic serves to highlight a broader principle in digital warfare: the power of attribution and verification. Leaks, when authenticated, can reshape narratives and empower audiences. Lies, when traced and exposed, can be neutralised. In both cases, the ability to identify and evaluate the source is central to managing the impact of information, whether true or false.

Seeding

This is another process that involves the deliberate movement of true information to a particular target, either through covert or more strategic pathways (Arce, 2024). This can be used to bolster the perception of credibility for a source, which in turn can be later harnessed to spread more information that is factually incorrect. The process can also be used as a method of distraction, diverting attention away from other, more important but less salient topics, as well as serving to manipulate public opinion. This could be observed in instances where a double agent produces some legitimate information to garner the trust of their target organisation, only to then pass on false information once this relationship has been established (Arce, 2024). Often, in the case of leaks, the originator of the information is revealed so that the material can be traced back to the original source, allowing for both trustworthiness and credibility to be established. This process contrasts with that of lies, where credibility is either manufactured as part of the disinformation process or hidden.

Revealing the identity of the originator is an integral part of the seeding process, as it preconditions the target audience to accept subsequent information from that source. This familiarity reduces the likelihood that individuals will critically evaluate the factual accuracy of the content. As a result, they become susceptible to the halo effect, a cognitive bias whereby the positive impression of an individual, source, or entity influences perceptions of their future actions. Coombs and Holladay (2006) noted that the halo effect can emerge during a crisis, where a favourable reputation prior to the event influences perceptions of credibility. They suggested that this effect acts as a shield, protecting the source from scrutiny and making people more likely to accept subsequent information at face value. In the context of disinformation, this means individuals are more inclined to trust content from a source they previously perceived as credible without engaging in critical evaluation, in turn overlooking potential errors or the presence of falsehoods. Confirmation bias may also play a role: if new information aligns with what the individual has already received from that source, they are even more likely to believe it. Additionally, this dynamic can serve as a distraction from more pressing issues, diverting attention towards trivial yet salient content that appears true (Arce, 2024).

Such a process is seen as a critical mechanism in Russian disinformation campaigns, often referred to using the term "Kompromat" (a shortened form of *Komprometiruyushchy*, meaning "compromising"). This is the practice of creating a dossier of damaging material that is either collected or falsified and then later released to target specific individuals of interest (e.g., government officials, business figures, and prominent public figures) in a direct attempt to discredit, blackmail, or manipulate them. Kompromat was a tactic widely used during the fall of the Soviet Union, where Stalin held a wide selection of information on his senior officials; this material ranged from information about their sexual activities, ethnicity, and unspent criminal convictions (Choy, 2020; Hübert & Little, 2022). Other examples include the creation of a *dossier cell* by the prime minister of Pakistan (two terms from 1971 to 1973 and 1973 to 1977), Zulfikar Ali Bhutto, which was established to act as a repository for the serious crimes and misdeeds of Pakistan's ruling elite (Choy, 2020; Darden, 2008). These more traditional mechanisms of collecting compromising information have now been afforded a new capacity and freedom with the rapid expansion of digital technology. Compromising information can now be farmed through emails, social media platforms, leaked documentation, or the use of technology to falsify media, which in turn can be disseminated through state-controlled actors and networks to shape public opinion on targeted individuals.

Cyber Smearing

One final tactic reviewed by Arce (2024) involves the deliberate spread of disinformation by concealed or anonymous sources. The primary aim is to damage reputations, manipulate public opinion, or divert attention from more pressing issues. These campaigns often rely on fabricated content such as deepfakes, fake quotes, or spoofed news articles, with the origin of the information obscured to avoid accountability. Cyber smearing is typically targeted towards ideologically aligned echo chambers, where the false information is more likely to be accepted and shared. This tactic is seen to exploit confirmation bias, reinforcing pre-existing beliefs and polarising discourse. As Hammond-Errey (2019) noted, smear campaigns rarely contain verifiable facts; their purpose is not to inform but to influence, whether it be the dominant narrative, public sentiment, or media focus. Strategically, these campaigns aim to discredit prominent individuals or organisations, especially those who challenge the views of the smear campaign's originators. They can also be used to sow doubt, confusion, and distrust in institutions, experts, and democratic processes (Arce, 2024). A further advantage is their ability to distract public attention from significant developments, such as the release of controversial government reports or decisions on divisive issues.

These processes connect with psychological phenomena discussed earlier in this book. For instance, the primacy–recency effect plays a crucial role in disinformation: the initial narrative, even if later disproven, can often have a lasting impact on perception and memory. This cognitive bias helps explain why false information can continue to shape beliefs long after it has been debunked (Unver & Arhan, 2023). In the short term, disinformation can erode trust, delay decision-making, and create confusion, particularly in fast-moving situations. Although digital disinformation tends to have a shorter effective lifespan due to the speed at which it can be discredited, it also benefits from a broader and faster reach compared to traditional methods of dissemination (Unver & Arhan, 2023).

Maskirovka

As a term and a concept, "maskirovka" is not new but has now evolved to be adopted by new methods and mechanisms in the context of the digital battlefield. The term is closely aligned to Russian military doctrine and includes the use of deception, decoys, concealment, and disinformation with the aim of reaping the strategic benefits of such (Bagge, 2019). Maskirovka is not only one tactic or construct but also involves the use of multiple different principles and methods that all form an integral part of the web of control and contradictions (Han, 2015; Stoica, 2020; Zehndorfer, 2022). These mechanics can include but are not limited to

1. Concealment and camouflage: while this may have more concrete references to traditional, kinetic warfare where troop movements might be hidden or key military assets are disguised, it can also be linked to activities in the digital warfare context. For example, any process that serves to hide an adversary's true intent or their current capabilities or movements can all be conducted in cyberspace with the main aims being to misdirect and misinform. This could include the use of proxies or virtual private networks (VPNs) to mask the origins of information or the use of false flag operations (claiming that an adversary is planning/has committed an offence to give legitimacy to later offensive actions).
2. Denial and deception: this refers to the active suppression or distortion of reality, often through the presentation of alternative narratives. It is a hallmark of maskirovka and has been prominently used by Russian officials during the Ukraine conflict. Key features include denying factual events (e.g., troop presence and civilian casualties), projecting blame onto opposing actors, and creating confusion through contradictory statements or staged evidence. The goal is to undermine trust, delay international response, and control the narrative, often by flooding the information space with conflicting accounts.
3. Disinformation (or dezinformatsiya) is the deliberate dissemination of information that is false and misleading and is seen as a core component of the maskirovka tradition. It is usually carefully created to manipulate public perceptions of current events, to influence decision-making, or to destabilise societal cohesion.
4. Reflexive control: reflexive control refers to the strategic manipulation of an adversary's decision-making process by shaping the information environment in such a way that the adversary makes choices that are predictable, favourable, or self-defeating, often without realising they are being manipulated (Zehndorfer, 2022). This is achieved through the deliberate use of perceptual cues, emotional triggers, and cognitive biases that influence how information is interpreted and acted upon. At its core, reflexive control exploits the mental models and expectations of the target. By feeding them misleading or selectively framed information, the originator can guide the adversary towards decisions that appear rational from their perspective but are engineered outcomes. Cognitive biases can be seen to be at work here, with anchoring bias using the initial information that has been presented to set the tone for all other judgements that might come afterward; confirmation bias means that the targets are more likely to be open to accepting manipulated information if it aligns with their current beliefs, and the framing effect means that decisions are being made not about the factual accuracy of information but about the way in which it is presented.

The use of maskirovka is not something that has been relegated to cold-war-era tactics, and current Russian military operations are replete with examples where these tactics have been used to great effect. The Russian annexation of Crimea in 2014 serves to stand as one of the clearest and most audacious uses of these tactics in modern times, and it served to blur the lines between direct military action and the use of digital warfare tactics, with deception, denial, and disinformation all being critical components of the campaign.

In February 2014, reports began to circulate on the internet and were later corroborated by mainstream news outlets (e.g., https://www.bbc.co.uk/news/) regarding the sudden appearance of unidentified military personnel on the streets of Crimea. These individuals wore unmarked green uniforms, lacked any official insignia, and did not display affiliation with any recognised military force. Their ambiguous appearance led to widespread references on social media to "Little Green Men," a term that quickly gained traction to describe these covert operatives. Despite their anonymity, the personnel were equipped with Russian military hardware and operated in accordance with Russian tactical doctrine, suggesting a high level of co-ordination and strategic intent.

The deliberate use of non-attributable forces introduced significant ambiguity into the operational environment. This ambiguity not only confused the local population but also disrupted the situational awareness of Ukrainian military leadership and complicated the international community's response. The inability to definitively attribute the actions of these operatives to a specific state actor delayed both diplomatic and defensive measures. This form of deception exemplifies a calculated strategy of plausible deniability, designed to exploit informational uncertainty and hinder timely decision-making (Hofirek, 2021; Tünde & Marian, 2014).

During this period, Russian officials orchestrated a deliberate campaign of denial and disinformation aimed at obscuring both the identity and strategic objectives of the unidentified armed personnel operating in Crimea. Russian state media, along with pro-Kremlin commentators, either ignored the presence of these operatives entirely or propagated alternative narratives. These included claims that the individuals were local volunteers acting independently to safeguard the population, thereby distancing the Russian state from direct involvement. Simultaneously, social media platforms were inundated with conflicting narratives, many of which were intentionally crafted to sow confusion and hinder attribution. This information environment, saturated with disinformation, served to paralyse decision-making processes by presenting a multitude of plausible yet contradictory explanations. The strategic deployment of such narratives effectively delayed both domestic and international responses to the incursion.

From an information operations perspective, Russian disinformation efforts during the annexation of Crimea extended well beyond official government statements. Much of the messaging echoed narratives disseminated through Russian state-controlled media, but social media platforms quickly became a central battleground for influence. Pro-Russian narratives were systematically amplified by a network of sympathetic bloggers, commentators, and co-ordinated online actors, creating an echo chamber that reinforced Kremlin-aligned perspectives.

Conversely, pro-Ukrainian narratives and those reflecting Western interpretations of the conflict were frequently ridiculed, discredited, or drowned out through co-ordinated information saturation. This asymmetry in narrative dominance contributed to a distorted information environment that favoured Russian strategic objectives. Additionally, numerous "false flag" stories emerged such as fabricated accounts of attacks on ethnic Russian communities in Crimea, which were strategically deployed to justify Russian military intervention under the guise of humanitarian protection. These disinformation tactics exemplify the use of narrative manipulation and PsyOPs to shape perceptions, manufacture consent, and obscure attribution in hybrid conflict scenarios.

The cumulative effect of Russia's disinformation campaign during the annexation of Crimea was a fragmented and delayed response to the presence of armed forces on the peninsula. This strategic ambiguity enabled Russian forces to consolidate control without engaging in overt military confrontation, thereby achieving key objectives through manipulation of the information environment rather than conventional warfare. The operation exemplifies the concept of maskirovka as a multifaceted doctrine of military deception, which in this case involved not only physical concealment (e.g., unmarked uniforms) but also the orchestration of narrative dominance across digital platforms. Rather than just being a singular tactic, maskirovka in the instance of the annexation of Crimea represents a broader strategic mindset, encompassing deception, denial, and psychological manipulation. The success of the campaign continues to be debated among military analysts, yet it is widely acknowledged that Russia managed to execute the annexation with minimal kinetic engagement, catching both Ukraine and the international community off guard. The ambiguity surrounding the identity and intentions of the so-called Little Green Men significantly delayed defensive and diplomatic responses. By the time Russian authorities formally acknowledged their involvement, Crimea was already firmly under Russian control.

This control was further legitimised through the dissemination of additional disinformation that framed the intervention that acted to protect ethnic Russian populations from alleged aggression. The operation has a clear link to digital warfare, where the control over dominant narratives, particularly on social media, played a central role in the campaign. While some physical elements of maskirovka were evident in the use of anonymous military personnel, the concurrent manipulation of the information domain was equally critical and allowed the Russian authorities the capacity to misdirect attention and blame away from themselves. Online disinformation not only served to sow doubt and confusion about the current presence of those little green men but also helped to provide a pretext for military action, reinforcing short-term strategic goals and shaping international perceptions in Russia's favour.

Psychological Tactics in Disinformation Campaigns

There are a variety of mechanics that are employed in the context of disinformation campaigns, many of which are based on methods of persuasion, the over-reliance on heuristics and engineering situations so that the deployment of cognitive biases is more likely. It would be very easy at this point to suggest that all disinformation campaigns are created equally and that most of the tactics suggested here are employed in a textbook way across domains. However, it is worth noting that research has demonstrated this is not the case, and the use of such tactics can be employed differently across different disinformation types. For example, Leite et al. (2025) noted that in four different disinformation domains (Islamic issues, COVID-19, climate change, and the Russian–Ukrainian conflict), there was a significant variation in the types of tactics employed. Some tactics, such as the use of doubt and loaded language, were common across all four domains. Doubt served to undermine trust in credible sources and information, in turn sowing the seeds of confusion and in turn providing fertile ground for acceptance of disinformation and false information (Leite et al., 2025). On the other hand, loaded language makes reference to the use of content that aims to engage strong emotive responses in individuals and fits into the emotive appeals strategy discussed below (Leite et al., 2025). In disinformation related to the Russian–Ukrainian conflict, the use of reputation questioning was more likely to be observed and fits into the use of *hahaganda* discussed in more depth below.

Emotional Appeals

The use of emotion and emotional appeals is a commonly leveraged tactic in the framing of disinformation, something that is ubiquitous to most forms of misinformation including fake news. Generally, any content that can evoke higher arousal can elicit a more viral response, building off emotional contagion within social networks (Berger & Milkman, 2013; Kramer et al., 2014). The use of emotion links back to the dual processing theory we explored in Chapter 9, where content employing a higher emotional valence is more likely to bypass more rational analysis and involve the use of heuristic mechanisms (Evans, 2006; Evans & Stanovich, 2013). The presence of emotion has been shown to have a wide-ranging involvement in the spread and propensity to believe misinformation (Garrett & Weeks, 2017; Weeks, 2015). Sentiment contained in misinformation has been shown to be a better predictor of how much engagement such content will generate, rather than the actual content of the information itself (Matalon et al., 2021).

This emotional dimension of disinformation therefore interacts strongly with cognitive biases and heuristic shortcuts. For instance, the presence of the negativity bias (Chapter 6) means that emotionally charged content framed around fear, anger, or outrage is more likely to capture attention and be remembered. This bias amplifies the reach of disinformation that leverages threats or moral violations, as such narratives resonate more deeply than neutral or positive ones. Similarly, the affect heuristic (Chapter 9) also plays a critical role: individuals often rely on their immediate emotional response to judge the credibility or risk associated with information, rather than engaging in systematic evaluation. When misinformation evokes strong affective reactions, it can shortcut deliberative reasoning, leading to rapid acceptance or sharing without verification. These mechanisms illustrate how emotional appeals not only increase engagement but also can serve to exploit fundamental cognitive tendencies that shape belief formation and decision-making.

Repetition and Familiarity

The repeated exposure to false claims can serve to increase their perceived truthfulness, a process that feeds directly into the illusory truth effect we reviewed back in Chapter 6. This also links to another closely associated concept, that of the *repetition-induced truth effect* (Unkelbach et al., 2019; Unkelbach & Speckmann, 2021). The repetition-induced truth effect is a process where an individual will believe information that is repeated in comparison to new and novel information that is factually correct (Unkelbach et al., 2019). Interestingly, the effect can be demonstrated with a wide range of information, including anything from generic trivia (Unkelbach et al., 2019) to fake news (Pennycook et al., 2018). The effect is also persistent over time and can occur when the repetitiveness of information occurs within the space of minutes or even months and still happens even when participants are given explicit warnings about the existence of such an effect (Unkelbach et al., 2019).

There have been a variety of explanations posited as to why repetition causes a greater level of belief in information being truthful, these including

- Frequency: the increased frequency with which an individual meets information in turn increases the likelihood that we believe that information is valid and reliable.
- Recognition: when an individual recognises information, they fall into the trap of believing it to be truthful, and this could be seen as feeding into the confirmation bias, with information that aligns with material that we have already seen being seen as reliable.
- Familiarity: a feeling of familiarity with information has been shown to influence our subjective perception of the truthfulness of that information. If we can recall information and therefore judge it as being more familiar, we are therefore more likely to see it as being truthful (Unkelbach et al., 2019; Unkelbach & Speckmann, 2021).

It is therefore no surprise that many prominent disinformation campaigns have used repetitive presentation of information to great effect. Moreover, such a mechanic can be enhanced using online media, including the viral distribution of information through social media platforms, as well as the potential to cascade the replication of such material on other platforms. As an example, let us look at the Spanish regional elections that took place in May 2023. During the process of the campaigns by the main candidates, it was noted that just under a quarter of the false claims related to political discourse were repeated an average of about four times (Larraz et al., 2024).

Similarly, during the 2024 U.S. presidential election, disinformation campaigns prominently targeted issues such as immigration policy, fabricated scandals, and widespread speculation about the health of both candidates, with these narratives repeated across multiple platforms to maximise exposure (Lemmon, 2024; West, 2024). The strategic repetition of these claims reflects a broader trend in political misinformation, where frequency serves as a proxy for credibility through the illusory truth effect. Beyond domestic politics, disinformation has played a central role in international conflicts, most notably in the Russian–Ukrainian war. Here, the Kremlin has consistently propagated the narrative that its military actions constitute a "Special Security Operation" that was intended to last only a few weeks, framing the invasion as both temporary and justified. This messaging is reinforced by persistent claims that Ukraine's government is illegitimate, controlled by neo-Nazis, and acting as a puppet of Western powers. Such narratives serve multiple psychological and strategic functions: they legitimise aggression, foster in-group solidarity, and delegitimise the adversary, while exploiting cognitive biases such as confirmation bias and motivated reasoning. The repeated dissemination of these themes across state-controlled media and social platforms illustrates how disinformation operates as a tool of cognitive warfare, shaping perceptions and sustaining long-term support for military objectives.

The Hahaganda

Hahaganda refers to a disinformation tactic that leverages humour, satire, and ridicule to delegitimise individuals, institutions, or political processes (Hutchings, 2025; Ivan et al., 2022). Rather than persuading through factual argumentation, hahaganda aims to erode credibility by rendering serious issues absurd or laughable. This strategy often manifests through memes, sarcastic commentary, and staged pranks and is particularly effective when disinformation actors are confronted with compelling evidence or robust counter-narratives. The goal is not to convince audiences of the literal truth of the joke but to foster cynicism, distrust, and disengagement through repeated mockery and humiliation. By exploiting the ambiguity of humour, hahaganda deflects criticism and avoids accountability, functioning as a psychological weapon in the digital information space.

Although it is becoming more readily referenced in the disinformation discourse, hahaganda remains under-theorised and lacks a formal definition in academic literature. Nonetheless, its strategic use, especially by pro-Kremlin actors, is well documented, with ridicule and humour deployed to trivialise serious topics and undermine adversarial narratives. There is an interesting thread of research that has been conducted in terms of disinformation that can shed light on why humour and ridicule are so effective in these campaigns. Harris (2025) challenged the dominant assumption that disinformation primarily aims to instil false beliefs, instead arguing that disinformation can be equally effective in *preventing* the formation of true beliefs. He suggested that part of this process involves the manipulation of *sub-doxastic states*, mental processes that influence cognition but are inaccessible to conscious reflection or rational evaluation. These states operate below the level of belief and play a critical role in perception, inference, and attribution of causality and blame (Stich, 2007). Sub-doxastic states are automatic, unconscious cognitive mechanisms that shape how individuals respond to stimuli. This influence is sub-doxastic; it shapes attitudes without forming explicit beliefs. For example, in language comprehension, individuals automatically apply grammatical rules to derive meaning from sentences, yet these processes are not consciously endorsed or interrogated. Similarly, facial recognition occurs even when the face is stylised or abstract (e.g., emojis), without forming a belief that the image is a real face. These automatic, unconscious processes illustrate how sub-doxastic states shape interpretation without engaging belief systems.

In the context of disinformation, sub-doxastic mechanisms are particularly vulnerable to manipulation. Repetitive narratives, such as claims that a public figure is corrupt or a particular product is dangerous, may be fiercely rejected at the conscious level but still influence judgements and emotional responses at a sub-doxastic level. Such a concept has a close link to heuristic processing and cognitive biases, where both familiarity and emotional salience can easily override rational scrutiny. Humour can function to take advantage of these states and act as a psychological Trojan horse: it serves to disarm critical thinking, lowers our cognitive defences, and embeds emotionally charged associations that persist even in the absence of belief. Hahaganda exploits these vulnerabilities by embedding ridicule and humour into repeated messaging. When serious content is consistently dismissed or mocked, it influences sub-doxastic interpretation, distorting cognitive coherence and weakening resistance to manipulative narratives. The result is a subtle but powerful erosion of trust, where individuals may not believe the disinformation outright but still internalise its emotional and associative cues. For example, a meme mocking a political leader may not be taken as literal truth, but repeated exposure can foster a vague sense of incompetence or distrust.

Moreover, humour can also create a psychological state of flow (Csikszentmihalyi, 1990), which is seen as almost total emersion in a process, akin to "being in the zone." Researchers have noted that humour can lead to such a flow experience (Bartzik & Peifer, 2021; Meany, 2007), so it is logical to assume that humour can serve to enhance the processing of information and in turn be adopted through sub-doxastic systems as a cue for truth. Satirical headlines, sarcastic commentary, and visual gags are processed quickly and remembered easily, making them ideal vehicles for disinformation. Because these messages are framed as jokes, they also benefit from plausible deniability: they can be dismissed as harmless entertainment while still reinforcing stereotypes, undermining institutions, or delegitimising opposing narratives.

The use of humour and ridicule can be used as a particularly potent mechanism in online environments, where humour is socially reinforced through likes, shares, and in-group bonding. However, ridicule and humour can also become a tool not only for persuasion but also for identity formation, drawing boundaries between "us" and "them." Such a tactic can also be seen to perpetuate in-group bias as well as out-group homogeneity effects. These social dynamics can also further entrench sub-doxastic associations, making individuals more resistant to correction and more susceptible to repeated exposure.

So, as you can see, the use of humour in disinformation campaigns can engage the more non-rational aspects of human cognition, as well as engaging mechanisms which do not lend themselves directly to conscious interrogation. In targeting sub-doxastic states, disinformation can shape public opinion, erode trust, and manipulate behaviour, all without requiring the audience to consciously believe the message. This underscores the need for a deeper understanding of cognitive vulnerabilities in the information domain, particularly those that operate beneath the surface of conscious awareness.

Fake Experts and False Testimonials

Anything that feeds into the consensus bias, the bandwagon effect, or the authority bias is a good bet for initiating belief and distribution of disinformation. If you can harness the power of expertise or present the illusion of commonality in terms of support for a particular cause or piece of news, you have a good chance of disinformation taking hold.

There are a variety of ways in which expertise can be created, and each of these types of experts has their own trademark hack or play that allows them to act as a spokesperson on a particular topic or issue. There have been a wide variety of attempts to define the categories into which fake experts can fit (Croce & Marsili, 2025; Fuhrer et al., 2021), and here we synthesise some of the key elements that have been attached to these categories and add some background research to inform these.

Faux experts: basically, anyone who assumes a title (e.g., doctor, professor, or admiral) but does not have any relevant expertise or experience in any given area. Fake expert networks have been seen in various spaces within cyberspace and are usually created as a wider initiative to generate credibility for their comments, in turn making that information appear as being more believable (CISA, ND). Faux experts can harness the use of false credentials or the appearance of real expertise to make their comments and content more believable to the public eye. Some faux experts will even go to the length of generating fictional research papers that support the disinformation they are discussing, in turn helping their claims look more legitimate.

Pseudo-experts: one example, although not directly related to that of disinformation, is that of the TV personality Gillian McKeith, who rose to prominence for her promotion of pseudo-scientific views about health and nutrition during the 2000s. Numerous aspects of McKeith's practices were not directly supported by medical research, including aspects of inspecting different body parts (e.g., the tongue) or looking at the consistency of a person's stools in order to determine if they have an underlying illness. Her fall from grace was quick and spectacular, with various members of the scientific community lambasting her ideas and asking pertinent questions about her qualifications. Later, it emerged that her PhD lacked any direct substance and was awarded to her by an unaccredited university in the United States, and she was forced to drop the *PhD* and *Dr* title in her work and advertising.

It is not hard for pseudo-experts to gain traction in terms of the reach and perceived credibility of their ideas. In the age of the internet, any individual can set themselves up as a self-proclaimed expert, using falsified qualifications and various aspects of manipulation to hide their lack of true expertise and experience. As the internet affords individuals a high degree of visibility and reach, positioning yourself as a pseudo-expert or pseudo-professional has become very easy and, again, is usually linked not to expertise but to how well you present yourselves online and how believable your current narrative is. As such, it means that this process becomes an easy one to harness when we look at discussions around disinformation and digital warfare, give yourself an impressive title, create a relevant background story, and generate a good narrative that you think people will buy into, and you are a pseudo-expert.

Junk expert: the framing of a junk expert is linked to their capacity to engage in practices that might use their existing expertise in questionable ways. Usually, there is an aspect of profit at hand in the motivations behind the junk expert, and they will be seen as some sort of sell-out, usually putting their name and creating bogus data and information to engage positive public opinions, in turn generating income. A prime example of this type of expert is clearly demonstrated in Andrew Wakefield and the MMR jab. In 1998, a British doctor published a study in which he made false claims that the measles, mumps, and rubella (MMR) vaccine was linked to cases of autism in children. The disinformation was widely reported in the mass media and caused widespread panic in parents who had already had their children vaccinated. It also gave rise to one of the single most pernicious conspiracy-like theories that persists today, that of the anti-vaccination movement. The paper that was produced by Wakefield and a collection of his colleagues presented data on a very small number of participants (12 in total), and the design as well as the conclusions presented by the paper were criticised by a wide range of experts in the field (Rao & Andrade, 2011). The report was later redacted by the publishing journal, and Wakefield, alongside his colleagues, was found guilty of fraud and falsification of data. In the end, it was noted that Wakefield and his co-workers were set to make a considerable amount of money from an alternative vaccine being marketed (Deer, 2010). So, in this instance, the use of existing professional qualifications was harnessed to dupe the public and the wider scientific community into believing disinformation, which in turn had wide-ranging effects, not only limited to the panic it instilled in individuals.

Epistemic trespasser: epistemic trespassing occurs when individuals with recognised expertise in one domain make authoritative claims in areas where they lack competence (Croce & Marsili, 2025). These figures leverage their credentials to gain trust, even though their judgements fall outside their field of expertise. A key example is Shiva Ayyadurai, an MIT-trained engineer with a PhD in biological engineering, who rose to prominence during the COVID-19 pandemic by promoting false claims about cures such as vitamin C and hydroxychloroquine (Croce & Marsili, 2025). Despite lacking expertise in virology or infectious diseases, Ayyadurai's status as an accomplished scientist lent unwarranted credibility to his assertions, appealing to conspiracist audiences.

Researchers have attempted to present definitions for epistemic trespassers, viewing them as individuals who have some level of competency or expertise in one field, but then they begin to "trespass" into other areas in which they have no objective expertise (Ballantyne, 2019). Not all forms of trespassing can be viewed as being harmful, and indeed, some cross-pollination of ideas and areas can result in some very productive collaborations. However, epistemic harm arises when trespassers persuade audiences to assign greater credibility to their testimony than it deserves. This harm is amplified when experts fail to qualify their claims, creating the illusion of authority in domains where they lack evidential support (Croce & Marsili, 2025).

Taken together, faux experts, pseudo-experts, junk experts, and epistemic trespassers illustrate the diverse ways in which authority signals are weaponised in disinformation campaigns. Each type leverages perceived expertise, whether through fabricated credentials, misapplied knowledge, or cross-domain trespassing, to lend legitimacy to false narratives. In the digital age, these tactics are amplified by social media algorithms and echo chambers, which reward authoritative-sounding voices regardless of accuracy. By manufacturing credibility, disinformation actors can bypass scepticism, foster trust, and embed falsehoods into public discourse. Understanding these mechanisms is critical for developing counter-measures, as the manipulation of expertise remains one of the most effective strategies for sustaining misinformation and influencing behaviour in both political and conflict-driven contexts.

Summary

In this chapter, we explored the strategic, psychological, and operational dimensions of disinformation and positioned it as a central component in digital warfare. Disinformation is distinguished from misinformation by its intentionality and strategic deployment. While misinformation often arises from cognitive shortcuts or a lack of verification, disinformation is engineered to deceive, destabilise, and manipulate. It frequently co-opts misinformation, amplifying it to serve political, ideological, or geopolitical ends.

Four core strategic aims of disinformation are identified, these being destabilisation, division, deception, and influence operations. Destabilisation involves undermining trust in institutions and creating uncertainty, particularly during crises or elections. Division is achieved by exploiting contentious issues to polarise communities, often through echo chambers and targeted messaging. Deception includes the use of deepfakes, impersonation, and fabricated evidence to obscure truth and confuse audiences. Influence operations leverage disinformation to shape public opinion and policy, often with long-term geopolitical objectives.

In terms of the mechanics for disinformation, there are a variety of tactics that can be employed as part of these campaigns. Lying involves direct falsehoods from identifiable sources, as illustrated by the Syrian gas attack hoax, where counter-narratives were rapidly deployed to neutralise international outrage. Leaks, while often truthful, can be weaponised to damage credibility or empower target audiences. Seeding blends true and false information to build trust and later manipulate, exploiting cognitive biases like the halo effect and confirmation bias. Cyber smearing uses anonymous sources to spread fabricated content, targeting echo chambers and reinforcing ideological divides. The Russian concept of maskirovka relies directly on a doctrine of deception, denial, and disinformation, as exemplified by the Russian annexation of Crimea, serving as a case study in strategic ambiguity and narrative control.

Psychological tactics underpin the effectiveness of disinformation. Emotional appeals exploit high-arousal content to bypass rational scrutiny, leveraging dual-process theories of cognition. Repetition and familiarity foster belief in false claims through the illusory truth effect, where repeated exposure increases perceived truthfulness. This tactic is especially potent in digital environments, where content is rapidly and widely disseminated. A particularly novel concept introduced is hahaganda, or the use of humour, satire, and ridicule to delegitimise individuals and institutions. Rather than persuading through argument, hahaganda erodes credibility by rendering serious issues absurd. It operates at a sub-doxastic level, influencing unconscious cognitive processes that shape perception and emotional response without forming explicit beliefs. Humour can therefore become a psychological Trojan horse, embedding associations that persist even when the literal message is rejected.

In sum, disinformation is presented not only as a communication problem but also as a psychological and strategic weapon. Its success lies in its ability to exploit cognitive vulnerabilities, manipulate emotional responses, and dominate the information environment. The chapter sets the stage for further exploration of counter-measures, emphasising the need for interdisciplinary approaches to resilience in the face of digital deception.

References

Arce, D. (2024). Disinformation strategies. *Defence and Peace Economics*, *35*(6), 659–672. https://doi.org/10.1080/10242694.2024.2302236

Bagge, D. P. (2019). *Unmasking Maskirovka: Russia's cyber influence operations*. Defense Press.

Ballantyne, N. (2019). Epistemic trespassing. *Mind*, *128*(510), 367–395. https://doi.org/10.1093/mind/fzx042

Bartzik, M., & Peifer, C. (2021). On the relationships between humour, stress and flow experience: Introducing the humour-flow model. In E. Vanderheiden & C. H. Mayer (Eds.), *The Palgrave handbook of humour research* (2nd ed., pp. 479–496). Cham, Switzerland: Palgrave Macmillan.

Berger, J., & Milkman, K. L. (2013). Emotion and virality: What makes online content go viral. *Insights*, *5*(1), 18–23.

Choy, J. P. (2020). Kompromat: A theory of blackmail as a system of governance. *Journal of Development Economics*, *147*(June 2019), 102535. https://doi.org/10.1016/j.jdeveco.2020.102535

Coombs, T. W., & Holladay, S. J. (2006). Unpacking the halo effect: Reputation and crisis management. *Journal of Communication Management*, *10*(2), 123–137. https://doi.org/10.1108/13632540610664698

Croce, M., & Marsili, N. (2025). Misplaced trust in expertise: Pseudo-experts and unreliable experts. *Social Epistemology*, *00*(00), 1–16. https://doi.org/10.1080/02691728.2025.2491104

Csikszentmihalyi, M. (1990). Flow: The psychology of optimal performance. In *Optimal experience: Psychological studies of flow in consciousness*. New York: Cambridge University Press.

Darden, K. (2008). The integrity of corrupt states: Graft as an informal state institution. *Politics and Society*, *36*, 35–59. https://doi.org/10.1177/0032329207312183

Deer, B. (2010). Wakefield's "autistic enterocolitis" under the microscope. *BMJ (Online)*, *340*(7751), 838–841. https://doi.org/10.1136/bmj.c1127

Evans, J. S. B. T. (2006). The heuristic-analytic theory of reasoning: Extension and evaluation. *Psychonomic Bulletin & Review*, *13*(3), 378–395. Retrieved from http://www.ncbi.nlm.nih.gov/pubmed/17048720

Evans, J. S. B. T., & Stanovich, K. E. (2013). Dual-process theories of higher cognition: Advancing the debate. *Perspectives on Psychological Science*, *8*(3), 223–241. https://doi.org/10.1177/1745691612460685

Filatova, O., & Bolgov, R. (2018). Strategic communication in the context of modern information confrontation: EU and NATO vs Russia and ISIS. *Proceedings of the 13th International Conference on Cyber Warfare and Security, ICCWS 2018*, March, 208–218.

Fuhrer, J., Cova, F., Gauvrit, N., & Dieguez, S. (2021). Pseudoexpertise: A conceptual and theoretical analysis. *Frontiers in Psychology*, *12*(November), 1–12. https://doi.org/10.3389/fpsyg.2021.732666

Garrett, R. K., & Weeks, B. E. (2017). Epistemic beliefs' role in promoting misperceptions and conspiracist ideation. *PLoS One*, *12*(9), 1–17. https://doi.org/10.1371/journal.pone.0184733

Gelfert, A. (2018). Fake news: A definition. *Informal Logic*, *38*(1), 84–117. https://doi.org/10.22329/il.v38i1.5068

Hammond-Errey, M. (2019). Understanding and assessing information influence and foreign interference. *Journal of Information Warfare*, *18*(1), 1–22.

Han, C. H. (2015). Maskirovka in the information age. *Pointer, Journal of the Singapore Armed Forces*, *42*(1), 39–50. Retrieved from https://www.mindef.gov.sg/oms/safti/pointer/documents/pdf/V42N1_Maskirovka_in_the_Info_Age.pdf

Harris, K. R. (2025). Beyond belief: On disinformation and manipulation. *Erkenntnis*, *90*(2), 483–503. https://doi.org/10.1007/s10670-023-00710-6

Hofirek, M. (2021). *Maskirovka's cognitive effects in crime and Donbas*. National Defense University.

Hübert, R., & Little, A. T. (2022). Kompromat can align incentives but ruin reputations. *American Journal of Political Science*, *66*(4), 871–884. https://doi.org/10.1111/ajps.12620

Hutchings, S. C. (2025). Uncovering the uncoverers: Identity, performativity and representation in counter-disinformation discourse. *Cultural Studies*, *39*(4), 546–573. https://doi.org/10.1080/09502386.2024.2384942

Ivan, C., Chiru, I., Buluc, R., Radu, A., Anghel, A., Stoian-Iordache, V., . . . Nastasiu, C. (2022). *Handbook on identifying and countering disinformation*, 1–266. Dominoes Erasmus+.

Kramer, A. D. I., Guillory, J. E., & Hancock, J. T. (2014). Experimental evidence of massive-scale emotional contagion through social networks. *Proceedings of the National Academy of Sciences of the United States of America*, *111*(24), 8788–8790. https://doi.org/10.1073/pnas.1320040111

Larraz, I., Salaverría, R., & Serrano-Puche, J. (2024). Combating repeated lies: The impact of fact-checking on persistent falsehoods by politicians. *Media and Communication*, *12*, 1–17. https://doi.org/10.17645/mac.8642

Leite, J. A., Razuvayevskaya, O., Scarton, C., & Bontcheva, K. (2025). A cross-domain study of the use of persuasion techniques in online disinformation. *WWW Companion 2025 – Companion Proceedings of the ACM Web Conference 2025*, 1100–1103. https://doi.org/10.1145/3701716.3715535

Lemmon, J. (2024). Disinformation as hybrid warfare and its strategic use in the United States 2024 election. *National Security and the Future*, *25*(2), 132–176. https://doi.org/10.37458/nstf.25.2.5

Matalon, Y., Magdaci, O., Almozlino, A., & Yamin, D. (2021). Using sentiment analysis to predict opinion inversion in Tweets of political communication. *Scientific Reports*, *11*(1), 1–9. https://doi.org/10.1038/s41598-021-86510-w

Meany, M. (2007). Humour, anxiety, and Csikszentmihalyi's concept of flow. *Creative Engagements: Thinking with Children-3rd*.

Pennycook, G., Cannon, T. D., & Rand, D. G. (2018). Prior exposure increases percieved accuracy of fake news. *Journal of Experimental Psychology: General*, *147*(12), 1865–1880.

Rao, T. S. S., & Andrade, C. (2011). The MMR vaccine and autism: Sensation, refutation, retraction, and fraud. *Indian Journal of Psychiatry*, *53*(2), 95–96. https://doi.org/10.4103/0019-5545.82529

Stich, S. P. (2007). Beliefs and subdoxastic states. In *Philosophy of psychology: Contemporary readings* (Vol. 45, pp. 559–576). https://doi.org/10.1086/288832

Stoica, A. (2020). From social influence to cyber influence: The role of new technologies in the influence operations conducted in the digital environment. *International Journal of Cyber Diplomacy*, *1*(1), 27–35. Retrieved from ijcd.ici.ro

Tünde, N., & Marian, C. (2014). The war which brings in the cold – Ukraine and crimea – Maskirovka and disinformatsia. *Research and Science Today*, *2*(August), 87–93.
Unkelbach, C., Koch, A., Silva, R. R., & Garcia-Marques, T. (2019). Truth by repetition: Explanations and implications. *Current Directions in Psychological Science*, *28*(3), 247–253. https://doi.org/10.1177/0963721419827854
Unkelbach, C., & Speckmann, F. (2021). Mere repetition increases belief in factually true COVID-19-related information. *Journal of Applied Research in Memory and Cognition*, *10*(2), 241–247. https://doi.org/10.1016/j.jarmac.2021.02.001
Unver, H. A., & Arhan, S. E. (2023). The strategic logic of digital disinformation. In *Routledge handbook of disinformation and national security* (Vol. 1, pp. 192–207). Routledge. https://doi.org/10.4324/9781003190363-17
Weeks, B. E. (2015). Emotions, partisanship, and misperceptions: How anger and anxiety moderate the effect of partisan bias on susceptibility to political misinformation. *Journal of Communication*, *65*(4), 699–719. https://doi.org/10.1111/jcom.12164
West, D. M. (2024). *How disinformation defined the 2024 election narrative*. Retrieved from Brookings Institute website https://www.brookings.edu/articles/how-disinformation-defined-the-2024-election-narrative/0/
Whaley, R. (1982). Toward a general theory of deception. *The Journal of Strategic Studies*, *5*(1), 178–192.
Zehndorfer, E. (2022). *Maskirovka: The weaponizing of misinformation*. Retrieved from Psychology Today website https://www.psychologytoday.com/au/blog/political-animals-and-animal-spirits/202203/maskirovka-the-weaponizing-misinformation
Zhou, Y., & Shen, L. (2022). Confirmation bias and the persistence of misinformation on climate change. *Communication Research*, *49*(4), 500–523. https://doi.org/10.1177/00936502211028049
Zhou, Y., & Shen, L. (2024). Processing of misinformation as motivational and cognitive biases. *Frontiers in Psychology*, *15*. https://doi.org/10.3389/fpsyg.2024.1430953

13 Online Radicalisation

Introduction

In the evolving landscape of digital warfare, online radicalisation has emerged as a powerful and deeply concerning mechanism for ideological recruitment and mobilisation (Garcet, 2021; Neo, 2016). However, radicalisation does not occur in isolation, nor is it solely an online process (Binder & Kenyon, 2022). It exists within a broader continuum that spans both digital and physical environments. Offline influences, such as community dynamics, personal relationships, and socio-political contexts, often lay the groundwork for susceptibility, while online platforms amplify, accelerate, and reinforce extremist narratives.

This chapter explores online radicalisation not as a stand-alone phenomenon but as a digitally enhanced extension of traditional radicalisation pathways. The internet has transformed the scale, speed, and subtlety with which extremist ideologies can be disseminated. Social media, encrypted messaging apps, and algorithmically curated content ecosystems allow radical actors to reach individuals across geographic and cultural boundaries, often by-passing conventional gatekeepers of information and social influence. Importantly, the interplay between online and offline environments creates a hybrid radicalisation process. Offline grievances, such as marginalisation, identity crises, or perceived injustice, can make individuals more receptive to online content. Conversely, digital engagement can lead to offline consequences, including behavioural shifts, social withdrawal, and, in some cases, violent action. This bidirectional flow underscores the need to understand online radicalisation within a broader psychosocial and cognitive framework.

Within the context of digital warfare, online radicalisation represents the strategic use of information and psychological manipulation. Extremist actors exploit cognitive vulnerabilities, emotional triggers, and identity needs to draw individuals into ideological echo chambers. These tactics are not random; they are deliberate, memetically engineered, and often supported by sophisticated digital infrastructures.

This chapter will examine the historical roots of radicalisation, the psychological and cognitive mechanisms that underpin its digital evolution and

DOI: 10.4324/9781003752400-13

the platforms and personas that facilitate its spread. Through case studies and theoretical analysis, it will explore how online radicalisation functions as a form of psychological warfare and how it can be countered through digital resilience, education, and strategic intervention. Ultimately, the chapter aims to integrate online radicalisation into the conceptual framework of digital warfare, highlighting its implications for security, society, and the future of conflict.

Defining Radicalisation

The origins of the politicisation of the term "radical" are contested and, while historically significant, have limited bearing on the core discussions within this chapter. Nonetheless, it is broadly accepted that the term gained prominence during the eighteenth century, when it became associated with political and social reform movements (Hessayon & Finnegan, 2013). It was frequently linked to figures involved in the French and American revolutions and often used to articulate opposition to prevailing political structures. Over time, however, *radical* came to denote individuals or groups espousing fringe beliefs that diverged markedly from mainstream societal norms (Awan et al., 2011).

A persistent source of confusion within the literature in this field lies in the distinction between *radicalisation* and *activism*. While both concepts involve efforts to challenge existing systems, they differ significantly in their methods and implications. Activism is typically characterised by lawful and non-violent political engagement aimed at effecting change. In contrast, radicalism is often associated with the willingness to engage in unlawful and violent actions as a form of ideological expression (Moskalenko & McCauley, 2021). However, this binary distinction has not been without its critics, with some arguing that such classifications are largely shaped by legal frameworks contingent upon geopolitical contexts, thereby complicating objective assessments of legitimacy (Schmid, 2005, 2013). Moreover, individuals may adopt radical positions in environments where democratic avenues for change are obstructed, particularly under authoritarian regimes. In such cases, actions deemed illegal within the prevailing legal order may nonetheless be morally or ethically motivated by a desire to pursue justice or reform (Schmid, 2013). This underscores the need for a nuanced understanding of radicalisation that accounts for both context and intent.

Malthaner (2017) noted that even though a variety of definitions have been presented for the term "radicalisation," they vary widely in terms of their presentation, often being vague and poorly constructed. What becomes classified as radical can be very subjective and depends entirely on the perspective of the individual making the judgements surrounding that behaviour (Malthaner, 2017). Radicalisation is often used as a lens through which Western societies frame and interpret the actions of extremist groups that sit in opposition to their dominant ideologies and actions (Malthaner, 2017). However, the term can also be used to refer to ideas and concepts that sit on the fringes of society, presenting a contrast to the current status quo.

It has been suggested that the internet now offers violent extremists a variety of new platforms to expand their propaganda beyond that of the more traditional, offline routes (Neo, 2016). Adversaries that have the desire to perpetrate extremist views have become very efficient at exploiting digital platforms as spaces where they can actively present their radical ideologies. Social media platforms can allow such groups to be targeted in very specific ways to groups that may be easily manipulated, perhaps due to pre-existing beliefs and currently held grudges. By harnessing the power of existing echo chambers, many extremist groups already have a readily available amplification system well-suited to their purposes, coming equipped with associated filter bubbles and respective cognitive biases that prevent counter-arguments from gaining traction. Digital platforms have become powerful tools for disseminating extremist views, enabling such content to reach broad audiences while bypassing the scrutiny typically associated with traditional publishing channels. This process links back to the disintermediation of gatekeeping that we discussed earlier in Chapter 10, meaning that anyone with an idea, a cause, or a vendetta can publish their ideas online without the rigour of more traditional publishing routes. This accessibility not only facilitates the spread of radical ideologies but also allows extremists to preserve and archive their core beliefs online, creating a lasting digital footprint of their movement (Conway & McInerney, 2008). Online publications that are produced by radical groups can offer a new platform for perpetuating their ideological beliefs in a targeted way, and one that can proceed without the direct scrutiny of more official and legitimate sources of information (Neo, 2016). As well as offering extremists a more diverse platform through which they can launch their ideals and narratives, the internet can also offer an excellent platform for distributing this material to those who might be sympathetic to their cause (Binder & Kenyon, 2022; Neo, 2016). The internet offers the opportunity to reach millions of individuals who could have a similar set of experiences or grievances with a target out-group, but in a way that serves to transgress geopolitical and geographical space, as well as step outside of the shackles of temporality (Neo, 2016).

With the freedom to publish unfiltered and unverified material online, another potential risk emerges. There is a potential for repeated exposure to radical extremist content to increase the likelihood that individuals will become susceptible to such ideological messages (Neo, 2016). If we think about the functioning of the illusory truth bias we explored in Chapter 6, bombarding any audience with repeated narratives around a particular topic can serve to influence their perception of that information as being true. Researchers have also noted that many online agents serve to action the use of social media to capture the attention of the younger generation, who in turn can present a highly mailable group of individuals and, as such, are generally more open to suggestions from extremist groups (Fernandez et al., 2014; Neo, 2016).

The threshold for individuals to engage in viewing advanced facets of radical extremism has been significantly diminished due to the widespread availability of information online. Resources such as bomb-making tutorials and detailed geographical data have made the planning and co-ordination of attacks considerably more accessible, reducing the physical and logistical barriers that previously existed (Cohen et al., 2014). A parallel concern lies in the ease with which individuals can now study and disseminate extremist ideologies, facilitated by unrestricted internet access and the absence of effective gatekeeping or online guardianship (Cohen et al., 2014).

However, it is essential to recognise that radicalisation is rarely a purely digital phenomenon. Numerous scholars have highlighted the interplay between online and offline influences in the radicalisation process. For instance, it has been observed that initial exposure to extremist ideologies often occurs in physical, offline contexts before individuals are directed to online platforms for further engagement (Binder & Kenyon, 2022; Mølmen & Ravndal, 2023; Neo, 2016). Neo (2016) further emphasised that the transition from offline to online radicalisation remains one of the least understood aspects of this process.

While extremist propaganda may reach thousands of individuals online, only a small fraction proceeds to enact these ideologies through violent means. This disparity may be attributed to varying levels of individual susceptibility, personal grievances, or differing thresholds for action. Some individuals may require more significant psychological or situational triggers before engaging in physical expressions of extremism (Neo, 2016).

Characteristics of Radical Groups

Even though there is a wide variety of radical extremist groups that exist, it has been demonstrated that they share core common elements (Doosje et al., 2016; Van Bergen et al., 2015). Doosje et al. (2016) summarised these key facets as follows:

1. Identification of an issue: all radical groups present the perception of a serious issue or problem within their current sphere of interest or may have current grievances with a specific target group or ideology. For each radical group, such an issue remains individual and unique but remains a constant feature across all groups.
2. Sense of resentment: each group comes from a position of resentment or dissatisfaction with the way in which current issues that have arisen as part of point 1 above are being dealt with. Such resentment may be the result of a perceived lack of direct action, a level of inaction, or the belief that such issues are being left largely ignored by those people who should be responsible for doing something about them. In turn, individuals who now occupy this position of resentment will form an inherent state of distrust

in the establishment and institutional processes that form the backbone of society, as well as creating a state of belief that those people in authority are ill-equipped to deal with such issues and are therefore illegitimate (Doosje et al., 2016).

3. Dominant ideologies: individual members of the radical group will assume that their normative values, captured in their ideology, are of greater importance than those of the out-group; this creates a persistent in-group–out-group bias, again serving to instil the didactic "us versus them" narrative that is so commonly exploited in radicalisation. Such a process can then be easily employed to enhance feelings of dehumanisation for the out-group, in turn allowing the moral justification of violence against them (Doosje et al., 2016).
4. Legitimisation of violence: one of the key elements that separates violent extremist groups from other forms of social activism is the active endorsement of violence as the chosen method for initiating change. It is here that the strong identification with the current in-group and the continued dehumanisation of the out-group make a perfect background for violence to be carried out as part of the group's main objectives (Doosje et al., 2016).
5. Only violence works: this is the final feature that is common to all extremist groups that engage in radicalisation, that being the core belief, and that only violence will provide the most effective means for initiating change. Therefore, violent actions are actively endorsed by members of the in-group and are seen as being the most productive means of obtaining the group's wider aims.

Understanding the foundational traits shared by radical groups, such as perceived grievances, ideological rigidity, and the legitimisation of violence, can provide a critical insight into how these entities operate and recruit. In the digital age, however, these characteristics are no longer confined to physical spaces or traditional forms of mobilisation. They are increasingly embedded within online ecosystems that amplify and accelerate radicalisation processes. The mechanics of online radicalisation build upon these core elements, leveraging digital platforms to manipulate cognitive biases, exploit emotional vulnerabilities, and construct persuasive ideological narratives. The following section examines how these psychological and informational tactics are deployed in the digital realm to transform passive discontent into active extremism.

The Psychological Mechanics of Online Radicalisation

Regardless of the specific mechanisms employed, online radicalisation remains one of the most potent ways in which the digital environment can be weaponised to influence, mobilise, and reshape the perceptions of individuals as to what is morally right and what is ideologically consistent with their beliefs. It involves the harnessing of social and informational biases, including in-group bias, out-group homogeneity effects, negativity bias, and the construction of echo chambers (see Chapters 6, 7, and 11). These mechanisms interact in combination, producing a cumulative effect as digital platforms amplify their psychological impact over time.

Radical ideologues exploit online spaces to disseminate their views rapidly and broadly, often shielded from detection until their messages have already gained traction. Algorithmic biases further reinforce these narratives by repeatedly exposing individuals to similar content, increasing the likelihood that extremist propaganda will resonate (Shin, 2024). Emotionally charged, repetitive, and salient messaging, particularly targeting individuals experiencing status loss or identity crises, can saturate digital platforms and activate cognitive biases such as those discussed in Chapters 6 and 7. The scale and virality of extremist content within the digital battlespace pose a significant threat to societal cohesion, making online radicalisation a critical concern in the context of psychological and informational warfare (Awan et al., 2011; Mutton et al., 2023; Neo, 2016).

As a strategic tool, online radicalisation is not a process that takes hold overnight and requires months, if not years, of planning and preparation to be effective. The key to the process is the development and evolution of ideological content and requires the crafting of persistent narratives that can stand the test of time.

Cognitive Dissonance and Radicalisation

As we have discussed in Chapter 6, cognitive dissonance (Festinger, 1957) presents the notion that individuals will start to experience levels of psychological discomfort when they hold two or more conflicting cognitions (e.g., attitudes, beliefs, and values). To reduce this level of discomfort, the individual becomes motivated to change their beliefs or behaviours so that they can regain some semblance of internal consistency. In terms of radicalisation, cognitive dissonance can be easily used so that individuals are forced into the trap of adopting more extremist narratives and ideologies (Baugut & Neumann, 2020; Koomen & Van Der Pligt, 2016; Nilsson, 2022). For example, in instances where an individual experiences feelings of isolation and marginalisation, they may experience dissonance between how they currently view themselves and their current inherent value to society. To resolve this conflict, extremist ideologies can offer a route out of this; they give an individual a narrative that can serve to validate their current feelings, as well as offering them a purpose and sense of belonging that they currently do not possess.

As individuals progress through the radicalisation process, their exposure to increasingly extreme content can trigger heightened levels of cognitive dissonance. For most members of society, acts of violence and killing are perceived as morally reprehensible. However, extremist narratives often frame such actions as necessary and justified means to achieve ideological or political goals. To reconcile this internal conflict, individuals may engage in cognitive reframing, allowing them to reinterpret violent acts as morally defensible within the context of their adopted cause. This process, known as *moral disengagement* (Bandura, 1990; Garcet, 2021; Moore, 2015), involves the rationalisation of ethically questionable behaviours through mechanisms such as moral justification, euphemistic labelling, or the displacement of responsibility, an element widely recognised as central to the radicalisation trajectory (Garcet, 2021). There are several ways that moral disengagement can be used by individuals to excuse morally questionable actions, which have been included in Table 13.1.

Additionally, individuals may encounter dissonance when confronted with contradictory information online. Extremist actors often seek to neutralise these cognitive threats through strategies of ridicule and delegitimisation, reframing complex moral and political issues into simplistic, binary oppositions. This reductionist narrative, which is typically structured around an "us versus them" dichotomy, serves to reinforce in-group cohesion while discrediting alternative perspectives (Nilsson, 2019; Garcet, 2021).

Table 13.1 Moral Disengagement and the Rationalisation of Violent Extremism

Type	*Function*	*Example*
Moral justification	Violent or harmful actions are reframed as serving a noble or moral purpose. For example, killing may be justified as a necessary act to protect a community or achieve justice.	"This violence is necessary to defend our people."
Euphemistic labelling	Language is used to sanitise or obscure the true nature of the act. This reduces emotional impact and moral scrutiny.	Referring to civilian casualties as "collateral damage" or calling torture "enhanced interrogation."
Advantageous comparison	The act is compared to something worse, making it seem relatively benign.	"What we're doing is nothing compared to what they've done to us."
Displacement of responsibility	Responsibility is shifted to authority figures or systems, allowing individuals to feel less personally accountable.	"I was just following orders."
Diffusion of responsibility	Responsibility is spread across a group, diluting individual accountability.	"Everyone in the group agreed to it – it wasn't just me."
Distortion of consequences	The harm caused by the action is minimised or denied.	"No one was seriously hurt," or "They deserved it."
Dehumanisation	Victims are stripped of human qualities, making it easier to justify violence against them.	Referring to the enemy as "vermin" or "infidels."
Attribution of blame	The victim is blamed for provoking the action, shifting responsibility away from the perpetrator.	"They brought this on themselves by refusing to cooperate."

Myth-Making and Narrative Bias

As we have noted in Chapter 6, when we introduced the narrative bias, individuals tend to pay more attention and perceive a higher level of credibility in information that is presented in a coherent way, usually something that forms a story (Allen & Preiss, 1997; Reinard, 1988). In instances where information is presented to individuals in the form of statistics, they find such information less persuasive compared to a story that presents the same information (Winterbottom et al., 2008). Most evidence suggests this occurs because narrative-based arguments activate heuristic processing, making them easier to comprehend compared to the more effortful, analytical evaluation required for statistical information (Winterbottom et al., 2008). While some researchers have commented that the evidence for such a benefit is limited, there are some clear examples where narrative information can be seen to bias judgements (Betsch et al., 2015).

Extremist perspectives are often heavily biased, positioning their views and ideological approaches at the extreme end of the neutrality spectrum. The radical elements embedded in these narratives, which are often conveyed through memes and online posts, have a strong potential to trigger cognitive biases, which in turn manipulate individuals into perceiving such views as valid and credible (Naderer et al., 2024). Extremist narratives often follow archetypal story structures such as heroism, victimhood, betrayal, and redemption that resonate deeply with individuals experiencing identity crises or social alienation (Mila et al., 2019). These stories are not only emotionally compelling but also cognitively efficient, enabling individuals to make sense of complex socio-political realities through simplified, emotionally charged frameworks. The persuasive power of such narratives is amplified by digital platforms that reward engagement and repetition, reinforcing belief through repeated exposure and emotional salience.

The Pathway to Radicalisation

Many researchers have engaged in the study of radicalisation and the process that it will take. For many individuals who engage in the journey towards radicalisation, there will be a specific goal that they will have towards which they will progress, such as martyrdom, honour, vengeance, and revenge. While it has been noted that there might be significant differences in the specific goal for extremists, these can be generally categorised under what has been termed a *quest for significance* (Kruglanski et al., 2014; Little et al., 2021). This is seen as a process through which an individual will strive to find a place within their current peer group, to find meaning, and at the same time to garner respect from their peers (Kruglanski et al., 2014). This quest for significance is not unique to those individuals who are engaged in the route to radicalisation and has been highlighted as being a fundamental human motivation for many of the things that we do daily (Maslow, 1954; Ryan & Deci, 2000). However, for most of society, the quest for significance does not involve the use of violent extremism as part of the tools that we will use to achieve that goal.

In terms of the initial steps towards radicalisation, researchers have proposed that there must be some form of tipping point where the quest for significance is initiated. The notion of tipping points has been studied in the field of psychology and is usually an unquantifiable and unpredictable point at which an individual will initiate some change (O'Brien, 2020). According to Kruglanski et al. (2014), one of the most significant motivations for engaging in a quest for significance is the individual experiencing feelings of isolation and a loss of position within society. This can occur when an individual or the group to which they belong becomes the target of public humiliation, perhaps because of conflict or other societal events. Loss of personal significance can arise from numerous sources, such as economic turmoil or changes in social and political environments. These circumstances can create an internal state in which the individual begins to believe they are not being given sufficient opportunities to achieve their personal goals, leading to feelings of helplessness and insignificance. Such conditions provide fertile ground for the awakening of a personal quest for significance. Socially based loss of significance may also stem from belonging to an in-group that has become the target of disrespect; in the context of radicalisation, Islamophobia is a prime example where socially based loss of significance acts as an environmentally linked trigger for this quest.

Accordingly, Kruglanski et al. (2014) suggested that the pursuit of violence and terrorism might present the individual with an ideal opportunity to regain some level of control and personal significance, such as giving them a place in history or presenting them as a hero in the eyes of their reference group. These authors noted that the pathway to radicalisation is presented as having three common elements:

1. *The motivational element*: this is the reason why the individual is engaged on the pathway to radicalisation and links directly to the quest for personal significance.
2. *The goal*: this is something that is directly related to the ideological narratives presented by the extremist group to which the individual belongs and is the main way in which the individual will be seen to regain significance. For example, this might be regaining territory or rights that were taken away as part of some form of political upheaval.
3. *Social processes*: networking and group dynamics form an essential part of the radicalisation process and are perhaps one of the key areas where digital technology comes into play more directly.

So, from this perspective, radicalisation often begins with a perceived loss of personal significance, which triggers a motivational drive to restore that sense of meaning and purpose. In seeking to regain this significance, individuals are drawn to ideologies that resonate with their grievances and offer a clear path to redemption. The reference group's ideology not only shapes their understanding of the problem but also legitimises the use of violence as a justified means to achieve their goals.

The Internet and the Path to Radicalisation

The use of the internet as a mechanism for initiating radicalisation of individuals has been the focus of concern for many social commentators. The capacity for information to emerge on the internet and thus be presented as commonly occurring narratives often encapsulates the presentation of extremist propaganda (Binder & Kenyon, 2022). Of key relevance to the processes involved in online radicalisation is the development and formation of echo chambers and relevant filter bubbles that maintain the persistent messages that are often presented by extremist groups. It is important to note that most of the prominent theories in this field present the notion that the internet serves as a mediator between the individual being radicalised and the actor promoting radical ideas. To this point, it is acknowledged that radicalisation is never wholly a purely digital process, and there are additional offline elements that serve to contribute to the process. This could include aspects such as social facilitation at in-person events, such as training events (Neo, 2016; Kruglanski et al., 2014). It has been noted that there is a great deal of sensationalism and hype around the potential for individuals to encounter extremist material and propaganda online and the associated influence this could have in swaying individuals towards a particular cause of action. However, it has also been noted that, taken in isolation, the consumption of online materials related to violent extremism is unlikely to be the sole cause of an individual turning to radical ideology. Others have argued that while the internet might form one part of the radicalisation process, real-world interactions offer a more powerful means of socialising the individual into the ideologies of the group (Neo, 2016).

Neo (2016) proposed a five-stage framework captured in the following elements: Reflection, Exploration, Connection, Resolution, and Operational (RECRO) to conceptualise the pathway to radicalisation, with the internet acting as a key mediating factor throughout the process. These stages are not strictly linear and often overlap, reflecting the fluid and dynamic nature of radicalisation.

1. Reflection
   The reflection stage is initiated by a significant personal or social disruption that undermines the individual's sense of meaning, identity, or belonging. Vulnerabilities such as psychological distress, social isolation, or perceived injustice increase the individual's receptiveness to radical content encountered online. At this point, the quest for significance, as conceptualised by Kruglanski et al. (2014), begins to surface, particularly when extremist narratives resonate with the individual's grievances. These narratives offer a

compelling framework through which the individual can interpret their experiences and begin to construct a new sense of purpose. A recurring theme in this stage is the experience of social disconnection, where feelings of alienation or exclusion make individuals more susceptible to ideologies that promise belonging, recognition, and a renewed sense of identity. Radicalisation, in this context, becomes a pathway to reclaiming significance and forging meaningful social connections.

At the reflection stage, the internet plays a pivotal role in facilitating exposure to a vast array of radical and extremist ideologies. It acts as a gateway to a diverse ideological landscape, allowing individuals to explore controversial content with relative anonymity. This anonymity serves as a protective mechanism, enabling users to engage with material that might otherwise carry legal or social repercussions. The internet also provides an environment rich in social reinforcement, particularly through echo chambers where specific narratives are continuously validated and normalised. Within these spaces, individuals are encouraged to express themselves in ways that align with their emerging belief systems, reinforcing their ideological shift.

As individuals become more embedded in these online communities, their susceptibility to further radical content increases. The internet thus becomes a transformative platform, especially potent during periods of psychological or emotional upheaval. The transition from passive browsing to active engagement with extremist norms and values may be subtle, yet it marks a significant shift in the individual's cognitive and ideological framework. This shift often results in a clear demarcation between their previous world-view and the newly adopted belief system, signalling a deeper commitment to the radical ideology (Neo, 2016).

2. Exploration

The exploration phase marks a critical juncture in the individual's psychological progression towards radicalisation. At this stage, the individual actively seeks out narratives and information that resonate with their emerging concerns and ideological leanings. This is not a passive process; rather, it involves deliberate sense-making, where the individual begins to interpret and integrate radical content with their existing world-view. The process is dynamic and often intertwined with the reflection phase, underscoring the non-linear and overlapping nature of radicalisation (Neo, 2016).

The internet plays a central role in facilitating this phase. It provides on-demand access to a vast array of ideologically charged material, often presented in diverse formats such as videos, memes, forums, and articles that are both attentionally engaging and emotionally provocative. These formats can trigger cognitive biases, such as confirmation bias, where individuals selectively attend to information that supports their emerging beliefs, and narrative bias, which leads them to favour coherent, emotionally resonant stories over complex or contradictory realities. The dominance of Type 1 processing, which is fast, intuitive, and emotionally driven, further reinforces the assimilation of radical content without critical scrutiny.

As individuals encounter narratives that align with their personal experiences or grievances, they begin to form deeper cognitive and emotional connections to these ideologies. This stage is characterised by active engagement, where individuals assess the relevance of new information to their evolving world-view. The internet not only facilitates this engagement but also amplifies it through algorithmic reinforcement and social validation, making the ideological shift more compelling and psychologically rewarding. In this sense, the internet can act as a mirror for their new beliefs while also serving to magnify their existing vulnerabilities and susceptibility to extremist propaganda (Neo, 2016).

In alignment with the exploration phase, Neo (2016) identified a critical tipping point in the radicalisation process, where the individual encounters violent extremist content online and is faced with a pivotal decision:

- Ignore the content: at this juncture, the individual chooses not to engage with the extremist ideology. Instead, they disengage and continue searching for material that better aligns with their existing beliefs, values, or psychological needs. This path reflects a rejection of the radical narrative and a preservation of their current world-view.
- Continue and integrate: alternatively, the individual finds resonance between the extremist narratives and their own emerging concerns. This alignment initiates a cognitive cascade, whereby the individual actively seeks out additional content that reinforces their evolving beliefs. The initial ideological reference point acts as a catalyst, encouraging further exploration and deepening commitment. This process is often reinforced by confirmation bias and selective exposure, as the individual increasingly filters information to support their new ideological stance.

This decision point is psychologically significant, as it marks the transition from passive exposure to active ideological integration. The internet facilitates this process by offering immediate access to a wide array of ideologically congruent material, often presented in emotionally compelling formats that heighten engagement and reduce critical scrutiny. As such, this phase underscores the importance of cognitive biases and emotional vulnerability in shaping the trajectory of radicalisation.

3. Connection

At this stage, the individual forms social bonds with like-minded individuals through online forums, chat groups, and social media platforms. These interactions reinforce their developing beliefs and provide a sense of community, further embedding the radical ideology into their personal identity. The connection phase marks the point at which the individual begins to form meaningful social bonds with others who share similar ideological perspectives. These connections are typically forged through online communities, forums, encrypted messaging platforms, and social media networks. The internet facilitates these interactions by offering low-barrier access to like-minded individuals, often within tightly controlled echo chambers that reinforce shared beliefs.

This stage is psychologically significant because it provides the individual with a sense of belonging, validation, and emotional support. The social reinforcement received from these communities strengthens the individual's commitment to the ideology and reduces cognitive dissonance that may arise from conflicting beliefs. The individual is no longer engaging with radical content in isolation; instead, they are embedded within a social structure that normalises and legitimises extremist views.

Moreover, the interactive nature of online platforms allows for real-time feedback, encouragement, and ideological grooming. These interactions often involve the sharing of personal narratives, group rituals, and symbolic language that deepen the individual's identification with the group. The social identity theory is particularly relevant here, as the individual begins to shift their self-concept to align with the in-group, often accompanied by increased hostility towards perceived out-groups.

4. Resolution

The individual now adopts the radical ideology as a core part of their belief system. This ideological commitment translates into a readiness to act, driven by a perceived moral obligation to support the group's goals and values. In the resolution phase, the individual transitions from ideological exploration to ideological commitment. The beliefs and values of the radical group are now internalised and adopted as central components of the individual's identity. This stage is marked by a psychological consolidation of the extremist world-view, where the individual perceives the group's goals as morally justified and personally meaningful.

The internet continues to play a crucial role by offering ideological reinforcement through curated content, propaganda, and peer validation. The individual may begin to engage in more structured activities such as participating in online campaigns, disseminating radical material, or mentoring newer recruits. This phase is often accompanied by a moral disengagement from societal norms, as the individual rationalises the use of violence or other extreme actions as necessary and legitimate.

Cognitive biases remain influential, particularly moral disengagement, in-group bias, and just-world beliefs that can help the individual justify their alignment with the group's objectives. The psychological momentum gained during this phase propels the individual towards action, as the ideological framework now provides both clarity and urgency.

5. Operational
   In the final stage, the individual becomes actively involved in planning or executing actions aligned with the group's objectives. This may include online activities such as propaganda dissemination or offline acts of violence, depending on the nature of the group and the individual's role within it. The operational stage represents the culmination of the radicalisation process, where the individual becomes action-orientated and ready to engage in behaviours that align with the group's strategic goals. These actions may range from online activities such as cyber-attacks, doxxing, or propaganda dissemination to offline behaviours including recruitment, logistical support, or direct involvement in violent acts.

   At this stage, the individual has undergone a complete ideological transformation, with their previous belief system replaced by a new, radicalised world-view. The internet serves as both a tool and a theatre for operational engagement, offering platforms for co-ordination, anonymity, and amplification of impact. Importantly, the transition to operational behaviour is often subtle and incremental. The individual may begin with low-risk activities and gradually escalate to more direct forms of involvement. The normalisation of violence, dehumanisation of out-groups, and perceived moral imperative to act are key psychological drivers in this phase.

   Neo (2016) emphasises that while the stages of RECRO are conceptually distinct, they are deeply interconnected, with feedback loops and overlaps that reflect the complex, non-linear nature of radicalisation – particularly in digital environments.

Digital Platforms and Radicalisation

Social Media

Social media is one of the most common platforms for distributing and consuming radical content. Estimates suggest that 80% of European teenagers have encountered material on social media that promotes violence or includes racist or xenophobic sentiment (Naderer et al., 2024). Even individuals searching for neutral or apolitical information online may inadvertently encounter violent extremist propaganda (Naderer et al., 2024). Schmitt et al. (2018) observed that users viewing counter-extremist content on platforms such as YouTube often encounter additional material aligned with extremist ideologies due to algorithmic biases. Consequently, information sources can become "poisoned," even when users seek content contrary to their current viewpoints, creating conditions for cognitive biases to take hold. As social media companies are typically slow to remove such content, if they act at all, individuals can face repeated exposure to similar narratives, deepening the illusory truth effect and reinforcing extremist beliefs.

Research indicates that exposure to radical online content is associated with extremist attitudes both online and offline, as well as an increased risk of violent political acts. This link appears across all types of radical propaganda, underscoring the need to address extremism in all its forms. Individuals who actively seek violent radical material are at greater risk of engaging in political violence compared to passive consumers, a pattern potentially linked to confirmation bias. The internet and social media act as catalysts by enabling at-risk individuals to access extremist content, join online and offline networks, and gather information for planning attacks. Online interaction with like-minded individuals can intensify extremist attitudes and foster negative perceptions of out-groups, particularly when combined with offline interactions with people holding opposing views. However, current evidence does not support the claim that online platforms operate independently of offline influences. Instead, the internet and social media appear to shape decisions in conjunction with offline factors, facilitating radicalisation processes, especially for active seekers of extremist content (Hassan et al., 2018).

Researchers have noted a connection between viewing radical extremist content online and the development of attitudes aligned with that material (Naderer et al., 2024; Hassan et al., 2018). This process can create a reinforcement loop whereby individuals are continually bombarded with extremist content, increasing the likelihood that such ideologies take hold in their cognitive processes (Naderer et al., 2024). Hassan et al. (2018) found some evidence that exposure to online content could lead directly to radicalisation, although Binder and Kenyon (2022) argue that there is no clear evidence detailing how much direct involvement is required for an individual to follow this path. Furthermore, Binder and Kenyon (2022) note that when online radicalisation is considered as the sole basis for engaging in violent extremism, the evidence remains very limited. Often, information about planned attacks is leaked online, which can be used to prevent these acts from crossing into the physical world (Binder & Kenyon, 2022).

Much of the research in this field remains conjectural, with a mix of anecdotal accounts and limited empirical evidence. However, there is an implicit recognition of cognitive biases as part of the radicalisation process (Naderer et al., 2024; Jensen et al., 2018).

Video Gaming, Gamification, and Radicalisation

A huge number of people play video games as part of their everyday lives, usually seeing it as a way of unwinding or socialising with people from all around the globe. Figures vary widely, but some estimates suggest that there are around 2.7 billion gamers globally (Clement, 2025), with higher estimates suggesting the figure is over three billion (Kumar, 2025). Debates surrounding the potential link between aggression in individuals and playing violent video games have been repeatedly raised, not only as a moral panic within the mass media but also within the collective research on the area. On the one side, we have the argument that there is a significant link between playing violent video games and aggression, as well as a reduction in prosocial behaviours. On the other side, we have the argument that there is no consistent link between the two, and where there are, such effects are minimal (Kühn et al., 2019). There have also been those who have suggested that while gaming presents a rather passive and enjoyable pastime, there is a darker and more disturbing side to gaming, this being a potential link between the presence of radical ideology in video games and violent extremism (Schlegel & Kowert, 2024; Schlegel, 2021).

On March 15, 2019, Brenton Harrison Tarrant, a 28-year-old Australian citizen, carried out a terrorist attack on two mosques in Christchurch, New Zealand, resulting in the deaths of 51 individuals and injuries to many others. Tarrant had extensively documented his radical ideology in a manifesto that he published online prior to the attack. This document revealed a range of extreme right-wing views, including white supremacist and Islamophobic beliefs (Lakhani et al., 2021).

During the first assault, Tarrant livestreamed the attack using a GoPro camera, deliberately mimicking the aesthetic and perspective of popular first-person shooter (FPS) video games. In such games, players typically assume the role of a combatant and engage in simulated battles against designated targets. His manifesto further incorporated numerous gaming references, including the use of structured "rules" for his actions and a system for tracking his progress through what he described as "levels," a framing that positioned the attack within a gamified narrative (Lakhani et al., 2021). The attack provoked widespread moral outrage and condemnation, as was entirely warranted given its horrific nature. It also sparked a broader discourse on the potential for gaming platforms and aesthetics to be co-opted in the service of violent extremism, raising urgent questions about the intersection of digital culture and radicalisation.

However, many researchers have highlighted that the use of video games in the context of radicalisation was prevalent as early as the 1980s, so this phenomenon is not a sudden by-product of the rise in digital technology. In their exploration of this area, Schlegel and Kowert (2024) noted that gaming platforms and game-like mechanisms, often referred to as gamification, are also widely employed within radicalisation strategies. These mechanisms serve not only as tools for ideological dissemination but also as immersive environments that can foster identity formation, group cohesion, and behavioural conditioning.

Games Used in Radicalisation

1. Bespoke games
   These are games specifically designed to reflect and promote the ideologies of extremist groups. A notable example is the Special Force series developed by Hezbollah in the early 2000s. In these games, players assume the role of fighters in the South Lebanon conflict. The training mode encourages players to shoot

at posters of prominent Israeli leaders, including Ariel Sharon, who served as prime minister of Israel from 2001 to 2006. Completion of in-game challenges is rewarded with virtual medals or certificates of honour, often attributed to Hezbollah's then-leader, Hassan Nasrallah. These rewards serve to reinforce ideological commitment and valorise participation in violent struggle.

2. Modded games
   Extremist groups have also exploited existing commercial games by modifying them (modding) to include radical content. These modifications can range from changing character skins and environments to inserting propaganda messages or altering game objectives to align with extremist narratives. For example, popular FPS games have been altered to simulate attacks on perceived enemies, turning mainstream titles into tools for ideological reinforcement. Others have noted that other popular gaming platforms such as The Sims and Minecraft have also been subverted to portray the attacks that took place in Christchurch, showing the extent to which extremist groups will go (Schlegel, 2021; Schlegel & Kowert, 2024).
3. Gamified training simulations
   Some groups have developed training simulations that mimic military operations, often using game engines to create realistic combat scenarios. These simulations are not always publicly distributed but may be used internally to train recruits in tactics, weapons handling, or strategic thinking. The gamified nature of these tools can desensitise individuals to violence and foster a sense of preparedness and legitimacy.
4. Online role-playing and social games
   Massively multiplayer online games (MMOs) and role-playing platforms have also been used as spaces for recruitment and ideological grooming. These environments allow for anonymous interaction, community building, and the gradual introduction of extremist ideas. The immersive nature of role-playing can blur the lines between fantasy and reality, making it easier for individuals to adopt radical personas and narratives.
5. Gamified propaganda platforms
   Beyond traditional games, some extremist groups have created web-based platforms that use gamification elements, such as points, badges, and progression systems, to encourage engagement with propaganda materials. Users may earn rewards for watching videos, sharing content, or completing ideological "missions," thereby reinforcing participation through behavioural incentives. These gamified platforms are particularly problematic because they serve to blur the lines among what could be classed as entertainment, education, and indoctrination into radical ideologies. Where groups begin to embed radical content into an attractive reward-based system that is highly social and competitive, it can foster a process of re-engagement with the ideology of that reference group, serving to create confirmation bias and positive reinforcement (Schlegel, 2021).

Why Is Gaming Such a Pervasive Lure for Radicalisation?

The potential reasons why gaming and gamification become so well-suited to the promotion of radical ideology link directly to the psychological mechanisms that underpin why we engage in playing them so much. One of the processes that can encourage an individual's alignment with the ideals and values of the extremist group is that of identity fusion. This is a process whereby individuals strongly align their personal identity to that of a cause or a group (Kowert et al., 2022, 2023). Identifying with fusion is a powerful psychological connection where an individual will be deeply involved with a group and become personally tied to other people within that group. It is a deeper dynamic than just thinking about the individual becoming part of the group but is better viewed as the group becoming part of the individual (Kowert et al., 2022). This process is set aside from the way in which we would identify with a group, which is seen as where we see ourselves as members of that group, but there is no suggestion that the individual manifests the group identity within their own. For identity fusion, the emotional bond between the group and members of that group is immensely strong and becomes akin to a family bond, where the individual will do anything to protect them. As such a strong connection exists, those who experience identity fusion are far more likely to engage in extreme activities to support it, even if this means they may put themselves and others at risk of harm. The strength of identity fusion has been demonstrated to predict the extent to which an individual would be willing to fight, make a sacrifice or even die for their in-group (Kowert et al., 2022). Most people know the difference between right and wrong, but just knowing what is right does not always mean someone will do the right thing, especially when doing so comes at a high personal cost, like risking their life. This is where identity fusion plays a powerful role. When someone feels deeply connected to a group, so much so that the group feels like part of their own identity, they are more likely to act on their moral beliefs, even if it means making a big sacrifice (Kowert et al., 2023).

In one study, people were asked to imagine a situation where they could save five members of their country by sacrificing themselves. Almost everyone agreed that the moral thing to do was to make the sacrifice. But only those who felt strongly fused with their group said they would do it (Swann & Buhrmester, 2015). Why would this be the case? Well, mostly because those who had strongly fused with the group were more likely to be driven by emotion and loyalty to their group. They did not need to think it through, as they felt it was the right thing to do. On the other hand, people who were not as emotionally connected to the group only considered self-sacrifice after weighing the pros and cons. So, while moral beliefs are important, they are not always enough. It's the emotional bond with others, especially through identity fusion, that often pushes people to take real, sometimes extreme, moral action.

Video games can create strong emotional bonds between players and the gaming community, providing an ideal environment for identity fusion to take place. Many games involve shared challenges, like teaming up to defeat powerful enemies that can feel intense and meaningful. Where people go through tough or exciting experiences together, they often form deeper connections. Research shows that friendships formed in gaming environments can be more personal and emotionally close than those made in other online spaces. Players often share more about themselves and build trust through teamwork and communication. These strong relationships and shared experiences can lead to identity fusion (Kowert et al., 2022). Other factors, such as personality traits that are inherent in those individuals who seek out gaming communities to fill a shortfall in social engagement. There is a wide variety of research that has examined the traits of gamers that make them more likely to look to online gaming for social interaction, including feelings of loneliness, insecurity, and aspects of anxiety (Kowert et al., 2022).

As part of their research, Kowert et al. (2022) explored the underlying mechanics that could be at work in the context of gaming and the propagation of extremist ideologies. In three separate studies, they demonstrated that at the heart of the emergence of radicalised ideologies, including the existence of being willing to fight and die for gaming culture, sexism, racism, and aggressive behaviour, was the fusion of identity with the gaming community. Those individuals who engaged in playing more extreme, violent, and competitive video games which had a high level of toxicity (e.g., in-game trash-talking, derogatory comments, flaming, and trolling) were more likely to have a stronger level of fusion identity in comparison to those who played less competitive, less violent, and less toxic games (Kowert et al., 2022).

In summary, the psychological dynamics of identity fusion, combined with the immersive and socially interactive nature of gaming environments, create fertile ground for extremist ideologies to take root. Gamification amplifies these effects by rewarding engagement and fostering a sense of achievement, which can be co-opted by radical actors to strengthen ideological commitment. When emotional bonds formed through gaming intersect with narratives of belonging and purpose, the result is a powerful mechanism for radicalisation, one that operates subtly yet effectively within digital spaces. Understanding these processes is critical for developing strategies to mitigate the exploitation of gaming platforms by extremist groups.

Summary

This chapter explores online radicalisation as a hybrid process within the broader framework of digital warfare, emphasising its interplay between offline grievances and online amplification. It begins by situating radicalisation as a continuum rather than a purely digital phenomenon, noting that identity crises, marginalisation, and perceived injustice often serve as offline precursors that make individuals susceptible to extremist narratives. Digital platforms act as accelerants, transforming traditional radicalisation pathways through scale, speed, and algorithmic reinforcement.

The discussion identifies core traits shared by radical groups, such as perceived grievances, ideological rigidity, and legitimisation of violence, and examines how these are embedded and amplified in online ecosystems. Psychological mechanisms such as cognitive dissonance, moral disengagement, and narrative bias are highlighted as key drivers, enabling individuals to reconcile violent acts with moral frameworks and adopt simplified, emotionally charged narratives. Extremist content often leverages archetypal story structures (heroism, victimhood, and redemption) and memetic strategies to exploit cognitive shortcuts, creating echo chambers that reinforce belief through repetition and emotional salience.

The chapter introduces Neo's RECRO model to conceptualise the pathway from initial vulnerability to active extremism, illustrating how the internet mediates each stage through anonymity, algorithmic curation, and social validation. It also examines the role of digital affordances such as social media platforms, encrypted messaging, and recommendation systems that serve to foster ideological grooming and operational readiness.

Emerging vectors such as gaming and gamification are explored as novel mechanisms for radicalisation. Immersive environments, identity fusion, and reward-based systems are shown to facilitate group cohesion and ideological commitment, blurring boundaries between entertainment and indoctrination. Examples include bespoke extremist games, modded commercial titles, and gamified propaganda platforms, all of which exploit psychological needs for belonging and significance.

The chapter concludes by underscoring that online radicalisation is not an isolated phenomenon but a strategic form of psychological and informational warfare. It calls for counter-measures focused on digital resilience, platform governance, and education, while recognising the complexity of mitigating processes that operate across both online and offline domains.

References

Allen, M., & Preiss, R. W. (1997). Comparing the persuasiveness of narrative and statistical evidence using meta-analysis. *International Journal of Phytoremediation, 14*(2), 125–131. https://doi.org/10.1080/08824099709388654

Awan, A. N., Hoskins, A., & O'Loughlin, B. (2011). *Radicalisation and media: Connectivity and terrorism in the new media ecology*. London and New York: Routledge.

Bandura, A. (1990). Selective activation and disengagement of moral control. *Journal of Social Issues, 46*(1), 27–46. https://doi.org/10.1111/j.1540-4560.1990.tb00270.x

Baugut, P., & Neumann, K. (2020). Online propaganda use during Islamist radicalization. *Information Communication and Society, 23*(11), 1570–1592. https://doi.org/10.1080/1369118X.2019.1594333

Betsch, C., Haase, N., Renkewitz, F., & Schmid, P. (2015). The narrative bias revisited: What drives the biasing influence of narrative information on risk perceptions? *Judgment and Decision Making, 10*(3), 241–264. https://doi.org/10.1017/s1930297500004654

Binder, J. F., & Kenyon, J. (2022). Terrorism and the internet: How dangerous is online radicalization? *Frontiers in Psychology*, *13*(October), 1–10. https://doi.org/10.3389/fpsyg.2022.997390

Clement, J. (2025). *Video gaming worldwide – statistics and facts*. Retrieved from Statista website https://www.statista.com/topics/1680/gaming/#topicOverview

Cohen, K., Johansson, F., Kaati, L., & Mork, J. C. (2014). Detecting linguistic markers for radical violence in social media. *Terrorism and Political Violence*, *26*(1), 246–256. https://doi.org/10.1080/09546553.2014.849948

Conway, M., & McInerney, L. (2008). Jihadi video and auto-radicalisation: Evidence from an exploratory YouTube study. *Lecture Notes in Computer Science (Including Subseries Lecture Notes in Artificial Intelligence and Lecture Notes in Bioinformatics)*, *5376 LNCS*, 108–118. https://doi.org/10.1007/978-3-540-89900-6_13

Doosje, B., Moghaddam, F. M., Kruglanski, A. W., de Wolf, A., Mann, L., & Feddes, A. R. (2016). Terrorism, radicalization and de-radicalization. *Current Opinion in Psychology*, *11*, 79–84. https://doi.org/10.1016/j.copsyc.2016.06.008

Fernandez, M., Gonzalez-Pardo, A., & Alani, H. (2014). Radicalisation influence in social media. *Journal of the Web of Science*, *6*, 1–15.

Festinger, L. (1957). *A theory of cognitive dissonance*. Stanford: Stanford University Press.

Garcet, S. (2021). Understanding the psychological aspects of the radicalisation process: A sociocognitive approach. *Forensic Sciences Research*, *6*(2), 115–123. https://doi.org/10.1080/20961790.2020.1869883

Hessayon, A., & Finnegan, D. (2013). Introduction reappraising early modern radicals and radicalisms. *Varieties of Seventeenth- and Early Eighteenth-Century English Radicalism in Context*, 1–30.

Koomen, W., & Van Der Pligt, J. (2016). The psychology of radicalization and terrorism. *The Psychology of Radicalization and Terrorism*, *30*(2009), 1–274. https://doi.org/10.1080/13537903.2016.1256667

Kowert, R., Martel, A., & Swann, W. B. (2022). Not just a game: Identity fusion and extremism in gaming cultures. *Frontiers in Communication*, *7*. https://doi.org/10.3389/fcomm.2022.1007128

Kowert, R., Martel, A., & Swann, W. B. (2023). You are what you play: The risks of identity fusion in toxic gamer cultures. *Games: Research and Practice*, *1*(2), 1–3. https://doi.org/10.1145/3604402

Kruglanski, A. W., Gelfand, M. J., Bélanger, J. J., Sheveland, A., Hetiarachchi, M., & Gunaratna, R. (2014). The psychology of radicalization and deradicalization: How significance quest impacts violent extremism. *Political Psychology*, *35*(Suppl.1), 69–93. https://doi.org/10.1111/pops.12163

Kühn, S., Kugler, D. T., Schmalen, K., Weichenberger, M., Witt, C., & Gallinat, J. (2019). Does playing violent video games cause aggression? A longitudinal intervention study. *Molecular Psychiatry*, *24*(8), 1220–1234. https://doi.org/10.1038/s41380-018-0031-7

Kumar, N. (2025). *How many gamers are there* (2025 Statistics). Retrieved from Demandsage website https://www.demandsage.com/gamers-statistics/

Lakhani, S., White, J., & Wallner, C. (2021). *The gamification of (violent) extremism: An exploration of emerging trends, future threat scenarios and potential P/CV solutiuons*. Luxembourg.

Little, R., Ford, P., & Girardi, A. (2021). Online self-radicalisation: A case study of cognitive vulnerabilities for radicalization to extremism and single actor terrorism. *Journal of Intellectual Disabilities and Offending Behaviour*, *12*(3–4), 112–123. https://doi.org/10.1108/JIDOB-03-2021-0006

Malthaner, S. (2017). Radicalization: The evolution of an analytical paradigm. *Archives Europeennes de Sociologie*, *58*(3), 369–401. https://doi.org/10.1017/S0003975617000182
Maslow, A. H. (1954). Motivation and personality. https://doi.org/10.1037/h0039764
Mila, M. N., Putra, I. E., & Umam, A. N. (2019). Stories from Jihadists: Significance, identity, and radicalization through the call for jihad. *Peace and Conflict: Journal of Peace*, *25*(2), 1–35.
Mølmen, G. N., & Ravndal, J. A. (2023). Mechanisms of online radicalisation: How the internet affects the radicalisation of extreme-right lone actor terrorists. *Behavioral Sciences of Terrorism and Political Aggression*, *15*(4), 463–487. https://doi.org/10.1080/19434472.2021.1993302
Moore, C. (2015). Moral disengagement. *Current Opinion in Psychology*, *6*, 199–204. https://doi.org/10.1016/j.copsyc.2015.07.018
Moskalenko, S., & McCauley, C. (2021). QAiion: Radical opinion versus radical action. *Perspectives on Terrorism*, *15*(2), 142–146.
Mutton, R., Lewis, J., & Marsden, S. (2023). *Full report online radicalisation: A rapid review of the literature*, (July). Retrieved from www.crestresearch.ac.uk/projects/contest
Naderer, B., Rieger, D., & Schwertberger, U. (2024). An online world of bias: The mediating role of cognitive biases on extremist attitudes. *Communications*, *49*(1), 51–73. https://doi.org/10.1515/commun-2021-0115
Neo, L. S. (2016). *An Internet-Mediated Pathway for Online Radicalisation*, (2007), 197–224. https://doi.org/10.4018/978-1-5225-0156-5.ch011
Nilsson, M. (2022). Motivations for Jihad and cognitive dissonance: A qualitative analysis of former swedish jihadists. *Studies in Conflict and Terrorism*, *45*(1), 92–110. https://doi.org/10.1080/1057610X.2019.1626091
O'Brien, E. (2020). When small signs of change add up: The psychology of tipping points. *Current Directions in Psychological Science*, *29*(1), 55–62. https://doi.org/10.1177/0963721419884313
Reinard, J. C. (1988). The empirical study of the persuasive effects of evidence: The status after fifty years of research. *Human Communication Research*, *15*(1), 3–59.
Ryan, R. M., & Deci, E. L. (2000). Self-determination theory and the facilitation of intrinsic motivation, social development, and well-being. *American Psychologist*, *55*(1), 68–78.
Schlegel, L. (2021). The role of gamification in radicalization processes. *Modus/Zad Working Paper*, (2019), 1–20.
Schlegel, L., & Kowert, R. (2024). *Gaming and extremism: The radicalization of digital playgrounds*. London, UK: Taylor & Francis.
Schmid, A. (2005). Terrorism as psychological warfare. *Democracy and Security*, *1*(2), 137–146. https://doi.org/10.1080/17419160500322467
Schmid, A. (2013). Radicalisation, de-radicalisation, counter-radicalisation: A conceptual discussion and literature review. *Terrorism and Counter-Terrorism Studies*. https://doi.org/10.19165/2013.1.02
Schmitt, J. B., Debbelt, C. A., Schneider, F. M., Schmitt, J. B., Debbelt, C. A., & Schneider, F. M. (2018). Too much information? Predictors of information overload in the context of online news exposure the context of online news exposure, *4462*. https://doi.org/10.1080/1369118X.2017.1305427
Shin, D. (2024). Artificial misinformation. In *Artificial misinformation*. https://doi.org/10.1007/978-3-031-52569-8
Swann, W. B., & Buhrmester, M. D. (2015). Identity fusion. *Current Directions in Psychological Science*, *24*(1), 52–57. https://doi.org/10.1177/0963721414551363
Van Bergen, D. D., Feddes, A. F., Doosje, B., & Pels, T. V. M. (2015). Collective identity factors and the attitude toward violence in defense of ethnicity or religion among

Muslim youth of Turkish and Moroccan Descent. *International Journal of Intercultural Relations*, *47*, 89–100. https://doi.org/10.1016/j.ijintrel.2015.03.026
Winterbottom, A., Bekker, H. L., Conner, M., & Mooney, A. (2008). Does narrative information bias individual's decision making? A systematic review. *Social Science and Medicine*, *67*(12), 2079–2088. https://doi.org/10.1016/j.socscimed.2008.09.037

14 Memetic Warfare: How Ideas Become Weapons Online

Introduction: It's All in the Meme

The concept of the meme was first introduced by Dawkins (2006) and has been more recently adopted to describe a visual stimulus that is distributed via the internet (McNamara, 2011; Shifman, 2019). A meme, in its simplest form, is a basic unit of cultural transmission and can be an idea, some form of behaviour, or a style that spreads from one person to another. Unlike genetic transmission, memes propagate through social interaction, yet they mirror biological evolution in striking ways. Dawkins' original theory positioned memes within a Darwinian framework, where cultural ideas compete for survival much like organisms in nature. Each meme must replicate to endure; those that fail to spread effectively will fade, while the "fittest," those with cultural resonance and emotional appeal, will thrive. This survival-of-the-fittest dynamic underscores the selective pressures acting on memes within digital ecosystems. Like biological organisms, memes also mutate as users remix and reinterpret them, enabling adaptation to shifting cultural landscapes and technological platforms.

A meme can be captured in any number of ways, and as McNamara (2011) pointed out, it can be "a word, a phrase, a riff, image, or gesture" (p. 1). Shifman (2019) offered a more nuanced definition that is directly tailored to memes in the digital age and described internet memes as

> a) a group of digital items sharing common characteristics of content, form, and/or stance, which (b) were created with awareness of each other, and (c) were circulated, imitated, and/or transformed via the Internet by many users.
>
> (Shifman, 2019, p. 41)

While this definition is well-rounded and presents a clear analysis of what constitutes an internet meme, others have argued that the positioning of the definition may be overly restrictive. For example, Wiggins (2019) argued that Shifman's original definition of internet memes was primarily focused on video-based memes. While this format was dominant in the early days of

DOI: 10.4324/9781003752400-14

the memeosphere, it has since been overshadowed by more diverse and adaptable forms such as image–text memes, GIFs, and an underlying remix culture. This shift highlighted the need for broader, more flexible definitions that reflect the participatory and iterative nature of contemporary digital culture, where memes evolve rapidly across platforms and genres. Wiggins (2019) adopted another definition, suggesting that an internet meme is a "remixed, iterated message that can be rapidly diffused by members of participatory digital culture for the purpose of satire, parody, critique, or other discursive activity" (p. 11). This definition is more flexible than that of Shifman (2019), and the inclusion of aspects related to undefined activities means that it can be applied to many different types of memes.

Internet memes tend to follow a generic format, usually images that are accompanied by some form of text, with the meaning being aligned to a collective idea or cultural reference. Usually, the meme is an image taken from popular culture, the realm of politics or an everyday occurrence, which is then reconstructed with relevant language (Osterroth, 2015). Other memetic types are also evident on the internet, such as videos and GIFs, but they tend to be less common than the staple image-language format. The typical structure of the most widely recognised internet meme aligns with five key elements:

1. Top text – Although this is often an optional element, there is usually some element that sets up the context or a question for the meme.
2. Image – Some form of central visual element, usually derived from popular culture or a reaction image that serves to grab attention.
3. Bottom text – This is the aspect that usually delivers the punchline, some form of commentary, or a twist.
4. Font style – Usually bold, white text with a black background.
5. Layout – Generally, the image occupies most of the visual space, and the text is overlaid on the image at the top and bottom of the image.

I have taken the liberty to create an example meme below using the very popular "distracted boyfriend" meme template in Figure 14.1. While this is a little different from some of the mainstream memes, the example should give the reader a flavour of what an internet meme looks like.

As can be extrapolated from the definitions provided by Wiggins and Shifman, internet memes rarely exist in isolation and are often grouped around a pivotal issue or discussion point. The meme can be seen as forming the singular, most basic unit of what could be termed a "memeplex," a structural constellation of interconnected memes (or aspects of cultural information) (McNamara, 2011). Memes in this environment can serve to evolve together and serve to reinforce each other as they share the same cognitive and social environment (Neklesova & Karpenko, 2023).

Figure 14.1 Example meme.

Memes are seen to possess three key properties that allow them to evolve, the first of these being *replicability*. Memes are spread by copying human behaviour and live in the world of human actions; what we say, what we do, what we share, and what we imitate all serve to allow memes to replicate. It might be a catchy dance move or a novel phrase, like these memes, which are passed from one person to another when someone else sees them and decides to copy them. With the advent of social media and digital technology, such sharing and replication happen much faster (McNamara, 2011). According to McNamara (2011), a meme must pass through several key stages for it to replicate itself. First, a meme must be assimilated into our perceptual system through whatever modality it is presented in (e.g., visual and auditory). It then must be retained in memory so that it can be recalled and then expressed in a format that others can understand and perceive. This last stage leads to the transmission of the meme to another person, thus leading to the replication process being repeated. Memes also possess a massive amount of variance, as is reflected in the different cultures which make up global society. As highlighted by the link to Darwinism, memes are also subject to natural selection, where reference points, terms, and concepts can be highly popular at one time and lost to the winds of time in a few days.

There are some key examples of more generic, not internet-based memes that exist within current society, some of which have had more permanence than others. For example, the "peace sign," or two raised fingers in a V for victory, has its origins in the first years of the Second World War. Victor de Laveleye, a WW1 veteran, will perhaps be best remembered for one single radio broadcast in January 1941. In this, he proposed that people adopt the "V" symbol as a sign of defiance against the occupation of Nazi forces across Europe, choosing it, as it was both the first letter in French for "victory" (*victoire*) and Dutch (*vrijheid*, meaning "freedom"). This meme was soon adopted more widely and gained more prominence when the then Prime Minister Winston Churchill started using the "V for victory" gesture as a mechanism for boosting morale. In a similar way, the Z symbol has been adopted as a mechanism for the demonstration of pro-Russian support for the invasion of Ukraine. Many theories have been postulated about the origins of this meme, but most likely it came about as people spotted Russian tanks daubed with the Z symbol, potentially as a clear indicator that they were indeed Russian to avoid friendly fire incidents. The adoption of the symbol was widespread and quick to reproduce, not only due to the use of social media but also the fact that state media were quick to capitalise on the presence of this meme (Kerley & Greenhall, 2022).

While the concept of an internet meme is usually seen as a mechanism for transferring a humorous message or a way of ridiculing someone in a way that is sarcastic, there is another side to them. Researchers have noted that memeplexes can be created by groups of people or state actors to deliver serious messages, some of which still retain an element of humour within them. The power of memeplexes is the blend of social commentary and overt humour, which means they become a perfectly adaptable form for digital expression and require very little effort to understand (Turk et al., 2025). Memes can easily become the fire-and-forget weapons of the digital battlefield; they can be created cheaply and quickly, they can be used to target specific groups or wider portions of society, they can be launched quickly, and you do not need to guide or support them.

The Life Cycle of a Meme

Understanding how memes evolve and spread is essential to grasping their power in digital culture and warfare. Drawing on the work in this area (Johann & Bülow, 2019; Shifman, 2019), we can conceptualise a meme's journey through a life cycle that mirrors both biological and cultural transmission. This framework helps explain not only how memes gain traction but also how they mutate, peak, and sometimes fade, only to be reborn in new contexts.

Stage 1: Creation

A meme begins with an original piece of content, which can be an image, phrase, video, or idea that in turn resonates with a cultural moment or emotional sentiment. This content is often humorous, provocative, or symbolic. This stage is governed by how easy the original meme is to open to being remixed and adapted.

Stage 2: Circulation

Once created, the meme is shared across digital platforms (e.g., Reddit, Twitter, and TikTok). Its spread is driven by its cultural resonance, or how well it connects with shared cultural values or emotions. Memes that are emotionally engaging or ideologically aligned with an individual or group are more likely to be shared.

Stage 3: Mutation

As the meme spreads, users remix or reinterpret it, often adding new captions, formats, or cultural references. This stage reflects the capacity for creativity in online communities. The meme becomes a "template" for expression, evolving into a memeplex, forming a cluster of related variants that reinforce a shared narrative or joke.

Stage 4: Peak Virality

The meme reaches a saturation point where it becomes widely recognised, often spilling into mainstream media or being referenced by public figures. At this stage, the meme may be used for political messaging, brand marketing, or social commentary, amplifying its cultural impact.

Stage 5: Decline or Recontextualisation

Eventually, the meme loses novelty and fades from prominence. However, some memes are recontextualised and can be revived in new formats or adapted to new events months or years after they originally appeared. Others become part of internet folklore, referenced nostalgically or archived in meme databases.

This life cycle model offers a valuable lens through which to analyse the strategic deployment of memes in digital environments. Whether used for humour, activism, or manipulation, memes follow a recognisable trajectory that reflects both their cultural relevance and adaptability. Understanding this life cycle is crucial for identifying how memes can be weaponised, countered, or sustained in the ever-evolving landscape of online discourse.

Meme Typology

The internet meme has emerged as a potent tool for digital communication and can be harnessed for humour, to expose an ideology, to inspire resistance, or to manipulate opinion and attitude. However, as humble and universal as the meme would appear to be at first glance, the task of trying to classify the multitude of forms memes can take is one that is fraught with some inherent problems. First and foremost, internet memes are not like traditional forms of media; they are an inherently fluid medium, making them infinitely adaptable to the current needs of the environment in which they are created. They are easily mutated into different forms that can change their meaning and appearance substantially from their origins. They are also highly context-dependent, meaning that once they are taken out of that specific context, they lose their coherence. So, overall, they lack the ability to apply a rigid classification system too. Then, add to this the realm of digital warfare, where memes can be used for both offensive and defensive purposes, harnessing the tactics of persuasion and influence to deceive and disrupt, and things become even more complicated.

Researchers have tackled the issues of classifying memes from several different perspectives, which in turn highlights the notion that the area itself is highly interdisciplinary. In an original conceptualisation, Brodie (2009) introduced a functional classification system that was heavily based on memetic theory and related categories to the action of the meme. For example, Shifman (2014) offered a way of categorising memes that used a communication-orientated framework that takes apart memes according to their content, their form, and their stance, in turn emphasising the notion that memes are participatory in nature and have transformative qualities, not only linked to the material within them but also their impact on the environment in which they are living. On the other hand, Baurecht (2020) used a multidimensional categorisation system that used aspects of the medium, the transmission format and the function the meme performs with culture, and by doing so, aimed to capture the full gamut of memetic variation.

Brodie (2009) suggested that memes can be differentiated according to their function within the memetic environment, where memes are seen to perform a set of fundamental actions.

1. Distinction memes: these embody the fundamental elements of cognition that humans use to categorise and label reality. Brodie describes them as the mental constructs that define what things are, from naming a geographical area a "state" to identifying oneself as a "human." They serve to create a distinction between concepts, shaping perception by creating boundaries and definitions. These types of memes are typically ones that are acquired through early language learning and cultural immersion and can include concepts such as "money," "nation," or "work," each of which is a socially constructed distinction.
2. Strategy memes: these memes encode beliefs about cause and effect, guiding behaviour and decision-making. They are often inherited from family, culture, or institutions and can operate unconsciously. As such, they often influence actions by suggesting what one should do to achieve desired outcomes. These memes are often passed on through the processes of socialisation with others, education and the media, such as the notion that "hard work leads to success" or "stranger danger." Brodie served to emphasise the importance of being aware of strategy memes that exist within our own cognitive systems, so we can explore if they align with our own current goals and values – only by deactivating maladaptive strategy memes can we take a step towards our own cognitive autonomy.

3. Association Memes: these memes link multiple sensory or conceptual elements, often in emotionally charged ways. They are particularly potent in advertising and propaganda because they bypass rational assessment and serve to appeal directly to instinctual drives. In terms of their function, they create an emotional resonance with the individual, enhancing the capacity for recall later. They are usually transmitted through a process of repetitive exposure and are a favoured weapon of choice for advertisers, as they are very easy to manipulate, relying on the core psychological trigger of sex. Examples can include memes such as "Sexy women and beer" or "Luxury cars and success."

However attractive this typology might appear, I would exercise a word of caution when exploring the memetic world using it. While having a list of categories for cataloguing meme types is useful, there is always the risk that outliers will emerge, leading to misclassification or dismissal as anomalies. This again highlights the inherent fluidity of memetic culture, where new forms can appear unexpectedly and challenge existing frameworks. Although such classification systems provide a helpful starting point for analysis, they currently lack robust empirical validation and should be applied with caution.

In Shifman's (2014) communication–orientation typology for memes, a three-dimensional system for the analysis of memes, which focused directly on the following characteristics:

1. *The content of the meme*: what are the main ideas and themes that are being conveyed within the meme?
2. *The form of the meme*: what is the shape of the meme, and what is its actual physical manifestation – for example, is it an image, is it text-based, or is it a video?
3. *The stance of the meme*: the positioning of the communication within the meme, such as the attitude portrayed within it, such as irony, mockery, or humour.

The beauty of this framework is useful when we are trying to delineate how memes and memeplexes function as a unit of digital culture, as well as having a grasp on how memes can evolve via the processes of imitation and transformation.

We can apply the tripartite model to the exploration of genre, where content relates directly to the thematic core of a meme; essentially, what the meme is about. The form element relates to the structure of the meme itself, or the medium in which it is communicated. Using these two dimensions alone, we can set about exploring genres of memes, particularly where recurrent formats or templates are used. These can include

- Reaction memes: these are typically images that are extremely expressive in nature, usually conveying some form of emotional response; typically,

Figure 14.2 A typical reaction meme, where the reaction is paradoxically linked to the presence of reaction memes!

the image is then paired with some text that highlights a reaction to an event or presents a common cultural reference. In most instances, there is a static image with the text content relating to some aspect of a relatable issue (see Figure 14.2).

- Advice animals: one of the authors' personal favourites, mainly because they are so ubiquitous and offer the capacity to present memetic information on so many levels. These are perhaps the most classic of meme genres and present a central character that is used to deliver a specific type of message, each of which can be highly tailored. The format for this type of meme is very rigid in terms of the template, and there is a high degree of predictability when it comes to the type of content that is conveyed. Usually, the central focus of the visual element is some form of animal (e.g., the *socially awkward penguin* or the *advice dog*, which portrays a Labrador puppy on a colour wheel background). However, advice animal memes can contain a plethora of other images, with the central theme being some form of advice or commentary on a topical social issue. An example of this type of meme is presented in Figure 14.3.
- Remix culture memes: remix culture memes represent one of the most dynamic and creative facets of memetic communication. They involve reworking existing media, whether iconic images, video clips, or cultural references, by inserting new captions, altering contexts, or combining disparate elements to create novel meanings. This process reflects the participatory nature of digital culture, where users are not passive consumers but active co-creators of content. The adaptability of remix memes makes them

Figure 14.3 The advice dog meme portrays some excellent, topical information around the use of memes for procreating misinformation.

particularly resilient; they can be rapidly updated to align with emerging cultural trends, political events, or social movements, ensuring their continued relevance in fast-changing online environments.

The appeal of remix culture lies in its infinite variability. Familiar templates such as *Distracted Boyfriend*, *Drake Hotline Bling*, and *Galaxy Brain* have been repeatedly repurposed to comment on everything from pop culture to geopolitics. This flexibility allows remix memes to function as powerful tools for satire, activism, and even propaganda. In the context of memetic warfare, remix culture becomes especially significant: its inherent creativity and recognisability enable actors to embed ideological cues within humorous or ironic formats, making persuasive messaging appear innocuous and entertaining.

Psychologically, remix memes exploit the ease with which familiar formats are understood and affect heuristics, which leverage emotional resonance to increase engagement. Their humour and novelty amplify virality, while ideological congruence strengthens perceived credibility. However, this same fluidity introduces ethical challenges. Remix memes can blur the line between parody and misinformation, and their capacity for rapid mutation makes them ideal vehicles for disinformation campaigns.

A popular example often cited within remix culture is the *Success Kid* meme (see Figure 14.4), which originated as a simple image of a triumphant child but has since been reinterpreted across countless contexts, from

Figure 14.4 The remix culture meme. In this instance, the well-known "Success Kid" meme has been remixed to be more context-relevant to our current discussion.

motivational messaging to political satire. This illustrates the core principle of remix culture: meaning is never fixed but continuously negotiated through creative recombination, making these memes both culturally vibrant and strategically potent.

At the third layer in Shifman's classification system (2009) is the stance element, which forms the ideological layer of the meme. This layer reflects the creator's point of view, their relationship to the content, and how they position that content for the audience. Stance is not merely stylistic; it is deeply tied to cultural and ideological meaning. It often aligns with the target audience's identity and values, embedding cues that signal belonging to a particular culture or subculture. In this sense, stance determines whether a meme affirms, mocks, or subverts dominant narratives, making it a critical factor in understanding how memes function as persuasive tools.

Ideological messaging becomes most apparent at this layer, and stance can manifest in several ways:

- *Irony or satire*: memes that mock political figures, ideologies, or social norms often use irony or satire to create distance between the creator and the subject. By adopting this stance, a creator can stake a position of plausible deniability and leave the interpretation behind the intention of the meme vague if they so wish.

- *Sincerity or affirmation*: some memes promote genuine beliefs or values, such as motivational memes or those supporting social movements. These often adopt a direct approach to the messaging contained within them and require very little in terms of interpretation to understand the ideological message they are trying to convey.
- *Parody or subversive*: these memes mimic information that is found in the common meme culture but subvert the format to critique or undermine dominant narratives. These are the memes that are perhaps the most used in the context of activist and countercultural spaces.

The stance layer of a meme is a crucial element in determining how a meme will be received, its intention, and whether it aligns with or challenges prevailing ideologies. It is often the case that the same meme template is used to promote opposing political views, which is entirely dependent on the stance embedded in its caption or context. Stance is also central to memetic warfare. The same template, such as *Distracted Boyfriend* or *Drake Hotline Bling,* can be weaponised to cater for opposing ideologies simply by altering captions to reflect different stances. This flexibility makes stance a powerful mechanism for embedding ideological cues within humorous or relatable formats, enabling persuasive messaging to appear innocuous.

Shifman's tripartite framework around content, form, and stance offers critical insights into how meme genres can be weaponised in digital environments. Each dimension plays a distinct role in shaping the persuasive power of memes:

- *Content* determines the thematic core of the meme, which can be manipulated to amplify ideological narratives or distort facts.
- *Form* influences accessibility and virality; familiar templates like reaction memes or remix culture formats are easily understood and widely shared, making them ideal for rapid dissemination.
- *Stance*, the ideological layer, is the most potent for strategic influence. It embeds subtle cues that align with or challenge dominant narratives, shaping interpretation and emotional engagement. Memes with a congruent stance to a target audience's identity often feel more credible and evoke stronger affective responses, increasing their likelihood of being shared.

From a weaponisation perspective, reaction memes can trivialise serious issues, reducing their perceived importance and fostering disengagement. Remix culture memes, with their inherent flexibility, can distort or reframe narratives by embedding ideological signals within humorous or ironic formats, making propaganda appear innocuous. Understanding stance allows analysts to detect these ideological cues and trace the emotional or cognitive strategies behind meme dissemination, such as exploiting affect heuristics or identity congruence to bypass rational scrutiny.

Psychological Triggers and Memes

Memes do not just sit in dormancy waiting for a specific time to be awoken. There must be a specific psychological trigger that drives the creation of memes, each of which taps into an underlying component of the human condition. Brodie (2009) identified several key psychological triggers that can be activated to make individuals inherently more susceptible to accepting and adopting memetic ideas. These are presented as follows:

Security: these are memes that offer safety or protection, often used in fear-based political messages. One key example of this could be the proliferation of the idea that immigrants are a threat to national safety and security, with memes offering the sense of protection through the creation of stricter immigration policies or better surveillance of individuals who enter the country illegally. This activates an emotive aspect that engages inherent anxieties that relate to safety and protection.

Belonging: memes that offer an individual the opportunity to be involved in a group identity, aligning with tribalism, nationalism, and culturally specific values. This could be embodied in something like "Real patriots fight for their country – join the fight." This not only offers the individual a position within a group but also provides an additional element to fight against an unspecified enemy. This type of memetic trigger can serve to reinforce current in-group loyalty while also ramping up hostility against an enemy out-group and is perfect for propaganda purposes.

Crisis: memes that serve to thrive in situations where information is sparse, or there might be some form of public emergency. These types of memes were virulent during the COVID-19 pandemic, such as the government hiding the truth about the virus, with people being encouraged to come to their senses before some impending doom collapsed in on them. Conspiracy theories are one form of memetic process that can serve to bloom using this psychological trigger, where individuals overwrite their capacity for critical thinking in favour of Type 1 processing due to the urgency of the situation.

Sex: the age-old notion that sex sells is even more relevant in the realm of memes. Memes that make a direct appeal to our reproductive instincts or serve to make us appear more attractive are an easy psychological trigger to push. Advertising memes are replete with such triggers and include slogans like "Drink this brand of beer and you will be irresistible to attractive people" or "Wear this make up, and you will be able to attract the person of your dreams." This trigger links products or behaviours to sexual desirability, a core evolutionary trigger for humans. Again, the psychological mechanism at work here serves to overwrite our rational thought processes to engage our instinctual processes.

Meaning: memes that tap into some form of existential crusade or provide some type of moral clarification to the individual. Captured in the notion of being born to fight for freedom from oppression, these types of memes can be found in radical, ideological, and activist-based approaches. They provide both a sense of destiny for the individual, as well as a higher purpose to their lives, and can be highly resistant to being extinguished.

These psychological triggers form the foundation upon which memetic strategies operate; by exploiting innate human needs for security, belonging, and meaning, actors can craft memes that do more than entertain but become deliberate instruments of influence. This psychological groundwork sets the stage for understanding how such triggers are weaponised in the concept of memetic warfare.

What Is Memetic Warfare?

The actual origins of the concept of memetic warfare are not entirely clear. The term "memetic warfare" has been used in several publications over the past two decades and has been used to describe several different concepts. For example, Prosser (2006) explored the use of memetics in the realms of U.S. military operations, where he stated:

> Tomorrow's US military must approach warfighting with an alternate mindset that is prepared to leverage all elements of national power to influence the ideological spheres of future enemies by engaging them with alternate means – memes – to gain advantage.
>
> (Prosser, 2006, p. 1)

In his thesis, Prosser (2006) observed that attempting to attack and defeat ideologies with conventional military force is largely a foolhardy endeavour, citing historical examples where such efforts have ended in failure. He highlighted the potential future use of memes in PsyOps and information warfare operations as a means of seeding information into target populations so that these ideas can grow and mature into accepted, dominant ideologies. This approach offers several attractive benefits when contrasted with conventional military tactics. First, it avoids the use of kinetic force, thereby preventing direct loss of life and destruction of infrastructure. Memetic warfare is a more subtle mechanism that preserves the physical structures of a society while working to overthrow the dominant ideologies that govern it. Another often-overlooked advantage of using memes as an offensive vector is cost: although not an immediate or direct method, creating memes is significantly cheaper and more cost-effective than many conventional options. Furthermore, memes operate within a grey space, a so-called shadow sphere of military operations that falls outside the obvious conventions of warfare. This allows them to be launched and monitored from a safe distance with minimal risk of direct reprisals against those responsible.

More recently and perhaps more contextually relevant for our current discussion, Munk et al. (2025) defined memetic warfare as

> a form of information warfare conducted online through memes and other tactics to achieve political, strategic, or ideological objectives. It involves the offensive or defensive circulation of content to influence public opinion, disrupt discourse, and advance the interests of those engaged in the campaign.
>
> (p. 3)

This definition frames memetic warfare as a subset of information warfare, emphasising its role in shaping narratives and influencing public opinion through low-cost, high-impact tactics. Unlike conventional warfare, which relies on physical force, memetic warfare operates in the cognitive and informational domain, exploiting the speed and reach of digital platforms to manipulate discourse. Its offensive and defensive dimensions highlight the key strategies employed in digital warfare, where actors seek to disrupt, deceive, and dominate the information environment rather than engage kinetically. By embedding ideological cues within memes, campaigns can bypass rational scrutiny and leverage emotional and identity-based heuristics, making them powerful tools for persuasion and polarisation. This aligns with the broader objectives of digital warfare: to weaponise information ecosystems, erode trust, and achieve strategic goals without direct confrontation.

Zakem et al. (2018) highlighted the keyways in which memes can be used in the context of the digital battlefield. Although not specifically linked to memetic warfare, their work positions itself within the sphere of influence operations, which has a very clear link to both defensive and offensive operations, even though they may not be specifically military in nature. In their conceptualisation, they present memes that are situated within this sphere as falling into three specific categories: *to inoculate*, *to infect*, and *to treat*. Based around the origins of memetic theory that borrowed heavily from biology, as well as incorporating models that had been developed to explore elements of terrorism and radicalisation, the main components are presented in Table 14.1.

Infecting the Host: Offensive Memetic Warfare

Employing the use of memetics in the realm of digital warfare has developed a great deal since the initial thesis produced by Prosser (2006), and while the actual classification of such strategies will often fall outside the official stance

Table 14.1 The Inoculate, Infect, or Treat Typology for Memetic Warfare (Adapted from Zakem et al., 2018)

	Inoculate	*Infect*	*Treat*
Purpose	Prevent or minimise the effect of adversary messaging.	Transmit messages in support of current interests.	Contain the impact of adversary messaging.
Distribution	Preventative: anticipatory	Offensive: stand-alone	Defensive: reactive
Definition	To use a meme to protect against a threat or anticipated attack. Using memes to pre-emptively address, with an emphasis on delegitimising or undermining a message or attack expected from another actor.	To use a meme to spread a specific message. To use memes to articulate a message, either positive (e.g., defending a value) or negative (i.e., disparaging an institution), that aligns with broader mission objectives.	To use a meme to treat an already circulating message. To respond. Memetically, either by mocking, disproving, or otherwise countering a message that has been spread by another actor.

of most nations, it is recognised that they are very much a thing. "Offensive memes" have been defined as

> strategically crafted visual or textual content designed to spread information pollution, manipulate narratives, and target individuals or groups with ridicule and harassment. They aim to polarise audiences, distort facts, and promote biased agendas by using humour, sarcasm, and provocation to incite conflict and confusion.
>
> (Munk, 2025, p. 5)

Munk's (2025) definition underscores the intentionality behind offensive memes: they are not accidental cultural artefacts but strategically engineered tools designed to manipulate narratives and amplify ideological agendas. This deliberate crafting aligns closely with the principles of digital warfare, where the battlefield is cognitive rather than physical. The concept of information pollution, or the flooding of online spaces with misleading or false content, serves to illustrate how memes function as low-cost, high-impact weapons to distort reality and obscure truth. By leveraging emotional appeals, repetition, and ridicule, memeplexes can exploit psychological vulnerabilities, fostering anger and division within echo chambers. These tactics mirror broader digital warfare strategies aimed at eroding trust, polarising societies, and reshaping discourse without kinetic force, making memes agile instruments for influence operations in the modern information ecosystem.

It is hard to tie down clear examples of offensive memetic campaigns, as many are conducted in a way that obscures the true adversaries responsible.

There are some more frequently referred to examples where experts have agreed that there has been direct involvement of state actors. For example, "The Great Meme War" that arose during the 2016 U.S. presidential election (Dafaure, 2020) has been noted as being a co-ordinated campaign that was designed to create a groundswell of support for Donald Trump while ridiculing and vilifying his opposition, Hillary Clinton. The internet is replete with memes that were used to sway the dominant narrative that surrounded the election candidates, where pro-Trump supporters formed various echo chambers on 4chan and Reddit (r/The_Donald), some of which are presented below.

The messages portrayed in both should be obvious; Figure 14.5 positions Hillary Clinton alongside the rest of the Democratic Party as having double standards when it comes to conflict, noting previous occasions where America, under their leadership, had taken up arms with other nations. In Figure 14.6, we have the use of iconography from a popular cultural reference, using a composite screen grab from Marvel's Captain America: Civil War, part of the Avengers franchise. There are two aspects to this: firstly, the expression that greets the suggestion

Figure 14.5 A typical example of a meme that has been employed for subversive purposes, taken from the 2016 Great Meme War.

Source: https://imgflip.com/i/kd57x

Figure 14.6 The Avengers: Captain America Civil War Meme.

Source: https://imgflip.com/i/qcnl4

that Hillary Clinton will be a good president is one of abject disengagement and shock; secondly, the inclusion of the iconography that accompanied the film suggests that the advent of having Hillary Clinton as the next U.S. president would result in some form of civil unrest, leading to the next American Civil War.

Memes as a Defence

There is an opposing side to the offensive use of memes in digital warfare, and there is a growth in research that is directly interested in the use of memes to counter misinformation and disinformation. Indeed, the typology presented by Zakem et al. (2018) identifies the use of memes as proactive agents that can serve to both inoculate individuals from pervasive messages and give them the capacity to treat existing ideologies that could serve to threaten societal cohesion. Munk (2025) defined "defensive memes" as

> visual and/or textual content designed to stop falsehoods, promote factual accuracy, boost the moral of those under attack, and foster critical thinking by using humour and simple messaging.
>
> (p. 505)

This definition highlights the significance of the counterposition that defensive memes can take, particularly in the battle against counterfactual information. Another feature of the defensive meme that is not often seen as a feature of the offensive meme is the capacity to enhance the morale of individuals who are in the direct path of conflict. In work that stands out as being isolated within the research space, Munk et al. (2025) presented a detailed exploration of the role defensive memes have had against the backdrop of the Russia–Ukraine conflict. In their report, they noted that the use of humour and satire has both been employed as key tools in the creation of memes by everyday people and adopted by officials to counter dominant narratives that have been exposed by the opposing side in the conflict.

Munk et al. (2025) stressed that memes should not be dismissed as merely facets of entertainment and casual online humour. Instead, they can be important strategic tools with significant reach and influence in the context of digital warfare and associated digital ecosystems. They further noted that memes, particularly in the context of digital warfare, can be used to mobilise societal support, build a sense of solidarity, not only within the embattled nation but also wider afield, and serve to bring sense to the often-chaotic narratives that can flood the digital battlefield.

The North Atlantic Fella Organisation (NAFO) exemplifies how memes can transcend trivial entertainment to become strategic instruments of digital resistance. Emerging as a grass-roots movement during the Russia–Ukraine conflict, NAFO uses humour and satire to counter Russian disinformation, maintain global attention on Ukraine, and mobilise solidarity. Central to its identity is the Shiba Inu avatar (see Figure 14.7), which was originally adopted from a Twitter user (@Kama_Kamilia), who functions as a unifying symbol, fostering group belonging and reinforcing in-group identity. NAFO's memes ridicule Russian propaganda while simultaneously serving practical purposes, such as fundraising for the Ukrainian military, illustrating how memetic content can blend activism with psychological triggers like belonging and meaning. By embedding ideological cues within humorous formats, NAFO leverages the stance dimension of Shifman's framework, positioning its messaging as ironic yet affirming of pro-Ukrainian values. This dual function, satirical critique and ideological reinforcement, demonstrates the potency of defensive memetic warfare in shaping narratives, sustaining morale, and influencing global discourse without resorting to kinetic force.

Figure 14.7 The Shiba Inu avatar that is often the central component of the North Atlantic Fella Organisation (NAFO) defensive memes.

As highlighted by Munk et al. (2025), defensive memes occupy a critical position in the digital battlefield, demonstrating that humour and simplicity can be powerful tools for resilience. Far from being trivial constructs, memes can serve multiple strategic functions: they counter misinformation, inoculate audiences against propaganda, and restore coherence in chaotic information environments. By leveraging psychological triggers such as belonging and meaning, defensive memes foster solidarity and morale, particularly in times of crisis. Their effectiveness lies in their accessibility and emotional resonance, qualities that enable rapid dissemination and engagement without requiring deep cognitive effort. Movements like NAFO exemplify this dynamic, blending satire with activism to sustain attention, mobilise support, and reinforce ideological clarity. Ultimately, defensive memes illustrate how digital culture can be weaponised for constructive purposes, transforming participatory humour into a mechanism for truth, resistance, and collective identity in the face of adversarial influence campaigns.

Dissecting the Power of the Meme

Memes have evolved from simple cultural artefacts into one of the most dominant forms of online communication. Wasike (2022) noted that memes created by others were the second most popular type of content shared by Gen Z and Millennials in 2019, and by 2021, memes ranked as the third most shared content across all U.S. demographics. This widespread appeal underscores their cultural significance and raises an important question: why are memes so universally engaging? Understanding this requires looking beyond their humorous surface to the psychological and social mechanisms that drive their creation, sharing, and transformation, which we will focus on in the remainder of this chapter.

There is ample evidence to suggest that not all internet users approach memes in the same way; some can see a meme and not engage with it, failing to understand the content or the sentiment within it. Others will engage in the dissemination of a meme through resharing, while others will actively modify the content of the meme for their purposes (Ling et al., 2021). We explored the mechanics of virality earlier on in Chapter 3, and there has been some associated work that has identified what elements of a meme's composition make it more likely to go viral, thus proliferating its reach further (Ling et al., 2021). On the one hand, there is evidence to suggest that specific personality traits can have a significant role in determining what individuals share online. For example, research has noted that individuals who have higher levels of conscientiousness are more likely to share information, while those people who exhibit higher levels of agreeableness are likely to be more trusting, which also impacts their likelihood to share information with others (Deng et al., 2017).

In contrast to exploring the role of personality traits, other work has focused more directly on the structure and the content of the meme, as well as the context into which it is born. One way in which to conceptualise the power and potency of a meme is as something that has been referred to as *intertextuality* (Molina, 2025). This is seen as the way in which meaning is generated through the juxtaposition of the text and the image within the meme. Molina (2025) also noted that memes can serve to harness the use of two heuristic processes that can also serve to influence the power of memes, one that taps into the affective element of the meme and another that taps into the credibility of the content. These should be familiar to the reader, as we have covered these extensively in other chapters of this book, but we will recap them here briefly in the current context.

The Affect Heuristic and Memetics

As we explored in Chapter 9, this mental shortcut is activated, where individuals will rely upon their current emotional state to influence their decision-making processes. According to Slovic et al. (2007), when we think about things (e.g., people, events, and places), these occurrences will often come attached with emotional tags that could be negative, neutral, or positive. When individuals make later attempts to make a decision, they will tap into this pool of emotional tags as an aid to guide their choices, often without having a full awareness that emotion could be guiding their decisions (Molina, 2025). Researchers noted that when they presented participants with the same event but manipulated the cause of the event to be either "human-caused" or "natural causes," individuals were more likely to judge the former type of event as being more severe, mainly because they had a more negative sentiment towards that event.

Molina (2025) was keen to note that the intertextual nature of many current memes is a crucial factor in determining how strong an emotional response will occur in individuals. In richer presentation formats where multiple modalities are tapped into (e.g., video that includes both sight and sound), there is an assumption that they are processed in a less systematic way and are in turn seen as being more credible (Molina, 2025; Sundar, 2008). As we reviewed back in Chapter 10, Sundar's MAIN model for exploring credibility online suggested that the more modalities that are used to present information, the more likely that information will be processed using heuristic methods. Moreover, the effectiveness of a meme also relies on the extent to which the content of the meme aligns with the identity of the individual who is viewing it (Molina, 2025). Heiskanen (2017) noted that more potent and powerful memes are those that are shared within peer groups among like-minded individuals. This again supports the formation of echo chambers where there is continuous reinforcement and renewal of dominant narratives, usually by memetic information. For any meme to reach its full potential, the individuals within the target group must have some form of insider knowledge related to the concepts being portrayed within the meme (Molina, 2025). Without such knowledge, there is a potential that such memes will fail to be understood, and their overall effectiveness will be quickly extinguished.

The Identity Heuristic and Memetics

This heuristic relates to the similarities between the ideological content of the meme and the identity of the individual. If a meme contains information that resonates with an individual's own beliefs and ideological perspectives, they will assume that this information is more credible (Molina, 2025). Research findings have supported this notion and noted that in situations where individuals were presented with identity-incongruent information in memes, they were less likely to view them as being effective and engage in a greater level of scrutiny when it came to their content (Huntington, 2020; Molina, 2025).

Molina (2025) reported findings that aligned closely with the three-dimensional model of meme structure presented by Shifman (2014), noting that, in terms of the stance of the meme, having a congruent ideological stance to that of the individual was a key predictor for potency. Such an effect was observed even if the form of the meme presentation (e.g., text-based or multimodal presentation) was considered. Those memes that were identity-congruent were also seen to create a more emotive response, evident in greater levels of anger experienced by the consumer of the meme. However, Molina (2025) also noted that individuals who did experience more anger because of seeing a meme were also more likely to view it as being less credible, perhaps because they search for information to identify the accuracy of the information contained within it, therefore reducing the reliance on heuristic processes. Similar results to this have been reported by other researchers, with Wong and Holyoak (2021) noting that politically congruent memes were more likely to be shared with others and seen as being more powerful.

Memes as Metaphors

Wong and Holyoak (2021) noted that memes are similar in some respects to common metaphors that are created by experts. This has been proven a popular framework for understanding memes, where researchers have suggested that memes are very similar to a visual metaphor (Molina, 2025; Huntington, 2020). However, memes, in contrast to metaphors, allow for a greater variety of artistic creativity and can be fashioned by everyday people who have access to a computer and the internet. It has been noted that the most influential factor in establishing the relatability of the meme and the humour contained within it is how well the image fits with the presented message, something they referred to as *aptness* (Wong & Holyoak, 2021). This matches what we generally see in the acceptable usage of metaphors, where the more closely a metaphor is aligned to an idea or context, the more likely we are to appreciate it (Wong & Holyoak, 2021). In the study by Wong and Holyoak (2021), they found that the most important predictor for comprehension and perceived humour of a meme was linked directly to the aptness, or the sense of how well the image matched the topic in question, as framed by the textual information in the meme. However, while the research also found a correlation between aptness and familiarity with a meme, familiarity did not significantly predict understanding or humour if aptness was controlled for. This means that the success of a meme is not only about an individual's capacity to recognise it but also about how well it conveys its intended meaning to the audience. In terms of sharing behaviour, Wong and Holyoak (2021) noted that apt memes are those that are more likely to be shared, showing that there is a clear relationship between content and potential virality.

Memes and Processing Fluency

Other research in the area has noted that the processing fluency with which an individual approaches a meme is a key cognitive component for the appreciation of internet memes (Ayele et al., 2025). The concept of processing fluency refers to the ease with which an individual can process information, which in turn is influenced by perceptions about the content and the capacity to make conceptual judgements about the content. The premise of fluency has been linked to positive affect, aesthetic pleasure (joy from the appearance of a meme), and the perception of truthfulness for that meme (Ayele et al., 2025). Memes that resemble familiar formats or structures are processed more fluently and are therefore liked more, captured in the notion of prototypicality. Prototypical information is processed more fluently and can also be linked to better appreciation in comparison to stimuli that sit outside the normal format for a meme (Winkielman et al., 2006). Fluency has also been linked to the "aha" experience we introduced earlier in this chapter. This phenomenon is characterised as a sudden and often emotionally charged event that brings clarity and focus to a problem that was previously confusing or seemingly unsolvable (Kounios & Beeman, 2009; Stuyck et al., 2021).

Following on from this, the research by Ayele et al. (2025) showed that internet memes, as with other forms of visual stimulus, are subject to a processing fluency bias. Memes that received higher positive ratings were those that were easier to understand, were processed faster, were seen as being more prototypical, were easier to replicate, and were perceived to have a greater sense of truth. In agreement with the earlier findings from Wong and Holyoak, the work also noted that aptness strongly influenced the ratings of the memes, but the authors of this work suggested that aptness served to enhance processing fluency; apt memes are more fluently processed, which in turn boosts their appeal. Ayele et al. (2025) also noted that humour and positive emotions were seen as important predictors of meme success, whereas negative emotions related to frustration and anger were associated with less successful memes.

Memetic warfare leverages the psychological and social potency of internet memes to influence beliefs, behaviours, and group dynamics within digital environments. Memes succeed not only because they are familiar or humorous, but also because of many of the heuristics and biases that we have explored throughout this book. By giving people something that is easy to process, easy to propagate and easy to modify, we create the perfect, self-contained packet of information that is easy to deploy in any given digital environment. Their inherent features make them feel intuitively true while also evoking an emotional resonance with their intended audience. This can trigger the "aha" experience, where a sudden moment of insight can serve to reinforce a belief or foster engagement. Memes can tap directly into affective and identity-based heuristics: emotional responses such as anger, humour, or fear can serve to guide judgements and increase the likelihood of sharing, while ideological congruence boosts perceived credibility. Multimodal formats can further enhance this effect by overwhelming critical scrutiny and increasing trust. When memes are shared within echo chambers, their potency is amplified through insider knowledge and social reinforcement. In this way, memes are not only accidental features of the new digital age but also can become strategic tools in digital conflict, capable of shaping narratives, reinforcing ideologies, and subtly manipulating public sentiment.

Summary

In this chapter, we examined how internet memes have evolved from humorous cultural artefacts into strategic tools of influence within digital warfare. Rooted in Dawkins' concept of memes as units of cultural transmission, modern memes thrive on replicability, adaptability, and emotional resonance, spreading rapidly through social media and forming interconnected "memeplexes" that reinforce shared ideologies.

The discussion introduced the life cycle of memes, from creation and circulation to mutation, peak virality, and decline, highlighting how these stages mirror biological evolution and enable memes to persist and adapt across contexts. Typologies by Brodie and Shifman were explored to classify memes by function (e.g., distinction, strategy, and association) and structure (content, form, and stance), revealing how memes can be weaponised for satire, affirmation, or ideological subversion.

Psychological triggers such as fear, belonging, crisis, sex, and meaning were shown to underpin memetic potency, enabling actors to bypass rational thought and exploit identity-based heuristics. The concept of memetic warfare was defined as the strategic use of memes to influence public opinion, disrupt discourse, and advance political or ideological goals. Offensive strategies involve disinformation and narrative distortion, while defensive memes aim to counter misinformation, boost morale, and foster solidarity, as illustrated by movements like NAFO during the Russia–Ukraine conflict.

Finally, the chapter examined cognitive mechanisms that amplify meme effectiveness, including processing fluency, aptness, and emotional resonance. Memes succeed because they are easy to process, evoke strong affective responses, and align with identity, making them highly shareable and persuasive. These features, combined with multimodal formats and echo chamber reinforcement, position memes as low-cost, high-impact weapons in the digital battlespace – capable of shaping beliefs, reinforcing ideologies, and manipulating public sentiment at scale.

References

Ayele, S. T., Cecchetti, L., & Reber, R. (2025). Ingredients for a good meme: Cognitive, emotional, and social factors of internet meme appreciation. In *Psychology of aesthetics, creativity, and the arts*. https://doi.org/10.1037/aca0000744

Baurecht, M. (2020). The categorisation of internet memes: A different approach. *Colloquium: New Philologies*, *5*(1), 135–152. https://doi.org/10.23963/cnp.2020.5.1.7

Brodie, R. (2009). *Virus of the mind: The new science of the meme*. Carlsbad: Hay House.

Dafaure, M. (2020). The "great meme war": The alt-right and its multifarious enemies memes and the metapolitics of the alt-right. *Angles: New Perspectives on the Anglophone World*, (10), 0–28.

Dawkins, R. (2006). *The selfish gene* (40th Anniv). Oxford UK: Oxford University Press.

Deng, S., Lin, Y., Liu, Y., Chen, X., & Li, H. (2017). How Do Personality Traits Shape Information-Sharing Behaviour in Social Media? Exploring the Mediating Effect of Generalized Trust. *Information research: an international electronic journal*, *22*(3), n3.

Hassan, G., Brouillette-Alarie, S., Alava, S., Frau-Meigs, D., Lavoie, L., Fetiu, A., . . . Sieckelinck, S. (2018). Exposure to extremist online content could lead to violent radicalization: A systematic review of empirical evidence. *International Journal of Developmental Sciences, 12*(1–2), 71–88. https://doi.org/10.3233/DEV-170233

Heiskanen, B. (2017). Meme-ing electoral participation. *European Journal of American Studies, 12*(2), 0–26. https://doi.org/10.4000/ejas.12158

Huntington, H. E. (2020). Partisan cues and internet memes: Early evidence for motivated skepticism in audience message processing of spreadable political media. *Atlantic Journal of Communication, 28*(3), 194–208. https://doi.org/10.1080/15456870.2019.1614589

Jensen, M. A., Atwell Seate, A., & James, P. A. (2018). Radicalization to violence: A pathway approach to studying extremism. *Terrorism and Political Violence, 32*(5), 1067–1090.

Johann, M., & Bülow, L. (2019). One does not simply create a meme: Conditions for the diffusion of Internet memes. *International Journal of Communication, 13*, 1720–1742.

Kerley, P., & Greenhall, R. (2022). Ukraine war: Why has "Z" become a Russian pro-war symbol? *BBC News*, (March). Retrieved from https://www.bbc.co.uk/news/world-europe-60644832#:~:text=In Russia%2C the %22Z%22 is fast becoming, symbol of President Putin%27s invasion of Ukraine

Kounios, J., & Beeman, M. (2009). The Aha! Moment: The cognitive neuroscience of insight. *Current Directions in Psychological Science, 18*(4), 210–216. https://doi.org/10.1111/j.1467-8721.2009.01638.x

Ling, C., Abuhilal, I., Blackburn, J., De Cristofaro, E., Zannettou, S., & Stringhini, G. (2021). Dissecting the meme magic: Understanding indicators of virality in image memes. *Proceedings of the ACM on Human-Computer Interaction, 5*(CSCW1), 1–24. https://doi.org/10.1145/3449155

McNamara, A. (2011). Can we measure memes? *Frontiers in Evolutionary Neuroscience, 3*(May), 1–7. https://doi.org/10.3389/fnevo.2011.00001

Molina, M. D. (2025). Do people believe in misleading information disseminated via memes? The role of identity and anger. *New Media and Society, 27*(2), 847–870. https://doi.org/10.1177/14614448231186061

Munk, T. (2025). Digital defiance: Memetic warfare and civic resistance. *European Journal on Criminal Policy and Research, 31*(3), 501–528. https://doi.org/10.1007/s10610-025-09613-4

Munk, T, Mahoney, I., Monastryrska, K., & Pristed, B. (2025). *The complex web in memetic warfare*. Nottingham Trent University.

Neklesova, V., & Karpenko, M. (2023). Memeplexes in the Ukrainian information landscape: An onomastic path. *Onomastica, 67*, 15–38. https://doi.org/10.17651/ONOMAST.67.2

Osterroth, A. (2015). Repositorium für die Medienwissenschaft Das Internet-Meme als Sprache-Bild-Text 2015. *Bildwissenschaft. Heft, 22*(2), 26–46. https://doi.org/10.25969/mediarep/16478

Prosser, M. B. (2006). Memetics: A growth industry in US military operations, Masters Thesis; United States Marine Corps, Quantico, Virginia.

Shifman, L. (2014). *Memes in digital culture*. The MIT Press.

Shifman, L. (2019). Defining internet memes. *Memes in Digital Culture*. https://doi.org/10.7551/mitpress/9429.003.0006

Slovic, P., Finucane, M. L., Peters, E., & MacGregor, D. G. (2007). The affect heuristic. *European Journal of Operational Research, 177*(3), 1333–1352. https://doi.org/10.1016/j.ejor.2005.04.006

Stuyck, H., Aben, B., Cleeremans, A., & Van den Bussche, E. (2021). The Aha! Moment: Is insight a different form of problem solving? *Consciousness and Cognition, 90*(2), 0–42. https://doi.org/10.1016/j.concog.2020.103055

Sundar, S. (2008). The main model: A heuristic approach to understanding technology effects on credibility. *Digital Media, Youth, and Credibility*, 73–100. https://doi.org/10.1162/dmal.9780262562324.073

Turk, N., Kaspar, S., & Kosseim, L. (2025). *On the Influence of Discourse Relations in Persuasive Texts*, (1), 1–12. Retrieved from http://arxiv.org/abs/2510.26124

Wasike, B. (2022). Memes, memes, everywhere, nor any meme to trust: Examining the credibility and persuasiveness of COVID-19-related memes. *Journal of Computer-Mediated Communication*, *27*(2), 1–30. https://doi.org/10.1093/jcmc/zmab024

Wiggins, B. E. (2019). *The discursive power of memes in digital culture: Ideology, semiotics, and intertextuality*. New York: Routledge.

Winkielman, P., Halberstadt, J., Fazendeiro, T., & Catty, S. (2006). Prototypes are attractive because they are easy on the mind. *Psychological Science*, *17*(9), 799–806. https://doi.org/10.1111/j.1467-9280.2006.01785.x

Wong, E. F., & Holyoak, K. J. (2021). Cognitive and motivational factors driving sharing of internet memes. *Memory and Cognition*, *49*(5), 863–872. https://doi.org/10.3758/s13421-020-01134-1

Zakem, V., Mcbride, M. K., & Hammerberg, K. (2018). *Exploring the utility of memes for U.S. government influence campaigns*, (April). Retrieved from https://imgflip.com/memegenerator

15 Conspiracy Theories

Introduction

At first glance, the inclusion of conspiracy theories as a main chapter in this text might seem somewhat disconnected from the rest of the material. Although conspiracy theories fit into the general typology of fake news and misinformation that is circulated online, can they be weaponised in a way that makes them strategically useful? I would argue yes, they can, and there are some clear examples of how this has been achieved over the past few years. While conspiracy theories are often thought of as fringe beliefs that only a small proportion of the population cling to, often seen as "crackpots" or individuals who are predisposed to delusional ideology, belief in them is more widespread than one might first assume (Douglas et al., 2017; Jolley et al., 2020; van Prooijen & van Vugt, 2018).

While we might view conspiracy theories as irritating and their believers as a group best ignored, the reality is that these narratives, when combined with the vast reach of the internet, can create another front on which digital warfare can be waged. Research has shown that exposure to conspiracy theories can influence an individual's judgement without their conscious awareness. It has been noted that individuals who were directly exposed to conspiracy theories were those who were more likely to endorse them, even while insisting that their views had not significantly changed (Douglas & Sutton, 2018, 2023). Therefore, understanding the psychological processes underlying susceptibility to and endorsement of conspiracy theories is critically important in the context of digital warfare.

On November 6, 2016, the hashtag *#Pizzagate* began trending on Twitter, with many individuals pointing to 4chan, a well-known hub for conspiracy theories. Some users had discovered leaked emails from John Podesta, then campaign manager for Hillary Clinton, who was embroiled in a fierce battle to become the next president of the United States. In a way, only 4chan members could interpret; elements of these emails were linked to satanic worship, sex orgies, child trafficking, and sexual abuse (Tuters et al., 2018). As part of the conspiracy theory, members produced visual materials suggesting connections between child-related businesses in Washington, D.C., owned by Democratic Party strategist David

DOI: 10.4324/9781003752400-15

Brock, and symbols allegedly associated with paedophile rings. They even created a map which, when joined by straight lines, formed a pentagram, a symbol often associated with the Devil (Tuters et al., 2018). At the lowest point of the pentagram sat a pizza parlour: Comet Ping Pong. On December 4, 2016, at around 3 p.m., Edgar Maddison Welch entered Comet Ping Pong armed with an AR-15 rifle and a .38 calibre handgun and fired shots inside the restaurant, some aimed at a locked door behind which he believed people were being held against their will. So, while on the surface the power of conspiracy theories may appear to be low-level with the assumption that only a few individuals share some of these beliefs, the reality is much more complex than we might first assume. As demonstrated in the #Pizzagate conspiracy, what started off as a discussion on 4chan quickly spilt over into mainstream social media, resulting in actual violent physical action by an individual. This is the real power of conspiracy theories, and while they might be seen as being confined to the fringes of society, those fringes, when suitably motivated, can and do result in dangerous physical consequences. In examples such as anti-vaccination theories, the impact of the belief in such information extends beyond that of the individual and could be seen as a direct factor in the spread of commonly occurring but controlled diseases (Uscinski et al., 2020).

In this chapter, we begin by exploring typologies that researchers have applied to classify conspiracy theories. While we might initially think of conspiracy theories as a unified whole covering a wide range of topics, the reality is far more complex. These theories can be differentiated along several key themes, which help us understand how they are constructed and in turn how they can be effectively weaponised for various purposes. We will also examine who believes in conspiracy theories and why they are so attractive to certain individuals, whether this is due to a psychological need for belonging or a deeper desire to make sense of events that fall outside conventional explanations. Finally, we highlight how these elements can be exploited offensively to give digital adversaries a strategic advantage.

Understanding the Typology of Conspiracy Theories

To better understand how conspiracy theories function within society and particularly within the context of digital warfare, it is useful to examine the different types that people commonly believe. Sambol et al. (2024) offer a detailed typology that categorises conspiracy theories based on their thematic content and psychological appeal. These categories reflect the diverse ways in which individuals attempt to make sense of complex or threatening events, often in ways that challenge official narratives and foster distrust in institutions.

Sambol et al. (2024) presented a typology of the most common conspiracy theories, these being:

1. *Government malfeasance*: this type of conspiracy theory suggests that government agencies are involved in activities designed to justify later sanctions

or actions. Examples include the alleged orchestration of terrorist attacks on civilian targets to create a pretext for sweeping restrictions on public freedoms or to distract attention from other pressing societal issues. To reinforce these beliefs, proponents often present spurious claims about fabricated official records or construct narratives about previously hidden government misconduct. A prominent example is the notion that the 9/11 attacks on the World Trade Center were planned and orchestrated by the U.S. government as a pretext for a renewed mission to eliminate Al-Qaeda and Osama bin Laden.

2. *Malevolent global manipulation*: these conspiracy theories focus on the involvement of unidentified or loosely defined groups operating on the fringes of society. Such individuals or collectives are alleged to manipulate world events for their own purposes and profit, often implicating organisations like the Freemasons, the Illuminati, religious sects, global elites, and technology giants. The purported aim of these actions is typically to usher in a "New World Order" or to consolidate existing positions of power. Believers in these theories frequently cite hidden symbols or coded messages as evidence of such activities and make unsubstantiated claims linking influential figures to events they perceive as orchestrated by these groups.
3. *The control of personal freedoms*: these conspiracy theories suggest that large corporations or governments employ various tactics to manipulate or restrict individual freedoms within society. Believers often express heightened paranoia about the potential use of technology as a mechanism for control, viewing it as a tool for surveillance and monitoring under vague or unspecified purposes.
4. *Extraterrestrial Cover-Ups*: although these conspiracy theories may seem less relevant to the current discussion on digital warfare, they still have the potential to spread disillusionment and distrust towards government institutions. Believers claim that government and military organisations are actively concealing the "truth" about the existence of extraterrestrial life. This includes alleged cover-ups of UFO sightings and alien abduction reports. At the core of these theories is the belief that such secrecy serves to maintain power and influence within society or that governments and militaries are harnessing alien technology for undisclosed purposes.
5. *The control of information*: this type of conspiracy theory argues that various agencies engage in active narrative manipulation to shape public opinion and perceptions while simultaneously suppressing dissent. A defining feature among believers is deep distrust of official channels for providing transparent and reliable information, coupled with disdain for narratives presented by such organisations. These individuals often advocate for alternative information sources they perceive as untainted by official doctrines.
6. *Health-related conspiracies*: although the typology presented by Sambol et al. (2024) focused primarily on conspiracy theories related to the COVID-19 pandemic, this classification is better understood as encompassing broader health-related conspiracy theories. Within the COVID-19 context, these

included claims about the virus's origins, the severity of the illness, and official responses to the pandemic. While this category is closely tied to a specific historical period, it reflects patterns common to other health-related conspiracies, such as those promoted by anti-vaccination groups. Many believers argue that COVID-19 originated from the accidental release of a bioweapon from a government-owned laboratory or that the pandemic was deliberately constructed by hidden global forces to enable social control and economic gain, with pharmaceutical companies portrayed as primary beneficiaries. Additional claims suggest that the pandemic was engineered to establish a more rigid societal infrastructure, linking its spread and susceptibility to technological factors such as 5G networks. Some theories even allege that vaccines were intended to implant microchips in individuals as part of a mass surveillance and control programme.

GIST Model of Conspiracy Theories

Conspiracy theories are often thought of as a singular, unitary construct to which individuals align their beliefs, each of which possesses its own ideology and distorted narratives. The reality of how conspiracy theories can be classified is less rigid and more nuanced, with research noting that there are distinct categories to which conspiracy theories are aligned. However, this is slightly different from the framework highlighted by Sambol et al. (2024), and Mao et al. (2024) presented the **G**roups, **I**deology, and **St**atus (GIST) framework, which is presented in Table 15.1.

The six categories outlined by Sambol et al. (2024), ranging from government malfeasance to health-related conspiracies, can be mapped onto the GIST model proposed by Mao et al. (2024), which classifies conspiracy theories based on three psychological dimensions:

- Groups: many of Sambol's categories (e.g., malevolent global manipulation and control of information) involve clear in-group/out-group dynamics, where shadowy elites or outsiders are blamed for societal problems.
- Ideology: theories such as government malfeasance and health-related conspiracies often align with, or challenge, deeply held political or cultural beliefs, making them ideologically charged and emotionally resonant.
- Status: several types (e.g., control of personal freedoms and extraterrestrial cover-ups) reflect upward conspiracies targeting powerful institutions or elites, while reinforcing feelings of powerlessness among believers.

By linking Sambol's content-based typology to Mao's psychological framework, we gain a more nuanced understanding of how conspiracy theories operate both cognitively and strategically. This dual perspective is especially valuable in digital warfare, where conspiracy narratives are crafted and deployed to exploit

Table 15.1 The GIST Framework for Classifying Conspiracy Theories, Adapted from Mao et al. (2024)

Facet	*Category*	*Example Conspiracy Theory*	*Key Antecedents*	*Key Consequences*
Groups	In-group	Own government hiding COVID-19 data	Internal threats (e.g., corruption and inequality)	Protest and hostility towards one's own government; decreased political participation
	Out-group	A foreign government created COVID-19 as a bioweapon	External threats (e.g., historical victimisation)	Support for one's own government; increased political participation; and hostility towards out-group
Ideology	Ideological	Climate change denial among U.S. conservatives	Threats to core values (e.g., political and religious)	Partisan hostility and polarisation
	Non-ideological	Flat Earth theory; anti-vaccine beliefs	General beliefs in the deceptiveness of authorities	Hostility and polarisation towards authorities, independent of ideology
Status	Upward	Elites conspiring (e.g., bankers, governments, and pharma companies)	Relative deprivation, precarity	Prejudice and power-challenging attitudes towards high-status groups.
	Downward	Migrants or minorities conspiring (e.g., the great replacement theory)	Threats to the majority group's traditional norms and values	Prejudice and hostility towards low-status groups

psychological vulnerabilities, reinforce ideological divides, and manipulate perceptions of power and truth.

What Drives People to Believe in Conspiracy Theories?

Understanding why people believe in conspiracy theories requires looking beyond the content of the theories themselves. Goertzel (1994) demonstrated that the belief in conspiracy theories is not defined by a single group category or personality trait that can be systematically applied to individuals across the board. It was demonstrated that belief in conspiracy theories was not linked to measures of gender, education level, or type of occupation, although a weak correlation was noted between age and belief in conspiracy theories, so as age increased, the belief in conspiracy theories decreased (Goertzel, 1994).

Research has identified three core psychological motives that drive conspiratorial thinking: epistemic, existential, and social (Douglas & Sutton, 2018, 2023; Douglas et al., 2017). These motives reflect our basic human needs to understand the world, feel secure and in control, and belong to a social group. Conspiracy theories often provide emotionally satisfying answers to complex or threatening events, especially when official explanations are unclear, contradictory, or distrusted.

1. *Epistemic motives*: to make sense of the world around us, individuals attribute events to causes they can understand, forming the foundation for an internally stable perspective of reality (Douglas et al., 2017). Epistemology relates directly to how we define knowledge and how it can be acquired. Many epistemologists refer to the notions of belief, truth, and knowledge when considering what it means to "know" something. From this perspective, epistemic motives in the context of conspiracy theories serve to provide individuals with something to believe in when no clear explanation exists or to reduce uncertainty in situations where information appears contradictory.

   Conspiracy theories differ from regular explanations of events. They often suggest that secret actions occur behind the scenes, involve co-ordinated efforts by multiple actors, and are difficult to disprove. In fact, attempts to refute a conspiracy theory may be interpreted by believers as evidence that the person challenging it is part of the conspiracy (Douglas et al., 2017). These theories allow individuals to maintain beliefs they value, even when strong evidence contradicts them. For example, someone who believes vaccines are harmful or that climate change is a hoax might claim that scientific research is part of a cover-up. This enables them to reject evidence without altering their core beliefs (Douglas et al., 2017).

   Many conspiracy theories are linked to cognitive biases that reflect a desire for explanations that align with what we know or *think* we know. For example, narrative bias (see Chapter 6) is a clear example of a bias that can initiate belief in something being true, particularly when a coherent narrative accompanies the explanation. Most conspiracy theories provide a structured framework for belief, including identifiable villains, their motives, and the plots underpinning events, thereby offering the meaning individuals seek. In the context of digital warfare, crafting narratives that tap into existing cultural fears or divisions makes them more likely to be integrated into belief systems. Similarly, epistemic motives often interact with confirmation bias, where individuals actively seek information that reinforces their existing views. When the flow of information can be controlled to emphasise causes aligned with an individual's interests, confirmation bias works in concert with epistemic motives, protecting cherished beliefs while dismissing contradictory evidence as part of the perceived conspiracy.

2. *Existential motives*: aside from providing explanations for events that allow individuals to maintain beliefs consistent with what they already know, conspiracy theories can also offer a sense of control (Douglas et al., 2017). In circumstances where individuals feel vulnerable or perceive a loss of control over their future in the face of global events, susceptibility to conspiracy beliefs tends to increase. There has been a wide variety of research that has noted a significant link between heightened anxiety and a greater likelihood of endorsing conspiracy theories, supporting this notion (Green & Douglas, 2018; Liekefett et al., 2023). Other studies echo these findings, suggesting that individuals often turn to the perceived control offered by conspiracy theories when they feel powerless, potentially highlighting a link to individual traits and locus of control (Douglas et al., 2017; Abalakina-Paap et al., 1999).

   Although people might turn to conspiracy theories to feel more in control, research shows that these beliefs often have the opposite effect. Studies have found that reading conspiracy theories can make individuals feel less in control and less motivated to take positive action, such as voting or engaging in their communities. Even more concerning, people often do not realise they have been influenced. After reading conspiracy content, they may believe they have always held those views, even if they did not beforehand (Douglas et al., 2017).

   Other researchers have noted external factors that serve to influence susceptibility to conspiracy theories. It has been observed that periods of social change can create an informational vacuum, leading to heightened uncertainty and upheaval (Federico, 2022; Papaioannou et al., 2023). Such processes can disrupt norms, beliefs, and values that govern society, straining the shared sense of reality that previously existed (Federico, 2022). In these circumstances, psychological stability may be challenged and manifested as fear and uncertainty. Individuals often seek easily accessible explanations, which conspiracy theories readily provide (van Prooijen & Douglas, 2017; van Prooijen et al., 2018). Stressful societal events can prompt people to react in ways that help them make sense of what is happening, often resulting in illusory pattern-seeking and the search for something or someone to blame.

3. *Social motives*: driven by a need to belong and identify with a cohesive social group, individuals may seek out communities where conspiracy theories are commonplace to avoid isolation and maintain a positive self-identity (Sambol et al., 2024). Using the backdrop of a conspiracy theory can serve to validate the individual and align them with a particular in-group, while simultaneously deflecting potential negativity towards the target of the conspiracy. Sambol et al. (2024) noted that individuals experiencing higher levels of social isolation and deprivation were more likely to endorse conspiracy theories. Similarly, greater social media use has been associated with an increased propensity to believe in conspiracy theories, potentially due to exposure to material that aligns with their need for belonging. Other research indicates that individuals who have experienced higher levels of social ostracism, perhaps due to lower socio-economic status or ethnic background, are also more likely to engage in and propagate conspiracy theories (Sambol et al., 2024; Douglas et al., 2017).

Conspiracy beliefs are not merely irrational curiosities; they serve deep psychological functions. Epistemic motives help individuals make sense of uncertainty, existential motives offer a sense of control in chaotic times, and social motives provide identity and belonging. However, these same motives can be exploited in digital warfare. Adversaries can craft and disseminate conspiracy narratives that align with these psychological needs, manipulating public opinion, deepening societal divisions, and eroding trust in institutions. By targeting these motives, particularly through social media algorithms and disinformation campaigns, digital actors can subtly shape beliefs and behaviours without individuals even realising they have been influenced.

The Cognitive Architecture of Conspiracy Thinking

It has been argued that seeing conspiracy theories as being linked to a function of "belief" in something is somewhat erroneous. Researchers have instead argued that conspiratorial beliefs are linked more directly to the cognitive miser element of human cognition. It is often the case that people need to simplify information that they are presented with so that they can fit it into what they already understand of the world around them. Conspiracy theories offer one mechanism of doing this, and people will tend to rely on them in times of uncertainty or when the information they are being presented with is too complex to understand (Gagliardi, 2025). From this perspective, it is suggested that the main driving force behind belief in conspiracy theories is more directly linked to the function of the Type 1 processing pathway we explored back in Chapter 4. It has been consistently reported in the research in the area that people who believe in conspiracy theories often rely on gut feelings rather than careful thinking (Bowes et al., 2023; Denovan et al., 2020; Pytlik et al., 2020). They will usually look for unusual or out-of-place information and treat it as proof of a hidden plot. For example, someone who denies climate change might point to a cold day and say, "See? It's freezing, so global warming must be fake," even though that one cold day does not disprove long-term climate trends.

There has been considerable research linking belief in conspiracy theories to heuristic functioning and cognitive biases, with many scholars identifying specific biases that play a critical role in their development and maintenance. This work focuses on how such cognitive biases play a role in both the development and maintenance of conspiratorial beliefs. In a review of the research in the area, Gagliardi (2025) highlighted several biases that fall into this category, some that we have already mentioned previously in this book and some that will be presented as new ground.

Conjunction Fallacy

This one is a bit tricky to get right in your head, but bear with me on this one. In the research by Tversky and Kahneman (1983), they found that individuals will rate the occurrence of a set of specific conditions as being higher in comparison to a single condition. This essentially violates the law of probability, which would state that the single occurrence is more likely in comparison to a combination of occurrences. In the "Linda" problem, they presented participants with a description of a fictional individual who was outspoken, single, and very intelligent. She had a degree in philosophy, and as a student, she was interested in issues related to discrimination and social justice; she also participated in anti-nuclear demonstrations. After reading this description, participants were asked whether Linda is more likely to be (a) a bank teller or (b) a bank teller and active in the feminist movement. Most people, erroneously, choose the latter option (b), which falls foul of the conjunction fallacy: the likelihood of two individual elements combined will always be lower when compared to the likelihood of one thing alone.

Individuals who are more susceptible to believing in conspiracy theories are also more likely to consistently fall foul of the conjunction fallacy. Gagliardi (2025) noted a wide range of research that demonstrated there is a link between belief in conspiracy theories and a tendency to be more prone to the conjunction fallacy, which could in turn suggest that they are looking for deeper explanations of complex events than they need to. Pattern-seeking behaviours might come into play here, where individuals who are susceptible to conspiracy theories are also more likely to seek hidden connections between events, therefore being more likely to already be predisposed to the conjunction fallacy (Brotherton & French, 2014; Müller & Hartmann, 2023; van Prooijen et al., 2018). As the belief in conspiracy theories has also been linked to the need for control and closure on events people have experienced, perhaps the more detailed explanations that are offered by conjunctions feed into this need, something that could also be linked to the proportionality bias we will discuss below.

There is an associated cognitive bias that also has relevance here, but one that was not mentioned in the work by Gagliardi (2025), that of *illusory correlation*. The illusory correlation occurs when an individual makes a connection between two independent variables, even though there is no evidence to support that connection. This can occur when events occurring in the person's immediate environment are rare or have very limited detailed information to support their interpretation. One prime example of this could be presented in the anti-vaccination movement, where individuals will isolate examples of someone becoming ill based on the notion that they have been previously vaccinated, even though the evidence for such a conclusion is typically a spurious connection (van Prooijen et al., 2018). People are very good at making concrete connections between two very discrete events, and this can easily come into play within the context of conspiracy theories. It also makes individuals more open to influence, as you can usually seed the idea that two events are connected without much persuasion or investment. For example, the link between COVID-19 and 5G telephone masts, celebrity deaths and government cover-ups, and weather manipulation and government control are all good examples of instances where illusory correlations can crop up in conspiracy theories.

Jumping-to-Conclusion Bias

The jumping-to-conclusion (JTC) bias is identified in situations where people stop searching for information that could support their decision-making efforts very early on in the decision-making process (Gagliardi, 2025; Moritz & Woodward, 2005). This bias is inherently linked to the functioning of the representativeness heuristic (see Chapter 9), where people will assess only very limited amounts of information, as they believe further information will only reflect what they have already found and would result in a futile use of cognitive resources with very limited return.

Several researchers have highlighted a link between JTC bias and beliefs in conspiracy theories. Pytlik et al. (2020) noted that individuals who exhibited the JTC bias were more likely to see conspiracy theories as being true, and this was in turn linked to a more intuitive, Type 1 style of thinking. Similar findings have been found in other studies where individuals who exhibited the JTC bias were more likely to believe in conspiracy theories directly linked to COVID-19 (Kuhn et al., 2022).

While JTC has been most widely explored in relation to clinical populations, such as individuals suffering from paranoia and psychosis, research increasingly shows its relevance to subclinical populations, particularly in the context of conspiracy theories. JTC, alongside other cognitive biases, does not occur exclusively in clinical groups; individuals outside these populations can still exhibit this tendency (Moritz & Woodward, 2005; Pytlik et al., 2020). In turn, digital environments can serve to amplify this vulnerability. The high-speed, high-volume nature of online information encourages active stop strategies, where individuals disengage from deeper searches due to cognitive overload (Hadlington, 2017). This accelerates acceptance of conspiracy narratives, especially when they align with pre-existing beliefs or emotional triggers. As Gagliardi (2025) noted, JTC bias interacts with other cognitive shortcuts, such as confirmation bias and proportionality bias, that can create fertile ground for disinformation campaigns.

In terms of how this translates into a weapon for us in the realms of digital warfare, such a tendency for individuals to cease exploring additional information around a topic can influence their susceptibility to disinformation. This is even more apparent when that information is aligned with conspiracy theories, and an individual who experiences a wide range of information online at the high pace at which it is presented may accept conspiracy narratives quickly and without any additional probing or questioning.

Proportionality Bias

Big events need to have big causes, or so goes the notion attached to the proportionality bias. This bias is exhibited in instances where individuals have a predisposition to assume the cause for an event should be equal to or larger in size than the scale of that event (Brotherton, 2013; Brotherton & French, 2014; Cassam, 2023). Proportionality bias has been linked to the functioning of the representativeness heuristic, where an individual will endorse the cause of an event when there is a match between the magnitude of the event and the cause (Brotherton, 2013). Research by Ebel-Lam et al. (2010) highlighted how the proportionality bias works in reality. In their study, they used a series of scenarios which described the outbreak of an infectious disease. In one condition, participants were told that hundreds of people had been killed, while a second group were told that only a small number of people had died. Participants were then asked to choose from four causes and rate them in terms of the likelihood of triggering the disease outbreak. Where participants had been told that the outbreak had resulted in a high number of deaths, they were more likely to choose a high-magnitude cause as being more probable (e.g., the outbreak of a biological weapon from a top-secret laboratory) versus a smaller-magnitude explanation (e.g., someone had become infected with the disease while travelling abroad).

Individuals who engage in conspiratorial ideation often exhibit a heightened need to detect patterns in ambiguous or uncertain events, even when no such patterns exist (van Prooijen et al., 2018). This cognitive tendency reflects a deeper epistemic motive, driven by the human need to impose order on uncertainty and make sense of ambiguous or threatening events. Individuals often seek explanations that provide coherence and predictability, even when those explanations lack empirical support. Conspiracy theories satisfy this need by offering structured narratives that reduce complexity and restore a sense of understanding in situations where official accounts seem incomplete or contradictory (Douglas &

Sutton, 2023; van Prooijen et al., 2018). Rather than accepting that some events may be accidental, random, or beyond personal or systemic control, individuals will gravitate towards causal explanations that feel coherent and intentional. In this context, conspiracy theories serve as narrative glue, binding unrelated occurrences into elaborate, often implausible, but emotionally satisfying frameworks.

This need for explanatory closure becomes especially potent in the digital age, where vast amounts of fragmented information are constantly circulating. Digital technologies, particularly social media algorithms, amplify this effect by surfacing content that aligns with users' existing beliefs, reinforcing perceived patterns and connections. In the realm of digital warfare, this cognitive vulnerability can be strategically exploited: adversaries may seed disinformation that plays into these pattern-seeking tendencies, encouraging individuals to adopt conspiratorial narratives that undermine trust, polarise communities, or destabilise democratic discourse.

Agency Detection Bias

Humans, beginning very early in the developmental process, tend to adopt explanations for events where some form of agent has been involved (Gagliardi, 2025). Now, this is not the James Bond, 007 version of an agent, but the notion that an intentional force (e.g., humans, animals, or supernatural forces) is behind events that occur, particularly those that defy direct explanation or are threatening. This cognitive bias can and does lead to individuals making a series of false attributions, such as the assumption that shadowy forces are behind events. Such biases are often interpreted as being reflective of learning experiences that have specific cultural significance, often seen as being a core part of many superstitions (Van Elk, 2015). The notion that some force or group is responsible for activities is a core feature of many conspiracy theories.

Researchers have explored the way in which people make assumptions about the causes of events and the tendency to assume they are linked to intentionality. This idea is called *intentionality bias* and is the tendency to believe that actions are done deliberately, even when they might not be. For example, Rosset (2008) noted we automatically assume actions are intentional and only later might consider an alternative explanation, such as it was accidental. This suggests our brains are wired to see purpose behind actions, especially when we see someone doing something. Brotherton and French (2014) tested this idea in the context of conspiracy theories using a list of short sentences describing actions that could be seen as either intentional or accidental (like "He set the house on fire" or "She kicked the dog"). They found that people who believed more strongly in conspiracy theories were also slightly more likely to assume these actions were done on purpose.

Another way researchers have explored how individuals detect agency is through the concept of anthropomorphism. This refers to the tendency to attribute human-like qualities, such as thoughts, intentions, or emotions, to non-human entities, including animals, objects, or abstract forces. Unlike intentionality bias, which focuses on how people interpret the actions of other humans, anthropomorphism extends this interpretive lens to non-human phenomena, suggesting a broader inclination to perceive purpose or intent where none may exist. It has been noted that individuals who scored higher on measures of anthropomorphism were more likely to endorse conspiracy theories (Bruder et al., 2013; Imhoff & Bruder, 2014). This supports the idea that people who are more attuned to detecting "hidden agents" behind events are also more susceptible to believing that powerful, covert groups are orchestrating outcomes behind the scenes. Similarly, van der Tempel and Alcock (2015) presented participants with descriptions of random life events, both positive and negative, and asked them to rate the perceived intentionality behind these occurrences. Their findings echoed previous research: individuals who were more inclined to see deliberate purpose in random events were also more likely to believe in conspiracies. This suggests that conspiracy beliefs may be rooted in a cognitive tendency to seek agency and assign blame, even in the absence of clear causal evidence.

Taken together, these cognitive biases, conjunction fallacy, illusory correlation, JTC bias, proportionality bias, intentionality bias, and anthropomorphism form a psychological architecture that predisposes individuals to conspiratorial thinking. Each bias reflects a deeper cognitive tendency to seek meaning, agency, and coherence in a complex and often chaotic world. While these mental shortcuts can be adaptive in everyday decision-making, they also create fertile ground for the acceptance of conspiracy theories, particularly when individuals are exposed to ambiguous or emotionally charged information. In the context of digital warfare, these vulnerabilities are not only academic but also become strategic targets. Disinformation campaigns can exploit these biases to manipulate public perception, erode trust in institutions, and sow division. Understanding the cognitive underpinnings of conspiracy beliefs is therefore not only essential for psychological science but also for developing effective counter-measures in an increasingly information-saturated and adversarial digital landscape.

Social Media, Social Proof, and Celebrity Endorsements

There have been some questions raised in the research literature on the topic of conspiracy theories around why some theories become more mainstream than others. Some have noted that belief in conspiracy theories tends to increase when there is a perception of some form of foreign threat or when there is a challenge to the political status quo within the individual's own country (Uscinski & Parent, 2014). Other mechanisms can also facilitate the spread and acceptance of conspiracy theories, including trends emerging from popular media and television that normalise their expression and belief. Such normalisation can serve as a coping strategy for many individuals, enabling them to regain a sense of control over their lives and current events that might otherwise cause significant distress (Kelley-Romano, 2008).

In terms of digital media, there has been some work that has demonstrated the role celebrity and influencer endorsements can have on the potential spread of conspiracy theories (Jennings et al., 2024). Much of this work builds on the concepts of normative influence and social proof that we explored in Chapter 8 when looking at social engineering. As a short recap, individuals will make an assessment about their own behaviour and what they should be doing in any given situation to understand what is socially acceptable. In terms of digital comparisons, people will often turn to online social proof, examining the norms and rules that other people online follow (Hilverda et al., 2018). Hilverda et al. (2018) noted that the number of comments or likes that social media posts received had a direct impact on the attitudes, feelings, and behavioural intentions of individuals. This was especially prevalent in instances where evidence of social proof was explicit and clear, with more positive attitude formation following positive social proof (lots of likes and positive comments), with the opposite being true for negative attitudes (Hilverda et al., 2018).

In terms of conspiracy theories, there is a certain stigma associated with belief in and endorsement of many such theories. While some individuals from the conspiracy theory community will often revel in this, for many outside of such groups, the belief in conspiracy theories is often accompanied by social ridicule and derogatory comments (Lantian et al., 2018). In instances where an individual dares to publicly endorse a conspiracy theory, they may experience a respective backlash, opening the possibility of social isolation and ostracism from their peers. However, as Jennings et al. (2024) noted, the increasing frequency with which celebrities and influencers actively endorse conspiracy theories, particularly on social media platforms, is making them more acceptable to be discussed in public. Jennings et al. (2024) noted that where celebrities actively endorse the existence of conspiracy theories on social media, this has a greater influence on both the spread and acceptance of such information than comments by other types of social media users. They also noted that celebrity endorsements on social media could result in a process of destigmatisation, in turn making it more socially acceptable for individuals to publicly acknowledge their own belief in conspiracy theories. So celebrity endorsements serve to act as a critical mechanism through which belief in conspiracy theories can be normalised, as well as lending greater legitimacy to those who may believe in them already (Jennings et al., 2024). While there is a consistent strand of research that exemplifies the role that individual characteristics can have in the belief and perpetuation of conspiracy theories, this work shows that you can move fringe beliefs to the mainstream with the use of social proof.

While numerous researchers have underscored the central role of social media in the dissemination of conspiracy theories (e.g., Jamieson & Albarracin, 2020), others have challenged its direct influence. For instance, Enders et al.

(2023) argued that merely exposing someone to social media does not inherently increase overall susceptibility to conspiracy theories. Instead, individuals must already possess a belief system or psychological predisposition that renders them receptive to such content. In this view, social media functions more as a facilitator than a causal agent that provides users with a vast array of conspiracy theories from which they can selectively engage, often reinforcing pre-existing biases.

This would suggest that social media platforms should not be viewed as the sole drivers of the proliferation of conspiracy theories. Rather, attention should be directed towards the underlying cognitive, psychological, and social characteristics that predispose individuals to believe in conspiracy theories. However, it would be premature to dismiss the role of social media entirely. The complex social dynamics, algorithmic amplification, and echo chamber effects associated with these platforms remain insufficiently understood and warrant further investigation. A more nuanced approach is needed, one that considers both individual susceptibility and the structural features of social media that may exacerbate the spread and entrenchment of conspiracy theories.

What Are the Implications for Digital Warfare?

The first point to reiterate is that the belief in conspiracy theories is not an isolated phenomenon and is not restricted to individuals who might be suffering from delusions or be of a subclinical population. Instead, conspiracy theories are often widely held, and even though many people shy away from publicly acknowledging them, they may still demonstrate some level of pluralistic ignorance. As we have seen from examples such as the Pizzagate conspiracy theory back in 2017, some of these theories rarely remain online and can have real-world consequences. The mechanics of echo chambers and filter bubbles, coupled with the myriad of cognitive biases, can serve to both create and maintain these conspiracy theories, ensuring they have both permanence and visibility. The power of the digital environment comes directly into play when what first appears to be fringe beliefs and groups are given the freedom to propagate such theories outside the initial echo chambers in which they have been incubated, serving to bleed into more mainstream digital platforms.

From an offensive standpoint, the strategic deployment of conspiracy theories in digital warfare is typically embedded within long-term, protracted campaigns that require careful planning and sustained effort. These tactics are not designed for immediate results; rather, they rely on gradual infiltration and amplification within the online information ecosystem. Crucially, the existence of pre-established echo chambers, digital spaces where conspiratorial thinking is already prevalent, provides fertile ground for seeding new or more disruptive conspiracy narratives. Research consistently shows that individuals who already endorse conspiracy theories are more likely to accept additional, related beliefs.

Therefore, targeting these echo chambers is both efficient and effective, reducing the need to cultivate entirely new audiences. Within these environments, confirmation bias plays a pivotal role, enabling new theories to be assimilated with minimal resistance and shielding them from counter-arguments or debunking efforts.

The strategic use of conspiracy theories alongside disinformation and misinformation campaigns has been widely acknowledged in the literature on digital warfare (Breedon, 2022; Paterson & Hanley, 2020; Wilbur, 2014). Online platforms amplify these narratives through a combination of technological design, psychological manipulation, and algorithmic reinforcement. Social media algorithms are engineered to maximise engagement by prioritising emotionally charged or sensational content (Schroeder, 2021; Zimmer et al., 2019). This dynamic fosters the creation of filter bubbles and echo chambers, reinforcing the illusion that fringe beliefs are widely held. For example, an individual who watches an anti-vaccination video may be algorithmically directed towards increasingly extreme content, reinforcing their beliefs through the illusory truth effect and bandwagon bias.

Digital environments also exploit cognitive biases that favour fast, intuitive Type 1 processing, especially when users are overwhelmed by information. The JTC bias is particularly relevant here: the rapid pace of digital content encourages users to make snap judgements without engaging in deeper, analytical reasoning. Similarly, narrative bias makes conspiracy theories especially potent, as they often feature compelling storylines with clear villains and motives and structures that are easier to process, remember, and emotionally engage with. These biases are not merely passive vulnerabilities; they are actively weaponised by adversaries in digital warfare to seed, spread, and entrench disinformation.

As demonstrated by Douglas et al. (2017), conspiracy theories are often engineered to appeal to existential and social motives, making them particularly potent during times of crisis. In such moments, individuals are more likely to seek control, certainty, and meaning, which are needs that conspiracy theories readily satisfy by offering simplified explanations for complex problems. This strategic timing is crucial: launching conspiracy narratives during periods of uncertainty increases their likelihood of acceptance and spread.

One of the key psychological mechanisms at play is social identity formation. Online communities frequently coalesce around shared beliefs, reinforcing in-group loyalty and fostering out-group hostility. Within these digital spaces, users find not only content but also validation and belonging. Likes, shares, and comments serve as social reinforcement, making individuals feel affirmed in their views and encouraging further engagement with conspiratorial material. Platforms such as Reddit, Telegram, and Facebook groups often act as incubators for conspiratorial ideation, providing both the infrastructure and the community needed for these narratives to thrive.

The low friction of content creation and dissemination in digital environments further accelerates the spread of conspiracy theories. Anonymity and pseudonymity allow users to share and promote conspiratorial content without accountability, while visual formats, such as memes, infographics, and short videos, distil complex ideas into emotionally resonant and easily digestible forms. These formats are particularly effective in capturing attention and triggering emotional responses. Moreover, conspiracy theories often propagate across platforms, moving from fringe spaces like 4chan to mainstream ones like Twitter/X, thereby increasing their reach and perceived legitimacy.

A critical challenge in countering conspiracy theories is their resistance to correction. Many operate on self-sealing logic, where attempts to debunk them are interpreted as further evidence of the conspiracy itself. This is compounded by a deep distrust in authority, which digital platforms inadvertently support by enabling alternative narratives to flourish unchecked. As a result, trust in experts, institutions, and traditional sources of information is eroded.

In the context of digital warfare, these dynamics have profound implications. Conspiracy theories can be strategically deployed by adversaries to exploit psychological vulnerabilities and algorithmic structures. Their ability to destabilise societies through a process of trust erosion, the polarisation of communities and inciting real-world action can make them a powerful tool in cognitive and informational conflict. Perhaps most concerning is their invisible influence: users often remain unaware that they are being manipulated, making conspiracy theories a subtle yet highly effective weapon in the digital arsenal.

Summary

In this chapter, we have examined conspiracy theories as potent instruments of cognitive and informational conflict rather than mere fringe curiosities. It begins by situating conspiracy theories within the broader typology of misinformation, highlighting frameworks such as Sambol et al.'s content-based classification and Mao et al.'s GIST model, which reveal their structural and psychological complexity. These narratives exploit deep-seated human motives, epistemic, existential, and social, providing simplified explanations, a sense of control, and group identity during times of uncertainty or crisis.

The discussion has emphasised how cognitive biases, including conjunction fallacy, illusory correlation, JTC bias, proportionality bias, and agency detection, create fertile ground for conspiratorial thinking. These biases interact with intuitive Type 1 processing, enabling individuals to adopt narratives that feel coherent and intentional, even when evidence is lacking. Social media platforms amplify these vulnerabilities through algorithmic curation, echo chambers, and influencer endorsements, normalising fringe beliefs and accelerating their spread. Mechanisms such as social proof and celebrity validation further legitimise conspiratorial content, reducing stigma and increasing public engagement.

From a strategic perspective, conspiracy theories are shown to be weaponised in digital warfare through long-term campaigns that infiltrate echo chambers, exploit psychological needs, and leverage emotionally charged content. Their resistance to correction, coupled with self-sealing logic and distrust of authority, makes them exceptionally resilient and dangerous. These dynamics can destabilise societies by eroding trust, polarising communities, and inciting real-world actions, as illustrated by cases like Pizzagate and anti-vaccination movements.

Ultimately, the chapter argues that conspiracy theories are not incidental by-products of the digital age but deliberate tools of influence. By mapping their psychological architecture and operational mechanisms, it underscores the need for counter-measures that address both individual vulnerabilities and structural features of digital platforms, reinforcing resilience in an increasingly contested information environment.

References

Abalakina-Paap, M., Stephan, W. G., Craig, T., & Gregory, W. L. (1999). Beliefs in conspiracies. *Political Psychology*, *20*(3), 637–647. https://doi.org/10.1111/0162-895X.00160

Bowes, S. M., Costello, T. H., & Tasimi, A. (2023). The conspiratorial mind: A meta-analytic review of motivational and personological correlates. *Psychological Bulletin*, *149*(5–6), 259–293. https://doi.org/10.1037/bul0000392

Breedon, K. (2022). An international law perspective on political informational warfare: The challenges of combating the weaponized use of conspiracy theories and disinformation to undermine democracy. *Update*, *2*(2009), 633–688. Retrieved from http://search.ebscohost.com/login.aspx?direct=true&db=e095mww&AN=532124&site=ehost-live

Brotherton, R. A. (2013). *Measurement issues and the role of cognitive biases in conspiracist ideation*, (October). Retrieved from http://research.gold.ac.uk/id/eprint/10428

Brotherton, R. A., & French, C. C. (2014). Belief in conspiracy theories and susceptibility to the conjunction fallacy. *Applied Cognitive Psychology*, *28*(2), 238–248. https://doi.org/10.1002/acp.2995

Bruder, M., Haffke, P., Neave, N., Nouripanah, N., & Imhoff, R. (2013). Measuring individual differences in generic beliefs in conspiracy theories across cultures: Conspiracy mentality questionnaire. *Frontiers in Psychology*, *4*(April). https://doi.org/10.3389/fpsyg.2013.00225

Cassam, Q. (2023). Conspiracy theories. *Society*, *60*(2), 190–199. https://doi.org/10.1007/s12115-023-00816-1

Denovan, A., Dagnall, N., Drinkwater, K., Parker, A., & Neave, N. (2020). Conspiracist beliefs, intuitive thinking, and schizotypal facets: A further evaluation. *Applied Cognitive Psychology*, *34*(6), 1394–1405. https://doi.org/10.1002/acp.3716

Douglas, K. M., & Sutton, R. M. (2018). Why conspiracy theories matter: A social psychological analysis. *European Review of Social Psychology*, *29*(1), 256–298. https://doi.org/10.1080/10463283.2018.1537428

Douglas, K. M., & Sutton, R. M. (2023). What are conspiracy theories? A definitional approach to their correlates, consequences, and communication. *Annual Review of Psychology*, *74*, 271–298. https://doi.org/10.1146/annurev-psych-032420-031329

Douglas, K. M., Sutton, R. M., & Cichocka, A. (2017). The psychology of conspiracy theories. *Current Directions in Psychological Science*, *26*(6), 538–542. https://doi.org/10.1177/0963721417718261

Ebel-Lam, A. P., Fabrigar, L. R., MacDonald, T. K., & Jones, S. (2010). Balancing causes and consequences: The magnitude-matching principle in explanations for complex social events. *Basic and Applied Social Psychology*, *32*(4), 348–359. https://doi.org/10.1080/01973533.2010.519245

Enders, A. M., Uscinski, J. E., Seelig, M. I., Klofstad, C. A., Wuchty, S., Funchion, J. R., . . . Stoler, J. (2023). The relationship between social media use and beliefs in conspiracy theories and misinformation. *Political Behavior*, *45*(2), 781–804. https://doi.org/10.1007/s11109-021-09734-6

Federico, C. (2022). The complex relationship between conspiracy belief and the politics of social change. *Current Opinion in Psychology*, *47*, 101354. https://doi.org/10.1016/j.copsyc.2022.101354

Gagliardi, L. (2025). The role of cognitive biases in conspiracy beliefs: A literature review. *Journal of Economic Surveys*, *39*(1), 32–65. https://doi.org/10.1111/joes.12604

Goertzel, T. (1994). Belief in conspiracy theories. *Political Psychology*, *15*(4), 733–744. Retrieved from http://doi.wiley.com/10.1111/0162-895X.00328

Green, R., & Douglas, K. M. (2018). Anxious attachment and belief in conspiracy theories. *Personality and Individual Differences*, *125*(December 2017), 30–37. https://doi.org/10.1016/j.paid.2017.12.023

Hadlington, L. (2017). *Cybercognition: Brain, behaviour and the digital world.* London: Sage.

Hilverda, F., Kuttschreuter, M., & Giebels, E. (2018). The effect of online social proof regarding organic food: Comments and likes on Facebook. *Frontiers in Communication*, *3*(August), 1–15. https://doi.org/10.3389/fcomm.2018.00030

Imhoff, R., & Bruder, M. (2014). Speaking (un-)truth to power: Conspiracy mentality as a generalised political attitude. *European Journal of Personality*, *28*(1), 25–43. https://doi.org/10.1002/per.1930

Jamieson, K. H., & Albarracin, D. (2020). The relation between media consumption and misinformation at the outset of the SARS-CoV-2 pandemic in the US. *Harvard Kennedy School Misinformation Review*, *1*(3). https://doi.org/10.37016/mr-2020-012

Jennings, F. J., Neville-Shepard, R., Jackson, D. B., Magusiak, A., & Sigrist, K. (2024). From fringe to mainstream: How celebrity endorsement on social media contributes to the spread of conspiracy theories. *Southern Communication Journal*, *89*(2), 119–131. https://doi.org/10.1080/1041794X.2024.2308892

Jolley, D., Mari, S., & Douglas, K. M. (2020). Consequences of conspiracy theories. In *Routledge handbook of conspiracy theories* (pp. 231–241). https://doi.org/10.4324/9780429452734-2_7

Kelley-Romano, S. (2008). Trust no one: The conspiracy genre on American television. *Southern Communication Journal*, *73*(2), 105–121. https://doi.org/10.1080/10417940802009509

Kuhn, S. A. K., Lieb, R., Freeman, D., Andreou, C., & Zander-Schellenberg, T. (2022). Coronavirus conspiracy beliefs in the German-speaking general population: Endorsement rates and links to reasoning biases and paranoia. *Psychological Medicine*, *52*(16), 4162–4176. https://doi.org/10.1017/S0033291721001124

Lantian, A., Muller, D., Nurra, C., Klein, O., Berjot, S., & Pantazi, M. (2018). Stigmatized beliefs: Conspiracy theories, anticipated negative evaluation of the self, and fear of social exclusion. *European Journal of Social Psychology*, *48*(7), 939–954. https://doi.org/10.1002/ejsp.2498

Liekefett, L., Christ, O., & Becker, J. C. (2023). Can conspiracy beliefs be beneficial? Longitudinal linkages between conspiracy beliefs, anxiety, uncertainty aversion, and existential threat. *Personality and Social Psychology Bulletin*, *49*(2), 167–179. https://doi.org/10.1177/01461672211060965

Mao, J. Y., van Prooijen, J. W., & Van Lange, P. A. M. (2024). Conspiracy theories: Groups, ideology, and status as three distinct bases for expressions in society. *Current Directions in Psychological Science*, *33*(6), 385–391. https://doi.org/10.1177/09637214241280742

Moritz, S., & Woodward, T. S. (2005). Jumping to conclusions in delusional and non-delusional schizophrenic patients. *British Journal of Clinical Psychology*, *44*(2), 193–207. https://doi.org/10.1348/014466505X35678

Müller, P., & Hartmann, M. (2023). Linking paranormal and conspiracy beliefs to illusory pattern perception through signal detection theory. *Scientific Reports*, *13*(1), 1–11. https://doi.org/10.1038/s41598-023-36230-0

Papaioannou, K., Pantazi, M., & van Prooijen, J. W. (2023). Is democracy under threat? Why belief in conspiracy theories predicts autocratic attitudes. *European Journal of Social Psychology*, *53*(5), 846–856. https://doi.org/10.1002/ejsp.2939

Paterson, T., & Hanley, L. (2020). Political warfare in the digital age: Cyber subversion, information operations and "deep fakes". *Australian Journal of International Affairs*, *74*(4), 439–454. https://doi.org/10.1080/10357718.2020.1734772

Pytlik, N., Soll, D., & Mehl, S. (2020). Thinking preferences and conspiracy belief: Intuitive thinking and the jumping to conclusions-bias as a basis for the belief in conspiracy theories. *Frontiers in Psychiatry*, *11*(September), 1–11. https://doi.org/10.3389/fpsyt.2020.568942

Rosset, E. (2008). It's no accident: Our bias for intentional explanations. *Cognition*, *108*(3), 771–780. https://doi.org/10.1016/j.cognition.2008.07.001

Sambol, S., Sans, E., Scarfo, J., Kirkovski, M., & Ball, M. (2024). A latent profile approach to the study of conspiracy belief: Identifying the role of executive functioning. *Personality and Individual Differences*, *220*(December 2023), 112537. https://doi.org/10.1016/j.paid.2023.112537

Schroeder, J. E. (2021). Reinscribing gender: Social media, algorithms, bias Reinscribing gender: Social media, algorithms, bias. *Journal of Marketing Management*, *37*(3–4), 376–378. https://doi.org/10.1080/0267257X.2020.1832378

Tuters, M., Jokubauskaitė, E., & Bach, D. (2018). Post-truth protest: How 4Chan cooked up the pizzagate bullshit. *M/C Journal*, *21*(3). https://doi.org/10.5204/mcj.1422

Tversky, A., & Kahneman, D. (1983). Extensional versus intuitive reasoning: The conjunction fallacy in probability judgment. *Psychological Review*, *90*(4): 293–315.

Uscinski, J. E., Enders, A. M., Klofstad, C., Seelig, M., Funchion, J., Everett, C., & Murthi, M. (2020). Why do people believe COVID-19 conspiracy theories? Research questions. *Harvard Kennedy School Misinformation Review*, *1*(3), 1–12.

Uscinski, J. E., & Parent, J. M. (2014). *American conspiracy theories*. New York: Oxford University Press.

van der Tempel, J., & Alcock, J. E. (2015). Relationships between conspiracy mentality, hyperactive agency detection, and schizotypy: Supernatural forces at work? *Personality and Individual Differences*, *82*, 136–141. https://doi.org/10.1016/j.paid.2015.03.010

Van Elk, M. (2015). Perceptual biases in relation to paranormal and conspiracy beliefs. *PLoS One*, *10*(6), 1–15. https://doi.org/10.1371/journal.pone.0130422

van Prooijen, J. W., & Douglas, K. M. (2017). Conspiracy theories as part of history: The role of societal crisis situations. *Memory Studies*, *10*(3), 323–333. https://doi.org/10.1177/1750698017701615

van Prooijen, J. W., Douglas, K. M., & De Inocencio, C. (2018). Connecting the dots: Illusory pattern perception predicts belief in conspiracies and the supernatural. *European Journal of Social Psychology*, *48*(3), 320–335. https://doi.org/10.1002/ejsp.2331

van Prooijen, J. W., & van Vugt, M. (2018). Conspiracy theories: Evolved functions and psychological mechanisms. *Perspectives on Psychological Science*, *13*(6), 770–788. https://doi.org/10.1177/1745691618774270

Wilbur, D. (2014). Strategic communicators to analyze conspiracy theories in the service of malign actors. *Journal of Military and Strategic Studies*, *23*(3), 186–195.

Zimmer, F., Scheibe, K., Stock, M., & Stock, W. G. (2019). Fake news in social media: Bad algorithms or biased users? *Journal of Information Science Theory and Practice*, *7*(2), 40–53. https://doi.org/10.1633/JISTaP.2019.7.2.4

16 Countering the Digital Threat

Strategies for Digital Resilience

Introduction

For most of the book, we have focused centrally on the offensive strategies within the domain of digital warfare. At this juncture, readers may rightly question the absence of a counterbalancing perspective that presents the defensive mechanisms that can be employed to mitigate such threats. This omission is not due to oversight or a lack of relevant material; rather, it reflects the complexity and subtlety inherent in psychological defence strategies. While some countermeasures have been introduced throughout the text, this chapter aims to more explicitly address the psychological dimensions of defence in digital conflict.

Rather than delving into technical solutions or the potential applications of artificial intelligence (AI), the focus here is on countering the psychological tactics that underpin digital manipulation. Although AI can certainly aid in identifying and responding to phenomena such as fake news and misinformation, the foundational elements of defence remain deeply rooted in human cognition. The strategies presented in this chapter are therefore curated with an emphasis on cognitive and behavioural processes. While not exhaustive, they offer a representative sample of approaches that can be employed to resist manipulation and maintain psychological resilience in the face of digital threats.

Many of the initiatives discussed in this chapter will draw directly upon principles from behavioural economics, which have underpinned much of the offensive strategies explored earlier in the text. These same principles can be repurposed for defensive ends. For instance, framing, a technique often used to manipulate perception, could be employed to highlight the benefits of secure online behaviour. By shaping narratives to emphasise gains in safety and digital literacy, we can foster proactive engagement and reduce susceptibility to subversive messaging.

This approach is particularly effective when contrasted with fear-based messaging, which research has shown to be largely ineffective in promoting sustained behavioural change. In fact, such messaging can provoke resistance or defiance, undermining its intended purpose. Instead, strategies that align with

DOI: 10.4324/9781003752400-16

individuals' values and perceived benefits are more likely to result in meaningful engagement and long-term resilience (S. Lewandowsky et al., 2020).

Ultimately, the mechanics of psychological defence in digital warfare are nuanced and multifaceted. There is no universal solution or training programme that guarantees immunity, but awareness has been posited as a key mechanism in terms of the fight against misinformation (Ecker et al., 2019; Ecker et al., 2011). By leveraging cognitive insights and behavioural strategies, we can begin to construct a more robust framework for resisting manipulation and preserving the integrity of individual and collective decision-making in digital environments.

Cognitive and Psychological Interventions

In this section, we will focus directly on the tactics that can be used to enhance the individual's awareness of the potential for manipulative techniques to be used on them and the goals that perpetrators of such have in mind. As many of the processes that occur in the sphere of psychological and cognitive warfare rely heavily on a lack of awareness of these tactics, giving detailed information on such threats can bolster their resilience.

In the context of digital warfare, there are two prominent strategies that could be implemented to prevent the spread of misinformation and the susceptibility of individuals to manipulation from subversive narratives. These are debunking (to present an argument that counters the misinformation that an individual has seen after it has been presented) or prebunking, which is linked to the presentation of counter-arguments prior to the subversive narrative being presented. We will now turn our attention towards each of these strategies and highlight their relevant advantages and disadvantages.

Debunking

In the research literature that explores the most effective ways of dealing with pervasive messages that are linked to false information or the presence of propaganda, there has been a detailed exploration of presenting information to disprove these falsehoods (Chan et al., 2017; van der Linden, 2024; Walter & Tukachinsky, 2020). There are some important factors that can contribute to the successful implementation of debunking strategies, and it has been noted that both the content and area of the misinformation, as well as specific factors related to the individual, can directly influence the success of debunking strategies. For example, Chan and Albarracín (2023) noted that in terms of science-related misinformation, the power of debunking was severely limited, demonstrating that this type of misinformation is particularly resilient to post-presentation correction. Such effects were noted to be much weaker than in other domains linked to the presentation of misinformation, such as those associated with political or health-related misinformation. However, Chan and Albarracín (2023) did note that where detailed information that corrected the misinformation was presented, this did have some limited success in debunking. Similarly, where the misinformation presented to individuals was negative and emotionally charged (so linked to fear-based or emotionally charged topics), individuals were far more likely to be open to post-presentation correction. The extent to which the misinformation was formed around strongly dichotomous arguments that can serve to create a strongly polarised debate was also seen as a significant factor in the effectiveness of debunking strategies for science-related misinformation, and simply refuting the misinformation with a respective counter-argument was seen as the least effective, often resulting in an increased resistance to debunking (Chan & Albarracín, 2023). In terms of the importance of individual differences in the context of the use of debunking strategies, aligning the counter-information with the ideological stance of the individual was seen as having a more successful outcome, potentially fitting into confirmation bias, where information that fits into contact with previous beliefs has been shown to be a key facilitator. Trust in the source for the debunking material has also been demonstrated to have a facilitatory impact on the individual's likelihood to accept such information, again demonstrating that simply presenting relevant counter-arguments is not a guaranteed, surefire way of countering misinformation (Bruns et al., 2023).

There are several key challenges that have been highlighted around the implementation of debunking programmes to nullify the effects of misinformation, where the actions can serve to strengthen people's resolve to believe in the material that you are actively trying to debunk (Ecker et al., 2011; Swire-Thompson et al., 2020; van der Linden, 2024).

The Backfire Effect

Sometimes it is referred to as the boomerang effect (Byrne & Hart, 2009). Researchers have detailed several prominent forms of the backfire effect, including the world-view backfire effect, the overkill backfire effect, and the familiarity backfire effect (Swire-Thompson et al., 2020). These mechanisms have been demonstrated to result in the reinforcement of false beliefs after corrective information has been presented, but both are reliant on different underlying psychological processes.

World-View Backfire Effects

It occurs when the corrective action to the presence of false or misleading information serves to challenge the individual's whole belief system. Accordingly, the effect is more likely to occur in instances where the information being challenged has a core importance for the individual or when they are deeply committed to the information being challenged (Swire-Thompson et al., 2020). This would suggest a course of action that relies on targeting those individuals who have not had sufficient time to incorporate prominent pieces of misinformation with counter-arguments, appealing to the group that is majority undecided, instead of a hard-to-move, stubborn minority (Lewandowsky, 2011; Lewandowsky et al., 2020). There is a particular bias, that of the *disconfirmation bias*, that comes into play in the case of the world-view backfire effect and is one that is seen as contrary to the confirmation bias (Edwards & Smith, 1996). This bias suggests that arguments that are presented as being inconsistent with our prior, core beliefs are subjected to a lengthier process of rejection and, in turn, are weaker positions than our existing, prior beliefs. In their study exploring disconfirmation bias, Edwards and Smith (1996) noted strong empirical support for the effect, demonstrating that arguments that served to contradict prior beliefs are generally judged to be less persuasive or weaker than those that align with their pre-existing beliefs. Aligned with this, they also noted that individuals will spend more time and energy critically evaluating beliefs that are inconsistent with their pre-existing beliefs, which suggests that individuals are engaged in more Type 2 processing rather than speedier, heuristic-based methods. Individuals were also seen to generate more arguments that served to refute contradictory information in comparison to supportive arguments when the argument challenged their prior knowledge (Edwards & Smith, 1996). This is interesting because it suggests that belief systems have a real resilience to change and offer an insight into the difficulties we face when trying to correct misinformation. This is particularly salient when information conflicts with either ideologically based or identity-based views, further exacerbating the capacity to debunk misinformation. So how do we resolve this issue in terms of messaging to individuals? Lewandowsky (2011) suggested that communication of counter-arguments needs to be couched in less threatening ways that do not immediately target an individual's existing beliefs and suggested that framing might offer a convenient way of doing this. A soft approach would seem more productive than a concerted effort to present counterclaims and would allow a more subtle process of opinion sublimination that avoids the risk of backlash effects emerging from pre-existing beliefs.

Overkill Backfire Effect

There have been some suggestions in the research literature that bombarding individuals with multiple counterclaims against misinformation could result in a similar refusal to engage in that counterclaim and, in turn, strengthen their commitment to the misinformation they had encountered (Ecker et al., 2019). However, the evidence for such an effect has been called into question, with researchers noting that when counterclaims are numerous and aligned with one another, they lead to a greater impact compared to when only a small number of counterclaims are presented (Ecker et al., 2019). In this instance, the adage "less is more" does not apply to debunking misinformation; rather, when counterclaims are carefully aligned, more is indeed more (Ecker et al., 2019).

Familiarity Backfire Effect

The familiarity backfire effect is grounded in the illusory truth effect, which we reviewed back in Chapter 6, a cognitive bias where repeated information is more likely to be judged as true simply because it feels familiar (Lewandowsky et al., 2020; Schwarz et al., 2007; Swire-Thompson et al., 2020). Accordingly, repeating misinformation, even in the context of a correction, can lead to an unintended consequence, which leads to the inadvertent increase in belief in the false claim by enhancing its familiarity.

While this concept has received attention in the misinformation literature, empirical support remains limited. The most frequently cited evidence comes from an unpublished study (Skurnik et al., 2007, as cited in Schwarz et al., 2007), which found that participants exposed to a "myths versus facts" vaccine pamphlet developed less favourable attitudes towards vaccines than those in a control group. However, subsequent studies (Ecker et al., 2019; Swire-Thompson et al., 2020) have failed to consistently replicate this effect.

One proposed moderating factor in this process is the novelty of the misinformation. Lewandowsky et al. (2020) suggested that corrections of novel misinformation, where an individual encounters claims that they had not previously encountered, might be the ones more susceptible to backfire. This is because the correction itself introduces the false claim, thereby increasing its familiarity from a no-exposure baseline. However, across multiple experiments, they found little evidence that correcting novel misinformation leads to stronger belief in the misinformation compared to no exposure at all (Swire-Thompson et al., 2020, 2023).

So, overall, there is very limited evidence to directly support the notion of a backlash effect against the presentation of factually true information to counter misinformation. Guess and Coppock (2020) noted that there was no direct evidence to support the backlash effect, even in large, nationally representative samples. However, even though there are multiple instances where the backlash effect has failed to be reliably elicited in research, it still exists as one of the most discussed barriers to the debunking of pre-existing information (Swire-Thompson et al., 2020). While many researchers maintain the perspective that it is a genuine and replicable effect that serves to create a real issue when it comes to the debunking of false information, others have suggested that it is only relevant in very specific situations (Lewandowsky et al., 2020; Swire-Thompson et al., 2020; Chan & Albarracín, 2023). However, that is not to say that these effects do not exist at all, and it would perhaps be dismissive to completely ignore them altogether. There are still relevant steps that need to be taken when we are considering messages presented to groups, with corrections needing to be carefully framed to avoid the potential for resistance to emerge through deeply engrained beliefs; a strategy that avoids direct confrontation would appear to be the best way forward. Similarly, given the potential for such resistance to emerge, mechanisms for prebunking would appear to be more attractive and build a level of resistance prior to the individual being subjected to the misinformation, meaning that such information does not get a chance to take hold.

Beyond the backfire effect, other phenomena illustrate the stubborn persistence of misinformation even after correction. One such mechanism is the *continued influence effect*, where individuals continue to rely on inaccurate information in reasoning and decision-making despite acknowledging a correction. This occurs because misinformation often provides a coherent causal narrative, and when no alternative explanation is offered, people default to the original falsehood. A related challenge is *belief regression*, in which individuals initially update their beliefs following corrective information but gradually revert to pre-correction levels over time. This regression is largely driven by memory decay; while the misinformation remains salient, the corrective details fade, allowing old beliefs to resurface. We will explore these now in the next section.

Continued Influence Effect

Individuals continue to use inaccurate information in reasoning and memory even after a credible correction has been presented (Ecker et al., 2011; Johnson & Seifert, 1994). There has been a long history of research that has noted that even though information has been discredited, it can have long-lasting impacts on decision-making and understanding of new information (Johnson & Seifert, 1994). In their study, Johnson and Seifert (1994) noted that a key finding was that people were more susceptible to misinformation when it had a direct impact on a story. For example, participants were more likely to make inferences about the cause of a fire being related to volatile chemicals, even if a correction to the contrary was made. Where the same materials were mentioned but in a non-causal way, participants were still likely to remember them but did not use them in their reasoning about the causes for the fire. This presented an important note about the framing of misinformation, showing that how it is causally linked to events can also influence thinking (Johnson & Seifert, 1994). Similarly, the researchers noted that misinformation is more likely to exert a direct influence on reasoning when it is presented as the sole available explanation for the event in question. (Johnson & Seifert, 1994). In situations where participants were given a correction in which the alternative explanation served to act as a causative link, they were less likely to hold the original misinformation as being relevant. Rather than individuals using misinformation in their decision-making processes because it is familiar (linking into the availability heuristic), it is more likely used because it feeds into the creation of a plausible causal narrative, in turn linking to the narrative bias; if no other information is available, misinformation fills the void individuals need to help keep the narrative alive, even when it has been discredited.

From this perspective, as we have seen in key discussions throughout this book, narratives that present individuals with information about current events that lack any specific real-world information are generally more likely to be believed. If we want to prevent this from happening, we need to ensure that individuals are being presented with clearly visible, plausible explanations where we are attempting to correct for misinformation. This means the potential gaps that could be filled with explanations from misinformation narratives are filled naturally but are ones that need to be engineered to ensure the coherence of information and not just the facticity of the alternative explanation.

Belief Regression

Individuals begin to update their beliefs after being presented with updated material, but the change in beliefs is not sustained over time (Swire et al., 2017; Swire-Thompson et al., 2023). While many people will correct their beliefs in line with corrected information, they are often quick to relapse to endorsing misinformation at levels that match pre-corrections levels (Swire-Thompson et al., 2020). The function of memory has been strongly implicated in belief regression, where participants who exhibited better memory for corrective information were less likely to believe in misinformation that had been presented prior to the corrective information, with this effect lasting for at least one month post-correction (Swire-Thompson et al., 2020). Swire-Thompson et al. (2020) noted that the functioning of memory explained regression in beliefs about the truthfulness of misinformation. Forgetting for the corrective information increased at a significant rate as a function of the time post-corrective information presentation, while the active rejection of misinformation was stable over the same period. In the group of individuals that still believed the misinformation at the post-one-month testing point, 57% of these still misremembered it as being true, which in turn suggests that it is memory, and not ideological resistance, that drives the re-emergence of false beliefs.

For prevention strategies in the context of digital warfare, such findings demonstrate how important it is to design corrective interventions that provide individuals with memorable information. Such information should be seen not as a one-shot, fire-and-forget strategy but as a one that needs continued maintenance so that individuals do not relapse into pre-corrective levels of misinformation belief. One-off corrections, given the issues linked to memory retention, would be seen not to be sufficient, but a programme of repetition and reinforcement would appear to be a more appropriate pathway (Lewandowsky et al., 2020).

Cognitive Inoculation

The concept of cognitive inoculation is analogous to the medical model of vaccination, wherein individuals are exposed to a weakened form of a virus to stimulate immunity against future infection (McGuire, 1964; Swire-Thompson et al., 2020). In the psychological domain, inoculation theory operates on a similar principle: by presenting individuals with a diluted version of a persuasive argument, one that reflects the core tenets of a potentially harmful narrative, alongside refutations, it is possible to build resistance to future, more persuasive iterations of that argument. This pre-emptive exposure activates cognitive defences, enabling individuals to critically evaluate and reject misleading or manipulative content when they encounter it in more potent forms (Compton et al., 2022; van der Linden, 2024). Where debunking forms a reactive strategy to correct the presence of misinformation, prebunking serves to offer a more proactive approach that prevents misinformation from taking hold in the first place.

There are some core mechanisms that are involved in cognitive inoculation, each of which serves to prepare the individual for the potential contact with misinformation.

1. *Threat component*: this includes giving individuals an opportunity to become aware of the potential for their own beliefs and ideology to become susceptible to attack via manipulation. This, in turn, can act as a significant motivating factor, triggering a defensive posture with people paying more attention to incoming information. This threat component is usually delivered to individuals via prominent warnings such as "you may be exposed to misleading information" or "information on this website has not been independently verified." Most of the time, individuals are generally unaware of their susceptibility to inaccurate information, and judgements generally highlight the influence of previously encountered misinformation (Salovich & Rapp, 2020).
2. *Refutational pre-emption*: this is where individuals are exposed to a weakened "dose" of the misinformation that is likely to be circulated or that they could potentially encounter. At the same time, the individual is also presented with relevant counter-arguments of information that refute the misinformation claims. This, in turn, should produce "cognitive antibodies" or strategies that allow individuals to resist the potential persuasive effects of misinformation in the future.
3. *Delay and reinforcement*: the process of inoculation becomes more efficient when there is a delay between the presentation of the inoculating information and the appearance of misinformation or a similar form of attack. A continued process of reinforcement by repeating the link between misinformation and the refutational material increases resistance and can feed into a positive illusory truth effect. This process also increases the potential for refutational information to be incorporated into memory.
4. *Active processing*: by getting individuals to engage in an active generation of counter-arguments to misinformation, this can serve to strengthen the inoculation process. In part, this process means that individuals are actively thinking about the counterpositions to misinformation, which in turn means that they are more likely to commit these to memory.
5. *Affective and identity anchoring*: resistance can become stronger where beliefs are tied to the identity, values, and emotions of the individuals. Any form

of inoculation message that taps into any or all these elements tends to create a more robust buffer between the individual and the misinformation (Compton et al., 2022; Lewandowsky & van der Linden, 2021; McGuire, 1964).

Prebunking

This is essentially the transport vehicle for delivering the cognitive inoculation discussed above. If we were to take the medical analogy to the extreme interpretation, prebunking can be conceptualised as the delivery mechanism for the inoculation process. There have been a variety of attempts to implement real-world mechanisms for the express purpose of prebunking, one of which was the "Bad News" game developed by Roozenbeek et al. (2020). In this game, individuals assume the role of a new producer who is charged with the creation of fake news. In the space of 15 minutes, the producer must recruit as many followers as they can to their channel without raising suspicions about the credibility of the information that they are presenting. The process of inoculation here is linked to the active reinforcement process highlighted above, where individuals are placed in control of the actual techniques that could be used to create fake news while at the same time allowing them to generate their own content (Roozenbeek & van der Linden, 2019; Roozenbeek et al., 2020).

The game presents players with memes or headlines to which they can engage in any number of ways. Their progress in the game is measured through two objective elements: the number of followers that have been recruited and their current credibility level. If players are to select a process that is consistent with a realistic content creator for misinformation, they, in turn, earn more followers and gain more credibility. However, if they initiate strategies that are in line with more credible content creation, or their tactics are seen as being far too obvious in terms of being linked to fake news, their number of followers is reduced, as is their credibility score (Lewandowsky & van der Linden, 2021). The Bad News game incorporates two key elements of inoculation theory reviewed above and includes details of forewarning or alerting individuals to the potential threats they might encounter, as well as being presented with weakened, diluted forms of misinformation. The latter element is done in a humorous, light-hearted way but serves to activate critical thinking and reflection without reaching the threshold for individuals to exhibit belief.

The Bad News game has garnered some impressive usage statistics from a variety of different academic sources. Roozenbeek and van der Linden (2019) conducted a large-scale evaluation of the game with 15,000 players and noted that individuals demonstrated a significant improvement in their capacity to spot misinformation as well as to resist the ingress of misinformation after gameplay. Such effects were demonstrated to be independent of other factors, such as age, gender, education, or political ideology. Others, such as Basol et al. (2020), showed that people who played the Bad News game demonstrated a significant improvement in their capacity to identify the techniques used in the creation of misinformation in comparison to a group that did not play the game. Players were also more likely to report an increase in confidence with respect to their judgements about misinformation, particularly when their judgements were reinforced by them making the correct observations. In terms of the permanence of these effects, Maertens et al. (2021) found that inoculation effects against fake news remained consistent for around three months, but only if the players were engaged in regular assessment and reinforcement. If players were not given relevant retesting or reinforcement through the gamified environment, the inoculation effects were reduced considerably after a two-month period.

While the success of the Bad News game is impressive, it demonstrates one of the key issues that impacts both debunking and prebunking strategies: they require continued maintenance for their effectiveness to be sustained. For organisations and governments looking towards a quick, simple fire-and-forget approach to cognitive inoculation, this is not the option that would fit with this remit. However, there are potential ways in which this process could be made more cost-effective, and perhaps normalising the capacity for individuals to engage in gamified activities that enhance critical thinking is a key method for increasing societal resilience. The question remains how much value we wish to place on the resistance of our citizens to the manipulation of misinformation and how much investment we are willing to commit to such activities.

Metacognitive Prompts

Metacognitive prompts are a subtle yet powerful tool in the arsenal of cognitive inoculation. They function by encouraging individuals to reflect on their own thinking processes, thereby enhancing awareness of how beliefs are formed, evaluated, and potentially manipulated (Flavell, 1979). Think of it as a process of thinking about thinking, where the individual is engaged in an effortful process of self-reflection, where they explore what they know. In the context of digital warfare, where misinformation often bypasses deliberate reasoning and exploits cognitive shortcuts, metacognitive prompts serve as a psychological "speed bump," slowing automatic acceptance and fostering critical engagement.

Metacognitive prompts are questions or cues that encourage individuals to reflect on how they know something, why they believe it, and whether the source or logic behind the information is trustworthy. These prompts do not provide answers; instead, they activate self-regulation and cognitive monitoring, which are seen as key processes for resisting persuasive misinformation. Researchers have suggested that metacognitive prompts can be direct or indirect (Graesser & McNamara, 2010; McCarthy et al., 2018). Direct prompts offer explicit instructions for evaluating knowledge or improving metacognitive behaviours (McCarthy et al., 2018) and could include things such as "What evidence supports this claim, and how reliable is the source?" or "List three reasons why this information might be misleading." On the other hand, indirect prompts subtly encourage the use of metacognitive strategies without overt instruction (Bannert et al., 2009; McCarthy et al., 2018) and include things such as "Does this remind you of something that you have seen before?" or "How does this information make you feel?" Additionally, prompts can be global, introduced at the end of a task to encourage broad reflection, for example, "After reading this chapter, which parts of it appeared to be most pervasive and why?" or "What strategies did you use to decide whether the information in this book was trustworthy?" Local prompts are embedded within specific stages of a task to guide moment-to-moment evaluation and could include "Before clicking on this link, what do you expect to find?" or "Whilst reading this paragraph, ask yourself: 'Is this fact or opinion?'" Research suggests that once individuals are subjected to metacognitive prompts, they are more likely to use those processes that have been initiated by them in the future, even in the absence of the same prompts (McCarthy et al., 2018). Similarly, Salovich and Rapp (2020) employed the use of a metacognitive reflection task that encouraged participants to engage in a process of reflection in terms of the information they had just read. Participants who were part of this condition were observed to make fewer errors in judgement about the facticity of the information they had just read compared to those who did not receive the metacognitive prompt.

In terms of digital warfare with the use of memetics, high-information volume that also consists of emotively charged narratives, the use of metacognitive prompts can be seen as a very low-cost but highly scalable mechanism for intervention. They can be easily embedded into a wide range of digital platforms, such as social media or educational contexts and are also used in gamified environments such as the Bad News game reviewed above. Using metacognitive prompts, individuals can become more involved, active processors of information they encounter, rather than just being the passive recipients, in turn presenting a fundamental shift in the mindset that shapes so much of our interactions online.

Behavioural Nudges

Behavioural nudges, introduced by Thaler and Sunstein (2009), make reference to subtle modifications in the decision-making environment, often labelled as *choice architecture,* that influence behaviour in predictable ways without restricting options or altering economic incentives. In the context of digital warfare, nudges offer a powerful, non-coercive mechanism for enhancing psychological and cognitive resilience against adversarial influence, manipulation, and strategic distraction. The mechanisms employed in the context of digital warfare often serve to exploit cognitive and dispositional vulnerabilities such as impulsivity, emotional reactivity, and social conformity to shape beliefs, behaviours, and group dynamics. Nudges counteract these tactics by redirecting attention, slowing automatic responses, and reinforcing reflective thinking. Below are key types of nudges and their implications for digital resilience:

- *Defaults*: setting the most protective or beneficial option as the default can guide users towards resilient behaviours with minimal effort. In digital warfare, default nudges can help encourage individual engagement with diverse information sources. They can also promote a focus on social media settings that enhance privacy or reduce exposure to algorithmic manipulation. They may also serve to reduce the perceived friction in adopting protective behaviours (e.g., opting into content provenance tools or critical reflection prompts). Defaults work because they reduce cognitive load and exploit the human tendency to stick with preset options (Lemken, 2024).
- *Commitment devices*: commitment devices are self-imposed psychological contracts that help individuals follow through on future intentions. Within the context of digital warfare, these mechanisms can encourage users to pledge to engage critically with emotionally charged content, support long-term goals such as reducing screen time or avoiding echo chambers, and promote behaviours like verifying sources before sharing. By reinforcing behavioural consistency, commitment devices make it harder for individuals to revert to passive or impulsive habits. Their effectiveness lies in the creation of internal accountability, which is difficult to reverse without incurring some form of psychological discomfort (Damgaard & Nielsen, 2017).
- *Accessible information*: simplifying complex information and making it actionable enhances engagement and reduces avoidance. In digital warfare, clear and easily interpreted cues can help users identify manipulation techniques, while visual summaries or interactive prompts can guide reflection without overwhelming the individual. Timely reminders can also interrupt automatic scrolling or reactive sharing. This form of nudge reduces cognitive friction, thereby increasing the likelihood that resilience behaviours will be adopted (Damgaard, 2020).
- *Framing*: as discussed elsewhere in this book, the way information is presented, whether in terms of loss or gain, or positive versus negative valence, can significantly influence perception and action. In digital warfare, positive framing, such as "Engaging with diverse sources strengthens your perspective," can promote open-mindedness, whereas negative framing, such as "Failing to verify sources increases your vulnerability to manipulation," can heighten vigilance. However, excessive negative framing may lead to apathy or fatalism, while overly positive framing may foster overconfidence. A balanced approach is therefore essential (de Bruijn & Janssen, 2017).
- *Social nudges*: social nudges leverage social norms and peer influence to guide behaviour. In digital warfare contexts, highlighting that "most users verify sources before sharing" can encourage conformity to resilient behaviours, while displaying group-level engagement with critical thinking tools

can normalise reflective practices. These nudges are particularly effective in uncertain environments, where individuals look to others for behavioural cues. This is especially critical in situations where information is scarce, and the potential for misinformation to take hold is high (Venema et al., 2020).

- *Incentives*: finally, incentives, both financial and non-financial, can reinforce desired behaviours. In digital warfare, gamified rewards such as badges for resisting clickbait or engaging with diverse viewpoints can motivate sustained engagement, while feedback mechanisms like performance scores for critical engagement can strengthen learning and self-efficacy. Loss-framed incentives, such as losing points for interacting with manipulative content, have been shown to be particularly effective in increasing vigilance (Goel et al., 2020).

While nudges are promising, their effectiveness varies. Meta-analyses show that default nudges are consistently the most impactful, while others depend on context, individual preferences, and prior beliefs (Hummel & Maedche, 2019). Nudges are less effective when individuals have strong pre-existing attitudes or when the environment is saturated with competing stimuli. However, in the context of digital warfare, nudges offer a low-cost, scalable, and psychologically sophisticated tool for enhancing individual and collective resilience. They can be embedded across platforms, educational systems, and public awareness campaigns to subtly shift behaviour towards critical engagement, strategic awareness, and cognitive autonomy.

Social and Peer Support

In the context of digital warfare, where adversarial actors seek to manipulate perception, fragment communities, and exploit cognitive vulnerabilities, social and peer-led learning offers a compelling and under-utilised strategy for building psychological resilience and collective defence. Traditionally associated with educational settings, peer-led learning can be repurposed to counter the effects of information manipulation and PsyOPs by fostering shared understanding, critical engagement, and trust within digital communities (Loh & Ang, 2020; Tran et al., 2019). One of the key strengths of peer-led learning is its ability to dismantle hierarchical barriers that often exist between information gatekeepers and everyday users. In environments where institutional and government-led messaging may be met with scepticism or apathy, learning from peers, individuals perceived as equals, can reduce resistance and increase receptivity. This dynamic is particularly relevant in digital warfare, where the perception of control and agency plays a crucial role in resisting manipulation. Peer-led approaches promote collaboration and mutual support, helping individuals feel less isolated and more empowered in their engagement with contested information (Parmar et al., 2025; Schürmann et al., 2024; Walker et al., 2021).

Peer-led learning typically involves a structure where individuals engage with a problem or topic through guided facilitation, discussion, and shared reflection. In digital warfare contexts, this might take the form of analysing viral content, deconstructing emotionally charged narratives, or exploring the psychological tactics embedded in memes and misinformation. The facilitator, who is often a peer rather than an expert, encourages participants to share experiences, question assumptions, and reflect on their own cognitive responses. This process not only deepens understanding but also normalises critical thinking as a communal activity (Parmar et al., 2025; Schürmann et al., 2024; Walker et al., 2021).

Research from educational settings has shown that peer-led learning increases motivation, engagement, and confidence in knowledge acquisition. These benefits translate well into digital environments, where individuals often feel overwhelmed by the volume and complexity of information. When users see their peers actively engaging with manipulative content and discussing its implications, they are more likely to adopt similar behaviours. This social modelling effect reinforces resilience and creates a ripple of informed scepticism across networks. However, the successful implementation of peer-led learning in the context of applications that relate directly to digital warfare depends on thoughtful design and facilitation. Without clear objectives or structure, the outcomes for such initiatives can become unfocused and counterproductive, feeding into the backfire effect we explored earlier in this chapter. The role of the facilitator is critical, not only in guiding conversation but also in maintaining a constructive tone and ensuring that misinformation is not inadvertently reinforced. Enthusiasm and credibility of peer leaders also play a significant role in shaping the effectiveness of these sessions.

In practice, peer-led learning can be integrated into online communities, gamified platforms, or civic engagement initiatives. It offers a decentralised, scalable approach to resistance, one that does not rely solely on institutional authority but instead builds resilience from the ground up. By encouraging individuals to become active processors of information rather than passive recipients, peer-led learning contributes to a broader cultural shift in how we engage with digital content under conditions of psychological and cognitive warfare. Ultimately, social and peer-led learning is not only a pedagogical tool but can also form a key strategic asset in the defence against digital manipulation. When embedded into digital ecosystems, it can foster solidarity, increase critical awareness, and share a commitment to truth, making it a vital component of any comprehensive resilience strategy.

Friction Design

In the fast-paced, emotionally charged environments of digital warfare, where information is weaponised and psychological manipulation is often subtle and instantaneous, friction-based design offers a strategic counter-measure. Normally, design processes focus directly on reducing the amount of friction an individual experiences when they are trying to complete a task, ensuring minimal distractions and maximum productivity. In contrast, friction-based design intentionally introduces small obstacles or delays into digital interactions to slow down impulsive behaviour and encourage reflection. These micro-interruptions serve to act as cognitive speed limiters and give users a moment to pause, reconsider, and engage more deliberately with the content they encounter (Jahn et al., 2023).

The logic behind friction-based design has its roots firmly planted in behavioural science, building off much of the work around heuristic processing. When individuals are exposed to emotionally provocative or misleading content, their natural response is often automatically driven by heuristics, biases, and affective cues. Friction disrupts this automaticity. For example, requiring users to confirm they have read an article before sharing it, or introducing a short delay before reposting a viral meme, can reduce the likelihood of impulsive engagement and increase the chance of critical evaluation. These interventions do not block behaviour; they simply make it more effortful, which in turn activates higher-order cognitive processes (Gordon-Tapiero et al., 2023; Hills & Menczer, 2020).

In the context of digital warfare, friction-based design can be deployed to counteract the rapid spread of divisive narratives, emotionally manipulative content, and co-ordinated influence campaigns. By slowing the velocity of information flow, friction creates space for metacognitive reflection, source evaluation, and strategic awareness, all of which are essential for resisting manipulation. This approach aligns closely with prebunking strategies, which aim to inoculate individuals against misinformation before exposure. Friction can serve as the delivery mechanism for prebunking prompts, embedding them at key decision points in the user journey.

The *Bad News* game (Roozenbeek et al., 2020) offers a compelling example of friction in action. While gamified and engaging, the game introduces deliberate pauses and decision points where players must choose how to manipulate their audience. These moments of choice are not instantaneous; they require consideration of tactics, consequences, and credibility. This slows down the learning process just enough to allow reflection, reinforcing the inoculation effect without overwhelming the player. In this way, friction becomes a pedagogical tool, one that enhances the effectiveness of gamified learning by embedding cognitive resistance into the gameplay itself.

Friction-based design can also be applied across digital platforms more broadly. Social media interfaces might include prompts before sharing emotionally charged content, search engines could require users to review multiple sources before accepting a claim, and messaging apps might delay the forwarding of unverified information. These interventions are subtle, scalable, and non-coercive, making them ideal for environments where user autonomy must be preserved, but manipulation must be mitigated. For example, Jahn et al. (2023) presented a model where friction-based design, coupled with a small amount of learning material, increased the quality of posts on social media. Similarly, Gordon-Tapiero et al. (2023) noted that the frictionless-based design format of many social media platforms has served to increase the ease with which individuals process and disseminate misinformation, often because of a lack of criticality when it comes to assessing the facticity of that information. One example of how this was countered was the implementation of limits on how many people's messages could be forwarded to at any one time (de Freitas Melo et al., 2020).

Ultimately, friction-based design is not about making digital experiences difficult; it is about making them deliberate. In an era where speed and simplicity are often exploited by adversarial actors, introducing thoughtful friction can help restore agency, promote critical thinking, and build the cognitive resilience necessary to navigate the complexities of digital warfare.

Gamified Learning

Gamification has emerged as a compelling strategy for engaging individuals in learning and behavioural change, drawing on the motivational power of game mechanics to enhance real-world activities. Originally developed within educational and organisational contexts, gamification involves the use of video game elements, such as points, levels, badges, and leader boards, to increase user engagement, motivation, and retention. Gamification has been viewed as the application of game design elements in non-game contexts to improve user experience and engagement and are something that has evolved to be used across training, health, and behavioural interventions (Deterding, Dixon, Khaled, et al., 2011; Deterding, Dixon, Nacke, et al., 2011).

In the realm of digital warfare, gamification offers a unique opportunity to build cognitive resilience and psychological immunity against manipulation, misinformation, and adversarial influence. It can accomplish this through the creation of immersive environments where individuals can actively engage with the very techniques used in information warfare, such as emotional manipulation, conspiracy framing, and polarisation – without being overwhelmed by them. This mirrors the logic of prebunking and cognitive inoculation, where exposure to weakened forms of manipulation helps individuals build resistance to more potent versions in the wild.

The Bad News game is another prime example of this approach, which we can revisit here. Developed by Roozenbeek et al. (2020), the game places players in the role of a fake news producer, challenging them to gain followers while deploying misinformation tactics. Crucially, the game uses humour and exaggeration to dilute the potency of these tactics, allowing players to recognise and reflect on manipulation strategies without falling victim to them. This gamified environment activates critical thinking and metacognitive awareness, reinforcing the psychological defences needed to resist real-world digital threats.

Gamification works by inducing a state of psychological flow, a deep, focused engagement with a task that enhances learning and retention (Csikszentmihalyi, 1990; Thatcher et al., 2008). Research has shown that gamified learning environments lead to higher levels of behavioural and emotional engagement compared to traditional methods, particularly when users feel immersed and challenged. This is especially relevant in digital warfare, where attention is fragmented and cognitive overload is common. By creating structured, goal-oriented experiences, gamification can help users stay focused, absorb complex information, and develop strategic awareness.

However, the effectiveness of gamification depends heavily on context, design, and user characteristics. Poorly implemented gamification, where game elements are superficial or disconnected from meaningful outcomes, can lead to disengagement or even resistance. In digital warfare contexts, this risk is amplified if the gamified experience fails to resonate with users' motivations or cultural values. For example, competitive mechanics like leader boards may appeal to some users but alienate others, particularly if the rewards feel arbitrary or irrelevant. Moreover, gamification is not a one-size-fits-all solution. Age, gender, cultural background, and psychological disposition all influence how individuals respond to gamified environments. Younger users may be more receptive to task-driven, rewards-based games, while older users may prefer socially oriented or narrative-driven experiences. Cultural differences also shape how achievements are interpreted and valued, which means that gamification strategies must be carefully tailored to their audience if they are to be effective in resisting digital manipulation (Dicheva, 2015; Hamari et al., 2014).

Despite these challenges, gamification remains a promising tool in the arsenal of digital defence. When thoughtfully designed and strategically deployed, it can transform passive users into active participants in their own cognitive protection. It can simulate adversarial tactics in safe environments, foster critical reflection, and reinforce protective behaviours, all while maintaining engagement and motivation. In combination with other resilience-building strategies such as metacognitive prompting, behavioural nudges, and peer-led learning, gamification can help cultivate a population that is not only aware of digital threats but also equipped to resist them.

Summary

In this, the last chapter of the current text, I offer a curated exploration of psychological and cognitive defence mechanisms designed to mitigate the impact of digital manipulation. Departing from the technical and AI-driven solutions often associated with online safety and security, the chapter focuses on human cognition as the primary battleground in digital warfare. In this chapter, it is argued that resilience against misinformation and subversive narratives must be cultivated through behavioural and psychological strategies rooted in awareness, critical thinking, and cognitive engagement.

Central to the chapter is the distinction between reactive and proactive interventions. Debunking, a reactive strategy, involves correcting misinformation after exposure. While it can be effective under certain conditions, particularly when misinformation is emotionally charged or ideologically aligned with the individual, it is fraught with challenges such as the backfire effect, belief regression, and the continued influence effect. These phenomena underscore the difficulty of altering entrenched beliefs and highlight the importance of message framing and source credibility. The chapter suggests that corrections must be carefully designed to avoid triggering defensive biases and should be reinforced over time to ensure retention.

In contrast, prebunking or cognitive inoculation is presented as a more promising proactive approach. Drawing on McGuire's inoculation theory, the chapter outlines how exposing individuals to weakened forms of misinformation alongside refutations can build psychological immunity. This process involves several components: threat awareness, refutational preemption, delay and reinforcement, active processing, and affective anchoring. These mechanisms collectively prepare individuals to resist future manipulative content by fostering critical evaluation and memory consolidation.

Gamified learning, exemplified by the "*Bad News*" game, is highlighted as an innovative method for delivering prebunking interventions. By allowing users to simulate misinformation tactics in a controlled environment, gamification promotes engagement, reflection, and strategic awareness. The chapter notes that such interventions are most effective when they are regularly reinforced and tailored to the user's cognitive and cultural context.

Further strategies include metacognitive prompts, which encourage individuals to reflect on their own thinking processes, thereby slowing automatic acceptance of information and promoting epistemic vigilance. Behavioural nudges, such as defaults, commitment devices, and social cues, are also explored as subtle yet powerful tools for guiding users towards resilient behaviours without coercion. These nudges exploit cognitive tendencies to promote protective actions and critical engagement.

The chapter also advocates for peer-led learning as a decentralised and scalable method for fostering collective resilience. By leveraging social trust and shared reflection, peer-led approaches can dismantle hierarchical barriers and promote informed scepticism within digital communities. Finally, friction-based design is proposed as a counter-measure to impulsive engagement, introducing deliberate pauses in digital interactions to encourage reflection and reduce susceptibility to manipulation.

In sum, hopefully, the chapter presents a nuanced and multifaceted framework for psychological defence in digital warfare. It emphasises the importance of cognitive engagement, strategic communication, and sustained intervention, arguing that resilience is not a static trait but a dynamic process that must be cultivated through thoughtful design and collective effort.

References

Bannert, M., Hildebrand, M., & Mengelkamp, C. (2009). Effects of a metacognitive support device in learning environments. *Computers in Human Behaviour*, *25*(4), 829–835. https://doi.org/10.1016/j.chb.2008.07.002

Basol, M., Roozenbeek, J., & van der Linden, S. (2020). Good news about bad news: Gamified inoculation boosts confidence and cognitive immunity against fake news. *Journal of Cognition*, *3*(1), 2. https://doi.org/10.5334/joc.91

Bruns, H., Dessart, F., Krawczyk, M., Lewandowsky, S., Pantazi, M., Pennycook, G., . . . Smillie, L. (2023). The role of (trust in) the source of prebunks and debunks of misinformation: Evidence from online experiments in four EU Countries. *Preprint*. Retrieved from http://www.biblioteca.pucminas.br/teses/Educacao_PereiraAS_1.pdf%0Ahttp://www.anpocs.org.br/portal/publicacoes/rbcs_00_11/rbcs11_01.htm%0Ahttp://repositorio.ipea.gov.br/bitstream/11058/7845/1/td_2306.pdf%0Ahttps://direitoufma2010.files.wordpress.com/2010/

Byrne, S., & Hart, P. S. (2009). The Boomerang effect a synthesis of findings and a preliminary theoretical framework. *Annals of the International Communication Association*, *33*(1), 3–37. https://doi.org/10.1080/23808985.2009.11679083

Chan, M. S., & Albarracín, D. (2023). A meta-analysis of correction effects in science-relevant misinformation. *Nature Human Behaviour*, *7*(9), 1514–1525. https://doi.org/10.1038/s41562-023-01623-8

Chan, M., Pui, S., Jones, C. R., Hall Jamieson, K., & Albarracín, D. (2017). Debunking: A meta-analysis of the psychological efficacy of messages countering misinformation. *Psychological Science*, *28*(11), 1531–1546. https://doi.org/10.1177/0956797617714579

Compton, J., Ivanov, B., & Hester, E. (2022). Inoculation theory and affect. *International Journal of Communication*, *16*, 3470–3483.

Csikszentmihalyi, M. (1990). Flow: The psychology of optimal performance. In *Optimal experience: Psychological studies of flow in consciousness*. New York: Cambridge University Press.

Damgaard, M. T. (2020). A decade of nudging: What have we learned? *Economics Working Papers*, 1–23. Retrieved from https://pure.au.dk/portal/files/191597643/wp20_07.pdf

Damgaard, M. T., & Nielsen, H. S. (2017). The use of nudges and other behavioural approaches in education. *EENEE Analytical Reports*, (29).

de Bruijn, H., & Janssen, M. (2017). Building cybersecurity awareness: The need for evidence-based framing strategies. *Government Information Quarterly*, *34*(1), 1–7. https://doi.org/10.1016/j.giq.2017.02.007

de Freitas Melo, P., Vieira, C. C., Garimella, K., de Melo, P. O. S. V., & Benevenuto, F.-C. (2020). Can WhatsApp counter misinformation by limiting message forwarding? *Studies in Computational Intelligence*, *881 SCI*, 372–384. https://doi.org/10.1007/978-3-030-36687-2_31

Deterding, S., Dixon, D., Khaled, R., & Nacke, L. (2011). From game design elements to gamefulness. *Proceedings of the 15th International Academic MindTrek Conference on Envisioning Future Media Environments – MindTrek '11*, 9–11. https://doi.org/10.1145/2181037.2181040

Deterding, S., Dixon, D., Nacke, L., O'Hara, K., & Dixon, D. (2011). *Gamification: Using Game Design Elements in Non-Gaming Contexts*, 4–7. https://doi.org/10.1145/1979742.1979575

Dicheva, D. (2015). Gamification in education: A systematic mapping study gamification in education: A systematic mapping study. *Educational Technology & Society*, *18*(June), 75–88.

Ecker, U. K. H., Lewandowsky, S., Jayawardana, K., & Mladenovic, A. (2019). Refutations of equivocal claims: No evidence for an ironic effect of counter-argument number. *Journal of Applied Research in Memory and Cognition*, *8*(1), 98–107. https://doi.org/10.1016/j.jarmac.2018.07.005

Ecker, U. K. H., Lewandowsky, S., Swire, B., & Chang, D. (2011). Correcting false information in memory: Manipulating the strength of misinformation encoding and its retraction. *Psychonomic Bulletin and Review*, *18*(3), 570–578. https://doi.org/10.3758/s13423-011-0065-1

Edwards, K., & Smith, E. E. (1996). A disconfirmation bias in the evaluation of arguments. *Journal of Personality and Social Psychology*, *71*(1), 5–24. https://doi.org/10.1037/0022-3514.71.1.5

Flavell, J. H. (1979). Metacognition and cognitive monitoring: A new area of cognitive-developmental inquiry. *American Psychologist*, *34*(10), 906–911. https://doi.org/10.1037//0003-066X.34.10.906

Goel, S., Williams, K., Huang, J., & Warkentin, M. (2020). Understanding the role of incentives in security behaviour. *Proceedings of the Annual Hawaii International Conference on System Sciences*, January, 4241–4246. https://doi.org/10.24251/hicss.2020.519

Gordon-Tapiero, A., Ohm, P., & Ramaswami, A. (2023). Fact and friction: A case study in the fight against false news. *UC Davis L. Rev*, *57*, 171–251.

Graesser, A., & McNamara, D. (2010). Self-regulated learning in learning environments with pedagogical agents that interact in natural language. *Educational Psychologist*, *45*(4), 234–244. https://doi.org/10.1080/00461520.2010.515933

Guess, A., & Coppock, A. (2020). Does counter-attitudinal information cause backlash? Results from three large survey experiments. *British Journal of Political Science*, *50*(4), 1497–1515. https://doi.org/10.1017/S0007123418000327

Hamari, J., Koivisto, J., & Sarsa, H. (2014). Does gamification work? A literature review of empirical studies on gamification. *Proceedings of the Annual Hawaii International Conference on System Sciences*, 3025–3034. https://doi.org/10.1109/HICSS.2014.377

Hills, T., & Menczer, F. (2020). The attention economy. *Scientific American*, *323*(6), 54. https://doi.org/10.1038/scientificamerican1220-54

Hummel, D., & Maedche, A. (2019). How effective is nudging? A quantitative review on the effect sizes and limits of empirical nudging studies. *Journal of Behavioural and Experimental Economics*, *80*(February), 47–58. https://doi.org/10.1016/j.socec.2019.03.005

Jahn, L., Rendsvig, R. K., Flammini, A., Menczer, F., & Hendricks, V. F. (2023). *Friction Interventions to Curb the Spread of Misinformation on Social Media*, 1–17. Retrieved from http://arxiv.org/abs/2307.11498

Johnson, H. M., & Seifert, C. M. (1994). Sources of the continued influence effect: When misinformation in memory affects later inferences. *Journal of Experimental Psychology: Learning, Memory, and Cognition*, *20*(6), 1420–1436. https://doi.org/10.1037/0278-7393.20.6.1420

Lemken, D. (2024). Options to design more ethical and still successful default nudges: A review and recommendations. *Behavioural Public Policy*, *8*(April 25), 349–381. https://doi.org/10.1017/bpp.2021.33

Lewandowsky, S. (2011). *Part 4: The world-view backfire effect.* Retrieved August 14, 2025, from The Debunking Handbook website https://www.shapingtomorrowsworld.org/debunking-handbook-part-4-world-view-backfire-effect.html

Lewandowsky, S., Cook, J., Ecker, U. K. H., Albarracín, D., Amazeen, M. A., Kendeou, P., . . . Zaragoza, M. S. (2020). *The debunking handbook 2020*, 19. Retrieved from https://sks.to/db2020

Lewandowsky, S., & van der Linden, S. (2021). Countering misinformation and fake news through inoculation and prebunking. *European Review of Social Psychology, 32*(2), 348–384. https://doi.org/10.1080/10463283.2021.1876983

Loh, R. C.-Y., & Ang, C.-S. (2020). Unravelling cooperative learning in higher education. *Research in Social Sciences and Technology, 5*(2), 22–39. https://doi.org/10.46303/ressat.05.02.2

Maertens, R., Roozenbeek, J., Basol, M., & van der Linden, S. (2021). Long-term effectiveness of innoculation against misinformation: Three longitudinal experiments. *Journal of Experimental Psychology. Applied, 27*(1), 1–53.

McCarthy, K. S., Likens, A. D., Johnson, A. M., Guerrero, T. A., & McNamara, D. S. (2018). Metacognitive overload! Positive and negative effects of metacognitive prompts in an intelligent tutoring system. *International Journal of Artificial Intelligence in Education, 28*(3), 420–438. https://doi.org/10.1007/s40593-018-0164-5

McGuire, W. J. (1964). Inducing resistance to persuadion: Some contemporary approaches. *Advances in Experimental Social Psychology, 1*, 191–229.

Parmar, J. S., Mistry, S. K., Micheal, S., Dune, T., Lim, D., Alford, S., & Arora, A. (2025). Peer support for improving student engagement and learning outcomes in postgraduate public health and health sciences: A qualitative study. *Education Sciences, 15*. https://doi.org/10.3390/educsci15050602

Roozenbeek, J., & van der Linden, S. (2019). Fake news game confers psychological resistance against online misinformation. *Palgrave Communications, 5*(1), 1–10.

Roozenbeek, J., van der Linden, S., & Nygren, T. (2020). Prebunking interventions based on "inoculation" theory can reduce susceptibility to misinformation across cultures. *Harvard Kennedy School Misinformation Review, 1*(2), 1–23. https://doi.org/10.37016//mr-2020-008

Salovich, N. A., & Rapp, D. N. (2020). Journal of experimental psychology: Learning, memory, and cognition misinformed and unaware? Metacognition and the influence of inaccurate information. *Journal of Experimental Psychology: Learning, Memory, and Cognition*, 1–18.

Schürmann, V., Marquardt, N., & Bodemer, D. (2024). Conceptualisation and measurement of peer collaboration in higher education: A systematic review. In *Small group research* (Vol. 55). https://doi.org/10.1177/10464964231200191

Schwarz, N., Sanna, L. J., Skurnik, I., & Yoon, C. (2007). Metacognitive experiences and the intricacies of setting people straight: Implications for debiasing and public information campaigns. *Advances in Experimental Social Psychology, 39*(6), 127–161. https://doi.org/10.1016/S0065-2601(06)39003-X

Skurnik, I., Yoon, C., & Schwarz, N. (2007). Education about flu can reduce intentions to get a vaccination. *Unpublished Manuscript.*

Swire, B., Ecker, U. K. H., & Lewandowsky, S. (2017). The role of familiarity in correcting inaccurate information. *Journal of Experimental Psychology: Learning, Memory, and Cognition, 43*(12), 1948–1961.

Swire-Thompson, B., DeGutis, J., & Lazer, D. (2020). Searching for the backfire effect: Measurement and design considerations. *Journal of Applied Research in Memory and Cognition, 9*(3), 286–299. https://doi.org/10.1016/j.jarmac.2020.06.006

Swire-Thompson, B., Dobbs, M., Thomas, A., & DeGutis, J. (2023). Memory failure predicts belief regression after the correction of misinformation. *Cognition, 230*(March 2022), 105276. https://doi.org/10.1016/j.cognition.2022.105276

Thaler, R. H., & Sunstein, C. R. (2009). *Nudge: Improving decisions about health, wealth, and happiness*. London, UK: Penguin.

Thatcher, A., Wretschko, G., & Fridjhon, P. (2008). Online flow experiences, problematic internet use and internet procrastination. *Computers in Human Behaviour*, *24*(5), 2236–2254. https://doi.org/10.1016/j.chb.2007.10.008

Tran, V. D., Nguyen, T. M. L., De, N. Van, Soryaly, C., & Doan, M. N. (2019). Does cooperative learning may enhance the use of students' learning strategies? *International Journal of Higher Education*, *8*(4), 79–88. https://doi.org/10.5430/ijhe.v8n4p79

van der Linden, S. (2024). Countering misinformation through psychological inoculation. In *Advances in experimental social psychology* (Vol. 69). https://doi.org/10.1016/bs.aesp.2023.11.001

Venema, T. A. G., Kroese, F. M., Benjamins, J. S., & de Ridder, D. T. D. (2020). When in doubt, follow the crowd? Responsiveness to social proof nudges in the absence of clear preferences. *Frontiers in Psychology*, *11*(June), 1–13. https://doi.org/10.3389/fpsyg.2020.01385

Walker, R., Chong, S., & Chong, J. (2021). Facilitating peer-led group research through virtual collaboration spaces: An exploratory research study. *Research in Learning Technology*, *29*(1063519), 1–21. https://doi.org/10.25304/rlt.v29.2520

Walter, N., & Tukachinsky, R. (2020). A meta-analytic examination of the continued influence of misinformation in the face of correction: How powerful is it, why does it happen, and how to stop it? *Communication Research*, *47*(2), 155–177. https://doi.org/10.1177/0093650219854600

Glossary

Agenda-setting theory: a communication theory explaining how the media influences what issues the public considers important, without dictating what to think.

Algorithmic amplification: the process by which algorithms increase the visibility of certain content based on engagement metrics, often reinforcing echo chambers and virality.

See also algorithmic manipulation, virality, and memetic warfare.

Algorithmic manipulation: the deliberate adjustment of algorithms to curate, amplify, or distort information exposure and user behaviour.

Affect heuristic: a mental shortcut where decisions are influenced by current emotional states rather than objective analysis.

Authority bias: the tendency to attribute greater accuracy or credibility to opinions from perceived authority figures.

Bandwagon effect: a bias where individuals adopt beliefs or behaviours because many others appear to do so, also called herding or conformity bias.

Behavioural economics: a discipline combining psychology and economics to study decision-making under uncertainty, emphasising cognitive biases and heuristics.

See also behavioural nudging, choice architecture, and heuristics.

Behavioural nudging: a subtle intervention in choice architecture that steers decisions without restricting options or imposing force.

Bounded rationality: a concept describing decision-making limited by time, information, and cognitive resources, leading to satisficing rather than optimising.

Bots: automated accounts programmed to amplify content, simulate engagement, or manipulate online discourse.

Choice architecture: the design of decision-making environments to influence choices without restricting options, often used in nudging strategies.

See also *behavioural nudging and bounded rationality.*

Cognitive dissonance: psychological discomfort arising from holding conflicting beliefs, often resolved through biased reasoning or attitude change.

Cognitive warfare: a form of conflict targeting mental processes such as attention, memory, and decision-making to influence behaviour and perception.

Conscientiousness: a Big Five trait associated with self-discipline, organisation, and goal orientation. Highly conscientious individuals may follow rules diligently but can be manipulated through authority cues.

See also personality and agreeableness.

Deepfakes: AI-generated synthetic media that convincingly imitate real people or events, often used for deception.

Descriptive norms: perceptions of what most people are doing in a given context, influencing conformity.

Digital psychological operations (DiPsyOPs): psychological operations executed within digital platforms to manipulate attitudes and behaviours covertly.

Digital warfare: strategic psychological, cognitive, and informational operations in digital environments aimed at influencing minds rather than machines.

Disinformation: false information deliberately created and spread to deceive or mislead audiences.

See also misinformation and propaganda.

Disintermediation: the removal or bypassing of intermediaries in a communication or transaction process, allowing actors to interact directly with audiences or consumers.

See also algorithmic amplification, social media platforms, influence operations, and propaganda.

Echo chambers: closed informational environments that reinforce existing beliefs and filter out dissenting views.

See also filter bubbles.

Emotional salience: the prominence or importance of emotionally charged stimuli, which enhances attention and memory encoding.

See also *emotional contagion and affect heuristic.*

Endogenous attention: goal-driven, internally guided focus based on intentions and expectations.

See also exogenous attention.

Exogenous attention: stimulus-driven, automatic attentional capture by salient external cues.

See also endogenous attention.

Extraversion: a Big Five trait associated with sociability, assertiveness, and positive affect. High extraversion often correlates with increased online engagement and exposure to influence tactics.

Cross-references: personality and agreeableness.

False consensus effect: the tendency to overestimate how widely one's own views are shared by others.

Flow: a psychological state of deep immersion and optimal experience in which an individual is fully absorbed in an activity, balancing high challenge with high skill. Flow is characterised by focused attention, diminished self-consciousness, and a distorted sense of time.

See also cognitive load, attention, immersion, persuasive design, and digital engagement.

Filter bubble: a personalised digital environment created by algorithms that restricts exposure to diverse viewpoints, reinforcing existing beliefs.

See also *echo chamber and normative influence.*

Framing theory: a theory explaining how the presentation of information influences interpretation and decision-making by emphasising certain aspects over others.

Hacktivism: ideologically motivated hacking aimed at promoting political or social causes.

Hahaganda: a form of propaganda that uses humour, satire, or memes to spread ideological messages, disinformation, or influence narratives. By embedding persuasive content within comedic formats, hahaganda lowers critical defences, increases shareability, and exploits emotional contagion to amplify reach. It is often deployed in social media environments to normalise extremist ideas or undermine opponents while appearing playful or harmless.

See also memetic warfare, news satire, news parody, propaganda, and virality.

Heuristics: mental shortcuts or rules of thumb that simplify decision-making but can lead to systematic biases.

See also *affect heuristic, availability heuristic, and cognitive bias.*

Illusory truth effect: a cognitive bias where repeated exposure to information increases its perceived truthfulness, even if false.

Illusory correlation: a cognitive bias where individuals perceive a relationship between unrelated variables, often reinforcing stereotypes or misinformation.

See also *confirmation bias and narrative bias.*

In-group bias: preferential treatment or evaluation of members within one's own social group.

Injunctive norms: perceptions of socially approved or disapproved behaviours within a group.

Information warfare: strategic control and manipulation of information flows to gain advantage, including misinformation and media framing.

Kompromat: a term originating from Russian intelligence practices, referring to "compromising material" collected to blackmail, coerce, or discredit individuals or organisations.

See also *disinformation, propaganda, influence operations, and social engineering.*

Locus of control: a psychological concept describing whether individuals attribute outcomes to internal factors (self-control) or external forces (fate and luck).

Loss aversion: a bias where losses loom larger than equivalent gains, influencing risk perception and decision-making.

See also negativity bias.

Machiavellianism: a personality trait characterised by manipulativeness, strategic exploitation, and disregard for morality.

Maskirovka: a Russian military doctrine term meaning "masking" or "deception," referring to a broad set of strategies designed to mislead adversaries about intentions, capabilities, or operations. In modern contexts, maskirovka encompasses both physical and informational tactics, including camouflage, disinformation, and PsyOPs, to create confusion and achieve strategic surprise.

See also disinformation, Kompromat, influence operations, and propaganda.

Meme: a cultural unit, such as an image, phrase, or symbol, that spreads rapidly through social networks, often evolving through replication and variation. Memes function as carriers of ideas, humour, or ideology and can be weaponised in memetic warfare to influence beliefs, amplify propaganda, and manipulate social discourse. Their simplicity, emotional appeal, and shareability make them powerful tools for virality and psychological influence in digital environments.

See also memetic warfare, virality, hahaganda, social contagion, and narrative bias.

Memetic warfare: the use of memes and culturally resonant symbols as tools for influence and ideological manipulation.

See also virality.

Misinformation: false or inaccurate information shared without intent to deceive.

See also disinformation and propaganda.

Narrative bias: a preference for coherent stories over abstract facts, even when narratives are inaccurate.

Narcissism: a personality trait marked by self-entitlement, dominance, and excessive self-promotion, often linked to overconfidence online.

Neuroticism: a Big Five trait reflecting emotional instability and susceptibility to stress. High neuroticism can amplify responses to fear-based messaging and misinformation.

See also personality and extraversion.

News satire: a form of content that uses humour, irony, or exaggeration to comment on current events or social issues, often mimicking the style of legitimate news. While intended for entertainment, it can be misinterpreted as factual, contributing to misinformation.

See also news parody, fake news, and narrative bias.

News parody: content that imitates the format and tone of news reporting for humorous or critical purposes, often without explicit disclosure of its fictional nature. Like satire, it can blur the line between fact and fiction.

See also news satire and fake news.

News fabrication: the deliberate creation of entirely false news stories presented as legitimate journalism, typically to mislead, manipulate, or provoke emotional reactions.

See also disinformation, fake news, and propaganda.

Normative influence: social pressure shaping behaviour through subjective, descriptive, and injunctive norms.

Optimism bias: the tendency to overestimate positive outcomes and underestimate risks.

Out-group homogeneity bias: the perception that members of an out-group are more similar to each other than they actually are.

Openness to experience: a Big Five trait characterised by curiosity, creativity, and willingness to engage with novel ideas. High openness can increase susceptibility to exploratory behaviours and risky online interactions.

See also personality and neuroticism.

Overconfidence bias: a bias where individuals overestimate their abilities, knowledge, or judgement, often leading to risky decisions.

Personality: a set of enduring traits and characteristics that influence an individual's thoughts, emotions, and behaviours. Personality plays a critical role in susceptibility to digital manipulation.

Photo manipulation: the altering of images using digital tools to mislead viewers or distort reality. In influence operations, photo manipulation is used to fabricate evidence, amplify narratives, or evoke emotional responses.

Cross-references: deepfakes and disinformation.

Pluralistic ignorance: a situation where individuals privately reject a norm but publicly conform because they believe others accept it.

Primacy–recency effects: memory phenomena where items at the beginning and end of a sequence are recalled better than those in the middle.

See also serial position effect.

Projection bias: the tendency to assume that current preferences or emotional states will persist into the future.

Propaganda: systematic communication aimed at shaping opinions and behaviours to achieve strategic objectives.

See also misinformation and disinformation.

Psychological warfare: the use of communication and psychological tactics to influence emotions, attitudes, and behaviours for strategic gain.

Rumour: unverified and speculative information that spreads informally, often amplified by emotional content.

Security fatigue: cognitive depletion caused by continuous security demands, reducing vigilance and safe practices.

Satisficing: settling for a solution that is good enough rather than optimal due to cognitive limitations.

Sub-doxastic states: mental states that operate below the level of explicit belief and are not directly available to conscious, propositional evaluation.

See also Type 1 processing, heuristics, cognitive bias, implicit cognition, perception, emotional salience, priming, and cognitive warfare.

Sunk-cost fallacy: the tendency to continue investing in a decision based on prior investment rather than future benefits.

Social engineering: psychological manipulation of individuals to disclose confidential information or perform actions that compromise security.

See also *authority bias and influence operations.*

Trolling: posting provocative or disruptive content online to elicit emotional reactions or derail discussions.

Type 1 processing: a fast, automatic, and intuitive mode of thinking that relies on heuristics and emotional cues. It operates largely unconsciously and is highly susceptible to cognitive biases, making it a prime target for manipulation in digital environments.

See also *heuristics, affect heuristic, cognitive bias, and emotional salience.*

Type 2 processing: a slow, deliberate, and analytical mode of thinking that requires conscious effort and cognitive resources. It is associated with rational decision-making and critical evaluation, often invoked to counter impulsive judgements driven by Type 1 processing.

See also *bounded rationality, choice architecture, and cognitive bias.*

Virality: the rapid and widespread dissemination of content through social networks, often driven by emotional engagement.

See also memetic warfare.

Index

For Product Safety Concerns and Information please contact our EU representative GPSR@taylorandfrancis.com Taylor & Francis Verlag GmbH, Kaufingerstraße 24, 80331 München, Germany